Volume 4

# ISSUES OF
# THE
# HEART

By

Rayola Kelley

Hidden Manna Publications

# ISSUES OF THE HEART
## Volume 4
### Copyright © 2014 and 2023 by Rayola Kelley

Featuring the Following Books:
*Hidden Manna (Revised)*
*Bring Down the Sacred Cows*
*The Manual for the Single Christian Life*
*Parents Are People Too*

You can obtain a study reference book to complement your studies of this volume at Gentle Shepherd Ministries' website at www.gentleshepherd.com.

Hidden Manna Publications
P.O. Box 3572
Oldtown, ID 83822
www.gentleshepherd.com

Facebook:
https://www.facebook.com/HiddenMannaPublications/

# DEDICATION:

I want to dedicate this volume to
the source of all my inspiration
and hope:  Elohim

# ACKNOWLEDGMENT:

I want to thank
Jo Reaves and Crystal Garvin for editing.

I also want to acknowledge the many people who
proofread the different books throughout the years.
Since there are so many of you to name,
please accept this acknowledgment
as my heartfelt thanks to each of you
for making this volume possible.

# CONTENTS

# INTRODUCTION

*Issues of the Heart* is the fourth volume in the Gentle Shepherd Ministries Advanced Discipleship Course. This fourth volume was written to deal with issues that should be close to our hearts. The main heart issue for all of us has to do with our relationship with God and others. If relationships are lacking, out of control, and sliding down into the abyss of destruction because of dishonorable attitudes, neglect, abuse, and selfishness, then the quality of our existence and life will also prove to be greatly lacking.

Relationships expose people's real heart condition. They will reveal what individuals truly value, prefer, and pursue. Sadly, relationships are on the bottom of the list for most individuals. Since the general consensus for most people is to consider how a matter will best serve them, they also regard relationships with the same self-serving premise as well. They do not understand that relationships demand personal investments that at times require a person to be selfless, sacrificial, and genuine in his or her commitment, devotion, and consideration.

Relationships also give people a sense of who they are in the scheme of things. This brings us to another important aspect about relationships. When people do not understand their place in light of their different relationships, they can experience an identity crisis. In order to properly address the issues of the heart, cycles, attitudes, and conduct must be challenged.

The fourth volume considers the prevalent challenges of today that are confronting relationships in light of Scriptural instruction. It is a volume that will challenge and test your way of thinking and doing. It will shake that which you have assumed, taken for granted, or have been indoctrinated in. It will reveal unhealthy attitudes that often prove to be the culprit behind failing relationships.

The first book in the volume, *Hidden Manna* has been revised to include updated information. This book has been in the making since 1986. It deals with personal cycles that not only find their source in a person's base nature, but in a person's type of rebellion. Man was created to reflect the image of God, but his base nature and potential has been marred by sin. This book eventually unveils a powerful revelation of Jesus that is hidden within humanity. However, this revelation cannot be revealed until people find their proper place in Jesus.

*Bring Down the Sacred Cows* is a sequel to *Hidden Manna*. This updated book considers cycles in light of the marriage and family relationships. It brings to light the scriptural purpose of marriage that was hidden until Jesus redeemed His Church. It challenges attitudes about marriage and children, as well as reveals the role that the old man and prideful expectations play in disrupting these relationships. *Bring Down the Sacred Cows* also encourages people to find their identity in Christ

8

rather than in their spouse and children. As pointed out in the book, when people look to others for purpose and identity, they exalt the person or relationship to an idolatrous position, producing dissatisfaction and often a perverted, parasitic, and unhealthy environment.

The third book in this particular volume deals with the challenges of being single in a world where normalcy, status, or worth is often judged by whether individuals are linked to a duo relationship. *The Manual for the Single Christian Life* confronts the different issues that plague single people in regard to their relationships with God, the opposite sex, and others. It addresses attitudes that often cause them to feel like outcasts, even in the Church, simply because they do not fit in with the normalcy established by culture and worldly philosophies.

This Christian manual will help single Christians come to terms with their real place in Christ, the church, and in society. It will help them resolve the issue of whether they have a gift of being single or a gift of marriage. Since the manual deals with every aspect and issue that might plague Christians in their single status, including death and divorce, it will also serve as an invaluable manual to others who need to understand the real heart issues as a means of dealing with and ministering to single people.

*Parents are People Too* deals with the relationship between adult children and their parents. Our earthly parents play a major part in determining our identity and the quality of our spiritual inheritance. In this book the author candidly discusses her own experiences in this area. She considers the games that are often played in this relationship as well as the unhealthy and unrealistic attitudes and expectations that exist between adult children and their parents. The author wades through confusion and guilt in order to establish scriptural boundaries in which believers, who are struggling with this issue, can discover that their real identity and inheritance is totally linked to their relationship and life in Jesus Christ.

# Book One

# HIDDEN MANNA
### (Revised)

# INTRODUCTION

What does it mean to be human? Does humanity constitute a mystery too great to comprehend? Is it like much of creation—simple in function, but profound in possibilities? And, how does the essence of human nature affect us in our spiritual pilgrimage here on earth? It might serve us all well to consider these questions.

It appears as though many Christians are earnestly seeking the answers to these questions without any resolution. They look to man's philosophies, worldly relationships, and belief systems to come to terms with life in the hope of understanding themselves.

In spite of all of their searching, the breakdown of family, local churches, and society is escalating. As many scramble to stop this destruction, lasting solutions are elusive.

For years, I have observed that people are in destructive cycles. Are these cycles a matter of habit or is there something behind their consistency? Cycles reveal that people respond a certain way to personal challenges and in their relationships with others. These predictable and clearly detectable responses can easily be observed in these individuals' reactions to reality and interaction with others.

Since cycles never deviate in attitude or action, there must be some kind of source or basis for the cycle other than habits. My conclusion was, if one could discover this base, the cycle could be stopped and consequences averted.

In 1986, the Lord, through various avenues, actually revealed to me the source behind the cycles found in people. This revelation was simple, but profound. I began to see how understanding the source of cycles would cut through the endless layers, facades, or cloaks people often hide behind to avoid accountability, repentance, and change.

As I began to confirm the information God had graciously revealed to me, a revelation of Jesus immerged. Obviously, God's heart was not to necessarily reveal the cycles of humanity, but to reveal Jesus in and through humanity. I was both awed and humbled by this reality.

The wickedness of the heart and the evil works of the flesh had hidden this revelation of Jesus that had been cleverly woven through the fiber of humanity. Even though this revelation can be seen in and confirmed by Scripture, it had been hidden from skeptical eyes and unbelieving hearts.

This unrevealed revelation brings us back to the formation of man in the Garden of Eden. Adam was created to reflect the glory of God. Sin marred the potential of man to serve as a reflection of God. Man eventually became a reflection of that which most influenced his selfish disposition and fleshly appetites.

When Jesus Christ died on the cross, it was God's way of restoring man to his original state of reflecting Him in the midst of a lost world. Sadly, many people fail to recognize what their position, purpose, and status is in light of God's eternal plan.

This book is to unveil the Hidden Manna of heaven. This material has the ability to call people back to the reality of God through the revelation of Jesus Christ. It will challenge readers to step outside of personal, destructive cycles to come higher in God, and to come to terms with their potential in the kingdom of heaven.

This information also gives viable solutions to help people become part of the answer instead of remaining part of the problem in destructive cycles. My prayer is that the reader will recognize his or her own particular cycle, step outside of it, turn around, call out to God, and begin to allow the very life and character of Jesus to be unveiled in his or her humanity for the glory of God.

# 1

# THE NATURE OF SOMETHING

Do you realize everything has a nature? In my study of this word and its definitions, I concluded that it means, *"unchangeable characteristics that identify or define something"*. For example, God is not God in title or name. God is God because of who He is. His attributes constitute His nature as being deity, which identifies Him as God.

The Word of God is clear that there is only one God by nature, "Howbeit then, when ye knew not God, ye did service unto them which by <u>nature</u> are no gods" (Galatians 4:8). (Emphasis added.) The apostle Paul was clearly stating that before we knew the true God of heaven, we were paying homage to those who were not gods by nature.

God will not step outside of who He is. In other words, He will never cease to be God. He will always work in accordance with who He is. Most people think of God in light of what He can do, rather than who He is. They see Him as a storehouse, rather than a Person or being whose power is disciplined by His unchangeable attributes. James 1:17 says, "Every good gift and every perfect gift is from above, and cometh down from the Father of lights, with whom is no variableness neither shadow of turning."

Hebrews 13:8 states, "Jesus Christ the same yesterday, and today, and forever."

Everything has a nature that identifies it. Every aspect of creation reacts according to its nature. An apple tree is an apple tree. It will never produce oranges regardless of similarities. A domestic cat may be part of a greater cat family that includes mountain lions, leopards, and tigers, but it will never be a mountain lion. The domestic cat is clearly distinguished from the rest of the species by certain characteristics, and it will never step outside of its nature or way of being.

Even though all animal and plant species fall into categories or families, they are clearly identified by their characteristics or nature. They stand distinct and unique in the midst of creation.

We know man stands unique in God's creation and heart. But, is there an order to man? Like the cat family, are there distinct categories among humanity? We know that man has been classified as homosapiens. Psalm 139:14 says this about man, "I will praise thee; for I am fearfully and wonderfully made: marvellous are thy works; and that my soul knoweth right well." As the different discoveries about our DNA are unveiled, one must conclude each person is fearfully and wonderfully made, as he or she personally stands distinct.

However, are there distinct natures found among people that clearly distinguish who they are and why they respond the way they do? Many shrug off such a possibility. They believe themselves to be emotionally and intellectually complex, making them an exception to the rule. By being such an exception, they can hide behind aloofness, as they believe no one understands. Of course, this elitism all points to pride.

The arrogance of man chooses to believe that not only are people different, but that there is no explanation for their consistent cycles other than habits, family, friends, or religious influences. But, behind this façade is fear. People are a dichotomy. Many become isolated because they are not understood, while on the other hand they fear to be understood because there will be a level of accountability. They bounce back and forth between these two extremes like a ping-pong ball.

Is man beyond comprehension or does he have a nature that clearly identifies him? Certain people who have tried to understand the differences, yet similarities, of groups of people have come up with some amusing conclusions based on personality. These conclusions provide a weak, surface observation without merit or divine purpose. However, they have rightly concluded that there are four different groups found among people. Going a step further, my question was could this imply that there are four distinct natures (not mere "personalities") among humanity? The implications of this would be incredible. By understanding the basic makeup or the nature of a person, could destructive cycles and behavioral patterns be exposed and properly dealt with?

Surprisingly enough, four distinct natures have been identified among mankind. How do people's nature work in the scheme of their outward temperament and personality? Here is a good illustration on the following page of how nature fits into the way we each express ourselves.

| Influence | Spirit | Motivation |
|-----------|--------|------------|
| Traits | Nature | Who I am |
| Heart | Disposition | Who I become |
| Environment | Prevailing Mood (Temperament) | Perception |
| Approach to life | Attitude | Manifestation |
| Fruits | Personality (Interaction/Reflection) | Who I allow myself to become |

As you can see, the spirit motivating us will influence how the traits in our nature will express themselves through our disposition. Disposition sets up the prevailing mood or environment that will determine the direction of our perception. Will it be within or upward? Our perception will determine how we approach life. Our perception about life and God will be manifested in our attitude. Our attitude will determine the quality of our personality. Our countenance will ultimately reflect our true disposition. The disposition will influence what type of decisions we make in regard to life. Such decisions will determine who we ultimately allow ourselves to become as a person.

It is vital that we understand that the spirit and disposition will determine how the traits of our nature will be channeled, determining how our inner man will express itself. If the spirit is wrong, the disposition will be wrong. If the disposition is not regenerated, it will operate out of a wrong spirit.

It is a selfish disposition that was passed down from Adam to the rest of humanity. This fallen disposition is inclined towards sin and has the tendency to justify sin. It opposes God's rule in our lives, while tacking Him on in other ways. The only means to deal with this old, ungodly disposition is found in John 3:3 and 5. A person must be born again of Spirit and Water (the Word). Born again means a new disposition (a new heart and spirit) is being placed within an individual.[1] The new disposition is that of the very life of Jesus. It is inclined towards God and will prefer righteousness to personal darkness. Such a new disposition points to being a new creation. However, we must give way to the right spirit to ensure this disposition is brought forth in our lives. Sadly, many hold to their old disposition, while trying to disguise it behind a cloak of religion and good works. Therefore, the disposition reigning in us will determine the spirit motivating us, as well as how our traits will manifest themselves in our interaction with others.

Although uniquely set apart by appearance, personality, and talents, people respond and act according to their basic nature. Their nature not only identifies their cycle, but it also associates them to one of these four natures that can clearly be distinguished among humanity.

By understanding a person's particular nature, one can know how he or she perceives situations around him or her. A person will be able to cut through others' so-called "complexity" and "excuses" to address the real core issues of a problem.

By understanding people's basic nature, you will know their *need*. Every living thing has specific needs in order to live properly. Humans are not an exception to this rule. However, peoples' needs go beyond physical existence to emotional and spiritual needs that produce well-being. A person's particular need in the area of emotional and spiritual well-being is his or her interpretation as to what constitutes love. A fulfilled need makes a person feel as if he or she belongs. It gives a person a sense of purpose and fulfillment.

There are three such basic *needs* found among people. They are *emotional love, acceptance,* and *recognition*. Recognition splits off into two different categories. For example, there are people who need to be recognized for what they are trying to accomplish. And, then there are those who need to be recognized for who they are.

These needs push people into cycles with others. It sets up the environment around them. Environments can prove to be challenging, especially if there is conflict intruding into people's comfort zones. Ultimately, environments will determine the person's *desire*. There are three desires: *to be loved, have peace, or know joy or happiness.*

The emotional desire of a person reveals what is going on in his or her environment. For example, if a person desires love, he or she is revealing that his or her environment has a high percentage of hatred or unforgiveness. If the individual desires peace, he or she is declaring there is a lot of turmoil in his or her atmosphere. If the person says he or she desires joy or happiness, there is much despair in his or her environment.

The reason for unhealthy relationships and environments comes down to sin reigning in a situation. Because of Adam's rebellion, every person possesses a wrong disposition. Wrong disposition expresses itself in sin. This sin mars people's perception, abilities, and pursuits. For

---

[1] Ezekiel 36:26-27; 2 Corinthians 5:17; 1 Peter 1:23

example, sin has perverted people's needs. This perversion causes conflict as people look to worldly relationships to get their needs met.

People clearly communicate love according to their own particular need. It is not unusual for them to be involved with others who have a different need. Therefore, as they communicate their perception of love to someone who has a different need, confusion, fear, and betrayal become byproducts. It is at this point that many conflicts arise in the relationship.

Conflicts or crises will cause people to respond according to their nature. This response begins in the attitude of self-sufficiency and responds in rebellion against God's authority. Rebellion points to independence. It is where a person "calls" the shots according to his or her terms. There are three main *attitudes* that point to self-sufficiency, and end in three rebellious corresponding actions. These attitudes set people up to act in the capacity of trying to be God in a matter. Such an attempt is a means of trying to control their reality or environment.

The first attitude is, *"I will deal with it, leave me alone."* This person *withdraws* into his or her mind to understand what is going on. Ultimately, reality is only changed in the mind, but it brings a false peace to the person as he or she becomes indifferent to what is happening around him or her. However, if understanding eludes the person, it throws him or her into confusion, fear, and depression.

The second attitude is, *"I can handle it, and I will prove it to you."* This individual struggles hard to handle all situations. People with this attitude try to control their environment or those in their environment, but most attempts end in defeat, producing frustration and anger. This person will avoid personal accountability by *justifying* unpleasant results at the expense of others or circumstances.

There are two forms of justification. There is the front door approach where the person is quick to up front justify away his or her actions with excuses. In fact, there is no end to this person's ability to fling out excuses. The second type of justification is where a person stands back, observes, and builds a case against the "culprit." In the right situation, this person will present his or her case and clear him or herself of all accountability while declaring the other party guilty.

The final attitude is, *"I will take care of it, and I'll show you."* This is where the person considers what is going on, adjusts the situation to his or her ideas, and *makes it right* in his or her own sight. This type of person will either display shock or intolerance when there is opposition because he or she cannot see how he or she can be wrong.

These self-sufficient attitudes and rebellious actions mark the start of destructive cycles. These cycles point to independence where a person steps outside of God's perspective and takes matters into his or her own hands. At the heart of independence is *pride*. Pride that reigns serves as an idol that torments and pushes a person. In fact, pride has four friends.

The first friend of pride is *fear*. Due to a fragile ego or an elevated perception of self, pride cannot afford to be wrong. Its fragile state causes it to operate in fear. Fear undermines power, love, and mental clarity.[2] There are four main fears that make people faint in their minds, hide from life, or run from reality. They are: *failure, rejection, incompetence,* and *losing control.*

*Confusion* is the next friend of pride. Pride does not deal in reality and when reality confronts it, the person will become confused. God is not a God of confusion, but of order.[3] Therefore, where confusion exists, one can find pride, the works of the flesh, or Satan.

*Unbelief* is another companion of pride. Since pride serves as an idol, it demands loyalty and obedience to its demands. As individuals put confidence in self, God resists them. Since God will be absent from much of the activity in their world, people begin to question His existence, commitment, or love, especially when consequences hit them. This doubt begins to undermine confidence in God, thereby, eroding away genuine faith. This will cause one to harden his or her heart towards God and walk in unbelief.

*Delusion* is the next prevalent friend of pride. It is opposite of truth. Truth is one of the greatest threats to pride. It will threaten, insult, and cause fear. It will reveal pride's wickedness and hypocrisy along with its many insecurities and insatiable appetites. There are three forms of pride found among people. They are: *conceit, selfishness,* and *pride* itself.

*Conceit* involves intellectual arrogance. It takes pride in what it knows and what it can do. It *focuses* on self while indirectly asking for attention. One of its clever ways to get attention is through fake nobility. Fake nobility states, "I know I am wretched, but aren't I humble about it." Even in depravity, this disguise of pride is exalted as being a helpless victim rather than a culprit. Once again, we are reminded that God resists pride and instructs and warns us to, "Be not wise in your own conceits" (Romans 12:16c).[4] When people encounter conceit, it often irritates them and causes the conceited person to lose credibility and appear foolish.

*Selfishness* is the next form of pride. It has to do with ego and vanity. This form of pride constantly *emphasizes* self. It wants your attention; therefore, it is always in competition and vying for top billing. For example, you may have had a bad day, but the person with selfishness will quickly rob you of the limelight by having a worse day or bringing up personal former successes in similar situations. This will cause tremendous frustration as you watch this selfishness either exalt itself or become a suffering martyr in every situation.

The third type of pride is what one would consider the epitome of arrogance, which is simply *pride* in all of its haughtiness. This type of pride operates within both the arenas of conceit and selfishness. For example, it operates from the conceits of the mind where it silently figures out how to be recognized, and then it plays the necessary game

---

[2] 2 Timothy 1:7
[3] 1 Corinthians 14:33
[4] James 4:6

of selfishness to get its ego and vanity fed. Such pride demands your attention and becomes *preoccupied* with self. Ultimately, it must be in control of the situation. If pride is not properly recognized, it will regress into self-pity. Pride often intimidates people as it insists that others comply with its demands or the person will pay.

Pride is greatly entangled with a person's need. People think very highly of themselves.[5] Such high opinions often drive people in various attempts to get their need met. This drive is based on the lie that one is worthy of personal adoration or worship that comes through love, acceptance, or recognition. It is at this point where people get into games of control and manipulation with others.

These games cause conflict and destruction in relationships. There are three means people use to get their way: *words, attitudes, and actions.* In some cases, there can be a combination of these forms of control, but the results are the same—resentment, anger, and the breakdown of the relationship.

Obviously, people must step outside of these cycles. The problem is that most people don't recognize their own cycle. It is natural for them to operate according to their nature. In many cases, they believe they are right and feel they must hold the line. They fail to recognize that the bedrock of their disposition is the selfishness of pride. It causes unnecessary strife and ends in casualties.

Pride often deludes its victims as to personal problems. This delusion prevents the person from recognizing personal cycles. Out of mercy, God allows crisis and problems. These challenges become a process. The process is geared towards the person's nature. The goal of this process is to bring the person to the end of his or her self-sufficiency and rebellion to face his or her need for God's intervention.

There are three different processes that individuals find themselves in. These processes are related to priceless gems: pearl, gold, or diamond. A *pearl* starts out as a grain of sand that finds its way into an oyster. This grain of sand begins to *irritate* the oyster, which in turn spits at the grain of sand. This simply means a pearl is hardened saliva, but it is desired and valued by many.

For people who go through a similar process, God will use a string of irritants that will cause them to snap under the pressure and seek one greater than self to understand the challenge. When they finally come to God, He can surround them with His perspective.

Other people go through a *gold* process. These people need to be separated from something. For some, they must go through a *sifting* process where they are separated from defeating factors in their lives. But, for others they must go through a *boiling* process where they must be separated from something that is intertwined with the very essence of self.

*Diamonds* begin as a piece of coal. Coal has some value, but is useless unless it is consumed by fire. However, a piece of coal has a

---

[5] Romans 12:3; Galatians 6:3

greater potential, that of becoming a diamond. For coal to reach its greater potential, it must go through extreme heat and pressure. People who go through this process often find themselves facing extreme situations that could bring them to the abyss of destruction.

The Lord's heart is for His people to reach their potential in Him. This involves a process, and when His people come out on the other side, they will be priceless gems. One day, He will take these gems and place them in a crown that will reflect His glory.

The spiritual process is to *confront, challenge, and channel* the traits of each nature in order to change the person's disposition and behavior patterns. Even though people have a tendency to adopt the traits of those around them, the traits of their particular nature will be evident. These traits can be traced from a person's particular form of rebellion, not necessarily their personality. As you study the different traits of each nature, you will realize how they must be properly confronted in order to discern whether their traits must be disciplined or challenged. Once challenged, some traits must be mortified, allowing the rest of the traits to be channeled and brought under the control of God.

It is important to correctly discern the nature of a person to determine where he or she might be spiritually. For example, what would be considered normal for one person would be abnormal for another. There are three levels that people can operate within. They are: *balanced, unbalanced,* or *extreme.*

If a person is under God's authority, he or she will be balanced in his or her attitudes and responses. If a person is unbalanced, he or she is focused on self, which makes him or her self-centered and operating in a small world of rebellion, self-pity, and disillusionment. If a person is operating in extremes, then you can conclude Satan is on the scene.

This brings us to a very important point: *Who is ruling in your life?* Either God or Satan is the ruler. If Satan rules, it means sin is enslaving you and self is being exalted. If God reigns as your Savior and Lord, you can be assured of salvation and the work of sanctification.

Examine the following table and consider what your need, attitude, and response are. See if you can get a glimpse into your nature. Keep in mind most people never perceive themselves in the proper manner. This is why it can prove hard for some to see personal cycles and failures.

| SIMPLE PICTURE OF HUMANITY | | | |
|---|---|---|---|
| Deceptive Levels | I will *deal* with it, Leave me *alone*. | I will *handle* it, I will *prove* it. | I will *take care* of it, I will *show* you. |
| Rebellion Levels | *Withdraw* into mind. | *Justify* to avoid accountability. | *Make it right* In own sight. |
| Needs | Acceptance | Emotional Love | Recognition |
| Desires | Love | Peace | Joy/Happiness |
| Forms of Control and Manipulation | Words | Attitudes | Actions |
| Forms of Pride | Conceit (Focuses-Irritate) | Selfishness (Emphasize-Frustrate) | Pride (Preoccupy-Intimidate) |
| Types Found in Natures | Balanced (Under God) | Unbalanced (Self-centered) | Extreme (Demonic Influence) |
| Processes | Pearl (Irritants) | Gold (Friction/Boil) | Diamond (Heat/Pressure) |
| Three C's | Confront (Rebellion-Discipline) | Challenge (Mortify the Flesh) | Channel (Under the Spirit) |

# 2

# INTRODUCTION TO THE NATURES

The nature information has been confused and compared with the four temperaments teaching and the worldly philosophy of psychology. It is neither. In the first chapter I made reference to the prevailing mood or temperament of a person. Temperaments determine the condition of one's environment. However, they can fluctuate according to situations, but people still react according to their nature.

The spirit and disposition will determine what a person becomes. This is why a person's disposition must be transformed and brought under the control of the Spirit of God to change any wrong prevailing temperament. Even though our temperament changes, we will continue to act according to our nature. The difference is that the Spirit is now regenerating our traits. People must recognize the tendencies and traits of their natures, and make sure they are properly confronted and channeled under the control of the Holy Spirit to reach their potential in Christ.

Psychology is the study of human behavior, and generally excuses away personal sin and accountability. As you study its origins, you can conclude that it falls into the category of the worthless philosophies of men, the world, and spirit guides. The Apostle Paul made this statement in Colossians 2:8, "Beware lest any man spoil you through philosophy and vain deceit, after the tradition of men, after the rudiments of the world, and not after Christ."

The questionable origins and spirit of psychology has made the use of it in the Church a heated debate in Christendom. The Word is clear that God is the true counselor, and that people can only be set free by His truth. Truth means a person realistically comes to terms with his or her disposition in order to overcome and reach personal potential in Christ. The nature information simply explains the behavioral patterns of the four different natures in light of how the selfish disposition of pride works within the person.

Is the nature information legitimate? One must test the spirit behind it to see if it lines up to the Spirit of God and the truth of the Word of God. I have been working with this information since it was revealed to me in 1986. Women from my Bible Study tested it out. They would take the information home and try it out on their families. The results often shocked them as they began to see through the maze of cloaks that even their own family members hid behind. As they cut through the games of rebellion and control, distinct consistent patterns immerged.

Amazingly, even in its infant stages, four distinct natures could clearly be identified.

Over the next four years the information expanded. It was discovered that individuals are not as complex as they often appear to be. By understanding the nature of a person, one could cut through the excuses and games to address, properly confront, minister, or call a person to accountability. Each time the information was tried or presented there was an expectancy that it would break down at any moment. However, each time it was confirmed.

The nature information even transcended gender, culture, and race. The information was presented to Koreans who still adhered to their culture. I expected to find inconsistency in the information due to cultural influences. Once again it was confirmed. The Koreans clearly identified their particular nature along with those of their friends. One Korean lady testified how she had felt isolated in America, but after attending the seminar she realized there were Americans with the same nature as her. She no longer felt alone or isolated.

Another interesting test had to do with gender. There is a well-preserved assumption or myth that women are more emotional than men. I personally questioned this logic because as a woman, my emotions come out last in my cycle, while I have met men who were clearly emotional. These men's emotions often manifested in frustration and anger. As a result, I witnessed confusion among the sexes, while occasionally questioning my own normalcy. Later I discovered that culture often defines people based on their gender rather than their person, character, and abilities. This has caused a tremendous amount of personal conflict, as well as identity crises.

In the unveiling of these natures, it was discovered that emotions surface at different stages for the different natures. For example, there is one nature that is emotional up front. Whether the individual is male or female, he or she feels very deeply about things, and displays emotional fervor in causes and beliefs.

On the other end of the spectrum, another nature goes through a process of mental evaluation until feelings are encountered. For people of this nature, it can actually take as much as a couple of weeks (or in some cases, years) for their emotions to emotionally catch up to them. In one incident, it took two weeks for a woman's sorrow over her grandfather's death to catch up with her. At the funeral she thought herself to be unfeeling. Two weeks later a minor incident caused her to fall apart. It was at this point that her grandfather's death had emotionally penetrated her.

In one of the Hidden Manna Seminars, I encountered a skeptic who questioned the information. He had come because of the insistence of his wife and friends. As I began to share the information, he started to relax. This man was the emotional type. In the past, he could not understand his enthusiasm, sensitivity, and his emotional fervor or outbursts. He had questioned his normalcy as a man. In the seminar he discovered that he was quite normal for his nature. In fact, God had used his emotional fervor to make him a bold witness. This brought tremendous peace to his soul, and even his daughter noticed that he possessed an inner peace that had not been there in the past.

The next weekend after the seminar, this man and his wife celebrated their wedding anniversary. Their time together was rewarding and precious because of the special insight they received about their individual natures. The following Tuesday, the man had a heart attack and went home to be with the Lord. His wife was thankful for the impact the nature information had brought to his life and their relationship in the short time they had remaining together.

On another occasion, an educator was ready to put her 13-year-old daughter into a detention center. She asked me to meet with her after she overheard me talk about the nature information. As she described her daughter, her nature was quickly identified. The mother was then advised how to properly confront her daughter according to the young girl's nature. The mother was also told that she would be pleasantly surprised to see that her daughter would probably display integrity. A couple of months later I touched base with the mother. She shared that her daughter was responding in a constructive way, and she was pleasantly surprised to discover that she had good character.

In one of my first seminars in Washington State, a woman recognized the nature of her daughter who had tried to commit suicide a few weeks earlier. She immediately applied the information, not only in regards to her daughter, but her whole family. She immediately witnessed results.

In another situation a young girl was acting contrary to her nature. In questioning her mother, she admitted that she and her husband suspected that the little girl had been molested. I realized that what she was displaying was shame. We ministered to her and dealt with her shame. The last time I saw her, the shame was gone and she was acting in accordance to her nature.

This information fascinates people and often appeases the intellect. Like the Word of God, when this information is kept on an intellectual plane and not put into practice, it becomes useless. Spiritual truths of God are meant to change attitudes and relationships. This is true for this information. When put into proper practice it has proven to stop destructive cycles, change the disposition of a person, and has been priceless in marriage relationships and for parents dealing with their children.

As previously stated, there are four distinct natures that are veiled in humanity. These four natures are:

**Submissive**

**Stubborn**

**Self-Assured**

**Strong-Willed**

Clear pictures or impressions come into people's minds when they hear or read the names of these natures. One individual asked me how I came up with them. She considered a couple of the names to be offensive.

I went to the Lord and asked Him the reason for the names. He revealed to me the names were based on the wall of protection. People put this wall up when they feel that someone does not understand them. Without proper understanding, a person does not feel that he or she can afford to be vulnerable because the individual in question cannot be trusted. Therefore, the person will put up a wall that will protect him or her from being hurt. For example, *submissive* people are not wimps, but they can quickly put up a wall of fear and submit to it.

The *stubborn* person is not always obstinate, but when threatened, he or she will put up an obstinate wall. In this state a stubborn person will not only refuse to move, but will dare anyone to try to knock down the wall.

The *self-assured* nature does not mean the person is sure of self. In fact, this type of individual can be very unsure of self and erect two different walls to protect or hide insecurities and uncertainties to maintain an outward facade. One wall can be emotional while the other one immovable and harsh.

The wall of the *strong-willed* person is actually comprised of all of his or her traits. This person can be dynamic, and will have a sense of infallibility. This individual's wall can be intimidating and immovable to those who encounter his or her wall.

By understanding a person's nature, you can know how to keep the person's wall down. This allows for communication and keeps open the avenue that will help to confront isolation, vain imaginations, moral deviation, and depression.

Each nature has different needs, forms of pride, and different means of manipulation and control. They process information differently, confront challenges according to their areas of strengths, and approach life from a different perspective. As a result, there are a lot of speculations and assumptions going on in people who have a different nature. People marry individuals with different natures. This often makes a spouse feel as if he or she has married someone from another planet.

The diversities in these four natures cause pride to raise its ugly head. This is where the judgmental "board" blinds a person to his or her own personal faults as he or she focuses in on what are considered the other person's offenses.[1] These misunderstandings or evaluations cause people to walk in judgmentalism or condemnation towards those they harshly judge. Both of these attitudes cause problems in relationships as they express themselves in fear, anger, or arrogance.

When people recognize natures, it not only allows them to confront or approach others affectivity, but it helps them to accept who they are. Some people compare themselves to others because they have a hard

---

[1] Matthew 7:1-5

time accepting the way God made them.[2] As a result, they find themselves in an identity crisis as they struggle to find their place in the kingdom of God and recognize their form of leadership. The Apostle Paul said this about such comparison, "For we dare not make ourselves of the number, or compare ourselves with some that commend themselves: but they measuring themselves by themselves, and comparing themselves among themselves, are not wise" (2 Corinthians 10:12).

It is only as people accept the way God made them that they can accept God for who He is. Because many people cannot accept themselves, they unknowingly question God's reasoning. In their mind they represent a flaw in God's plan, rather than the potential to express Jesus Christ in a unique way.[3]

The beautiful discovery is that Christ is veiled or hidden in humanity. Once the Manna of heaven is unveiled in a person, he or she will discover the beauty of life, and will be able to impart this Manna to others.[4]

The question is, are you ready to discover in what way Jesus can be expressed in your humanity? Are you ready to take the journey through your inner person to see how you respond? Are you open enough to discover the makeup of your cycle so you can step outside of it and become a solution rather than part of the problem?

As you begin this journey of personal discovery, there are a few facts you need to remember.

You have only <u>one</u> nature. Many people become confused because they display traits of other natures. People of other natures do influence us, and we tend to adopt some of their traits. I call these <u>secondary traits</u>. You must discover your own basic nature, and then you can properly begin to distinguish the traits of your particular nature. This means you must come to terms with your form of rebellion and need. It is hard for people to recognize their rebellion because it is so natural for them to respond the way they do. In fact, it seems logical, practical, and justifiable, but rebellion comes down to dealing with, handling, or taking care of a matter in one's personal strength. Personal strength points to pride, self-sufficiency, and independence.

When people first learn this information, they do not like what they see about their nature. Some become very upset and depressed. It proves what the Bible has long advocated, that there is no good thing in man's flesh.[5] The purpose of this information is to recognize the different aspects of our nature so we can reach our potential in Christ. The explanation of each nature is based strictly on how the particular nature operates when it is in its unregenerate state.

If you are a mature Christian, it might be hard to recognize yourself. Self-denial, the application of the cross, and the sanctifying work of the

---

[2] Psalm 139:14-24
[3] Romans 8:29; 2 Corinthians 3:18
[4] John 6:32-40; Revelation 2:17
[5] Romans 3:10; 7:18

Spirit can change much in your disposition, but the nature is still in place, but now it will be transformed to reflect Jesus, rather than the old man.

Keep in mind; we are the ones who least know ourselves. People have an unrealistic idea of who they think they are. Sometimes it is hard to recognize one's own nature, but those who live with us know us quite well. If you are in confusion about your nature, ask those around you how you really act and respond in situations.

With these points in mind, it is time to begin this incredible journey to discover how God made you, and what He wants to accomplish in you. Your life will never be the same, your relationships will change, and your perception of God will be enlarged to embrace the revelation and unveiling of Christ in your life.

# 3

# SUBMISSIVE NATURE

People with a submissive nature often come across as *sweet* and *quiet*. They are considered the most compliant child or one of the nicest of individuals. This outward sweetness usually hides a great deal of fear. In fact, the walls of protection that people erect hide some form of fear, but for submissive people, their actual rebellious wall is *fear*. This wall is quickly erected in situations that the submissive person does not understand or may have to *confront*.

Due to the sweet exterior and the inward fear, submissive people can send confusing messages to others. Confusion causes problems in their relationships because these people need to be *accepted*, but often feel they are accepted only if they are compliant. This makes them feel as if they must earn acceptance by being good, which may produce resentment, anger, and rebellion in them.

A submissive person seeks to understand the mechanics of something. They have a mind like a computer. It is full of compartments that contain various "file cabinets." Within these "cabinets" are options that can be explored or considered in the right situation. Because of how they process information, they are very *persevering* in their attempts to find the best solution to their problem or challenge.

Submissive people have great confidence in their ability to figure something out. Their attitude is, *"Leave me alone, I will deal with it."* When faced with a challenge, they *withdraw* into their mind and begin to *analyze* possible options. James 4:8 states, "Draw nigh to God, and he will draw nigh to you." This person is actually drawing away from God instead of closer to Him. However, the submissive people's great confidence in their ability to reason something out blinds them to the reality that they are in competition or opposition against God's wisdom.

Submissive people are very *methodical* in their approach to a problem. Their speed of processing information also determines the speed with which they do all of their activities. They will only move as fast as their mind is able to process information. I have seen people of this nature with different speeds. Some move fast, others have a medium speed, and others are slow. They usually have one consistent pace. In fact, if this person is pushed to move beyond his or her speed, he or she can become overwhelmed. This is when you might find this type of individual parked behind a wall of fear. Each time you try to push the submissive person to move or go faster, the wall of fear can often be reinforced.

These individuals will seek out the best option, method, program, or diplomatic way to deal with a problem. Sadly, submissive people do not realize that exaltation of their mind is idolatry. An unregenerate mind is at enmity with God.[1] It is unable to discern the things of God, causing a person to walk in the flesh rather than in the Spirit.

The *mind* is where the submissive person's rebellious cycle begins. It leads the person down a path of *dramatization* and depression as he or she loses perspective. These people actually begin to develop ruts in their mind. As different challenges confront them, they stick every challenge, bit of information, or conclusion in a compartment to consider or deal with it later. Amazingly, these people can even have a compartment for the things they choose to ignore.

Eventually, all of the compartments become full. When this happens, submissive people cease to be compliant and even-tempered, and become *obnoxious*. Attitudes begin to stick out as they become *unmanageable* in their responses, intense as they hide further behind their wall of fear, and unbearable to live with. By this time, they are out of control and out of perspective. For this type of individual, it is like falling off an emotional cliff into a pit; and, climbing out of it will take everything in them to come once again into emotional balance. This is why Proverbs 3:5 serves as a valuable instruction to these people, "Trust in the LORD with all thine heart; and lean not unto thine own understanding."

Emotions are the last reaction that comes out of this person. When this type of person begins to show emotions, you know that situations are catching up to him or her, and will eventually overwhelm him or her. In fact, these people's mental compartments usually fill up with unresolved issues that have been put on the shelf until another day. At this stage of the cycle, understanding is clearly eluding the submissive person, making him or her feel that his or her life is out of control. It is from this premise that these individuals have a tendency of withdrawing even deeper into their mind.

The biggest problem with submissive people is that all of this mental exercise comes down to them *avoiding outright confrontation* with someone, or simply facing the reality of an environment that is becoming confusing as it increasingly spins out of control. This avoidance is very self-centered and self-serving, but it is often considered noble by the submissive person.

Submissive people refuse to see that their unwillingness to face problems up front has nothing to do with protecting or watching out for the other person, but with protecting self of possible conflict or consequences that might inevitably make them appear as a *failure*. Such avoidance is a form of control and manipulation that refuses to face the selfishness behind the game that is being played. This *fake nobility* that is displayed often covers up the submissive people's greatest initial fear—that of failure. Their unwillingness to confront problems because of

---

[1] Romans 8:5-8

their fear of failure throws them into cycles in their relationships with others including God.

This cycle begins with the submissive person trying to avoid, comply, or please someone to keep the peace as a means to avoid conflict. Such a response requires a submissive person to play the game to avoid confrontation. The natural tendency for people in a relationship with a submissive person, who has avoided properly confronting them for wrong attitudes or actions, is to take advantage of him and her. When the submissive person plays these people's game, it usually unleashes the monster of pride and selfishness in them rather than subduing it. These individuals become more demanding, abusive and disrespectful towards the submissive individual. The submissive person struggles with how to properly deal with the other person or issue as the matter escalates, while striving to maintain his or her sweetness and nobility. As these individuals struggle, they devise well-planned statements that are meant to stop the other person in his or her tracks, thereby, avoiding confrontation.

Submissive people are good at using *words* as a means to control and manipulate. In some cases, it works, while in other situations, it simply prolongs a matter. In the end, submissive people are left with a lot of *unresolved issues* that will develop into a tidal wave that will eventually threaten to destroy their mental and emotional well-being and their relationships.

Unresolved issues will eventually bury these individuals. This is where the submissive person will give up and spiral downward into depression. These individuals can retreat behind barricades of eating disorders, alcoholism, drug abuse, and imaginary or exaggerated physical problems. These excessive behaviors have three possible sources behind them: 1) They serve as forms of control; 2) they are a means of getting attention; and 3) they become ways of self-destruction.

Extreme behaviors in submissive people that are not properly challenged can cause the submissive person to toy with the option of *suicide*. When a submissive person is at this point, he or she is in major depression. It is a sign that the person is out of perspective and needs to be properly confronted. Sadly, this person rarely shares what he or she is thinking about. Suicide, therefore, is often this person's dangerous little secret.

# Pride in Action

A submissive person's form of pride is hard to detect. In fact, his or her pride would be considered a covert pride. Because these people's pride is not obvious, they actually view themselves as superior to others whose pride may be more obvious.

Submissive people's arrogance can clearly be observed in relationships. I knew of a submissive woman who displayed steady calmness in most situations. Her husband, who was more expressive about his feelings, would especially vent in traffic. She viewed his actions as unacceptable and felt superior to him. This woman was blinded to her form of pride, a sin that God resists. In fact, it is the covert sins that will sink a person more than outward disobedience.

The pride that motivates a submissive person is *conceit*. Although conceit has a certain air about it and causes *irritations* in others, it is hard to detect in this type of individual because it is not expressed in obtrusive self-exaltation. In fact, this individual is often considered to have a low or no self-esteem, and will nobly throw the attention elsewhere to avoid being noticed. The reason is that the submissive person wants to be left alone in his or her world. If submissive people do emerge from their self-made mental world, they will want you to know how smart, humble, sweet, wise, or good they are. Conceit ultimately translates into intellectual pride. It takes pride in what it knows and can do.

These people perceive themselves to be *wise* in all their ways. They will try to reason with others about their way of doing things. If they encounter someone who will not agree or tolerate their reasoning or condescending air, they will nobly give way to the other person and become a suffering martyr. This fake nobility still leaves them on top of the game because it exhibits more honor than the one who refuses to receive wise instruction.

Even though submissive people outwardly give way to someone else's perception, they never give in mentally. They usually maintain their way of thinking, and will go back to the drawing board to devise a cleverer argument for the next encounter. If the issue is not resolved according to their way of thinking, they will end up overanalyzing, which causes them to appear unreasonable, foolish, or obsessive. In fact, people who are trying to deal with a submissive person at this state would refer to him or her as being *pigheaded*.

Conceit's greatest disguise is *false humility*. False humility is nothing more than worldly remorse.[2] Worldly remorse will take some accountability for failure, but it is to make such individuals feel they have properly conceded on a matter. Since they have come to terms with it in their mind, they figure that you need to get off their back and leave them alone.

The reason most submissive people fall short of true repentance is because they simply work it out in their mind. They perceive that now that they have worked it out in their mind, it is reality. These people have failed to realize that they have not changed their mind. They have simply added another conclusion to one of their compartments. Since they have not changed their mind, their heart maintains the same inclinations that keep them on the same path or course. In other words, nothing has changed.

Changed lives are the fruit of true repentance. When those around submissive people do not see the change, they will not give them the desired acknowledgment. After all, submissive people work hard to bring

---

[2] 2 Corinthians 7:10

everything together in their mind. To not be recognized for such a feat is considered unfair. This is when fake nobility turns into self-pity. These people began to feel sorry for themselves because they have done everything to play the game and cannot understand why others will not recognize their attempts. Once again, these individuals come out on top in their minds as they become victims.

Like all pride, unchallenged conceit will eventually lead its devoted followers into delusion. This delusion creates a sick little world of depression, obsession, and utter ridiculousness. Ultimately, the submissive person becomes a fool in his or her own conceits.

# Overcoming

Submissive people must come to terms with their traits in order to overcome. They must be surrounded by God's perspective much like the grain of sand is when being formed as a *pearl*. One of the traits they must honestly *confront* is their sweetness. This trait is not part of the fruit of the Spirit. Rather, it is part of their selfish disposition. This sweetness gives a false sense of goodness to these people. They hide behind it to avoid confrontation. Their unwillingness to confront falls in with the sins of omission, where righteousness is being omitted in a matter. This unwillingness is also a subtle form of unbelief because it shows that those who avoid confronting life do so out of fear and complacency. Submissive people must realize that their sweetness often serves as a cloak to cover up their true depravity.[3] It is not an expression of Jesus, but a means to receive desired acceptance and undeserved recognition. Therefore, this trait must give way to the sanctifying work of the Holy Spirit.

Certain traits must be disciplined. For the submissive person, he or she must discipline his or her analytical mind. Overanalyzing causes this person to *dramatize*. In order to keep their minds balanced, submissive people must withdraw into God. This allows their earthly wisdom to give way to the true wisdom of heaven.[4] Godly wisdom means one will have God's perspective. And, it is His perspective that ensures balance in a submissive person's life.

There are other traits that must be *mortified* or put to death. The submissive traits that fall into this category are fear and conceit. Fear demands worship from its subject. As long as submissive people give in to it, they will be hindered from reaching their potential in Christ. When submissive people encounter fear, they must step back from the wall, decide to step through it, ask Jesus to take their hand, and leave fear behind as they take steps of faith through fear's darkness.

Submissive people must realize that their conceit is perverted and earthly wisdom. Once they agree with God's evaluation about it, they must ask Him to reveal how it works in their life and to give them a

---

[3] Galatians 5:22-23; James 4:17; John 15:22
[4] James 3:13-17

hatred for it. Pride can only be overcome by a repulsive hatred towards it. Submissive people must realize that conceit does not make them wise, but sets them up to play the fool.

There are traits that must be *channeled*. Submissive people must learn to withdraw into God. This means they will be putting their confidence in Him, rather than in their minds. This allows the Holy Spirit to properly channel all information, in order to bring forth God's perspective. Once the mind is transformed, the submissive person will gain an understanding of God's way. It is this understanding that establishes the submissive person on the immovable Rock of Ages and brings peace to his or her mind.[5]

# Confrontation

How do you properly confront a submissive person? You must first recognize when he or she is in his or her cycle. There are two indicators that this type of person is in a destructive cycle. The initial sign are bad attitudes. Submissive people do not have strong attitudes per se. Therefore, any sign of an attitude means that they are overwhelmed and their compartments are full.

The second indicator is unbalanced or extreme behavioral patterns. For example, if a submissive person is overly emotional or obnoxious, there is something amiss in his or her world. Obviously, there are unresolved issues that are filling up his or her compartments.

If the submissive person is very withdrawn, this is a big warning signal. You must not allow him or her to remain in his or her world unchallenged. Such extreme behavior points to depression, which can include suicidal thoughts and plans. These people will be tight-lipped about such plans unless asked. However, if you show *acceptance* and firmly challenge their perception with the facts, they will simply do their submissive thing by automatically withdrawing and considering what you have presented.

As you consider how you confront different people, you will begin to see how you actually use a person's nature against him or her in confrontation. You do this by using the person's need and way of processing information to get their attention. Once you have people's attention, you can effectively speak into their lives. For example, you show a submissive person acceptance to keep his or her wall down. By understanding that such an individual analyzes all information, you must be ready to firmly give these people the facts. These facts will challenge the submissive person's perspective. Granted, these people will try to occasionally deter you by being obnoxious or running you around with reason. Do not be sidetracked by either detour. Once the submissive person gains perspective, he or she is most likely to admit when he or she has been out of line.

---

[5] Isaiah 26:3

When giving this nature the facts, avoid being harsh or placating. If you are harsh with this type of individual, you will encounter his or her wall of fear. If you try placating the submissive person, he or she will perceive it as a game and will lose respect for you.

# 4

# STUBBORN NATURE

The greatest struggle for the stubborn-natured person is with his or her *emotions*. Unlike submissive people whose emotions come out at the last part of his or her cycle, emotions are the first thing you encounter with the stubborn individual. In fact, these people wear their emotions on their sleeves.

The emotional level of a stubborn people makes them *personable*. Often this front hides insecurities and doubts while keeping others at a distance. It is also a means for some stubborn people to con others. This is a form of control and manipulation that will eventually be exposed for the game it is, causing them to lose credibility.

The emotions of stubborn people run deep, and will cause confusion and conflict in their worlds. These emotions have almost a tormenting force behind them that often causes these people to seek after relief, pleasure, and satisfaction through various avenues. They can become *impulsive* about filling up their worlds with things or activities that make them feel good, or will satisfy their need to bring meaning and purpose to their often-chaotic world. These means are always temporary, which can send them on unusual or sporadic searches. Needless to say, trying to bring undisciplined emotions under control can prove to be very overwhelming to these people. As a result, they often live in a dream world while unsuccessfully trying to manipulate and adjust their world to their particular fantasies. If stubborn people run out of fantasies or the means to satisfy their emotions due to harsh reality that remains constant, they will close down their emotions. This will create a zombie who will be expressionless due to utter hopelessness.

Stubborn people need to feel *love*. This love is an emotional love where others actually enter into the emotional world with them. For the other three natures who do not understand the emotional plight of these people, it can be both frustrating and traumatic. They do not know how to calm the emotional beast that often rises up within stubborn people. This beast can become explosive and abrasive.

This type of individual feels the need to earn this emotional love. There are four reasons for this outlook: 1) Stubborn people feel vulnerable in the area of love because of being gullible; 2) they strive to be indispensable to others to avoid experiencing rejection; 3) they have high standards that demand reformation; and 4) they need proof of love; therefore, they conclude they must earn love. The gullibility of a stubborn person comes down to his or her need to be transparent with others.

This is to ensure that people will simply love him or her for who he or she is.

Stubborn people try to become indispensable to those they love and care about because of their own insecurities and fears. Their greatest fear is *rejection*. They do everything to avoid this feeling, only to find rejection haunting them as they are misunderstood and often taken for granted.

People of this nature have very high *standards*. These standards not only put unrealistic pressure on them along with those in their environment, but they actually box them in. Such standards are meant to bring discipline to the stubborn person's emotions and environment, but instead of bringing order to the environment, these standards often cause these people to become hard and unmerciful. These high standards make them very judgmental and skeptical about anything that does not initially line up with their unrealistic values or undisciplined emotions.

The stubborn person requires proof of love. Sadly, this proof may be insatiable and unrealistic. These people can put up a fuss or fight, and expect those who care about them to fight for them, not with them. Even though they want others to fight for them, they either put up resistance to such attempts, or they emotionally run people around. Those who are dealing with this type of nature find themselves fighting with these individuals. This causes those who are trying to contend with them to throw up their hands in utter hopelessness or walk away in frustration.

The emotional stubborn person feels deeply about personal beliefs. These people can be *persistent* in their pursuits. This happens when they get caught up with causes that will rob them of valuable time, take them on detours, or lead to obsessions. It is not unusual for these people to get caught up with the causes of the underdog because they have a deep sense of loyalty, as well as hate unfairness. In the process, such causes can turn into obsessions that often throw common sense and reality out the door. These obsessions imply total indifference and delusion about reality.

Stubborn people can display common sense. Their *practical* approach to life, decisions, and situations can cause those with a different nature to experience frustration and anger. In most cases, a balanced and realistic stubborn person does see the end result of situations, but due to his or her emotional level, others rarely take this individual seriously. Problems, therefore, are not averted and the stubborn person is proven to once again be correct. This can cause resentment and jealousy with those who did not understand or respect the practical, simple side of this type of individual.

The stubborn individual strives hard to maintain or control his or her environment to keep on top of his or her emotions. This need to control the environment to keep emotions intact is often considered controlling and manipulative by others. Such a perspective will cause more *friction* for the stubborn person who has failed to realize he or she must bring personal emotions under control before his or her world can have order.

Stubborn people are consistent in their emotional patterns. The emotional cycle usually starts when *plans* are *interrupted*. These people try hard to organize their day so they can complete the many demands or responsibilities of their world. For example, a stubborn person may have 20 different activities on his or her list. These people actually can make plans in their mind right down to the last minute as to what they are going to do. Then, someone adds one more demand; the *pressure* begins to build because this individual no longer feels emotionally on top of it. This becomes obvious as he or she begins to *complain* about all of his or her responsibilities. This is followed by *strong attitudes*.

If the emotional momentum is not properly dealt with, *explosive anger* follows. This anger breeds insult, offense, hurt, and anger in others. The results leave the stubborn person experiencing doubts, insecurities, and *guilt*. Satan starts to support this case of guilt, opening the door of condemnation. *Condemnation* will send this person into hopelessness or *depression*.

Stubborn people feel the depths of depression. They often fear it, and will do everything to avoid this unbearable pit. They actually run from it through activities, relationships, and substance abuse.

Due to the fickleness of their emotions, stubborn people are often *misunderstood*, causing them personal hurts and wounds. These people perceive themselves as *handling* any situation, and given enough time will *prove* it to others. Eventually, reality will collide with their world in the form of interrupted plans or rejection. They stand in confusion as they consider everything they did to get the necessary *approval* from those around them. After all, they have been giving, complimentary, and gone out of their way to become indispensable. When stubborn people do not receive the necessary acknowledgement or reaction from others, they can feel rejected, used, and abused. These feelings will produce hurt that turns into anger and *complaints*. These complaints can cause others around the stubborn person to scramble in an attempt to change a stubborn person's environment to keep the monster of selfishness at bay. To handle these emotions, a stubborn person will stuff them. Unresolved issues will create frustration, moodiness, and attitudes.

Once the stubborn person has stuffed an unresolved issue, he or she becomes a time bomb as the emotional momentum begins to build up like a volcano. It is a matter of time before something will cause him or her to explode, leaving others in a state of confusion and chaos.

This is when stubborn people come to the harsh reality that they cannot handle it. They begin to *justify* their reactions at the expense of their environment. For example, if it was not for so or so, or this or that, they would have never exploded. Quickly, they release themselves from personal responsibilities while trying to handle the guilt they feel under the barrage of excuses. These excuses allow them to erect a *stubborn* wall of protection. This wall declares that no one will pass beyond it. It implies the stubborn person must maintain their justification about a matter and will not sway from his or her stand. At this point stubborn people are viewed as being *bullheaded*. Not only do they refuse to be moved, but if challenged, they will charge and push back all opposition. But, in spite of the justification and wall, the guilt remains intact.

Stubborn people desire to be stopped at the point of justification in order to silence their guilt. Although they can act unreasonably when confronted, the stubborn person does not know how to stop him or herself after a certain emotional point or silence the onslaught of personal excuses. In my experience with these individuals, I have found that their excuses are a means of trying to convince themselves that they are not guilty. If they do not come to truth about their personal involvement in a situation, they can become deluded. This means they create ruts in their mind where excuses become a truth rather than a point of self-justification and self-delusion. When stubborn people are in this type of rut, their bullheadedness becomes apparent as the truth is pushed aside, and they become defensive, unreasonable, angry, and in some cases bullies.

Due to their *undisciplined emotions*, these people desire proper discipline, but will rebel against any form of control and manipulation. Although these people can come across as pushy, they will not tolerate being pushed or controlled by others. Sadly, those who are around them try to control or manipulate them because they are afraid of how they might react in different environments or situations. To stubborn people, such attempts are like putting a red flag in front of a charging bull. Needless to say, they will oblige.

# When Pride Hits the Scene

Pride is the last trait that enters the scene in the stubborn person's cycle, but when it does, it leaves quite a mark or impression. *Selfishness* is the stubborn person's form of pride. It works off of the ego and vanity of the stubborn person.

Stubborn people take pride in what appears to be selfless giving, when in reality, there is usually a self-serving motive behind it. The main motive behind this flurry of giving, besides the good feeling it provides, is often to receive the desired love or approval. They *want* people to exalt them in order to feel needed, understood, and important. Selfishness rears its ugly head in this nature after attempts of love and approval are not properly returned. This makes this type of person feel used and unappreciated. This is when selfishness becomes offended.

Offense produces frustration, which is verbally expressed by *words* that are followed by strong *attitudes*. These words are complaints or excuses that will escalate the momentum of selfishness. Selfishness begins to *emphasize* self blatantly. Such an emphasis becomes an appetite that cannot be satisfied. This inability to quiet selfishness and to keep it from exploding often causes frustration in those who are trying to contend with it.

Eventually, selfishness will build such a case in the stubborn person's mind that it begins to see and define the lack of response as treacherous and a form of betrayal. Due to the fact that their touchy emotions are taking center stage in their world, stubborn people take everything personally; therefore, in their mind everything is directed at them. They perceive betrayal as personal rejection. This will create the disguise of selfishness: that of the martyr syndrome.

As a martyr, the stubborn person becomes a suffering victim with an attitude. This bleeding, wounded victim may display self-pity and sarcasm. The end of this cycle is *depression*.

# Overcoming

Those who are stubborn by nature must go through a *gold* process. This is where God allows friction in their world to sift or separate them from their unending excuses. This friction causes confusion and brings them to a point of total frustration. God wants stubborn people to realize they cannot handle life on their terms. All of their means of trying to substantiate their worth proves to be disappointing and depressing. These individuals must realize that they are only justified at the point of the blood of Jesus. This justification can only occur through repentance and faith.[1]

Stubborn people must learn to discipline their emotions and not their environment. This means they must first come under the control of the Holy Spirit. The Holy Spirit creates an attitude of meekness. This meekness produces self-control or temperance in the soul area.[2]

Self-control is very important for a stubborn person because he or she judges reality according to feelings rather by than the Word of God. Once the emotions are lined up with the Word of God, the stubborn person will have stability in his or her reality and world. If the emotions come under control, then the impulsive drive, persistence, and loyalties will be channeled in the right way.

It is also important for stubborn people to not take everything personally. They need to keep in mind that the world does not revolve around them. Much of what is happening around them is the evidence of human nature in operation, and not a personal affront against them. They must learn to discern between such matters by getting past touchy feelings, and properly discern what is going on in their environment.

Another trait that must be disciplined is the *stubborn* wall. Stubborn people must be careful about where they erect their wall. They need to be stubborn towards and for the things of God, but never in relationship to personal pride.

Selfishness must be mortified through neglect. It is hard for stubborn people to identify their pride because they are so giving. The test does not lie with outward actions, but inward motives.[3] The motives constitute

---

[1] Luke 13:5; Romans 4:5; 5:18
[2] Galatians 5:22-23
[3] Proverbs 16:2

selfishness; therefore, stubborn people need to rightfully discern their motives to avoid self-justification and delusion.

Stubborn people must mortify their standards or they are in danger of becoming bigoted, self-righteousness, dogmatic, and opinionated. Their unusually high standards are not realistic or obtainable. Ultimately, these standards will box this individual into a narrow, judgmental, self-centered world that becomes the means by which stubborn people judge all matters, including God. The Word tells us God's ways are not the standards of the stubborn person. These standards may be high and rigid, but God does not ordain them. These narrow rulers become burdens too great to bear, as they comprise a yoke too heavy to carry. These people need to exchange their standards with Jesus' yoke and burden.[4]

Stubborn people must give up their need to be loved by others and allow the love of God to fill up that insatiable vacuum. The desire to find approval from others can prove to be a grave snare.[5] Because of this desire, many stubborn people accept ungodly relationships in order to get this need met. It is a dangerous trap.

These people must learn how to discern between conviction and condemnation to properly confront their guilt. The Holy Spirit convicts in order to bring a person to forgiveness and restoration, while Satan condemns. In condemnation, there is no hope for forgiveness and restoration, just hopelessness and judgment.

# Confrontation

Stubborn people operate according to a consistent cycle. It is easy to observe them and discover this cycle. The key to effectively entering in with stubborn people is one's ability to recognize this cycle and enter in at the right time.

Due to the emotional roller coaster of a stubborn person, it may appear difficult to determine when these people are actually in their cycle or whether they are venting emotions in order to keep things in perspective. If they are venting emotions because the frustration has built up in them, allow them to vent. Avoid getting in their face because you will be causing greater frustration.

To discern if a stubborn person is in his or her cycle, test his or her spirit. There is a decisive attitude behind these people's emotional momentum. Emotional venting comes in outbursts that indicate the person is working their way through the emotional maze, but in the stubborn cycle, it expresses itself in complaining. Complaining is different from the form of explanation and reasoning that often takes place in venting. Complaining is the means for this person to work up his or her emotional momentum in order to justify reactions.

---

[4] Isaiah 55:8-9; Matthew 11:28-30
[5] Proverbs 29:25; 1John 4:16-19

If the stubborn person is working his or her way up into an emotional lather, you must effectively confront him or her at the point of *frustration*. The stubborn person will emotionally run over you past this point. The key is to get him or her to recognize what truly ails him or her. This could be interrupted plans or hurt feelings that have been stuffed. Due to a stubborn person's ability to stuff points of frustrations and hurts, he or she may run you around, but you need to continue to bring him or her back to reality. Eventually, the source of his or her agitation will be revealed. Once a stubborn person can get the source out in the open, it can be resolved, stopping the cycle and allowing the stubborn person to emotionally land.

Keep in mind that to enter in with stubborn people means you are emotionally entering in with their emotional struggles. If your motive is to calm this person so you can have peace, he or she will see through it and throw up his or her wall of mistrust. If you are condescending towards these people because of their emotions, or trying to manipulate them to get a desired affect, it will backfire on you. Godly confrontation is always about the other person and not for self-serving reasons. A right attitude in confrontation will ensure that the person's dignity will remain intact.

# 5

# SELF-ASSURED NATURE

Self-assured people take pride in the idea that others cannot figure them out. They are *reserved* and will only let people in so far. They are also *unpredictable*. They can change in midstream when it comes to decisions, attitudes, and direction. This often causes confusion, chaos, and frustration for others.

Amazingly, self-assured people are easy to understand. The key to unlocking the mystery and confusion surrounding them comes down to something called *images*. Self-assured people have an image for every responsibility or role in their lives. For example, they will have an image for being a son or daughter, a sibling, friend, spouse, and parent. Each responsibility or demand requires a distinct, separate image. These different images are very detailed and demand perfection. Due to the need for perfection these people's greatest fear is *incompetence.*

These people can only maintain one image at a time. Tremendous frustration and anger arises when their different images begin to collide. You can actually witness them mentally scrambling to adjust their image according to the people that surround them. This conflict with images forces them to prioritize their images. The image that takes a back seat is usually that of the spouse.

Needless to say, the changing of image sends a mixed or confusing message to those who are contending with these people. Not only do they see the self-assured person change emphasis and attitude, but his or her course. This unpredictability causes confusion, insecurities, and conflict in the relationships of self-assured people.

In observing self-assured people, they use the confusion they create in their personal world to gain the upper hand over others. They use insecurities to lord over those in vulnerable positions, and conflict to control their space. In the end, it does not matter what kind of problems or conflicts they cause in their relationships, they will come out on top, or *justified* in their own sight.

This brings us to the self-assured motivation: pride. These people can display the very epitome of *pride*. Detailed concepts and high standards comprise their images. They can be very judgmental toward others. They not only personally operate according to images, but they have images for everyone and everything from their parents, spouses, and children to how their environment should look and function. When they encounter any inconsistency in any of these areas, they will become very judgmental and critical. In most cases, if one thing is out of order, they will zero in on the discrepancy while ignoring that which is right.

Their reactions to such discrepancies are often manifested in *cruelty*. They become very cutting or demeaning in their remarks. In their mind the situation is obvious to any thinking person; therefore, there will be no excuse for any inconsistency, and judgment will be rendered and demanded.

Self-assured people have a *lawyer's mind*. Each discrepancy is added to their list of offenses. This list can be literally written on various items, such as a piece of paper, on a calendar, or simply mentally erected in their minds.

These people have a *reservoir of anger*. When the reservoir is filled up, they will feel justified in taking actions against the culprit. Violence, cruelty, and mocking in various proportions are justified. It is not unusual for these people to shred those "culprits" whom they have a list against into hundreds of condescending pieces with their "list of evidence." Even though they leave their victims devastated, they feel justified. This justification makes them indifferent to the fruits of their personal actions, while changing their image makes them believe themselves to be guiltless of all wrongs committed by their previous expressions of anger, cruelty, and indifference.

Changing image simply means the person will change present reality. The image these people change into is either the "*good guy*" image or the one of a *victim* due to others' incompetence or injustice. Both the justification and image keep the self-assured person from ever being called to personal *accountability*. After all, his or her actions are justified, and due to the present image, he or she is not accountable for actions that occurred under another image.

Unless self-assured people have integrity at the point of their images, they can be good liars, especially to themselves. They will delude themselves by believing that their images truly represent their character and reality.

As you can see, images are everything to the self-assured person. However, these images are a means of hiding something. What are these images concealing? In fact, if you confront them, they will erect two walls to protect that hidden part of self from discovery.

The *first* wall is an *emotional wall*. When images begin to fail the situation, mass confusion hits the self-assured person. This confusion implies that this person's world is out of control. This will cause frustration that can express itself in an outburst of wailing or tears of *self-pity*. At the end of this wall is fear of incompetence, which immediately turns into anger. This anger is expressed in the second wall: that of *pride*. The wall of pride proves to be a harsh *unyielding* wall. This is where you discover that this person refuses to be wrong at any point, regardless of how much evidence can be provided as to his or her guilt.

The refusal to be wrong causes this individual to come across as being *mule-headed*. The difference between being bullheaded and mule-headed is that those who are bullheaded push their way through situations. Those who are mule-headed cause a fuss, which results in conflict and chaos among others in their environment. This redirects the focus from them, and puts it elsewhere.

It takes everything within self-assured people to admit when they are wrong. They often operate in generalities when it comes to personal injustices that they are directing at others. This unwillingness to be found, or proven, wrong causes them to be *indecisive* in making decisions. In fact, they often cleverly manipulate others around them to make desired decisions for them. For example, they present self-serving options. As they discuss these options with you, they cleverly nudge or push you towards the most preferred choice with their *logic* and strong *attitudes*. In the end, you usually make the decision they desire. The logic behind this game is that if anything goes wrong, guess who is to blame?

What are these people hiding behind their images? There are two traits they are hiding. The first trait is their incredible pride. This pride expresses itself throughout the self-assured person's many other traits. Pride is the essence of self. Therefore, whenever you encounter the pride of any nature, you have come to the end of that person. Unless this pride has been replaced with integrity, there is no character or substance behind it. It is at this point that you find out how deep or shallow a person is. This reality is clearly brought out in the self-assured person who has not developed integrity. Past these people's images, they can prove to be shallow vacuums that have no substance. They have nothing of importance or significance to offer.

The second trait self-assured people are hiding is their *fierceness*. They are fierce people. This can be expressed and seen through their *anger*. This fierceness is the force behind hiding and protecting both their pride and images. It is the unrelenting source behind justification. It causes intimidation through strong *attitudes*.

These people control and manipulate by using their *attitudes*. They can communicate volumes without saying a word. When accused of something that has not been made obvious through word or deed, they can deny it, laugh it off, mock, or become angry at the perceived injustice. Because of the strength behind these attitudes, people do adjust to them to avoid encountering the self-assured person's fierceness and possible repercussions.

If a self-assured person does make a decision without proper perspective, anger or vengeance often inspires it. These people can be very *persevering* in situations where they plan to make a statement, get their way, or an upper hand in a matter. They often leave a path of self-destruction without considering the devastation or consequences.

Once a self-assured person pays the consequences for personal actions, he or she will immediately take on the victim image, and display *self-pity*. Self-pity is the manifestation of fake nobility and worldly repentance. This can be seen in the lives of Esau and Judas Iscariot. Worldly repentance will always express itself in tears, while blaming others or circumstances for personal actions. This approach falls short of true repentance.[1]

# Confrontation

Self-assured people can be quite miserable in their existence. Needless to say, this misery finds company with those who have to live or contend with them. In fact, the more miserable they are, the stronger their attitudes will become and the more difficult they are to contend with. The struggle can become so great within these people that they can appear close to insanity, especially if they are constantly trying to adjust or change images.

Images can cause a lot of confusion and chaos. These people naturally believe that those around them should bow down, adjust, and worship their images. When their image does not get the desired response, these people will take offence on behalf of their image. Therefore, how can you get past the image to minister to the person?

Depending on whether you are trying to minister to them or confront them will determine the strategy you use. If you are ministering to them, you have to *recognize* their images in order to keep their walls down.

These people desire *recognition* for what they are trying to accomplish through their image. By recognizing the image that is the most important or prevalent at that time, you can discern what they are trying to accomplish in the situation or relationship. This will keep the walls down so you can address their rigid, unrealistic standards, and reason with their emotional side. The goal is to get them past their images to clearly see the fruits of their lives. These people must see the contrast between where they are and what they are striving for. This contrast will help them to realize that their standards are unrealistic and unobtainable. Such contrast is important for them to see that their unrealistic standards cause fear, frustration, and anger.

When in confrontation with a self-assured person, never argue with him or her. Since these people have a *lawyer's mind,* they perceive themselves to be *logical.* You will never win an argument with them because they have cleverly built a case against you in their minds that they will use to justify their deviant actions at your expense. They will use their "list" against you every time.

Self-assured people use their strong attitudes to draw people into their legalistic trap. The key is not to venture their way regardless of how pouty or moody they become. Leave them alone in their small, self-centered worlds and go about your business. Like the groundhog, they will eventually have to raise their heads out of their self-pity and come to you. This means they are coming to you on your terms. When they do, hold the line. In other words, make them responsible for their personal attitudes and actions no matter how much they try to throw the blame on you or others. Emphasize the fact that they are responsible for their own

---

[1] Matthew 27:3-9; 2 Corinthians 7:10; Hebrew 12:15-17

disposition and actions, and one day, they will stand before God and give an account for their ways and deeds.

This allows you to put up the contrast and declare that you will not take responsibility for them. Confrontation with self-assured people calls for firmness, authority, and brutal honesty. You cannot let them off the hook for one second, and you cannot move from off the line of truth until they realize that you are not budging. It is as though you must gain the necessary respect each time you confront them to silence the case they have collected against you or others.

# Overcoming the Image

Pride is the main trait that the self-assured people must overcome. Since pride is the very essence of who they are, it can require an intense process. This is why these people's process is related to that of *gold* where it must be *boiled* to separate the precious material from the impurities that are mixed with it. This boiling process is not only intense, but it can be quite drawn out.

As a reminder, pride loses its influence through neglect.[2] This simply means it must be replaced with integrity, and then ignored when it raises its head to demand obedience. Integrity helps a person discern between reality and the façade that such images create.

It is important that self-assured people fill up the vacant area behind pride with character that is produced by integrity. As they allow character to be worked in them by the Holy Spirit, their fierceness will be disciplined and channeled. Once channeled, this fierceness can be directed towards the work of God. This will bring forth powerful leadership in the kingdom of God.

Self-assured people must get rid of their lists of offences they are keeping to justify their attitudes and actions towards others. These people not only keep lists against others who have offended them, but against themselves for imperfections in their lives. These lists are opposite of love and faith. Love proves a person is of God, while faith is the only thing that truly pleases God.[3]

These people need to ask God to show them each of the lists that they have developed against others, as well as against themselves. These lists serve as seeds that will breed bitterness and unforgiveness. These two sins will end up breaking a pure heart and making a person into a judgmental, self-serving skeptic.

The self-assured person needs to discover his or her real potential in Christ. This will bring his or her fierceness and standards under the control of the Holy Spirit. Such discipline will enable self-assured people to reach their potential in the kingdom of God.

---

[2] Matthew 16:22-26
[3] 1 Corinthians 13:4-8; Hebrews 11:6; 1 John 4:15-21

# 6

# STRONG-WILLED NATURE

The biggest struggle for the strong-willed person is to let go of control of his or her atmosphere or world. In fact, *losing control* is the greatest fear of this person. It creates intensity and fear that can completely drive him or her into destructive behavior patterns.

These people operate in *extremes*. Even though strong-willed people give you an impression that all is calm, behind the scenes they are emotionally like bouncing balls. This extreme environment can be seen in their personality and atmospheres as well. For example, they can be very outgoing or very quiet. They can have a very orderly environment or they can live with an abundant amount of clutter. Either way, they are usually cognizant of what is affecting their world.

Strong-willed people are *decisive*. They make decisions that become concrete lines. These lines serve as boundaries in which these people perceive they can confidently operate. These boundaries form *ideas* that seem factual. Since these people perceive themselves as possessing facts, they cannot fathom the possibility of being wrong. Everything to them is black or white, and any shades of gray are either ignored or discarded. When these lines or ideas are challenged, these individuals will *make themselves right* in their own eyes regardless of the validity of the challenges.

These people maintain control by lining everything up in their world. They are people of *action*. Although much of what they do can prove to be nothing more than a bluff, they have a very intense atmosphere around them that causes others to line up or carry out their ideas. In fact, people around them can be intimidated by the strength that seems to permeate their sphere.

Strong-willed people's ability to get things done makes them appear to be *dynamic*. This dynamic appearance gives the impression that they are fearless. A great deal of this has to do with their *sense of infallibility*. Due to their factual perception, they believe there is no way they could be wrong about the decisions they have made or the conclusions they have come to. Since they are right, success awaits them. This success is usually just a matter of getting others to see it their way. Their ability to intimidate and bluff their way through situations serves as a powerful means to get others to line up to their way of doing or thinking. In fact, some of these people can bulldoze others over with their intensity, their sense of who they think they are, and their dynamic abilities to take on the impossible.

This brings us to the strong-willed person's need. This individual needs to be recognized for who he or she is. This *recognition* is a form of respect. Without this respect, strong-willed people will display mistrust towards others or lack confidence in their relationship with others. Mistrust will cause the strong-willed person to put up his or her wall.

The wall of mistrust is comprised of all of the traits of the strong-willed person. This wall can prove to be very immovable, and can make this type of person appear *hardheaded* when trying to reason with him or her. It also gives this individual a sense of infallibility. And, when the wall is erected, it is to maintain control of his or her world. This form of protection hides the tremendous fear that often drives this person to be impulsive or rash. The catalyst that holds this wall together is the strong-willed person's form of pride.

# Immovable Will

The strong-willed person has an iron-clad will. This will is tied up in his or her need to control, as well as his or her form of pride. It serves as an immovable barrier that this individual cannot get around no matter what is happening in his or her world.

Interestingly, strong-willed people can be motivated by any one of the three forms of pride. These different forms of pride are what bring distinction among those who are strong-willed. It is obvious what form of pride drives each strong-willed person because it will be extreme

Although strong-willed people appear to be strong, they can prove to be very *fragile*. This is obvious when they encounter confusion. Confusion means that reality is colliding with their world. Confusion is unacceptable and will not be tolerated by these people. It is at this point that you can begin to see how the will works in the strong-willed person.

When reality fails to fit within the ideas of strong-will people, they basically will ignore it as if it was a lie or discard it as silly, heretical, or unrealistic. This ability may maintain personal reality for a season until challenged again, but it causes hardship on those around them. It is the people around these individuals who must pick up the pieces or deal with the consequences of the strong-willed person's unwillingness to realistically confront challenging reality.

When reality catches up to the strong-willed person, it can cause tremendous self-pity. These people *avoid the emotions* of others because they feel that such emotions will confuse the issue. They often act as if they are afraid of others' emotions, or will not tolerate them because they consider such emotions to be nonsense. However, when these people lose control, they can be very emotional. In fact, they can be extreme in their emotional responses.

I have been shocked at these people's ability to adjust reality. In a way, they become clueless. This is a form of denial or fantasy. These people have an uncanny ability to actually turn off their minds to anything that will not fit within their concrete lines. It is not unusual for this person to ask the same question numerous times. When this happens, it simply means that he or she had not heard the desired answer. It is as if he or she is waiting for reality to adjust to his or her perception or conclusion to a matter.

Sadly, these people can lose a lot of credibility. People, who do not understand how the strong-willed nature processes reality, will question these people's intelligence, hearing, and mental functioning. Strong-willed people usually miss viable details that would change the present facts or situation. There are four possible reasons as to why they miss such details: 1) These details may not fit within their lines; 2) they are considered insignificant in light of present circumstances; 3) there is too much activity going on in their environment, causing a state of confusion; and/ or 4) they assume others will take care of the details as they continue to confront greater issues. If these individuals do not have integrity, they will bluff their way through situations they do not understand because of their concrete lines and need to control.

# Overcoming

Strong-willed people will be taken through a *diamond* process. The diamond starts out as a piece of coal. It appears as if it has worth, but coal is a piece of material that is ready to be consumed in the fire. On the other hand, the diamond represents a precious jewel that will be established in extreme heat and pressure. This means that a strong-willed person will go through an extreme process to ensure that he or she ceases to be a piece of coal ready for judgment, and becomes a diamond that is being made ready to reach its potential.

These people often find themselves in extreme situations because they are not sensitive to what is happening in their reality. Because of their immovable lines, they have very limited vision, leaving them open to fall into Satan's various snares.

The real battle for strong-willed people begins with their will. They must exchange their iron-clad will for the will of the Father. This is very difficult since pride and control is mixed up in it. The will of the strong-willed person must be submitted before his or her *lines* can be properly adjusted or disciplined according to God's purpose. As long as the will is intact, these individuals' lines remain immovable. Once the lines can be adjusted, these people can be lined up to God's will and purpose.[1]

Strong-willed people must mortify their *obsession to control or rule.* This strong desire exalts them as God in their life. This is idolatry that will cause rebellion and set them up for a fall. In order to put to death this obsession, they must give way to the control of the Holy Spirit. This means walking according to the Spirit and not their personal boundaries. The leading of the Holy Ghost will take away the hardness of their lines,

---

[1] Luke 22:42; John 4:34

and will bring tremendous liberty to them as they walk by faith according to the life of the Son of God that must be developed in them.[2]

Strong-willed people must keep in mind that they are not infallible. They must not take themselves too seriously. This reality will keep them humble enough that others may be able to warn or instruct them. I encourage strong-willed people to surround themselves with godly counselors or advisers whom they respect and trust.[3]

These people must learn to challenge their focus. Their ideas keep them very limited from perceiving reality around them. They must discipline their attention to embrace reality. This will help them to properly respond to and function among those around them.

In many cases, these people will surround themselves with those who will see it their way, ridding themselves of possible challenge or instruction. Strong-willed people can view any challenge as disrespectful instead of a necessity to maintain checks and balances in their lives and decisions. Beware of such strong-willed people because they harbor fragile egos due to fear, and are untrustworthy because there is no integrity or character.

Strong-willed people need to keep in mind that becoming a diamond is just part of the process. They must not only be completely changed from their lesser state to reach their potential, but they must be cut and polished. This process symbolizes their need to maintain a complete dependency on God to ensure that the remaining extreme traits of their nature will be properly disciplined and channeled for the glory of God.

## Confronting the Diamond

Strong-willed people demand respect and shun emotions. If respect is missing, they will discard you as an insignificant nuisance. They want the facts, and in their book, emotions confuse the issue. In fact, avoid anything to do with feelings. Even the statement, "I feel this way about something," can be a big turn off to the people of this nature.

The main thing those who contend with strong-willed people must determine is what constitutes respect to these individuals. First of all, showing any fear or intimidation is not considered respect, but a weakness. A person must not only show respect to the strong-willed person, but also have his or her respect. The way you gain respect from this nature is to drop all emotions and signs of weakness.

If you have their respect, *look them in the eyes.* These people like eye contact. In their initial meeting with you, they size you up on the basis of whether you make eye contract with them. This is hard for other natures who may feel intimidated by them, but is vital if you are going to have any authority to speak into their lives.

Once you have their attention, firmly and decisively give them the facts. Avoid any type of explanation or rhetoric. You will immediately

---

[2] 2 Corinthians 3:17; Galatians 5:16-18
[3] Proverbs 11:14

lose them. Keep it to the point and then back off. These people will make up their mind. Do not take it personally if they fail to respond to your warning or advice. If these people love God, it will be up to Him to confirm and adjust their lines.

# In Review

Let us now compare the differences between these four natures. You will be able to see how distinct they are from each other. The differences are simple, yet they are far reaching when it comes to how each nature responds in crises and in their relationship to God and others. Consider the following table on the next page.

| TRAITS | SUB-MISSIVE | STUBBORN | SELF-ASSURED | STRONG-WILLED |
|---|---|---|---|---|
| PROCESS | Pearl | Gold/Sifting | Gold/Boiling | Diamond |
| REBELLION | Withdraws | Justify (Front Door) | Justify (Back Door) | Make it Right |
| RESPONSES | Analytical | Impulsive | Unpredictable | Decisive |
| CHARACTER | Sweet | Personable | Reserved | Extreme |
| CONTROL | Words | Word/ Attitudes | Attitudes/ Actions | Actions |
| APPROACH | Persevere | Persistent (Aggressive) | Persistent (Logical) | Dynamic |
| PERCEPTION | Wise | Practical | Logical | Factual |
| PRIDE | Conceit | Selfishness | Pride | Any of the Three Forms Of Pride |
| WALL | Fear | Stubborn | Emotional/ Pride | Infallibility |
| NEED | Acceptance | Emotional Love | Recognition for their accomplish-ments | Recognition for who they are |

# 7

# REALITY VS. PERCEPTION

Each nature perceives him or herself as being reasonable and realistic in his or her conclusions about present reality. In fact, each of these natures cannot perceive how they could be wrong about any matter they have carefully considered. This conclusion is in opposition to the words of Isaiah who declares that man's thoughts are not God's thoughts.[1]

God's thoughts consist of simple truths that are profound. The profound aspect of God's truths often causes people to complicate them in order to understand them. This complication actually is what perverts or defiles the truths of God. It is at this stage that man begins to hold the truth in unrighteousness, which is considered a serious offence in the Bible.[2]

Regardless of what nature a person may be, he or she has a selfish disposition. Unchallenged, selfishness always gives way to the lust of the flesh, the pride of life, and the lust of the eyes. When selfishness reigns, the pride of life is the motivation that reigns supreme when it comes to a person's perception. Pride perverts present reality and adjusts it according to personal conclusions. This pseudo reality often avoids personal accountability and responsibility, and falls short of coming to the truth of Jesus Christ.[3]

People look to self to understand the workings and happenings of the world around them, rather than looking to God. The Apostle Paul talked about the unregenerate mind in Romans 8:6, "For to be carnally minded is death; but to be spiritually minded is life and peace."

Romans 12:2 states that the mind must be transformed. Transformation of the mind by the Holy Spirit will produce the mind of Christ. God is the only one who can bring a correct perspective to a person, but few ever take into consideration their need to have their minds transformed. They fail to believe that they know in part and see through a glass (flesh) darkly. They believe that God gave them a brain to find solutions. This conclusion causes them to lean on their own understanding.[4] Looking within for the answer causes introspection. Introspection points to a self-centered perspective.

---

[1] Isaiah 55:8-9
[2] Romans 1:18
[3] John 14:6
[4] Proverbs 3:5-7; 1 Corinthians 13:9, 12; Philippians 2:5

Amazingly, people are surprised when they find out that their conclusions are not trustworthy and far from the truth that can make them free. They cannot fathom how their way of processing information could be far from reality. Even though there are Scriptures that warn each of us of the extent of our intellectual arrogance, we apply them to others.[5] This makes us indifferent to our reality. We quickly judge others' conclusions as being ridiculous, without realizing that we are making that evaluation according to our own perverted conclusions.

In dealing with people, you will find that their reality hinders the work of God in their lives to bring them to restoration. They will often insist on their reality regardless of the fruit that is being produced in their relationships. They will deem other people's perceptions as being ridiculous and out of touch, while maintaining the reasoning behind their reality.

It is important for each person to understand how he or she processes information. Conclusions outside of God's perspective leave people in despair, disillusionment, depression, and delusion.

Consider the following diagram:

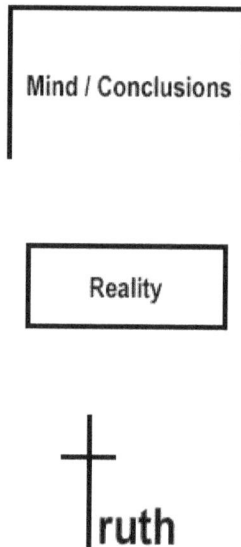

```
┌─────────────────────────┐
│                         │
│                         │
│   Mind / Conclusions    │
│                         │
│                         │
└─────────────────────────┘


       ┌──────────────┐
       │              │
       │   Reality    │
       │              │
       └──────────────┘


            ┼
            │ruth
```

Notice how you cannot come to truth without facing present reality. Sadly, most people refuse to face reality, and will go into their own minds to create a desired reality. The problem with this scenario is that others will not share in that perception. They have their own perceptions. As a result, others are always challenging the personal reality of these individuals. This causes frustration, resentment, anger, and bitterness.

Let's consider how each nature changes their reality. This is important because people insist on their personal reality, while letting life

---

[5] John 8:32-36; Romans 12:3; 1 Corinthians 10:12; Galatians 6:3

pass them by. They either live in the past or the future, but few ever properly deal in the present.[6]

Submissive people use their *analytical* process to come to an understanding about a situation. They actually run around in their different compartments to collect the necessary data to consider all of their possible options. When they have combined all of the information together, they make a decision. To these individuals, this conclusion seems *wise* and unshakable. They conclude that this is the *way things should be*, and there is no way that they can be wrong since they have considered all of the pertinent information.

These people underestimate the depth of darkness that is attached to their intellectual conceit. Conceit perverts reality and truth. It is a product of human wisdom. Human wisdom is earthly, sensual, and devilish. It may be based on experience and common sense, but it lacks God's perspective. All the submissive person has succeeded in doing is *recreating* his or her own reality. These individuals can become wise in their own conceits as they fail to connect with the reality around them.[7]

God does not choose human wisdom to reveal His wisdom. The Apostle Paul made this statement in regards to how God will expose the vanity of the wisdom that is inspired by this present world in 1 Corinthians 1:27, "But God hath chosen the foolish things of the world to confound the wise."

God uses the means of simplicity, not intellectual evaluation to reveal His truths. The Apostle Paul expressed real concern about those who complicate the truths of God, "But I fear, lest by any means, as the serpent beguiled Eve through his subtlety, so your minds should be corrupted from the simplicity that is in Christ" (2 Corinthians 11:3).

The analytical ways of the submissive person will fail to solve the problem. When understanding or resolutions fail him or her, he or she will begin to create a rut in his or her mind. This rut will develop into a pit of dramatization and depression.

Consider the following diagram:

---

[6] For a more detailed presentation on how people handle reality, see *Battle for the Soul*, by the same author.

[7] Romans 12:16; James 3:13-18

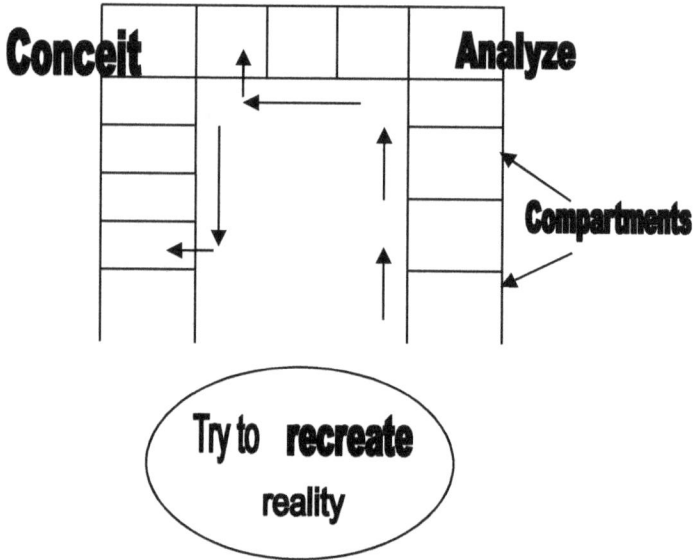

Stubborn people believe themselves to be *practical* about how they view and approach life. Information is not put into a mental box like the submissive person. Rather, they have an uncanny ability to pull it out of the hat when needed. The reason for this is because their information is often interpreted by how something makes them feel. Emotions and their environment make up a big part of how these people process information. Since these people can feel deeply about something, they perceive it as truth.

Standards are also used by stubborn people to process information. These standards serve as a means of bringing discipline to their environment. They determine *how something should be*. These rulers are a product of pride. In their mind, these standards are practical, even though they grow in requirements and demands. Eventually, these standards become harsh and unobtainable. If not kept in the right perspective, these standards will cause the stubborn person to become unloving, unrealistic, judgmental, skeptical, and unreasonable.

When you combine standards with emotions, you will have individuals who will *adjust* their environment to fit the reality they perceive is right. This reality can be aggressive to those who have to deal with it. It can be opinionated, dogmatic, and immovable when challenged.

The Apostle Paul tells us that God has chosen, "…base things of the world" (1 Corinthians 1:28). Base things seem unlikely and impractical, but they make up a burden that is light and reachable by those who are sincere in heart. They will bring individuals under the yoke of Jesus, rather than serve as an unbearable yoke to those who are struggling with the demands of life.[8]

Consider the following diagram:

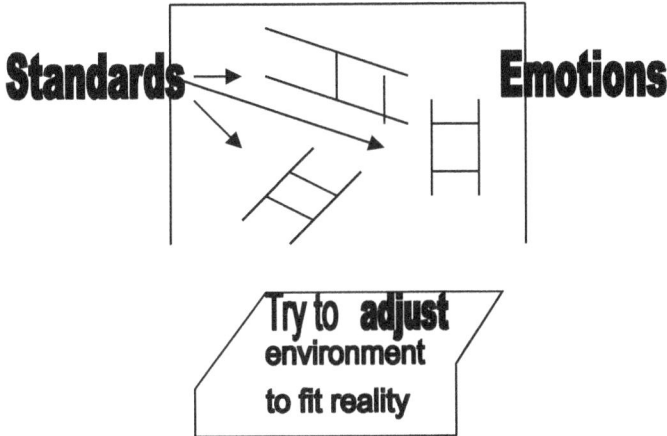

**Standards** → **Emotions**

Try to **adjust** environment to fit reality

Self-assured people perceive themselves to be *logical* in their conclusions. These conclusions are based on their *images*. These images are forever trying to get others to *adjust* to their perception of reality. This is different from the stubborn person who tries to adjust his or her environment to his or her reality.

These images are made up of tough *standards* that demand perfection. They determine *the way things must be*. The problem with these images is that if self-assured people perceive themselves as failing to live up to a particular image, they simply change to another image. Each image becomes their reality. Meanwhile, they expect others to adjust to their image and confirm this reality. Since these images constantly change, reality becomes fickle and confusing to those who are contending with this person. They often do not know which way to turn. They realize the person has changed in midstream, but they see it as hypocrisy, rather than the "changing of the guard."

When people fail to adjust to the reality of a self-assured person, their reservoir of anger begins to fill up. This reservoir will eventually allow them to adjust their reality to justify any ungodly or immoral actions towards those who fail to reinforce their images. This can be a frightening reality to those around this type of individual, because this person is not only unrealistic, but also unreachable. All the reasoning in the world will be shot down by his or her justifications.

The Apostle Paul tells us that God has chosen, "..things which are despised" (1 Corinthians 1:28). God uses what many would consider contemptible or far from perfection. In the end, His character and truth

---

[8] Matthew 11:28-30

will be upheld, not surface images that show contempt towards those who refuse to worship them.

Consider the following diagram.

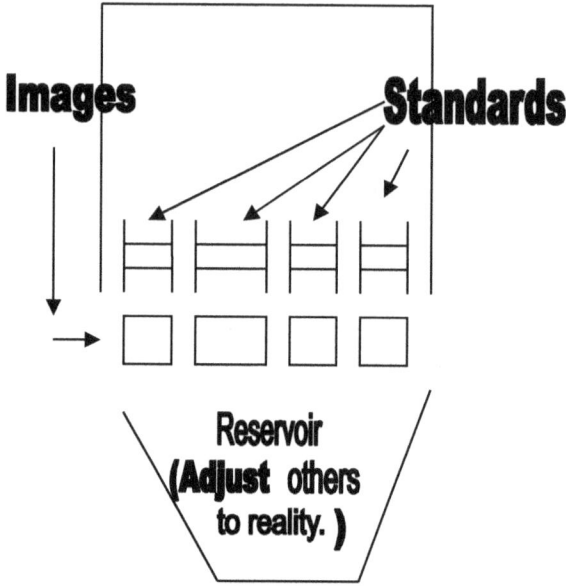

**Images**    **Standards**

**Reservoir
(Adjust others
to reality. )**

Strong-willed people *reshape* reality to fit within their *ideas*. These ideas establish *how things will be,* and are made up of lines of facts. These people perceive themselves as having all the necessary facts to determine the proper reality. Since they conclude that what they know is true, these lines become cemented into their perception. They actually use the lines to reshape all information to their ideas. If any information does not fit within these lines, it is often ignored or discarded. As previously stated, these people can ask the same question over and over again. It is their way of seeing if the information has been adjusted in any way, so that they can fit it into their world. Apparently, they must conclude that if they ask the same question enough times, that particular reality will change, and line up to what they perceive to be the only acceptable reality.

It is amazing to watch these people reshape their reality. They consider all the angles in which they can approach a subject. They use each approach as if they are trying to herd or corral you into their neat, controlled reality. Their attempts can become elaborate and manipulative. Sadly, this is what they do with their understanding of God as well. If they run out of angles, then they become confused and resort to intimidation.

The Apostle Paul tells us that God has chosen, "...things which are not, to bring to nought things that are" (1 Corinthians 1:28). God chooses things that seem insignificant and unimportant to bring forth His truth and message. Strong-willed people need to realize that reality does not rest within their concrete ideas, but in simple truths that will not always fit into their perception.

Consider the following diagram

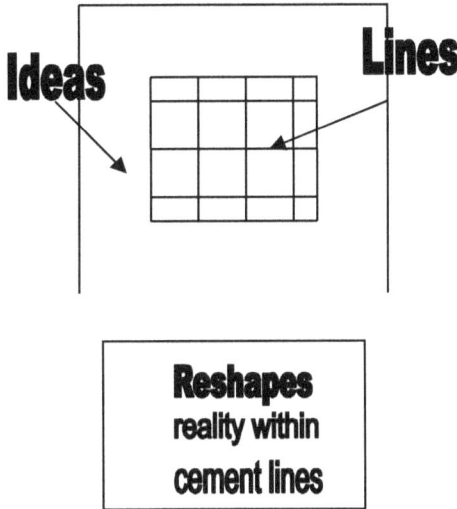

**Ideas** **Lines**

**Reshapes**
reality within
cement lines

Each nature is in search of a particular reality. Much of this search has to do with vainglory. This vainglory is about receiving recognition for wisdom or intelligence, and in personally determining what constitutes reality and truth. For the submissive, they desire *wisdom,* while stubborn people want to be *righteous* about their decisions. The self-assured seeks after *perfection*, while the strong-willed desires *completion* and *certainty*. Sadly, what each of these natures do not realize is that their particular form of reality can only be found in a relationship with God through Jesus Christ, as they yield completely to His Lordship.

The Apostle Paul brought this out in 1 Corinthians 1:29-31, "That no flesh should glory in his presence. But of him are ye in Christ Jesus, who of God is made unto us wisdom, and righteousness, and sanctification, and redemption: That, according as it is written, he that glorieth, let him glory in the Lord." Jesus serves as wisdom to the submissive and is the essence of righteousness for the stubborn. To the self-assured, He is sanctification who points to perfection through servitude. For the strong-willed, He is the point of redemption that is certain and complete for all who will come to Him on His terms.

Man's desire to glory in self, keeps him from realizing his life in Christ. His desire to control his reality, keeps him from coming to truth. His insatiable need to reign prevents him from reaching his potential in Christ.

What are you seeking after? How far away from truth are you? Is your perception worldly or heavenly? If you are operating outside of Jesus, you are already on a dead-end road.

# 8

# COUNTERFEIT REPENTANCE

The study of man's fallen condition confirms God's evaluation of it, which is found in His Word. It is easy to quote Scripture concerning the sin that plagues man's relationship with God, but few ever receive a personal revelation of their own depravity. Until a person does receive such a revelation, he or she will maintain there is something good or beneficial in him or her person that is worth salvaging. As long as he or she maintains this delusion, he or she will not see the need to totally sell out to God.

Total abandonment comes out of brokenness before God. This brokenness is a result of coming face to face with this depravity. As one discovers the depths of his or her fallen condition, he or she becomes crushed under the weight of hopelessness. Once a person comes to this point, he or she can do one of two things: repent or perish.

Jesus said in Luke 13:3, "I tell you, Nay: but, except ye repent, ye shall all likewise perish." One cannot get to heaven without repenting. This is why it is God's will that all come to repentance to avoid spiritual separation and ruin.[1]

Repentance is a simple matter of a complete change. It means turning from the present way of thinking, feeling, and being, towards God's way of thinking and responding. Sadly, the selfish disposition complicates repentance, preventing people from coming to true repentance. People do not know how to repent because it does not involve a formula, but humility and brokenness that is contrary to selfishness. In fact, each nature provides a counterfeit repentance that can delude its victim and somewhat deceive others. But, eventually it is exposed as a counterfeit because there is no evidence of fruits that are fit for repentance.[2] This simply means there is no inward change of character that would be evident in real repentance.

2 Corinthians 7:10 talks about the two types of repentance that are in operation, "For godly sorrow worketh repentance to salvation not to be repented of: but the sorrow of the world worketh death." Real repentance involves godly sorrow. Sorrow points to heaviness. For those who have godly sorrow, this heaviness is not only great, but also is repulsed towards sin and an unacceptable attitude towards deviant conduct.

---

[1] 2 Peter 3:9
[2] Matthew 3:8

People with godly sorrow will come to the cross of Jesus, seeking the means of rolling off this heaviness through forgiveness and cleansing; thereby, resulting in reconciliation, restoration, and salvation.[3]

Worldly sorrow expresses itself in personal penitence, tears of self-pity, and the victim syndrome.[4] This type of sorrow is seeking personal recognition by showing how much it is suffering for deserved consequences. This suffering is fake nobility that holds onto its personal dignity regardless of the extent or damage that personal sin has cost God and others. It is a form of pride with the appearance of repentance, but it refuses to submit to the work of the cross of Jesus. As a result, it leads to death or separation from God.

To clearly see the contrast between these two types of repentance, you can study the parable of the Prodigal Son in Luke 15:11-32, and Judas Iscariot's handling of his betrayal of Jesus in Matthew 27:1-5. The prodigal son recognized the condition he was in after squandering his inheritance and wallowing with the pigs. He concluded that being a servant in his father's house was greater than his present situation. He humbled himself, ceased from his way of thinking and doing, and went back home. Before his father, he acknowledged his sin and was willing to accept the consequences of his action by becoming a servant. He knew he was not worthy of his status as a son. His repentant attitude and action caused his father to rejoice, as well as allowed him to restore him as a son.

Judas Iscariot displayed worldly sorrow after he realized the gravity of his actions. He went to the religious leaders and confessed his error to them, rather than to the one he had offended. He admitted that he had betrayed an innocent man. This declaration still showed that Judas did not believe Jesus Christ's declaration about His true identity. Jesus was not just an innocent man; He was and is the Son of God, the promised Messiah. Judas failed to see that his sin was against God. Repentance involves coming into agreement with God's evaluation about a matter. When the leaders failed to absolve Judas for his actions, he threw the coins down, ran out and hung himself. At every point, we see where Judas sought man's absolution rather than God's forgiveness. In the end, he took matters into his own hands and hung himself.

Obviously, godly repentance turns to God, while worldly sorrow turns to self or others to make it right. Godly sorrow takes full responsibility for personal actions, while worldly repentance becomes noble in the situation. Worldly sorrow throws a bone by confessing wrongs, while maintaining the same ungodly mannerisms, attitudes, and practices. Godly repentance will turn to God with an open heart in humility and confession, seeking reconciliation with Him. Such repentance will cause the person to cease from ungodly attitudes and actions; and become changed in his or her disposition, as he or she submits to discipline.

---

[3] Matthew 11:28-30
[4] Hebrews 12:16-17

True to his deceptive form, fallen man's tendency is to always resort to worldly sorrow. It cleverly counterfeits repentance in such a way that those who are trying to come to repentance often mistake it for godly sorrow on their part. This delusion causes these individuals to walk in deception about their life before God and the destructive path they are still on.

Worldly repentance expresses itself differently among the four natures. Each nature has its own form of repentance and delusion. In order for people to overcome their sin, they must understand how they counterfeit repentance.

*Submissive people* withdraw into their minds. They run around in each compartment trying to figure out where they went wrong. If they discover that they were indeed foolish, they begin to go through mental whippings. This is a way of chastising themselves. In this process, they may confess outwardly the gravity of their actions, but they are busy trying to devise a means by which to avoid the same scenario in the future. This is a type of *flattery* that appears sincere outwardly, but is a form of deception.

The problem is that since submissive people work it all out in their mind, they perceive it as repentance. They can even acquire a peace about the situation, but the peace is a result of them coming to an understanding about it and not because they have repented. Since they have a personal understanding about it, they feel they have resolved it, but this resolution is temporary. Although they may have *complied* outwardly, their patterns and fruits remain unchanged. Each time they encounter failure in the same area, their patterns of repentance and rebellion get shorter. In spite of the obvious failure that comes from seeking resolution in their mind, they fail to come to the foot of the cross of Jesus seeking forgiveness, cleansing, reconciliation, and restoration.

*Stubborn* people's worldly sorrow can involve two different responses. First, they will adjust their standards even higher as a means to discipline themselves. This discipline will supposedly keep them from committing the same unforgivable error. Or, they will resort to emotionally whipping themselves by deprivation or some form of abuse to resolve their guilt. This whipping can be intense, but it is their way of getting back into God's good graces. In a way, it is the same as *reformation*. However, such reformation is surface, thereby, misleading. Therefore, it is not unusual to witness them in the same repentant process, while justifying the same wrongdoings at the expense of others.

Such justification wins out, and they begin the process of putting their world back together. The problem is that these people often live in a fantasy world. They do not deal in reality concerning their relationships with others. This is where their incredible ability to *con* themselves, as well as others, comes into play. The attitudes and problems that have brought them to the state of incredible guilt, rejection, or failure remain intact, but their fantasy keeps them from facing this reality. Reality eventually challenges them and they fall back into the same patterns.

Each time stubborn people find themselves in the same pattern, it causes them to be overwhelmed with greater condemnation. When the condemnation becomes too great, they will find themselves being pushed by guilt and fear. For some to rid themselves of these intense feelings, they fine-tune their justification in such a way that they begin to operate in delusion, anger, obsession, and insanity.

If stubborn people would come to the cross of Jesus, they could calm the intense feelings of guilt and fear by embracing His forgiveness. But, if their standards are reigning, these people feel they cannot come to the cross until they right the situation. This gives Satan an inroad to lie, deceive, or condemn them even more. They could silence the many lies of Satan by allowing Jesus' blood to justify them. They could ultimately know liberty from condemnation as they experience His abiding mercy and grace.

*Self-assured* people fake repentance by adjusting the standards behind their images. This is nothing more than a *performance* on their part that gives the outward appearance that they have changed, while *concealing* the reality that nothing has changed in their disposition. As they adjust their reality, they begin to *delude* themselves as well as others about what is genuine. They are still hiding their deviations behind masks, while holding on to their right to maintain their lists, rights, and games of control and manipulation.

In most cases these people will not admit when they are wrong. I had a self-assured person admit that she will apologize for something she is not guilty of, rather than take responsibility when she is wrong. Even in the area of accountability, these people will play games with you. They can afford to own up when they are not in the wrong because they can give an impression of being noble, but will refuse to admit any incompetence in situations where personal wrongdoing is obvious. In my encounters with these people, they will admit they are wrong in a generic sense, but will fall short of ever taking accountability for individual sins.

Jesus talked about taking away the cloak to reveal sin, and even declaring secret words from the housetop.[5] Obviously, sin cannot be hidden. The Light of the world will reveal all secret thoughts and sins. It would be wise for people to quit trying to conceal sins and bring them to the cross in humility and brokenness in order to experience forgiveness and restoration. As Proverbs 28:13 states, "He that covereth his sins shall not prosper: but whoso confesseth and forsaketh them shall have mercy."

*Strong-willed* people work worldly sorrow from two angles. The first angle is that they will fit their interpretation of a discrepancy into their lines. Once this happens, the issue becomes automatically resolved even though there is no change. The second approach is that they will appear to agree up front that it may not be right, while maintaining their lines. Basically, this is throwing a bone for the purpose of getting a person off their back and winning confidence. This is a form of outward

---

[5] Luke 12:2-3; John 15:22

*conformity*, but its goal is to maintain control or get control of a situation. It is all part of their game plan. In addition, if it does not work, they will try to bluff or intimidate a person to line up to their reality.

The reason strong-willed people avoid genuine repentance is because they must lose control and come under the authority of Jesus. Therefore, their worldly sorrow strives to maintain personal control to conform people or situations to their atmosphere.

The predominant fruits of worldly sorrow are self-righteousness and self-pity. If people manage to succeed in changing their worlds around them through the fallacy of counterfeit repentance, they become very self-righteous. After all, they managed to change the situation in their own power. Therefore, these individuals have a right to glory in it and lord it over others.

The reality that one faces in genuine repentance is that only God can change the heart, disposition, and perception of a person. Godly repentance brings to focus the person's need for God's intervention to save him or her from the arrogance and delusion of self.

When worldly sorrow fails to get desired results, self-pity raises its ugly head. After all, each nature has striven hard to deal with, handle, or take care of their particular discrepancy. When they encounter an unresponsive response from others, they perceive themselves to be victims. They conclude people just do not understand their situation. This conclusion causes these souls to perceive themselves as an exception to the rule, and such hypocrisy ultimately exalts them above Scriptural accountability and reason.

There is one virtue that allows people to discern between these two forms of repentance: integrity. Integrity will honestly evaluate self according to personal fruits rather than personal opinions or fantasies. It will line up to God's evaluation of a matter, and will not be content until it is resolved before the throne of grace.

King David was a man who walked according to the integrity in his heart.[6] When he was confronted about his different failures, he never counterfeited repentance. He came to God, humbled himself, confessed his sins, and threw himself on His mercy. This is clearly revealed in his famous prayer of repentance found in Psalm 51.

Integrity has to be applied at certain points depending on a person's nature. For example, integrity must be applied at the end of a *submissive* person's conclusions. If integrity is reigning, the submissive person will conclude that he or she cannot trust personal conclusions. The final analysis will be that he or she has been leaning on his or her own understanding, and that God's thoughts are much higher and beyond personal evaluation and comprehension.[6] This conclusion will take the intensity and reality out of this person's understanding and put the emphasis back on gaining God's perspective.

---

[6] 1 Kings 9:4
[6] Proverbs 3:5; Isaiah 55:8-9

*Stubborn* people must apply integrity at the point of their overwhelming emotions. Emotions often create present reality for a stubborn person rather than the Word of God. These people must avoid giving in to the cycles of their emotions, and actually pull themselves up to consider what the Word of God says about a matter. This requires them to make a choice in the will area to seek out God's understanding by first disciplining their emotions. The key for the stubborn person is not to ignore or close down his or her emotions, but face their instability in discerning reality. These individuals must choose not to give in to the false reality they create by choosing to put their faith in God's Word.

*Self-assured* people must institute integrity up front before they give way to the false reality of their images to ensure godly repentance. They must recognize the hypocrisy and deception that each of their images create. They must hold each image lightly, and test themselves according to the fruit that is being manifested when they encounter challenges to their reality, disrespect in relationship to images, and adversity.

*Strong-willed* people must apply integrity at the point of their motivation and lines. Few strong-willed people test their motivation behind their atmosphere, attitudes, and actions. They see themselves as being right and cannot imagine how they could be wrong. However, if the motivation or spirit, behind something is self-serving, or serves as a means of controlling others, it will be considered wrong and unacceptable to God. These individuals must realize their lines do not constitute motivation, nor do they establish reality.

It is vital for strong-willed people to test the spirit behind them, and allow God to adjust their lines to His way of doing. This means they must take their conclusions lightly until they can be properly tested. They must relinquish to God their need to control in order to ensure uprightness.

The question is this, have you come to real repentance, or are you operating in a counterfeit repentance? Have you properly applied integrity or are you walking in fake humility, personal justification, and self-delusion?

# 9

# THE PROCESS

God's Word is quite clear. Christians must overcome. The message to the seven churches in Revelation 2-3 confirms that overcoming is not an option, but a requirement to possess all that God has for His people. Revelation 21:7 gives this promise, "He that overcometh shall inherit all things; and I will be his God, and he shall be my son."

As we have taken this journey through the fallen ways of man, it has become obvious that many people want to fake spiritual victory, rather than pay the price to know God. They want to put a cloak over sin, rehabilitate the old man (the flesh) while still placating its appetites, and subtly give way to the idolatry of pride by disguising it behind fake humility. Many such individuals are hoping they can slide into heaven without anyone discovering that they have been operating according to the ways of the flesh, instead of walking in righteousness. These people devise ways to take the path of least resistance, while giving the appearance of repentance, obedience, and sacrifice.

Sadly, this scenario is the epitaph of the fallen condition. Like the rich man in Luke 16, the old man seems to trip over that which seems insignificant, to only taste the reality of hell. Man is forever tripping over the filthy rags of his righteousness, the so-called insignificance of justified sins, and the compromise of the world. What seems petty or unimportant to the old man becomes the open door to spiritual ruin and defeat.

There are three things that the Word of God commands His people to overcome: the world, the flesh, and the devil. The world is capable of entangling people in its destructive web. This represents a challenge because the world consists of doing that which is *necessary*. The necessities of life are neither good nor evil, but they can be exalted improperly. Such exaltation will allow the needs and demands of the world to choke or drown out God's Word. These cares can clutter the real issues of life.[1]

A person who gives in to the world begins to lose perspective. Wants are viewed as needs, and life begins to consist of worldly possessions, rather than Christ. Eventually, the demands of the world grow to such proportions that they suck the spiritual life out of a person as they pervert what is holy, pure, and acceptable.

---

[1] Matthew 13:22; Luke 12:15; 2 Timothy 2:3-4

Jesus instructed His followers to not fear the world for He overcame it. Since believers' lives are hid in Christ, they do not have to fear the world or fall into its various traps. In fact, the solution to overcoming the world is for a person to grow in his or her testimony of Jesus. This maintains a growing relationship, ensuring a right focus and perspective.[2]

The flesh is the next predominant enemy of our souls. It serves as the main open door to spiritual oppression. The confusion with this area is that the flesh represents doing that which is *natural*. How could something that is so natural and brings such pleasure, be so wrong to God? It comes down to the harsh reality that the flesh defiles the things of God and results in spiritual death.[3]

Total abandonment from the dictates of the flesh is the means of overcoming it. This abandonment points to consecration. Consecration is where the person physically separates self from that which is unholy, for the purpose of emotionally and spiritually being separated unto God.

Separation unto God is the work of sanctification. It involves a cleansing. We already know that the blood of the Lamb cleanses believers. Revelation 12:11 reminds us that followers of God overcome with the blood of the Lamb. The blood of the Lamb points to a new covenant. This covenant allows us to be children of God. It sets us apart because a seal of identity is upon us, a heavenly inheritance awaits us, and the right to enter into the throne room without fear of judgment is before us. With this new covenant of redemption, we can walk in the light and experience fellowship with God and others.

The Holy Spirit is the One who does this inward, transforming work of sanctification. This ensures fellowship, growth, and victory over Satan. To ensure the work of sanctification, a person must submit to God. As he or she submits, priorities and focus change. Eventually, the ways of the flesh will become unnatural and repulsive, while the ways of God will be perceived as normal.

The final enemy that must be overcome is Satan. He causes activities that are *unnatural*. In fact, he pushes everything into extremes. Extremes of this nature cause oppression or bondage. Such bondage keeps a person from moving forward in his or her relationship with God. The three means of overcoming Satan are clearly stipulated in Revelations 12:11, "And they overcame him by the blood of the Lamb, and by the word of their testimony, and they loved not their lives unto the death."

Walking in the New Testament covenant will help Christians overcome the flesh. Properly applying God's Word will enable believers to overcome the world. By closing down these two avenues, Satan has no inroads. But, before these avenues can be dealt with, one must cease to love the life that is associated with the world around us.

The world and the flesh are associated with life as we know it. Jesus made this statement in Matthew 16:25, "For whosoever will save his life

---

[2] John 16:33; 1 John 5:5; Revelation 12:11
[3] Romans 8:13

shall lose it: and whosoever will lose his life for my sake shall find it." Man's greatest desire and struggle is to maintain life as he knows or perceives it. This life is based on self, the flesh, and the values of the world. Self has rights, the flesh has its many wants (lusts), and the world has various counterfeits that cleverly replace the need for God. Such counterfeits are pagan and idolatrous.

People cling to this life because it offers happiness and seems so logical. However, Jesus stated that if people are not willing to lose life as they know or perceive it, they will lose it all in the end—meaning their very souls.

Each nature must go through the process in order to lose the essence of identity of self to reach its potential in God. For example, *submissive* people find their identity in their ability to analyze. Eventually, their ability is proven incapable of changing the face of life as they fail to intellectually resolve problems. These unresolved problems begin to create *irritations*.

As submissive people file each fact away or ignore each problem, this combination creates a tidal wave that eventually catches up to them, leaving them foundering in a whirlpool of failure and despair. It is only after submissive people run out of options that they might look up from their pit of depression to seek God's perspective. As God surrounds them with His perspective, they start being formed as the *pearl* that He intends them to be.

Submissive people avoid coming to terms with the depravity of their fallen condition. They do this by running away from reality in their mind or wallowing in a world of fake nobility and self-pity. In their conceited way, they can create a reality that feeds their pride as they imagine how they would direct the world and the people around them. They will attempt to make their world comply, and when they fail to accomplish this task, they translate it as failure. Instead of taking accountability, they will strive to maintain the dignity of their arrogance. They do this by hiding behind fake nobility or becoming a suffering victim.

*Stubborn* people must be separated from their *self-justification*. For this to happen, their environment must become overwhelming, out of control, and chaotic. Environment is practically everything to these people. In fact, the environment of a stubborn person will determine his or her identity. This environment reflects this type of person's emotional stability. The more chaos, the greater stubborn people attempt to control their environment. This will cause tremendous pressure for everyone who enters the stubborn person's world. They will feel the pressure to *reform* according to the stubborn person's expectations put upon them by complaints or attitudes. Even if people reform, the pressure continues to escalates due to the fact that there is something amiss in the inward environment of the stubborn person. Pressure of this type will produce a *sifting* or *friction* process.

Friction eventually wears down the resolve of the stubborn person. This process is capable of bringing the stubborn person to the end of self where either submission to God or emotional suicide, are the only two choices left. If God is allowed to have His way in this person, he or she will come forth as *gold* that is ready to be shaped for His work. Sadly, some stubborn people opt for emotional suicide where they close down and become zombies.

*Self-assured* people must be separated from their images. Images determine these people's ever-changing reality. They are always trying to get others to perform according to their images. However, people rarely perform, and life will not be adjusted, causing the process to either begin or escalate for these individuals. The process includes a *boiling* process of adversity that will eventually separate them from their various images to establish them in reality.

These people must be brought to the end of the fallacy of their images. Once they face the hypocrisy and fallacy of their images, one of three things will occur: 1) They will become angry and vengeful, 2) they will become apathetic with underlying anger and self-pity ready to erupt, or 3) they will develop integrity and come forth as pure *gold*.

*Strong-willed* people often give themselves no other choice but to experience the extreme process of a *diamond*. This extreme pressure comes when the strong-willed person loses control. The heat is turned up when others refuse to conform to this person's world and play his or her games of control. The more the struggle to control those in his or her world, the greater the process escalates until the strong-willed person is brought to a place of being in a fragile or vulnerable state. This state can drive these people into one of two directions: 1) Either they will go into total delusion about their spiritual condition, which brings them to the brink of destruction, or 2) they will be broken and forced to run into God.

Sadly, very few people accept the challenge of their process. They try to fake it or give the impression that they have paid the necessary price to become priceless heirlooms in God's kingdom. The problem is that there is no change, and when they pay the consequences, they groan and moan about how great the price is. The truth is, when one is truly paying the price to know God, it is not a source of great suffering, but one of great privilege and identification. In other words, there is no moaning or self-glorification, but an abiding peace in the reality of possessing in greater measures the precious treasure of heaven.

Jesus gave simple instruction to all of his disciples in Matthew 16:24 to ensure this process, "If any man will come after me, let him deny himself, and take up his cross, and follow me." Self-denial works within two avenues: 1) Not giving in to self and 2) obedience to what is right.

When a person refuses to give in to self, he or she will neglect the demands and vain imaginations of pride and submit to the work of the Holy Ghost. Such work points to abandonment to self, which is a form of consecration. Consecration allows one to submit to the work of sanctification that is done by the Holy Spirit.[4]

Self-denial is the first step because without it the selfish disposition in us will become a noble, suffering martyr when the cross is applied. The

---

[4] Romans 15:16; 1 Peter 1:2

cross represents death. The flesh with its disposition must be put upon the cross daily.[5] As the flesh is daily mortified, a person becomes crucified to the influences of the world. The Apostle Paul confirmed this in Galatians 6:14, "But God forbid that I should glory, save in the cross of our Lord Jesus Christ, by whom the world is crucified unto me, and I unto the world."

Once self is denied and the personal cross applied, a person will have the discipline to follow Jesus. Some Christians believe that it is easy to follow Jesus, but they do so in foolish zeal and ignorance.[6] Eventually, they take detours or get ahead of Jesus. Godly discipline can only come by way of neglecting the essence of the pride of self and properly applying the cross.

Each nature has a different challenge when confronting self and applying the cross. For example, *submissive* people must neglect giving in to the arrogance of their conceits. They become so top heavy in knowledge that they forget to be realistic and sensitive to others, as well as the world around them. They eventually become so certain and deluded in their intellectual conclusions, they become fools.

They must cease from taking their conclusions seriously and seek after God's perspective. This means submissive people must apply the cross to their concepts or notions about what constitutes reality and *wisdom*. Application of the cross at this point will do away with identity based on personal understanding, allowing them to seek identity in God's incredible wisdom.

*Stubborn* people must neglect the insatiable demands of their selfishness to control their environment to feel loved or on top of their emotional life. Controlling environment implies they have to get those in their environment to bow down to their perception and demands. The problem with this is as others react to the stubborn person's attempts to control their world, these unsuspecting individuals will begin to define or establish the stubborn person's identity. In other words, this identity will come down to how others make a stubborn person feel about him or herself.

Once stubborn people discipline their emotions by neglecting their selfishness, they can apply the cross to their unrealistic standards. These standards serve as a form of personal *righteousness*, but they create tremendous yokes and burdens that are too harsh and cruel to bear. In fact, these unrealistic yokes and burdens make stubborn people critical, skeptical, and hard towards others who fail to agree or adhere to them.

*Self-assured* people must avoid giving in to realities established by their images. They must realize that these different realities do not constitute fruit, integrity, or truth, but a façade that keeps them from properly functioning in the world around them and in relationships. Ultimately, it will keep them from entering into the kingdom of God. By

---

[5] Luke 9:23
[6] Romans 10:2-3

neglecting the demands of the different realities that are created by these images, they can effectively apply the cross to each of their images.

These people search for perfection in their images can only be realized in the work of *sanctification*. Sanctification can only take place when their images are properly dealt with. Therefore, it is important to mortify these images because they serve as the essence of self. They actually determine the variety of confusing and unpredictable identities these people interchange or display.

*Strong-willed* people must neglect the sense of infallibility created by their pride. In other words, they must not give in to its perception. This infallibility determines their identity. The identity gives them a false sense that they possess truth. Therefore, they must learn to take their conclusions lightly because this infallibility puts them on a collision course with reality. This will make them not only fallible, but also fragile.

Once strong-willed people put their infallibility in a correct perspective, they will be able to apply the cross to their immovable ideas. This allows God to properly adjust their lines to His truth, allowing them to experience the fullness of His complete work of *redemption*.

As we can see, the ideal or essence of self often determines people's identity. The process creates an identity crisis as it reveals each nature's inability to change personal reality. This fleshly, worldly identity must give way to following Jesus. Following Jesus implies totally becoming identified with Him. Jesus begins to serve as a person's identity. This means He will become his or her wisdom, righteousness, sanctification, and redemption.[7]

As a person gives way to this new identity in Jesus through self-denial, death to the flesh, and walking in the fullness of Christ, the new man will be resurrected and manifested. Romans 6:4-5 clarifies this,

> Therefore we are buried with him by baptism unto death: that like as Christ was raised from the dead by the glory of the Father, even so we also should walk in newness of life. For if we have been planted together in the likeness of his death, we shall also in the likeness of his resurrection.

The Christian life is contrary to our old man. The old man declares it must live, but the way of the cross states that he must die. The old man wants to slide into heaven without death to its rebellious, contrary ways, but the cross declares it must cease to reign through suffering and death. This suffering and death come through neglect, deprivation, tribulation, and adversity.[8]

The cross of Jesus is a harsh revelation of the old man and what he does with the things of God. He will try to use, defile, or destroy what is of God in our lives. However, life past the cross of Jesus is about the new man being developed in us, and coming forth in power and victory for the glory of God.

---

[7] 1 Corinthians 1:30
[8] John 16:33; Acts 14:22; 2 Timothy 3:12

The Apostle Paul put it this way in 2 Timothy 2:11-12, "It is a faithful saying: For if we be dead with him, we shall also live with him: If we suffer, we shall also reign with him: if we deny him, he also will deny us." Have you allowed the process of God to bring you to your true identity in Christ? If you haven't, you will be brought to an identity crisis for the sake of your soul.

# 10

# FINDING OUR PLACE IN CHRIST

To reach our potential in Christ, we must find our place in Him. After all, our lives are hidden in Him, and we are positionally seated in high places with Him.[1] Sadly, our fallen condition keeps us from realizing this potential.

The selfish disposition makes people vulnerable to fall into various traps. They become established in their arrogance by the world. Their self-sufficiency gives them a false sense of their spiritual condition as they try to create an earthly utopia that is void of God's reign and one that will revolve around them. Their flesh feeds their ego and gives temporary pleasure as a means of enticing them into greater darkness. Eventually, reality reveals their inability to possess a utopia where they reign as god. This creates an identity crisis, causing many to fall into utter despair, resulting in some giving way to anger and aggression.

The percentage of people who come to God out of complete need or desperation is small. Most people ignore, avoid, or deny facing their mortality and their need for God. This need is not only in light of their present state, but their past and future. Each person needs to be cleansed of his or her past sins, and to be presently established in righteousness in order to be overcoming in the present, and victorious in the future.

This is what it means to experience wholeness in Christ. To accomplish this, a person needs to recognize his or her nature. Since each nature has different strengths and weaknesses, God establishes each person in His kingdom according to his or her strengths and weaknesses.

The Bible points out that man's undisciplined strengths will set him up for a fall. On the other hand, submitted weaknesses become the greatest avenue of strength in God's kingdom.[2] These strengths and weaknesses also determine the type of leadership a person will bring to the kingdom of God. For example, a submissive person may desire the leadership qualities of a strong-willed person, but does not possess the same strengths or weaknesses that will define such leadership. Such a comparison will cause frustration, despair, and condemnation.

The Bible condemns such comparisons. The Apostle Paul said this about this matter in 2 Corinthians 10:12, "For we dare not make

---

[1] Ephesians 2:6; Colossians 3:3
[2] 1 Corinthians 1:29-31; 2 Corinthians 12:9-10

ourselves of the number, or compare ourselves with some that commend themselves: but they measuring themselves by themselves, and comparing themselves by themselves, are not wise." It is not wise to compare yourself with those who appear or boast of having a greater measure of spirituality.

Christians are only given one example by which to test or discern themselves, and that is the Person of Jesus Christ. His disposition marks the real quality of leadership. His life marks both the righteous walk and what constitutes an acceptable sacrifice. In order to become this example, He had to become a servant of all. As a result, He was exalted above all.[3]

The secret to finding our place in Christ begins with accepting the way we are made. Our fallen condition always mocks our weaknesses and exalts our strengths above God. But Jesus gave up His strength and became weak and poor. He took on the disposition of a servant. He instructed us to take on the same disposition. In fact, we are told to learn of Him.[4]

This brings us to what we need to do about personal strengths and weaknesses. As each person realizes strengths must be subdued through submission to the Holy Ghost and weaknesses redefined through the grace of God, he or she can begin to accept how God has designed him or her. The main purpose of this design is to reflect the glory of God.

As the character of Christ is defined through a person's weakness, he or she can begin to discover his or her leadership and place in His Body. As he or she presents his or her body as a living sacrifice, the Holy Spirit will discipline and channel personal strength, as well as transform the person's mind. This mind will take on the disposition of Christ, therefore, expressing itself in Christ-like character, attitude, and conduct. It is the reality of Christ in the person that serves as an acceptable fragrance to God, becomes a source of edification to the Body of Christ, and a distinct challenge to the unsaved.[5]

If each person found and took his or her rightful place in the kingdom of God, the Church would become distinct, powerful, and unstoppable. Sadly, many Christians are lost. They are in an identity crisis that makes them feel as if they are being swallowed up by the demands of life.

Due to the invasion of heresy in the Church, Christians are also falling prey to wolves in sheep's clothing, doctrines of demons, and "another spirit." As a result, some are chasing after other Christs and believing another gospel. This hodgepodge has caused confusion, defilement of the holy, and has indoctrinated people into super spiritual delusion and great darkness.[6]

---

[3] Matthew 11:28-30; Philippians 2:5-11
[4] Matthew 11:28; John 13:13-17; 2 Corinthians 8:9
[5] Romans 12:1-2; 2 Corinthians 2:15-16; Philippians 2:5
[6] Matthew 7:15-16; 2 Corinthians 11:1-4; 1 Timothy 4:1

This heretical invasion has thwarted the effectiveness of the Church and the unveiling of the image of Christ in His people. The Body of Christ needs to be revived by catching a vision of its real purpose in this world. One of the ways this can be accomplished is by studying the leadership of each nature.

To ensure the spirit behind this information, I asked the Lord to scripturally confirm it. He graciously obliged me by showing me examples of each nature in Scripture. This revelation opened the Word up to me in greater ways. As I studied and meditated on each scriptural example, I could see how God dealt with these individuals according to their nature. It was both exciting and humbling. Interestingly, I found that people often related to the writings and lives of those who had like nature. If you are not sure of your nature, consider the Scriptural examples that you most relate to. These examples might reveal your nature to you.

# Submissive Nature

Submission is considered a weakness in most societies. But, godly submission in the kingdom of God is the greatest point of strength and leadership. Jesus made this clear in Matthew 20:27, "And whosoever will be chief among you, let him be your servant."

For submission to become this strength, submissive people must be in submission to Jesus. He must become their focus in order to be established on the immovable Rock of ages. Once they are established on the Rock, they will become pillars in His kingdom. Interestingly, Revelation 3:12 says this, "Him that overcometh will I make a pillar in the temple of my God..." The term "pillar" was ascribed to the Apostle John, the beloved, in Galatians 2:9.

The *Apostle John* fits the qualification of a submissive person. His Gospel and epistles reveal someone who presented the truth in an analytical way, by building up a clear presentation as to Jesus' identity. He did this by emphasizing Jesus' teachings in his Gospel.

We see John becoming obnoxious at one point when he wanted to call fire down from heaven upon the Samaritans. But, we also see a sweet, sensitive side when he laid his head on Jesus' chest.[7] In his first epistle, he talked about his personal encounter with Jesus,

> That which was from the beginning, which we have heard, which we have seen with our eyes, which we have looked upon, and our hands have handled, of the Word of life; (For the life was manifested, and we have seen it, and bear witness, and shew unto you that eternal life, which was with the Father, and was manifested unto us;) (1 John 1:1-2).

John's perspective was the Son of God. It established him as a pillar in Jesus' kingdom. He was a strong leader of the new Church. He proved

---

[7] Luke 9:51-56; John 13:23

to be bold in his declarations of Him, and ready to offer himself up for the furtherance of His kingdom.

The Apostle John had been surrounded by the reality of Jesus. He was a man compelled by a personal revelation of His Lord, upheld by the reality of His presence, and refined by his identification with Him. However, in Revelation, he would be confronted with a greater revelation of his Lord and Savior that would bring him to his face.

If submissive people fail to have Jesus as their focus, they will give way to fear. We see this happening to *Elijah*. He was a great prophet of faith. He had stopped the heavens from raining for three years and taken on the prophets of Baal, but when he took his eyes off God and put them on Queen Jezebel, he fled in fear and fell into self-pity.[8]

In spite of his struggles, God met him. Once again, Elijah gained the right perspective that enabled him to finish his course. This is the key behind victory. Submissive people, who have a balanced perspective because of God, can stand and withstand. However, they must be surrounded by His perspective and ways, rather than running in the ruts of their mind to gain understanding.

The means of success for the submissive person can be observed in the life of *Daniel*. He was faced with death more than once. Instead of fainting before the prospects of it, he withdrew into God. God did not fail him and honored him before Gentile leaders. He truly rested on the Rock because he had purposed early in his life to believe Jehovah God and obey Him.[9]

If submissive people have the eternal perspective, they can be entrusted with much. After all, they are pillars. *Isaiah* had a vision of the Lord in Isaiah 6. He was entrusted with what many consider a miniature Bible within the Word of God. His book reveals the birth, ministry, death, and reign of Christ.

Another submissive person who was entrusted with much was *Mary*, the mother of Jesus. She was sincere in her faith and pure in heart. As a result, God entrusted her with the Messiah.

We also see this in the case of Daniel and the Apostle John. They were given many details about the future or what we know as the end-day events, which are presently unfolding before our very eyes.

Are you submissive? Is your focus on self, fear, or Jesus? The answer will determine the extent of your perspective, and how much God will entrust to you.

## Stubborn Nature

Stubborn people need proof from God. This is a quality that is often criticized. Surprisingly, God will give the necessary proof as He did to *Gideon* and *Thomas*. Few criticize Gideon for putting out a fleece concerning a matter that had been commanded by God. He not only

---

[8] 1 Kings 17:1; 19:1-15
[9] Daniel 1:8; 3, 6

asked Him to confirm it once, but twice. But, when it comes to Thomas wanting Jesus to prove His existence in the midst of his despair, he is considered "doubting Thomas."[10]

Many stubborn people are misunderstood because they show uncertainty in the midst of challenging times. The problem concerning their uncertainty is that it is much more obvious with them than it is with other natures. The other natures can cover up doubt or uncertainty with wisdom, diplomacy, masks, and games, but stubborn people's struggles are "all out there" for others to see.

Take Peter for example. He is the only one who got out of the boat and walked on water to meet Jesus. However, because he took his eyes off Jesus as the waves loomed in front of him, he is made a constant example of how doubt works. Few ever note that the rest of the disciples stayed in the boat and avoided the fiery test of their faith. This is probably why Peter could effectively address the test of faith in his first epistle.[11] It is easy to be a spectator and critical in these matters, but opinions mean little unless one has been tested. Those who have been tested tend to avoid judging others because of their own personal experiences.

Peter is often pointed out for his denial of Jesus. Once again, few note Judas' betrayal of Jesus, while the rest of His disciples abandoned Him altogether. Again, Peter blatantly failed the test, but so did the rest of humanity. Jesus was a test to many types of people during His ordeal to Calvary. If they weren't denying Him, they were beating Him. If they were not betraying Him, they were crucifying Him.

The reason for instability and inconsistency in stubborn people is their emotional makeup. It causes them to be on an emotional roller coaster; therefore, they do not always trust their decisions. They seek proof to confirm what they perceive or have been told.

*John the Baptist*, in his darkest ordeal, sent his disciples to ask Jesus if He was the Promised One. Jesus did not reprove him for the question. He simply sent the necessary proof back to John to assure him of His identity.[12]

Although stubborn people's emotional instability can cause much grief, it also can serve as an asset. King David was able to express every known emotion in the book of Psalms to reveal the personal, inner struggles that we all face because we live in the flesh. However, his final conclusion was the same: God is real and reigning.

The secret to victory for stubborn people is lining up all their emotions to the cornerstone (examples and words) of Jesus Christ. This will bring the necessary discipline or stability. Emotional stability allows the Holy Ghost to channel their momentum and energy level into bold leadership in the kingdom of God.

---

[10] Judges 6:36-40; John 20:24-29
[11]Matthew 14:26-33; 1 Peter 1:6-9
[12] Nehemiah 4:9-18; Jeremiah 4:3; Matthew 11:2-11; John 20:1-18

We see this boldness in Gideon, David, Nehemiah, John the Baptist, Peter, and even Thomas. The combination of boldness and their sense of fair play can cause these people to become abrasive plumb lines in the Church. Like the prophet, *Jeremiah*, they will tear up the fallow ground of unregenerate hearts. And, like Nehemiah, they will erect necessary walls of protection, while holding a sword to ensure God's work is done. In the case of *Mary Magdalene*, they will become bold witnesses to His presence and reality in the midst of fear and doubt.[13]

Stubborn people bring a powerful, stable leadership to the kingdom of God. They are able to hold the line of righteousness as they challenge and contend for the souls of others. They will do all they can to line up the living stones of Jesus' Church to the true spiritual Cornerstone.[14]

Another aspect that stubborn people must discern and discipline is their emotional sensitivity. These people can be sensitive to the spiritual realm. Like Joseph, Jesus' stepfather, God can communicate with them in dreams.[15] But, if they aren't careful to discern the spirit, they can abuse what some consider man's sixth sense. They will open themselves up to the kingdom of darkness, allowing them to be influenced by demonic powers and doctrines of demons.

Are you stubborn? If so, are you lining up to the Cornerstone, Jesus Christ, so that you are able to bring a bold leadership to God's kingdom?

# Self-Assured Nature

Images cause self-assured people to become unpredictable. In fact, if they do not have a vision of the destination or end results of something, they will not finish the course. This is why God must give them distinct vision beyond their images or they will end up taking detours. We see this in the case of Moses. *Moses* was a self-assured person who had the necessary integrity for God to use him. The reason we know this is because of what Hebrews 11:24-25 says, "By faith Moses, when he come to years, refused to be called the son of Pharaoh's daughter; choosing rather to suffer affliction with the people of God, than to enjoy the pleasures of sin for a season."

Moses went through a great boiling process in the wilderness. He had been demoted from the courts of Pharaoh into a base, abominable shepherd. What images he then had fell to the wayside. By the time God met him in the burning bush, Moses' images and identity were pretty well dealt with by his 40-year process.[16]

Moses was now an insecure man who was vulnerable. This vulnerability made him pliable in the Potter's hands. God took his uncertainty and put authority in its place. He took his silent voice and caused it to ring through the corridors of Pharaoh's courts. He replaced

---

[13] John 11:16
[14] 1 Peter 2:5, 9
[15] Matthew 1:20; 2:19-20
[16] Genesis 46:34; Exodus 2:9-15; 3:1-6

his staff with a rod. He exchanged the sheep in the wilderness with the children of Israel. He took an insignificant shepherd and caused His glory to be unveiled before others.[17]

This is the key to victory of the self-assured person. An exchange has to be made in his or her life. We see such an exchange happening in Moses' life. The courts of Pharaoh were exchanged for the wilderness. The wilderness gave way to Mount Sinai. On Mount Sinai, the vanity of idols and paganism were exposed and replaced by the Law.[18]

We also see an exchange occur in *Jacob's* life. He was a plain man of the tent. He may have appeared to be quiet, but underneath his exterior he had a desire for position and purpose greater than what he possessed in the present world. He understood the character of his brother, Esau. And, at the right time his clever qualities came forth. Jacob managed to get his brother to sell his birthright for a bowl of pottage.[19]

Later, he conspired with his mother to possess the blessing. These actions on the part of Jacob put him in a questionable light. But, God knew what was in Jacob's heart. The word "plain" in Exodus 25:27 implies gentle and dear, coupled with perfect, undefiled, and upright.[20] It would take twenty years to bring this disposition forth, but once it was unveiled, it revealed a man of tremendous leadership—a man who ended up blessing the Pharaoh.[21]

An exchange had to be made in Jacob's life. This exchange could not occur until after the process was complete. Esau's murderous attitude towards Jacob forced him to leave his home in search of a new life. The spiritual part of the journey would last two decades. In a sense, it would begin at Bethel when he was on his way to his uncle's place. There, God revealed Himself. Jacob did something of great significance at Bethel in recognition of His encounter with God. He erected a pillar and anointed it with oil. Then, he made a vow to God that if He brought him home, he would make Him God of his life.[22] This means that Jacob was vowing to become a servant of Jehovah God.

Jacob could not develop a servant's disposition on his own. Only God could work this attitude in him. God used Jacob's uncle to accomplish this feat. He would serve as a mirror to Jacob. He was deceptive, shrewd, and sneaky. He concealed certain matters and managed to manipulate Jacob into the position of a servant. In spite of this treatment, Jacob showed integrity and God blessed him. In the end, Jacob would serve his uncle for 20 years, while maintaining righteousness.[23]

---

[17] Exodus 3:9-16; 4:2-3; 34:28-20
[18] Exodus 20
[19] Genesis 25:27, 29-34
[20] Strong's Exhaustive Concordance of the Bible; #8535
[21] Genesis 27:5-30; 47:7, 10
[22] Genesis 28:11-22
[23] Genesis 30:33; 31:1-18

Possible retribution from Esau awaited Jacob on his return to his homeland. Alone, Jacob faced the possibilities. He had crossed over Jabbok. Jabbok means "emptying". Here he met a heavenly being. He wrestled all night with this being to secure a blessing. This is when an incredible exchange took place. He ceased to be Jacob, "the supplanter," and became Israel, "the prince that prevails with God." Jacob was no longer Jacob, but a man of God, a servant of God who had overcome.[24]

The disposition of a servant brings us back to Jacob's action in Bethel. He erected a pillar and anointed it. Once self-assured people are emptied of their prideful ways, Jesus, the Rock of Ages, can be erected in their lives. At this point, they can become the anointed servants of God. Interestingly enough, God refers to godly self-assured people as His servants.[25] We see this in the case of Job.

Job had a righteous life that could clearly be seen by others. His life before God caused God to point him out to Satan as an example. Satan rose up to wipe that perfect, undefiled image out by testing Job in areas that would cause the best devotee of God to fall into disbelief and anger. Satan touched Job's possessions, his family, and his health.[26]

Job encountered questions, confusion, and accusations throughout his trial, but He never cursed God. As he struggled with beliefs that were proving limited and inept, he held on to the character of God, knowing that one day he would be resurrected into His unending and glorious presence. He maintained that he was being refined as gold through this process, and declared that even if God should slay him, he would choose to trust Him. Job was indeed righteous **before** God, but the process would make him righteous **in** God.[27]

Job did all the right things, but he failed to realize that the source of all righteousness was found in God. God had given Job the heart, the means, and the vision to be righteous before Him. Job could never take credit for the righteousness that was being manifested in his life through disposition and actions. At the end of his ordeal, he could only declare, "I have heard of thee by the hearing of the ear: but now mine eye seeth thee. Wherefore I abhor myself, and repent in dust and ashes" (Job 42:5-6).

When self-assured people's fierceness is channeled in a right way, they will wrestle in prayer and ensure the promises of God are upheld in integrity. For example, Moses interceded on behalf of Israel when God threatened to destroy Israel after the people refused to enter the Promised Land. Sarah, the wife of Abraham, protected Isaac's inheritance. She knew Isaac was not to share his inheritance with Ishmael. She demanded that Abraham send Ishmael and his mother away. God commanded Abraham to obey her.[28]

---

[24] Genesis 32:22-32
[25] Job 1:8, see also Exodus 14:31
[26] Job 1 & 2
[27] Job 13:15; 91:25-27; 23:10
[28]Genesis 21:1-13; Numbers 14

Fierceness that is properly channeled will enable the self-assured person to make the commitment to become the strong leader in God's kingdom. This will allow the Holy Ghost to transform his or her perception and agendas by aligning his or her standards to the disposition and example of Jesus. This will cause the self-assured person to become singular in heart and vision.

Pride remains a big issue for these people. Their images along with indecisiveness and fear of incompetence can place them at precarious places of judgment. Moses failed to circumcise his sons and almost lost his life. At the end of the journey through the wilderness, he gave way to his anger, allowing self-sufficiency to arise. In this state, He disobeyed God concerning the rock in the wilderness, and never entered the Promised Land. As he was instructing the people of Israel about the Law of God, he blamed them for his judgment. However, God set the record straight when He sent Moses up to Mount Nebo to die. He clearly stipulated that the judgment was the result of what Moses did.[29]

We can also clearly see the results of pride in King Saul and King Ahab's lives. As you study Saul's life, you see where he had no inclination to obey God as he walked according to the flesh. He showed worldly remorse when called to accountability by the prophet Samuel, but he never really repented or changed his way of being. Eventually, the Spirit of God departed from him.[30]

Ahab was idolatrous and greedy. He was moody when he didn't get his way. But, Ahab walked lightly before God when confronted by Elijah over the murder of Naboth.[31] However, this only lasted for a season, and Ahab was back to his old ways.

These people display self-pity when called to accountability. Self-pity is nothing more than worldly sorrow. This can be observed in the lives of Cain and Judas Iscariot. Cain killed his brother, but felt sorry for himself when God called him to accountability. Judas Iscariot regretted that he betrayed an innocent man (the Son of God), and tried to give the money back to the priests. When the Chief Priest refused to free him of his guilt, he hung himself.[32]

Self-assured people can be assured of one thing, God will call them to accountability whether in this present world or at the last judgment. They need to test themselves according to fruits rather than images. Repentance must get past the images and emotional level down into the heart where integrity must prevail. They must wrestle before God to become empty, in order to become a servant in disposition.

Once self-assured people get past the façades, God can meet them in truth. At this point, they will receive a vision that will enable them to finish the course. After all, Jacob witnessed the ladder between heaven and earth, Moses knew God's presence and saw His glory, and God

---

[29] Exodus 4:24-26; Deuteronomy 3:23-26; 32:49-51
[30] 1 Samuel 15; 16:14
[31] 1 Kings 21:29
[32] Genesis 4:8-15; Matthew 27:3-10

revealed Himself to Job. These men possessed heavenly visions beyond this world. And, what powerful leaders and examples they became in the kingdom of God.

# Strong-Willed Nature

Strong-willed people bring decisive leadership to the kingdom of God by bringing clarity to the things of God. For example, the Apostle Paul brought decisive instructions to the new Church in his many epistles. He instructed them in the ways of righteousness.

The key behind the validity of a strong-willed person's leadership is determined by who he or she is serving. These people will reflect the very attitudes and attributes of those they follow. This is brought out in the leaderships of Deborah, the judge and prophetess, and Queen Jezebel. Deborah displayed the righteousness and the victory of Jehovah God, while Jezebel reflected the demonic influences, wickedness, and practices of her idolatrous, pagan god, Baal.[33]

God's dealing with these people is distinct as well. The Apostle Paul started out persecuting Christians. On the road to Damascus, he encountered the real Jesus. He was not only brought down to his knees, but he lost his eyesight. This proud Pharisee had to be led by the hand. Talk about an extreme process! But, this incident turned Paul around to walk in the light of Jesus.[34]

The prophet Jonah and King Nebuchadnezzar are other examples of strong-willed people doing an about-face because of extreme processes. God prepared a fish for rebellious Jonah. Needless to say, the fish changed Jonah's mind and direction, bringing him into obedience to God.[35]

After being warned by Daniel about taking credit for his kingdom, Nebuchadnezzar was driven into a field where he ate grass as an ox for seven years.[36] At the end of seven years, his senses returned. This was his humble declaration, "Now I Nebuchadnezzar praise and extol and honor the King of heaven, all whose works are truth, and his ways judgment: and those that walk in pride he is able to abase" (Daniel 4:37).

Strong-willed people, who are being ruled by God, prove to be trustworthy. We see this in the life of Jacob's son Joseph. Betrayed and sold into slavery by his brothers, he maintained his uprightness. Even after being falsely accused and imprisoned, he upheld his integrity. Through his ordeal, God gave him favor until he was exalted as a powerful leader in Egypt.[37]

In both the lives of the Apostle Paul and King Nebuchadnezzar, we read about the rock. In Nebuchadnezzar, the rock or stone came as

---

[33] Judges 4 & 5; 1 Kings 16:28-33; 19:1-3; 21:17-25
[34] Acts 9
[35] Jonah 1-3:1
[36] Daniel 4
[37] Genesis 37:8-36; 39-41

judgment on all earthly kingdoms, giving way to an eternal King and His kingdom. Jesus talked about being the Stone that man would trip over and be broken, producing eternal life, or else be utterly crushed by Him in judgment. [38]

The Rock in Paul's case was the one found in the wilderness that was struck by Moses. It miraculously gave water to the thirsty people. This incident pointed to Jesus who was struck by man in the wilderness of suffering and death. Out of Him, came rivers of Living Water for all who will come to Him.[39]

The reality of this Rock is that it will either bring life to the thirsty or judgment to those who discard and abuse its provision. Such judgment points to separation.

The cross of Jesus brings a separation and decisiveness to the world. A person will not leave this world untouched by this Rock. It will either break him or her, bringing him or her unto repentance, or in judgment, it will grind him or her into powder. Godly strong-willed people have the ability to cause this decisive separation in the kingdom of God. They will reflect God's attributes as well as cut away at the heart of personal justification and compromise.

These people's ability to bring powerful, decisive leadership is clearly exposed by Joseph, Jonah, and the Apostle Paul. Joseph was used to save his family, Jonah's preaching saved a whole city, and the Apostle Paul opened up the kingdom of God to the entire Gentile world.

Strong-willed people's potential can only be discovered when they give up their need to rule their worlds. This means they must come into obedience under the rule of God.

Are you strong-willed and under the control of God's Spirit, or are you subjected to other masters? This will determine whether you reach your potential in God's kingdom or waste your life, causing you to reap the consequences for eternity.

---

[38] Daniel 2:44-45; Matthew 21:44; 1 Corinthians 10:4-10
[39] John 7:37-39

# 11

# THE REFLECTION OF CHRIST

My co-laborer, Jeannette, was at first suspicious about the spiritual validity of the nature information. She was leery of self-help programs or information that found its roots in psychology or the four temperaments. In spite of her doubts about the information, she remained a true friend because she knew we had agreement in almost every other scriptural matter.

She patiently listened to my ramblings about the nature information while silently wondering if I was operating with a mixed spirit. In other words, whether at different times I was operating with the right spirit while occasionally coming under a wrong spirit. However, God eventually put the nature information to a test where she was concerned.

We were in a precarious situation where Jeannette had to consult with a pastor about another minister. To ensure effective results, I told her how to approach this pastor based on his nature. She followed my instructions. To her surprise, it was an effective meeting. She began to earnestly listen to me, as well as ask questions. A new world opened up to her as she began to understand her relationships with others.

It was not long before Jeannette became an enthusiastic supporter of the Hidden Manna information. As a result, God began to give her insight into the natures. In fact, she was given one of the most humbling and powerful revelations of Jesus Christ.

It is not my cause to promote the Hidden Manna information. It is simply a tool that has helped others, as well as me, to effectively minister to people. My main heart is Jesus Christ and Him crucified. Jesus is the only One who can save. He heals the broken hearted and sets the captive free.[1]

Therefore, my main spiritual search is not to understand human nature, but to find Jesus in His Word and creation, as well as to witness His attitude and life in His Body. Because of this desire, He has never failed me as far as substantiating and revealing Himself in Scripture, as well as in the nature information. In this case, He revealed to Jeannette how these different natures put together in the Body serve as a powerful revelation of Him. And, through a series of situations, He revealed the name or reference to the nature information: *Hidden Manna*.

I was reminded of the manna of old. It came from heaven. The Israelites perceived it as a foreign substance, but God told them to

---

[1] Luke 4:18; 1 Corinthians 2:2

gather it and partake of it. It not only gave them life, but also proved to be satisfying. Jesus confirmed that this manna pointed to Him as the bread from heaven.[2]

There are so many aspects about Jesus that are hidden.[3] The Holy Ghost unveils each revelation about Him and bids His followers to partake of it. Each nugget brings greater meaning to life, producing satisfaction and contentment in the soul.

There are also treasures or nuggets of Jesus that are veiled in humanity. Only through the work of the Holy Ghost can these treasures be uncovered. As the Lord began to reveal this gold mine hidden in humanity, I was reminded of Revelation 2:17, "He that hath an ear, let him hear what the Spirit saith unto the churches; To him that overcometh will I give to eat of the hidden manna, and will give him a white stone, and in the stone a new name written, which no man knoweth saving he that receiveth it."

Jesus' followers must overcome to truly eat of the manna, and to receive the stone that has a new name written on it. The manifestation of this overcoming will be the unveiling of Jesus in power and glory in the believer's life.

Jeannette received this information when we were about to minister in an obscure place in Arizona. Immediately, we implemented it into the Hidden Manna Seminar. This revelation has overwhelmed, humbled, and brought sobriety to those who have heard it. Those who hear the Hidden Manna information begin considering what it means for them to get beyond acceptable religious boundaries and scale the heights that God has divinely ordained for each nature in the Body of Christ.

Keep in mind that in the beginning, God made man in the image, likeness, and resemblance of Himself. Therefore, man was to reflect the glory of God. When Adam disobeyed God, he fell into darkness. Needless to say, the ability to reflect God's glory was darkened and marred. As Romans 3:23 says, "For all have sinned, and come short of the glory of God."

Jesus Christ put off His former glory or capacity as deity and took on the shape of man. He reflected the Father and served as a mirror to mankind. Through His redemption on the cross, He established the way in which people can once again serve as a reflection of God. Granted, the veil must be taken off of a person's heart and mind, but Jesus is able to accomplish this. This allows freedom for the Spirit of God to work Jesus' life in His followers, thereby, reflecting Him in and to the world.[4]

Christians who give way to the Holy Ghost's work will reflect Christ. Depending on their nature, they will reflect various aspects of Jesus in different ways. These different reflections do not contradict one another, but simply add dimension to His character and reality.

---

[2] Exodus 16:4, 11-36; John 6:32-40
[3] Colossians 1:26-27, 2:2-3
[4] Philippians 2:6-8; 2 Corinthians 3:13-18; 4:3-5

The Apostle Paul tells us that God takes each believer and places him or her individually in the Body of Christ.[5] If each believer allows the reality of Christ to shine forth, what kind of reflection or image would emerge in Jesus' incredible Body? You would have a powerful, complete picture of Jesus Christ.

This was brought to light by two Scriptures: Ezekiel 1:10 and Revelation 4:7. These Scripture verses are in regards to the four beasts: the lion, the ox or calf, the man, and the eagle. These four beasts represent the universal reign of Christ over all of creation, therefore encompassing all four directions of the earth.

There are also four Gospels. As you study these four Gospels, you realize that each of these four symbols or aspects of Jesus' reign is represented in the Gospels. As you consider the four creatures in light of the four natures, once again, you can see these four representations in the natures. Each of these creatures give much needed insight into what each nature must overcome to personally and collectively become the reflection of Christ in this lost world.

As a person associates the creature to the right nature, he or she will unveil the Gospel that was written for his or her particular nature. As each line connects with the dots, a powerful revelation of Jesus is uncovered along with the potential of the Body of Christ in this world. This potential is immeasurable. However, for the Body to reach its heights in God, each nature must overcome that which would mar Jesus' reflection in his or her life, and allow God to fit him or her into the Body.

Let us now consider this incredible revelation.

# Strong-Willed Nature

The first Gospel is Matthew. It was written to the Jews to prove that Jesus was and is their Promised King and Messiah. It revealed that He is from the tribe of Judah and of the lineage of King David. As the oldest son of Joseph, Jesus was in line to the throne of David. This lineage was of the uttermost importance, because a king was promised from the lineage of David. This king would establish David's throne forever.[6]

Jacob also made reference to this leader when he prophesied over Judah,

> Judah is a lion's whelp: from the prey, my son, thou art gone up: he stooped down, he couched as a lion, and as an old lion; who shall rouse him up? The scepter shall not depart from Judah, nor a lawgiver from between his feet, until Shiloh come; and unto him shall the gathering of the people be (Genesis 49:9-10).

This prophecy is pointing to Jesus, the Lion of the tribe of Judah. This reveals the symbol associated with the Gospel of Matthew, the *lion*.

---

[5] 1 Corinthians 12:18
[6] 2 Samuel 7:12-16

Matthew not only establishes Jesus' identity as King and the lion prophesied in *Genesis* by recording His lineage, but he also confirms His identity by pointing out how seven prophecies were fulfilled concerning His coming in the first four chapters of this Gospel.[7] As one considers the facts, decisiveness, and emphasis of the Gospel of Matthew, he or she can see how it is written to the strong-willed person.

The lion is also the symbol that strong-willed people gladly embrace. He is considered the king of all the wild beasts. He is powerful, and can intimidate or bring fear to the hearts of almost all who cross his path. Strong-willed people can prove to be both powerful and intimidating leaders. They have the potential of ruling much, but can easily display improper leadership when not being ruled by the King of kings and Lord of lords.

This brings us to the dangers of the lion. Strong-willed people may like the concept of being a lion, but they must keep in mind how dangerous this beast can be. It preys on other creatures in order to rule. It can be indifferent, ruthless, and cruel regardless of the circumstances. This can also be true for strong-willed people who are not under the control of the Holy Ghost. They prey on other people in order to control their worlds. They can be indifferent to needs, ruthless in pursuits, and cruel in their handling of matters. Such attributes are contrary to the disposition of Jesus.

There are four distinct attributes associated with a powerful reign: *authority, royalty, strength,* and *power.* All of these attributes are attractive to a strong-willed person, but the secret is that there must be balance that comes in the form of godly boundaries.

Scripture reveals this balance by always presenting the lion in conjunction with the lamb. We see this in the case of Jesus. In Revelation 5:5-6, the Apostle John is ready to behold the Lion of Judah, but what he beholds is the Lamb that was slain before the foundation of the world. Interestingly, the Lion of Judah is always depicted in conjunction with the meek, sacrificial Lamb. This means that proper balance can only come to the strong-willed person when he or she takes on the disposition of the lamb.

How does one with the capabilities of a lion develop a disposition of the lamb? And, how can he or she display the attributes of leadership that will benefit the Church and bring glory to God? For example, it is easy for a lion to possess natural authority, but how does a lamb display that authority?

Scripture tells us through gentleness. "Thou hast also given me the shield of thy salvation: and thy right hand hath holden me up, and thy gentleness hath made me great" (Psalm 18:35). The word great means "to increase or be in authority."[8] This shows that godly authority is established through the attitude of gentleness and not intimidation or aggression.

---

[7] Matthew 1:23; 2:5-6, 14-15, 17-18, 22-23; 3:3; 4:14-16
[8] Strong's Exhaustive Concordance #7235

*Royalty* means "to rule sovereignly, kingly, and a foundation of power or dominion."[9] How does one gain the position of royalty in God's kingdom? This position can only be obtained through humility. Matthew 5:3 says, "Blessed are the poor in spirit; for theirs is the kingdom of heaven." The word "poor" in this text means "beggar" or "cringing pauper."[10] Such an attitude points to one who is in need and is vulnerable. Such a concept is far from the strong-willed person who insists on putting confidence in personal strength, rather than regress and trust God. But, to those with the disposition of a lamb, meekness is a natural response.

*Strength* is the third trait. It implies to fasten upon, seize, conquer, withstand, might, and prevail.[11] In what way does a strong-willed person display strength? Matthew 5:5 tells us through the disposition of meekness, "Blessed are the meek: for they shall inherit the earth." Meekness implies that a person's strength is under the control of the Holy Spirit. Therefore, it will never be abusive and destructive.

Strong-willed people want to rule their worlds and often display an *unruly spirit* that opposes God's authority. Until they become properly ruled, they become the ones who will eventually be conquered by their own fear. This fear will cause them to pull their world down around them. In other words, their own strength will end up destroying them. It is only by taking on the disposition of the lamb that their strength can be used in a proper way to inherit all that God has for them. This disposition means total surrender to the real King of kings.

The final attribute of a king and a lion is power. Strong-willed people can only display power in a proper way when they are under right authority. They must remember where real strength and power come from, "...Not by might, nor by power, but by my spirit, saith the LORD of hosts" (Zechariah 4:6).

When strong-willed people are unruly, they will draw their own lines and rules. These lines may run parallel to God, but they will not be within the righteous boundaries or ways of God. Interestingly, one of the definitions of rule is to mark with parallel lines.[12] These people will always have lines or boundaries, but God must be the One who establishes the location of these lines.

Strong-willed people must give up the need to control, and submit to the gentle guidance of the Spirit. The Apostle Paul brought this out as he instructed believers to follow him as he followed Christ. Paul had lost his strength as a lion on the road to Damascus, but found real life and authority in Jesus.[13] He became a meek, obedient lamb that willingly followed the Lion of Judah. In the end, he was able to make this declaration:

---

[9] Ibid #4467
[10] Ibid #4434
[11] Ibid #202, 3581
[12] Webster's New Collegiate Dictionary
[13] Acts 9; 1 Corinthians 11:1

For I am now ready to be offered, and the time of my departure is at hand. I have fought a good fight, I have finished my course, I have kept the faith: Henceforth there is laid up for me a crown of righteousness which the Lord, the righteous judge, shall give me at that day:... (2 Timothy 4:6-8).

# Stubborn Nature

*Mark*, the second Gospel depicts Jesus as the burden bearer or the sacrificial ox that carried our sins to the cross. It is a fast-moving Gospel, and is full of proof as it speaks of the many miracles of Jesus. Many believed the stubborn Peter dictated this Gospel to Mark. These aspects of this Gospel all point to the stubborn person. Therefore, the ox or calf serves as the symbol for this nature.

Stubborn people have a problem with the ox representing their nature. It often causes sobriety rather than joy. They initially see themselves as free spirited, ready to embrace and experience the world in glorious ecstasy, rather than being tied to a cart or plow. They feel more like a wild stallion that refuses to be caught or tamed, instead of an ox ready to be led to the altar of sacrifice. Feeling like a wild horse is nothing more than a fantasy, but these people can stubbornly hold onto it.

The reality behind these people is clearly revealed when they are challenged, abused, hurt, and wounded. They don't run like a horse to escape the situation, but will charge like a raging bull. As a result, they often leave a path of confusion and destruction behind them.

Because stubborn people enjoy their fantasy about being a wild horse, they often balk at the concept of being nothing more than a cow, prepared to be offered up as a sacrifice. Their response is normally in compliance with their *undisciplined spirit*. It also explains what God wants to do with stubborn people by using the contrast of the ox. The ox is the king of all the tame beasts; therefore, God truly wants to discipline the emotions, purpose, and walk of this individual to bring forth his or her potential in the kingdom of God.

Two things must occur for stubborn people to experience godly discipline: 1) They must become yoked with Christ, and 2) they must be willing to be sacrificed. The reason for this is because stubborn people have the ability to plow up the fallow ground of people's hearts with their honesty and bluntness. Even when stubborn people try to be diplomatic about the truths of God, they still manage to cause friction. In turn, those offended will turn around and sacrifice them. Unless stubborn people realize that this sacrifice is an affront against truth and righteousness, they will take it personally and interpret it as rejection.

This brings us to the importance of the yoke. Stubborn people must be yoked with Jesus to keep matters in perspective. If these people remain under the yoke of Jesus, they will be able to confidently hide in Him regardless of the attitudes, expressions, and actions of others.

Jesus' yoke will also bring stubborn people to the altar of the cross. This yoke points to the disciplined walk of self-denial and death. As stubborn people submit to the yoke, they begin to take on the disposition of Jesus. As they give way to the work and the leading of the yoke, they become identified with Him in His sufferings. This identification will make them into leaders who have been consecrated to reign with Him.[14] It is in this disciplined walk that Jesus deals with their selfishness.

Once selfishness is dealt with, stubborn people can become the acceptable sacrifice. They will be ready to be offered up at all times for the sake of Christ. Hebrews 12:2 reveals Jesus' attitude about the sacrifice He made on our behalf, "Looking unto Jesus the author and finisher of our faith; who for the joy that was set before him endured the cross, despising the shame, and is set down at the right hand of the throne of God." He endured the cross, joyfully knowing the outcome. Likewise, stubborn people can joyfully endure the cross, knowing that victory awaits them.

There is also another significance to Hebrews 12:2. Scholars believe that this Scripture verse refers back to the sacrifices that were offered up by the Levitical priests. The priests were required to examine each part of the sacrifice. As one considers each area in light of stubborn people becoming yoked with Christ and walking out the sacrificial life as a living sacrifice, they can begin to understand those areas that must be disciplined.

The first area that was examined on the sacrifice was the *head*. Head represents the intelligence and thoughts. Everyone has to recognize the need to discipline the focus of their intelligence in order to control their thoughts. Since stubborn people have an emotional momentum that leads them into a world of fantasy, they must avoid the tendency to go with their feelings. The key to this discipline is found in Philippians 2:5, "Let this mind be in you, which was also in Christ Jesus." The word "let" implies discipline. This discipline occurs when one gives way to the work of God.

The second part that needed to be examined was the *fat*. The fat represents the general vigor or excellence of the sacrifice. To the Christian, the fat represents what he or she is offering. Much of what the American Church offers is unacceptable because it is not marked with a price tag. In other words, the sacrifice never comes out of one's need, but one's leftovers or abundance. Such a sacrifice represents second best, which is marred, blemished, and unacceptable to God. This blemish is a product of selfishness. It is marked by a lack of devotion to God and marred by the absence of genuine sacrifice.

King David made an important point to Araunah in regard to obtaining the land to offer a sacrifice to stay judgment upon Jerusalem. Araunah had offered David the land free of charge. David's reply was, "Nay; but I will surely buy it of thee at a price: neither will I offer burnt

---

[14] 2 Timothy 2:12

offerings unto the LORD my God of that which doth cost me nothing" (2 Samuel 24:24).

If a stubborn person gets past selfishness, he or she will be liberal in his or her sacrifice. Such sacrifice is acceptable and pleasing to God.[15] Scriptures make reference to this liberality. Proverbs 11:25 tells us that the soul shall be made fat, and he that waters shall be watered. Psalm 92:12-15 implies that the righteous shall be fat and flourishing. Fat in these Scriptures means "to anoint, to satisfy, to be rich, and fertile."[16]

Obviously, if a person brings the best to God, He will anoint it for His use. God will then satisfy him or her with a greater reality of Himself. His manifested life in the person will cause him or her to be rich with heavenly treasures, and will cause him or her to be productive for His kingdom.

The third area the priests examined of the sacrifice was the inward parts. This represented the motives and affections. Colossians 3:2 instructs believers to set their affections on things above and not on things on the earth. If the affections of the stubborn person are directed at the right source, the motivation will eventually come into line with Jesus' heart. At the core of His heart is sacrificial love that was expressed in obedience. This love is devoid of self and alive with steadfastness to carry out God's will as a servant and as a burden bearer.

Finally, the priest examined the legs of the sacrificial animal. The legs represent the *walk*. The Apostle John stipulates how one must walk in 1 John 2:6, "He that saith he abideth in him ought himself also so to walk, even as he walked." This is in relationship to Jesus.

Jesus serves as our example. He left us with two examples: that of servitude and suffering.[17] As a servant, He submitted to the will of the Father. As a sacrifice, he became obedient to the suffering of the cross.

Jesus' walk led Him up the narrow path to Calvary. The Christian walk leads up the same narrow path in servitude and sacrifice. This brings His followers in line with God's way, and in obedience to His will. Therefore, stubborn people must consider if they are under the yoke of Christ to ensure the reality of His sacrifice. These two points of discipline will actually discipline their walk.

Interestingly, the strength of the ox must be disciplined before it can become the king of the tame beasts. Discipline helps this animal reach its leadership potential in God's scheme of things. Otherwise, this beast is subject to those things which will prey upon its weakness, leaving it unprotected.

Jeannette discovered some interesting facts about the ox. Discipline for the ox must start at day one. If a calf is not handled immediately, it will become a roaming beast that will become impossible to discipline. Oxen will not respond to brutal treatment, but can be trained to respond

---

[15] Hebrews 13:15-16
[16] Strong's Exhaustive Concordance #1879
[17] John 13:14-16

to vocal commands. Oxen do not need elaborate harnesses and bits like horses. Just a simple yoke can guide their steps and ensure effective work.

The Apostle Peter understood the necessity of this yoke. Jesus told him that one day he would be guided where he had no intention to walk.[18] This was to stipulate his sacrificial death. This assured him that no matter how his emotions fluctuated, he would stay the course and become an acceptable sacrifice to God.

If you are stubborn, are you yoked with Jesus? Are you becoming an acceptable sacrifice that is ready and willing to be offered up for the glory of God?

# Self-Assured Nature

The third Gospel of *Luke* is where Jesus is portrayed as the Son of man. His lineage went back to both Adam and God. This brings us to the conclusion that the third Gospel is associated with the man in the four beasts. Jesus as man reflected what the normal, perfect man would have become before sin entered the picture. But, He also served as the visible image of God.[19] The words "reflection" and "image" immediately identify the nature that is represented by this particular Gospel and symbol—the self-assured nature.

Man is the crowning glory of creation. Adam was formed to reflect the glory of God in the midst of creation. When he sinned against God, that image was marred, preventing him from reaching his ultimate potential.

Jesus was fashioned as a man; therefore, He was capable of representing the perfect man in creation. Hebrews 7:26 gives us insight into this perfection, "For such an high priest became us, who is holy, harmless, undefiled, separate form sinners, and made higher than the heavens."

This Scripture verse says four things about what constitutes perfection. A person must be holy. This means he or she must be upright in disposition and conduct. A person must be harmless, or in other words, innocent, simple or unsuspecting in attitude. He or she must be undefiled or unsoiled by the world. And, he or she must be separate from sinners in every area of his or her heart, mind, and lifestyle.

Many people can respect the qualities of the perfect man, but maintain that Jesus could only fit such qualifications. Once again, the Word refutes this argument. There is a man that fits this criterion. His name is Job. Job 1:1 gives this insight into his character, "There was a man in the land of Uz, whose name was Job; and that man was perfect and upright, and one that feared God, and eschewed evil."

---

[18] John 21:18
[19] Luke 3:23-38; John 14:7; Colossians 2:9; 1 Corinthians 15:44-49

Job was considered perfect in his generation. This means he was complete, pious, gentle, dear, and undefiled.[20] He was complete in his devotion, pious in his actions, gentle in attitude, dear or precious to God, and unspoiled by the world.

Job was also upright. This means Job was straight, direct, fit, and seem good.[21] Being upright pointed to his walk. He stood upright before God. He was consistent in his life, steadfast in his course, fit for God's use, and morally upright.

Job feared God. Such fear serves as a point of discipline. At the heart of this fear is humility. It causes people to show discretion in their walk. This discretion is a manifestation of godly wisdom. Psalm 111:10 states, "The fear of the LORD is the beginning of wisdom..."

Finally, Job hated evil. To hate evil means to hold the line of righteousness regardless of what it personally costs. Job would not turn to the left or right, but maintained his life, testimony, and walk before God.

Job's perfection expressed his inward disposition. His perfection pointed to how complete his commitment was to God for there was no deviation in his faith. His uprightness once again pointed to a walk that was straight in conduct and practices. Fear of the LORD represented his perception, and hatred of evil speaks of his attitude towards the holy and the unholy. As a result, Job represented a sanctified man who stood perfect before God.

Job stood perfect before God, but he was not a perfect, sinless man. Jesus is the only One who remained sinless. This sinless man, who is considered the second man or second Adam, went to the depths of the grave and death so that man could reach perfection in Him.

Let's now consider the first and the second Adam. The first Adam was created in the image of God. He had the ability to reflect the glory of God. The fact that he had the capacity to reflect the image of God implies that he was self-assured by nature. Do the rest of his actions confirm his nature? He had a choice between the tree of life and the tree of knowledge of good and evil. The fact that he failed to choose either one of them up front points to indecisiveness. When confronted over his sin, he blamed both Eve and God. In his bid to claim independence from God's reign, he exchanged his ability to reflect the glory of God with an angel of light image. This image can be religious, but remain independent and *unyielding* towards God's reign. Instead of operating in a right spirit, it hides behind a beguiling spirit that will strive to seduce people into worshipping an image instead of God. Rather than being upright, this image is crafty and shrewd due to its self-centeredness. Instead of being steadfast, it is unpredictable, causing confusion. Rather than being faithful to God, it becomes treacherous in its motives and dealings. This religious image gives the impression of perfection, but

---

[20] Strong's Exhaustive Concordance #8535
[21] Ibid #3474

lacks the inward work of sanctification. -It becomes a sick substitute for what is real and acceptable.

In the future, the world will have to contend with such an image. This person will come across as the Promised Messiah, but behind the façade is someone who is crafty, beguiling, and seductive. His whole goal is to get the world to bow down and worship him. We know him as the antichrist.

This brings us to the second Adam, Jesus. Jesus was fully God and fully Man. You can only have one nature; therefore, as the Man, what is Jesus' nature? Is it the same as the first Adam? Jesus gives us insight into this subject when He told Philip that He was the physical representative of the Father. He actually reflected the Father's heart, mind, and will. We, therefore, can only conclude that Jesus Christ is self-assured by nature.

If you noticed, the spiritual examples given in the previous chapter for the self-assured were all from the Old Testament. When Jesus' nature as man was being unveiled as being self-assured, I realized why I was not given any New Testament examples. In the Old Testament, Job proved that one can stand perfect before God, but Jesus in His humanity revealed how one becomes perfect in God. He revealed the complete work of sanctification.

The desire of self-assured people is to be perfect. This is why they develop different images, but Jesus' example reveals that they only have to have one image—His. All these people have to do is yield to the work of the Spirit and He will change their disposition from an *unyielding*, independent spirit to that of a servant. Keep in mind that Jesus emptied Himself of His glory and took on the disposition of a servant and was fashioned as a man.[22] To be a perfect person, a self-assured person must get rid of his or her vainglory displayed in images and allow the Holy Spirit to develop the disposition of Jesus. Once His disposition is erected, he or she will reflect the perfect man in this world.

The ability to reflect this perfect man gives a small insight into this nature's potential. The potential to reflect the unhindered glory of Jesus in this dark world is incredible. Is it any wonder that Satan tried to wipe this image out by coming against Job? And, consider how he came against Jesus. Satan will do anything to wipe the true image out of the world whether he has to drown it out, counterfeit it, or destroy it.

Luke is a Gospel of contrasts. This nature needs contrast. For example, there is the contrast between the first Adam and the second Adam. The first Adam provides the harsh reality and hypocrisy that is evident with any façade, while the second Adam, Jesus, brings a contrast by defining the disposition and attitude that promotes godliness and perfection and reflects the glory of heaven.

These contrasts are brought out in Luke's many parables. One can discover incredible insights in studying these stories. They bring out the

---

[22] Philippians 2:6-8

clear differences that convey instruction concerning acceptable attitudes and godliness.

Are you self-assured? Are you reflecting the image of Jesus? If you don't reflect His image, consider if you have applied the cross to your images and yielded to the work of the Holy Spirit. In order to do this, you must exchange your logic with integrity and offer up all of your vainglory.

# Submissive Nature

Perspective is everything to a submissive nature. The person with this nature will either prove to be a turkey that is earthbound or an eagle that soars in the heavenly realms. This brings us to the fourth Gospel, John.

The Gospel of John is written to unveil Jesus as the Son of God. In order to do this, it opens by giving a heavenly perspective, "In the beginning was the Word, and the Word was with God, and the Word was God" (John 1:1). Not only is Jesus revealed in His pre-incarnate state in the first chapter, but He is also declared the life and light of man, as well as abounding in grace and truth. This incredible revelation continues as Jesus' teachings are intertwined in this Gospel. We are given insight into His wisdom, and we can only conclude that He is wisdom Personified. We witness His first known miracle of turning water into wine. It is in this Gospel that we find Jesus' last teachings and prayer the night He was betrayed. It reveals His heart as He leaves His disciples with indelible examples, as well as simple, life-changing truths and instructions.

The eagle is the only beast that could symbolize this heavenly and incredible perspective. The eagle is the king of all birds. This may seem insignificant in light of the other three creatures unless you realize some simple facts. Lions may claim to be the king of all the wild beasts, but they cannot reach the heights of an eagle. The ox can speak of its strength and sacrifice, but an eagle manifests the ability to find sources of power and strength that will enable it to reach down from great heights to glean from the depths of streams, rivers, and valleys. Man has the ability to reflect the glory of God, but an eagle has the ability to witness God's unhindered glory from the heights of the air currents.

When Jeannette considered how the fearful submissive person had the potential to be an eagle, she marveled. How could people who run in mental ruts reach such heights in God? The answer rests with their ability to seek out such heights and embrace an eternal perspective. For example, Isaiah's perspective was God's glory as His train filled the temple. The Apostle John had a revelation of Jesus in His power and glory. These different perspectives brought these two men low in humility so that they could be brought higher in their understanding and life before God.[23]

Submissive people can be *unmanageable* unless they have an eternal perspective. They become bogged down in their mind. This causes great frustration and depression. As they look to their mind,

---

[23] Isaiah 6; Revelation 1

unresolved matters begin to take over as they ignore, file away, and try to figure out how to resolve issues. Eventually, their conceit and understanding are brought low in the form of failure. It is at this point that they can look up to embrace God's wisdom.

Submissive people's fear also brings them to the end of self so they can be lifted up. Their need to understand brings them to grave depression. This causes desperation. At this point, many submissive people will look up, allowing their understanding to be channeled upward towards the eternal rather than the earthly.

This much needed heavenly perspective for the submissive person is brought out by using the example of the eagle. Job 39:27-29 says, "Does the eagle mount up at your command, and make her nest on high? She dwells and abides on the rock, upon the crag of the rock, and the strong place. From there she sees the prey, and her eyes behold afar off." Jesus must be the Rock and strong place for the submissive person. If he or she lifts up Christ, He will lift him or her up, giving His perspective.

Once eagles begin to soar on the wind, they can go higher, even above storms. Submissive people can endure the storms when they understand the ways of God. This understanding gives them assurance about their immovable Rock.

Isaiah 40:31 says, "But they that wait upon the Lord shall renew their strength; they shall mount up with wings as eagles; they shall run, and not be weary; and they shall walk, and not faint." Submissive people must withdraw into Christ to be established on this immovable Rock. When they become established on and in Christ, He will become their strength. As these individuals are brought higher by Jesus' wisdom, they will also be enabled to reach deep into His immovable truths.

Finally, the eagle is fearless. Under the power of the Holy Spirit, submissive people can truly move in freedom. In fact, Jesus talked about how the wind cannot be controlled or understood. The wind is often symbolic of the Holy Ghost. Submissive people must step outside of their mind, and put their wings out in faith, and allow the wind of the Holy Ghost to lift them above the limited, earthly perspective to embrace God's perspective for the Body of Christ.

Are you submissive? Do you act like a turkey, or do you possess the intensity of an eagle who has an eternal perspective? Are you living in your mind or are you soaring in the liberty of the Spirit?

The challenge for each Christian is to personally reflect Jesus to edify the Body and bring glory to God. In order to reach this potential, believers must come higher in their life in Christ.

# 12

# EMITTING THE
# FRAGRANCE OF CHRIST

2 Corinthians 2:14-16 says,

> Now thanks be unto God, which always causeth us to triumph in Christ, and maketh manifest the savour of his knowledge by us in every place. For we are unto God a sweet savour of Christ, in them that are saved, and in them that perish: To the one we are the savour of death unto death; and to the other the savour of life unto life. And who is sufficient for these things?

Obviously, the Church has what it takes to make a difference and conquer that which opposes it. Yet, many Christians appear to live in defeat. Is God's Word incorrect or are some of His people clearly missing it?

Any triumph a Christian might experience can only be found in Christ. This means that it is no longer the person who lives, but Christ lives in and through him or her.[1] It is Jesus' life that is powerful and attractive. It is His life that serves as a fragrance to God, the Church, and the world.

Therefore, Christ must be lifted up in each life in order to serve as an acceptable fragrance to God. This points to the voluntary sacrifices found in Leviticus 1-3. These sacrifices were not required like the sin and trespass offerings.[2] These sacrifices were freely given. They had to be anointed. As the fire consumed the sacrifice, the smoke and fragrance would ascend towards heaven. This smoke and fragrance brought pleasure to God.

Jesus served as a mandatory sin offering on the altar of the cross, but a voluntary sacrifice in His service before the Father, and toward others. As the Lamb of God His sacrifice was required by God to deal with our sin. Since Jesus became the mandatory offering, Christians are to serve as living sacrifices, constantly emitting a perpetual fragrance of His life to God. The living sacrifice points to a sacrifice that is being consumed by self-denial, the application of the cross, obedience to the Word, and the reality of Jesus. As the life of Jesus comes forth, it emits a fragrance that brings pleasure to God.

---

[1] Romans 8:37; Galatians 2:20
[2] Leviticus 4 & 5

This fragrance also brings life to the Church. The life of Christ is the living bread that can be imparted to others for edification. His life is the light of man that can expose all sin, hindrances, and enemies. The life of Christ also points to resurrection life and power that enables one to be established in a relationship with the Living God. His life is the means to bring forth reconciliation between God and man.[3]

Finally, the fragrance of Christ's life signifies death to those who are unsaved. The unsaved are those who remain on the outskirts of God's salvation and reign. This fragrance becomes a harsh reality of judgment and wrath. Although the unsaved would like to brush the reality of Christ aside, this fragrance signifies His eternal life and becomes a haunting challenge.

Each Christian is called to express Jesus. Their lives must become the expression of His disposition. Their hearts must serve as an altar that constantly emits His fragrance, while their faith must become refined in their lives to bring them forth as priceless heirlooms that will crown Jesus' glorious head. Their dispositions must mirror or reflect His majesty. This is what it means for Christ to be in all and to become all in all to those who name His Name as Lord and Savior.[4]

Scripture reveals what needs to happen for Christ to be unveiled in our lives before we begin to emit the fragrance of Christ for God's pleasure, the Church's edification, and a reality check to the unsaved. The greatest hindrance in emitting the fragrance of Jesus is self. Self wants to be honored and exalted as God. It wants to be served. It resents challenges, cries over adversity, and feels picked on when paying consequences. It wants the world to revolve around it, and failure to do so results in anger towards God and self-pity.

Self is forever avoiding personal accountability. In other words, self refuses to grow up and become responsible for personal attitudes and actions. Irresponsibility is an expression of what ails self—the desire to do nothing but what is convenient, comfortable, and feels good. It does not want to face the darkness, wickedness, and vanity of its ways. This is why it pursues fantasies that keep it from taking personal accountability. After all, if it has to face itself, it will have to be responsible to deny self, pick up the cross, and follow Jesus. Self expresses itself differently in each nature.

# Submissive Nature

Submissive people can bring much needed heavenly perspective to the Church. The problem with these people is that until they become an eagle who soars on the wind of the Holy Spirit, they display an *unmanageable spirit*. When this natural spirit is in operation, these people become *self-absorbed*. Underneath self-absorption is complacency. This complacency wants nothing more than to be

---

[3] John 1:3-11; 3:19-21; 6:35; Romans 6:1-9; 2 Corinthians 5:18-19
[4] Romans 8:29; 2 Corinthians 3:15-18; Galatians 2:20; Philippians 2:5

constantly satisfied so that it never has to stir itself up to do that which is uncomfortable. In other words, everything must be absorbed and made to submit or fit into mental compartments to comply with their small worlds. When challenged to step into uncharted territories to properly confront reality, complacency responds in fake nobility. If the fake nobility fails to get the desired recognition, self-pity follows.

These people operate so much in their minds and self-absorbed world, that they begin to act more like turkeys who never get off the ground because they are stuck in their mental ruts. They are unable to get beyond their own conclusions, reality, and worldly wisdom to realize that they are not soaring above the situation; rather, they are buried by it.

Without a heavenly perspective, the Church will not have the wisdom of Christ. This means the pillars will be shaky rather than grounded on and in the Rock of Ages. Therefore, submissive people must get beyond their intellectual comfort zones and stir themselves up to explore the depths and heights of God. After all, they are meant to express the wisdom of Christ in confidence. This means they are reaching high to gain God's perspective, as they reach deep into His truths and ways. Such a pursuit will allow God to surround them with His perspective. Each time a submissive person is surrounded by His presence and glory, he or she reflects God.

Sadly, the cords of fear and personal concepts bind many submissive people to their mental ruts. They do not know how to move beyond either to gain God's perspective. This keeps them from reaching their potential in Christ and emitting His fragrance to others. As a result, they fail to become the eagle. This condition simply means the submissive person will fail to reach great heights in God.

The heights of God allow submissive people to guard the ways of God with heavenly wisdom. This will edify the Church as these heights represent the victory of the cross, which comes by way of liberty in the Spirit.[5] As they are established in the ways of God, they become pillars that will uphold the ways and character of God. As pillars, submissive people will help others to discover the enduring, everlasting foundation of the Christian life: Jesus Christ.

This is why God cannot afford to let submissive people off the hook. He is calling them higher, but they must forget self by denying the credibility of their intellectual conceit and subduing their fear. They must exchange their natural, earthly wisdom for the heavenly wisdom from above.

The way that submissive people deny self is by choosing to love God with their entire *mind*.[6] This love will penetrate every compartment and override every concept. Once this occurs, the intense fleshly or worldly focus of these people will change from the earthly to the heavenly. The change will redefine their desire to understand the world around them with the need to know Jesus. As submissive people pursue the

---

[5] 2 Corinthians 3:17
[6] Mark 12:30

knowledge of Jesus, they will begin to soar in greater revelations of Him. Greater revelations of Jesus will give submissive people the authority to stand sure in the Body of Christ, as others seek wisdom and truth from their example.

When it comes to fear, submissive people must realize that it serves as an immovable wall. To overcome this fear, they must step back from the wall and look up towards the One who is able to draw near to them. Once these people stand back, look upward, and cry out for help, God can lift them out of their mental pit.

Revelation 1:9 says four things about the Apostle John. He was a brother, committed to the well-being of others in God's kingdom. He was a companion in tribulation, identified with others and capable of bringing consolation to those in despair. He was in the kingdom and patience of Christ, which meant he was an heir of salvation and identified with Christ in suffering and fruits. He was being persecuted for the Word of God and for the testimony of Jesus Christ. As a pillar, John would not waver from the Word, and as an eagle, he had victory because of his testimony of Christ.[7] What a beautiful picture of the submissive person who is soaring in the heights of God, while firmly planted on the Rock. Such a person is trustworthy and reliable. These people can be immovable due to their foundation. Yet, they are unstoppable in regards to the heights they can reach in Christ because of the Holy Spirit.

Sometimes the Church tries to control or dictate the heights a submissive person is to reach in God. This is a grave error because it will close down or hinder the heavenly perspective. Perspective has to do with vision. This vision is in relationship to perspective outside of self and the Church. Keep in mind people without such vision will perish.[8]

If you are submissive, are you bound by fear or are you creating a mental rut? Are you a turkey, flopping around in the wind, or are you soaring with it like an eagle? Are you striving to reach the heights that God has prepared for you, so that you can bring a heavenly perspective to the Church regardless of what is going on in this world? Or, are you living in your own personal world? The answers to these questions will determine if you are reaching your potential in Christ, thereby, emitting His fragrance.

# Stubborn Nature

The stubborn person has an *undisciplined spirit* until he or she becomes yoked with Jesus. It is very *selfish*; therefore, it insists that everything that enters its environment be designed for its personal use, needs, and desires. Selfishness often hides laziness. This laziness is indolent in attitude; therefore, it avoids anything that might result in pain or uneasiness. As a result, these people end up running in circles to avoid the reality that challenges their fantasies. If these people fail to properly

---

[7] Revelation 12:11
[8] Proverbs 29:18

face reality or allow their reality to be challenged, they become lazy and unreasonable. They will only act according to their emotions, and not according to reality and responsibility.

Stubborn people often refuse to grow up. They want their fantasy world. Their attitude is that they will either slide by or con their way around anything that does not serve their emotional purpose or come into compliance with the world they so desire. This is nothing more than laziness. Laziness reveals itself in rebellious attitudes and moodiness that leads to depression.

These people's unwillingness to face reality can be hidden behind their many excuses. They want everything to adjust to them, so they can feel good about themselves and their life. When they do not get their way, they become angry and rebellious. All too often, these people remain immature and foolish because they refuse to take responsibility for their emotions.

Stubborn people's undisciplined spirit can drive them mad with activities and endless commitments and pursuits. They naturally take on causes, but many of these causes have to do with making them feel better about self or creating the right environment. Once again, we see the need for these people to be yoked with Jesus, so that they can become like a tamed ox, a beast that will only shoulder the burdens put on by their Master. As the tamed ox, they will properly shoulder God's work, as well as always be ready to be offered up as an acceptable sacrifice for God's glory.

For most people, this type of disciplined life would not hold much significance. However, for the stubborn, it holds the key to liberty, purpose, and satisfaction. Although stubborn people fight to be free to do as they will, their need is to have their emotional momentum, aggression, and strength properly disciplined or channeled. They know if this strength is not properly channeled, it will prove to be chaotic and destructive for them. This is why they develop high *standards*.

These standards serve as their personal yoke that will bring what they consider to be the needed discipline to their environment. Rather than bringing discipline, these standards eventually cause overwhelming burdens that create a frustrating, condemning cycle.

The real conflict for stubborn people comes down to maintaining their freedom, while ensuring that their emotional strength is under proper control. Again, it comes down to the yoke they bear. If it is Christ's yoke, it will bring freedom through proper discipline.

This disciplined, sacrificial life does not point to fairness, but it does develop righteousness. It may not represent the free spirit that many stubborn people desire, but it does constitute the security that they so often seek and desire in their life. Like most people, what stubborn people often pursue is contrary to what they need to live a meaningful life.

It is hard for stubborn people to come to terms with godly discipline because they feel so deeply about their perception of their needs, as well as what is right and wrong and what would constitute real life to them.

Yet, these deep feelings are what bring the greatest instability into their lives. This instability not only creates havoc for them, but also prevents them from serving as a fragrance to God, the Church, and the unsaved.

Stubborn people who are disciplined by the yoke of Jesus bring stability to the kingdom of God through bold leadership. They are meant to plow the way for the seeds of the Gospel to be planted in people's hearts. They prepare the way to the cross by example of an acceptable sacrifice. They establish other Christians in their faith as they serve as a plumb line to the righteous Cornerstone, Jesus Christ.

Therefore, God will not let stubborn people off the hook. They must become yoked with the One who became a sacrifice. This identification will give them the liberty to follow Jesus up the paths of righteousness. But, how do stubborn people submit to such rigid discipline? First, they must realize that Jesus' yoke is the only way that the Holy Ghost is able to produce in them a specific character or pattern of behavior. Until this character or pattern is established in stubborn people, they will always figure a way around paying the necessary price to become identified with Christ in every way. To avoid the price means they are avoiding the cross and identification.

Identification brings us to sacrifice. Stubborn people must sacrifice their need to be loved by choosing to love God with all of their *hearts.*[9] This sacrifice will align their affections towards heaven, thereby, changing their pursuits. As their affections become established in Christ, their life will become yoked with Him.

The yoke of Christ will channel stubborn people's emotional momentum in the right direction. They will plow up the hard turf of hearts, challenge conventional ways of man's religion, and display righteous indignation as they hold the line of righteousness against the works of wickedness.

Sadly, the Church fears stubborn people who display this momentum and righteousness. This fear causes those in position to try to control stubborn people's momentum. Ultimately, they muzzle the ox, preventing these people from being the prophetic voice in the Church. Silencing this voice could mean destruction for the Body, for this voice brings vital warnings and instructions.

People who encounter the bold leadership of a stubborn person must not try to muzzle him or her; rather, they must discern whether the person is truly yoked with Christ and serving as His voice. If the stubborn person is yoked with Christ, stand back and let Jesus lead that individual where He desires. The results will not only prove to be interesting, but beneficial and necessary.

Are you stubborn? Are you yoked with Christ, bearing the burden of His kingdom, while always ready to be offered up as a sacrifice for His glory? If not, you will fail to reach your potential and serve as that incredible fragrance of Jesus. Remember the fragrance that is emitted

---

[9] Mark 12:29-31

comes out of sacrifice that is being burned by the purging fires on the altar.

# Self-Assured Nature

Self-assured people have the highest potential in the kingdom of God. The reason is that they have the capability of reflecting the very image of Jesus. This means they have the ability to take on His disposition of a servant. Taking on a servant's disposition can only occur when self-assured people exchange their pursuit for perfection with the Lord's will. When this happens, these people can become an avenue by which Jesus' compassion is expressed, His fiercest leadership displayed, and His righteousness and purpose manifested to others.

The problem with self-assured people is that the ability to reflect Jesus is often enslaved by images, fear, and rebellion. These people have an *unyielding spirit* towards authority. Their unyielding spirit covers apathy that allows them to remain uncaring towards reality. This lack of concern enables them to maintain their pride or appearance of perfection no matter what it may cost them or others around them. Their unyielding spirit makes them *self-centered* and cruel. Self-centeredness demands that everything must be about them, and when it is exposed, it manifests itself in anger and vindictiveness.

These people, therefore, must totally yield everything to the Holy Ghost, but they often refuse to do so. Self-assured people will play the game in order to maintain their image and means of control. They will devise clever ways to avoid yielding their will or ways in order to hold on to their rights. They will substitute outward conformity for inward commitment. They will do anything except completely surrender.

Self-assured people's unwillingness to surrender prevents the Holy Ghost from completely sanctifying their body, soul, and spirit.[10] Without the work of sanctification, Jesus Christ will not be erected as the pillar or source in their life and reality. As a result, they will fail to reflect the image of Christ, do the will of the Father, and bring a consistent leadership to the Church. If Jesus is not erected, self-assured people will never become the anointed servant in God's kingdom. Without the anointing, they will never bring trustworthy or strong leadership to the Body. Ultimately, this will mar the part of the Body that serves as the crowning glory of God in a dark world.

The struggle for the self-assured person comes down to yielding or surrendering images, standards, rights, and life as he or she perceives it. The aspect of surrendering is a terrifying prospect for these people. If yielding is a terrifying prospect or the last resort, how do self-assured people become a fragrance? The answer is obedience.

Godly obedience requires self-denial and submission. As self-assured people choose to obey, because it is the logical and righteous response, they will give way to the work of the Spirit. The Holy Ghost will

---

[10] 1 Thessalonians 5:23

begin to change their desires and pursuits as He sanctifies the different aspects of their character.

This brings us to the acceptable motivation. Godly obedience is a response of love.[11] Self-assured people must choose to love God with all of their *souls*. This means to obediently love Him at the point of their wills, minds, and emotions. They must determine to do His will, to allow the Holy Ghost to develop Jesus' mind, and to permit the Spirit to channel their fierceness and authority as a means to produce compassion and consistency in their lives and leadership.

God will not let self-assured people off the hook. They must take on the full character of Christ. This means pride must give way to humility. Their independence must be replaced with meekness. They must submit their unyielding disposition to the Holy Ghost. They must exchange their images for God's will, and their defiance with the mind of Christ.

If self-assured people give way to the leadership of Jesus Christ, they will bring strong leadership to the kingdom of God. Sadly, many Christian practices encourage self-assured people to become enslaved to religious masks, façades, and games. Such slavery has marred the powerful reflection of Christ. As a result, self-assured people fail to sow the Gospel seed into hearts. They fall short of reflecting the product of the cross: the image of Christ in His unwavering love, commitment, and obedience. Without the ongoing reality of Christ, His life is never established inwardly. Without His reflection, His life will never be manifested outwardly in the Church or to the world.

If you are self-assured, make sure you yield or give way to the reality of God. This will ensure that you will reach your potential. Your life will serve as a fragrance that will please God, challenge the Church, and shake the foundation of the unsaved.

# Strong-Willed Nature

Strong-willed people may be a lion in attributes, but they must become a lamb in disposition if they are going to become part of the fragrance of Christ to the Church and in this world. The biggest obstacle for strong-willed people is their *unruly spirit.*

The unruly spirit is very *self-serving*. It makes them obtuse or insensitive towards any reality that might challenge their sense of infallibility. Everything must adjust and line up to the strong-willed person's world. This need to rule causes strong-willed people to strive for control, so that they can rule their world in accordance to their reality. This is to ensure that everyone lines up to their reality in order to serve their purpose and reach their goals. They want people to automatically recognize their abilities, power, and authority, and submit. But, if people fail to do so, they will try to cage them into their world by playing games or bluffing their way to subdue and overwhelm. If their reality is

---

[11] John 14:15

consistently challenged, these people can become bullies who will make the person pay who refuses to line up to their way of thinking.

Their goals, power, and authority represent lines that bring them into competition with God, and serve as the means that will ultimately *cage* them into a rigid, unforgiving world that renders them useless to God. This closes down, perverts, or limits decisive leadership in His Body. It prevents strong-willed people from preparing the way for the Gospel by bringing clarity and distinction to God's work and man's spiritual condition. These peoples' unruliness can keep them from showing the way and the work of the cross through example. Ultimately, they will fail to lead others to Christ to establish them on the right foundation and line them up to the Cornerstone.

For this reason, God will not let strong-willed people off the hook. They are a vital part of the Body and revelation of Jesus. To overcome their dominating nature, strong-willed people must become lambs in disposition. This disposition will bring godly leadership, discipline, and authority. Proper discipline will keep their sense of infallibility in the right perspective. It is this controlled disposition that will ultimately emit the fragrance of Christ.

To develop this disposition, strong-willed people must give way to the authority of God, and choose to love Him with all their *strength*.[12] They must allow the Rock of judgment to destroy their natural strength in order to embrace the reality of the complete work of Christ's redemption.

It is only as strong-willed people's strength is properly channeled that they become the strength and authority in the Church. Their strong, decisive leadership will bring confidence and direction to God's sheep. This clarity of leadership will prove that they have exchanged their personal crown of strength and authority with their personal cross. Such a cross points to regression. Regression in personal strength and confidence will develop the disposition of meekness and servitude. Application of their personal cross will mark their walk with straight, parallel lines, as they follow the King of kings.

Strong-willed people must, out of recognition of who God is, become lambs that follow the Lion of Judah. The meekness of a lamb will allow them to see their inability to do what is wise, righteous, and acceptable to God in the power of His Spirit. It will make them realize that all lasting accomplishments are a manifestation of His work and power.

Are you strong-willed? If so, are you a caged lion due to your cement lines or are you a lamb following the Shepherd? Are you striving for personal control and recognition, or have you given up your identity to press forward to the high calling in Christ Jesus? If you are failing to press forward, you will never become a fragrance acceptable to God, beneficial to the Church, or serve as an effective reality check to the doomed world.

---

[12] Mark 12:29-31

# 13

# THE OVERCOMING CHURCH

Overcoming is not an option, but a visible expression of salvation. 1 John 5:4-5 confirms this, "For whatsoever is born of God overcometh the world: and this is the victory that overcometh the world, even our faith. Who is he that overcometh the world, but he that believeth that Jesus is the Son of God?

In *Hidden Manna*, I have been revealing why Christians fail to overcome. They simply give into their fallen condition. In other words, they do that which is natural. For example, it is natural in our fallen condition to rebel against the authority of God. It is natural to resist, avoid, and ignore what is righteous when it does not properly fit into our comfort zones. It is natural to bow down to personal pride, justify the flesh, and compromise with the world. Since it is natural for carnal Christians to give way to their selfish disposition, they have a hard time perceiving why God would not see it their way and bless them in all of their religious attempts.

God's evaluation about the fallen condition of man is clearly recorded in the Scriptures. Sadly, our fallen condition blinds us to the fruits of our personal spiritual condition. We clearly see the ways of the flesh and the arrogance of pride in others, but we cannot see these active influences in ourselves. We actually remain indifferent to the personal devastation plaguing us from within.

Sadly, we cannot overcome until we come into line with God's evaluation of our fallen condition. We must recognize how our rebellion manifests itself, and our pride disguises itself. We must acknowledge how our flesh operates and the world affects us. Such enlightenment will mean the veil will fall off of our minds, so we can see the true face of our spiritual condition and properly respond to God.

One might wonder why people fail to see God's evaluation since it is clearly presented in Scripture. There are five reasons for this failure:

1) Due to pride, people must come out either as the savior or the victim in their world. In the kingdom of God, there is only one Savior, Jesus Christ, and there are no victims, just losers who refuse to pay the price of submission to know God. Pride refuses to acknowledge Jesus as Lord, and hides behind self-righteousness as it views the fleshly ways of others as ridiculous and foolish.

2) A person must have an open heart before God can reveal such matters to him or her. Hearts that are closed to God become hard towards those things that do not fit into their personal understanding.

3) Some people want to believe that there is still some good in them; therefore, they are deserving of blessings and happiness. But, if this were so, Jesus would not have had to die on the cross.

4) People want to believe that they are an exception to the Word rather than responsible to it. Subsequently, they are justified in ignoring it, claiming ignorance towards it, or disobeying it.

5) People do not want to take personal responsibility for their life, attitude, and practices; therefore, they operate in self-delusion and self-justification.

God must reveal the depth of our depravity, but we must be willing to look at it and agree with His evaluation. Such agreement lines us up to God's ways and thoughts. Once we come into a mental agreement with God's evaluation of our condition, we will begin to see the destructive path we are on, and turn from our way of doing and being to walk towards God. This is repentance.

Repentance is turning from our old way of living, and beginning to walk in the ways of obedience and righteousness before God. Obviously, without changing the direction of our walk to be converted to the ways of righteousness, we will never overcome.

Once the face of our fallen condition is revealed, we can give way to the work of the Spirit, resulting in regeneration and sanctification. God is able to begin the work of changing or regenerating us from within. This regeneration does not mean our nature is changed. Rather, it points to our traits being properly realigned as certain characteristics are mortified, and others are disciplined and channeled or sanctified by the Holy Ghost.

Obviously, to overcome, we must develop a relationship with God, rather than practice a religion. Each nature has a different way of expressing religion, while Jesus is clearly missing in their lives.

*Submissive* people major in knowledge about the Word, rather than coming to the knowledge of the Living Word, Jesus. This makes Christianity a religion of controllable facts and formulas, rather than a relationship. Jesus becomes a *concept* that is complimented by the uniqueness of the Word of God with all of its facts, history, and spiritual insights. However, this knowledge never gets past the mind. Since it stops at the mind, submissive people can remain indifferent about the reality around them, including their own spiritual condition.

To ensure that Jesus becomes real, submissive people must recognize that their conclusions do not represent the wisdom or truth from heaven. They must bring all thoughts into captivity and into obedience to Jesus, and begin to seek Him out as the Living Word in order to possess Him as a *living* and *personal Savior*.[1]

---

[1] John 1:1; 2 Corinthians 10:5

Since minds serve as their personal lord over submissive people's reality, they must step past their minds and make the Person of Jesus, Lord. This is a hard battle for them because while they are struggling in their minds to not go into their minds, they become weary and overwhelmed. They cannot imagine themselves functioning outside of their minds. It is as though they first must run out of compartments and options before Jesus can step on the scene and lift them out of their endless mental pit.

*Stubborn* people often create a Jesus according to their emotional feelings. This Jesus becomes a contradiction of religious notions as He is constantly being adjusted to present emotions or environments. For example, they perceive Him as loving, but if He fails to perform according to their feelings, they conclude He does not love them. Sadly, the Jesus these people create is nothing more than an unrealistic fantasy or a harsh, unloving Savior that is unfair, prejudicial, and who appears to constantly toy with people's emotions.

When Jesus fails to prove His undying love for them according to their standards, they put up a wall of skepticism against Him. Skepticism causes them to play the religious game by becoming religious, dogmatic, and legalistic in their beliefs. They become plagued with doubts and pushed by self-righteousness, causing them to become judgmental towards others. Ultimately, they will perceive themselves to be suffering martyrs.

The Jesus whom stubborn people often erect is fickle and weak in crisis, uncertainties, and changes. This is why they must know Jesus as a *Powerful Savior* who cannot be controlled by emotional whims or changes according to environments. His life and ways prove that He remains the same, and that nothing can sway Him from Who He is and His commitment to His followers.[2] Since emotions serve as the master of stubborn people, they must allow God's Word to master or discipline their emotions, as they choose to allow it to serve as their final authority.

Stubborn people must also avoid taking Jesus' "so-called" failure to comply with their standards and whims as personal rejection. Jesus' proof of His love for each of us can be seen by His own sacrifice on the cross. Therefore, it is not up to Him to wade through the endless parade of a person's emotions to prove His commitment when He has already done so on the cross.

*Self-assured* people erect an image of Jesus that serves as their personal religious image. This image of Jesus is not realistic because it lacks His disposition. For example, self-assured people see Jesus as a perfect image, but not as a perfect Man who truly lived and breathed. The key to Jesus' perfection as man was His disposition as a servant. He was totally yielded to the will of the Father. Without the reality of this disposition, both the face and spirit behind Jesus would be changed as He is robbed of His humanity and made unobtainable or untouchable by mere man.

---

[2] Hebrews 13:8

Once self-assured people bring down the religious image, they can accept Jesus' work of grace as the *Perfect Savior* on the cross in order to make Him Lord of their life. They will see that all He does in His followers' lives is a matter of grace and not a situation where they obtain some personal level of perfection.

*Strong-willed* people make Christianity a matter of facts that are shaped according to their personal understanding. They see Christ as black and white, but there is no dimension or personality to Him. A person's disposition serves as the reflection of someone's character, but personality is how a person will manifest his or her disposition. Therefore, without this dimension or personality, Jesus remains an idea to strong-willed people, rather than a living reality.

This allows strong-willed people to be indifferent to spiritual matters or concepts. They often act outside of religious matters or beliefs in order to reshape them according to their perceptions. Their lifeless perceptions of Jesus make their life before God not only religious, but also controllable. Jesus inevitably becomes someone who can be understood and reshaped to fit the situation. In other words, they are always trying to fit God and His activities into their world.

It is vital that strong-willed people come to terms with Jesus as their *Promised Savior*. Promise points to something that will be accomplished. This not only implies action, but a certainty or reality. Jesus not only came as the Promised Messiah and suffering Savior the first time, but He is coming back as the victorious King and Lord. These people need to realize that everything about their life in Christ must line up between these two decisive realities about Jesus.

For example, strong-willed people must line up their ideas to who Jesus is. They must allow Him to become Lord in their activities, the Anointed One in ministering to others, and the only Savior in light of redemption. After all, strong-willed people always try to figure out how to save the day to bring their world into order and under control. Such a pursuit is often driven by their need to receive recognition and honor from those around them. They need to give this need for recognition to God in worship and to others in ministry.

Once the relationship with God is on track, each person must come to terms with how his or her flesh operates.

# The Flesh

The flesh represents the natural tendencies or inclinations of the fallen condition. When a person understands how the flesh operates, he or she can get a small glimpse of how far the unregenerate disposition is from the glory of God. It is overwhelming, sobering, and frightening. In fact, the reality of this could drive people mad if they fail to understand it in light of God's forgiveness. God's forgiveness does not take away the sorrow or despair that such a personal revelation can bring, but it does offer hope in spite of it. This hope leads to God's provision of salvation.

The first factor we must recognize about the flesh is that it refuses to submit to any authority. It will devise games to get around authority. These games give an impression of obedience and humility, while maintaining the rights of the flesh to call the shots, as well as determine the terms of what it will subject itself to.

These games are deceptive, but they serve as a point of control and manipulation. They feed pride in order to use people. They flatter in order to reign. These games toy with people's emotions in order to control. They lack integrity, but many play them in the name of harmony, family, personal agendas, and success.

These games toy with souls as they wrap up lives and the world in a perverted reality. In spite of how many Christians justify such games, they are fleshly and worldly. They avoid or oppose the work of the Spirit. This opposition puts them in the ways of separation from God and spiritual ruin. Therefore, how can a person know if he or she is operating in the flesh or walking by the Spirit?

*Submissive* people can automatically know they are operating in the flesh when they withdraw into their minds to seek wisdom, understanding, and direction. God does not speak to the mind, for it will pervert or limit the affects of His truth. Rather, He speaks to a person's spirit. Once a truth reaches into the spirit of a person, it will enlarge his or her mind to embrace the truth. This is why submissive people must know that their conclusions outside of God's perspective are fleshly and untrustworthy. They must avoid *complying,* not only to their mental ruts, but also with those in their world. These people must choose to hold all conclusions lightly and bring all of their thoughts into obedience to Jesus.[3]

*Stubborn* people can know that they are operating in the flesh when they give way to their emotions. These people are always trying to *reform* themselves and their environment to get their emotional needs met. Many stubborn people perceive that these emotions are from the heart. This is incorrect. These emotions are operating according to the appetites of the flesh and the vain imaginations of the mind. Stubborn people must remember how fickle and unrealistic the reality can prove to be that are created by their undisciplined emotions.

When stubborn people begin to recognize that their emotions are beginning to escalate, they must avoid going there. After all, it does not take much for these people to fall victim to the tidal waves of their emotions. All they have to do is take their emotional temperature. Since they feel deeply about a matter, they will feel justified going with the momentum and conclusions of their undisciplined emotions. The only source that can bring a proper reality to their undisciplined emotions is the Word and character of God. Therefore, stubborn people must make a heart determination to believe God, rather than allow their emotions to reign.

---

[3] 2 Corinthians 10:5

*Self-assured* people who walk according to the reality of their images are simply giving in to the flesh. These people will *perform* according to their images to get desired responses. However, images are in competition with God and unrealistic. Those who walk according to their fragile reality or images are trying to reach maturity or perfection in their own strength.

These people will fail miserably in their attempt to be perfect, but sadly those around them pay for their inability to reach this perfect state. Frustration, anger, bitterness, and hatred often flow out from self-assured people towards others.

When *strong-willed* people rely upon their facts or ideas, they are operating in the flesh. The works of the flesh are expressed in their need to control their world. They resort to different methods to gain the desired control. They first try playing a game or adjusting to the situation. They do this by *conforming* to a situation. They may approach a situation from different angles, always adjusting their approach or maneuvers. But, the motivation behind all of these attempts is to win confidence so they can gain control. If this doesn't work, they can display self-pity or become aggressive and intimidating because of frustration and anger.

God will not bow down to the understanding of the submissive person, wade through the emotions of the stubborn, or compete with the images of the self-assured to try to bring a person to truth. He will never adjust so that He can fit into the world of strong-willed people, nor will He allow Himself to be defined and controlled by their facts or lines. It is up to each individual to recognize the operation of the flesh in his or her life, and to step outside of the destructive cycle.

This brings us to the next area that must be properly examined: that of the spirit.

# The Motivation

People are always judging others by their outward conformity, rather than discerning their spirit. We are told that we can only interact with God from the premise, influence, and leading of the Holy Spirit. However, there are three main spirits in operation in the world. There is the Spirit of God, but each person also has a natural spirit that operates in them. If the individual does not discipline or rule his or her spirit, he or she will become like an unwalled city that is broken down and will not have the walls of safety to properly protect him or her. This brings us to the third spirit, which is of this present world. We know the god of this world is Satan. He is the prince that rules the unseen kingdom that opposes God and works within those who are disobedient.[4]

It is vital to understand how spirit works. It motivates the different attitudes and approaches of a person. It determines the intent or purpose behind an individual's activities. It will determine what each of us comes

---

[4] Proverbs 25:28; 2 Corinthians 4:3-4; Ephesians 2:2-3; 1 John 4:1

into agreement with, as well as personal preferences and attractions. It actually sets up the inner and outer environments in which people operate. The spirit behind people's motivation and intent will manifest itself in the fruits that will be produced in their lives.

Needless to say, the unchecked natural spirit of man and the spirit of the world represent the wrong spirits. They are motivated by the same source, as well as possess the same intent, goals, and fruits. If man's spirit is not properly ruled, Satan will find the necessary inroads to oppress the soul of man or possess his spirit, soul, and body.

These wrong spirits must be properly confronted in order to overcome the flesh and Satan. For example, the natural spirit will toy with sin, justify it, and give way to its temptation. As a result, a person must repent to bring the natural spirit into subjection to the Holy Spirit. Satan throws well aimed darts at our minds, such as lies to confuse us. In such confusion he is able to seduce a person into another reality. James 4:1-10 tells us about the types of influence the flesh and the world has on each of us, and what it will take to overcome such influences. Repentance results in cleansing, while submitting ourselves unto God will cause Satan to flee. In other words, we take authority over him by coming under the authority of God. Sadly, people often repent of what Satan is behind, and try to take authority over their flesh. The wrong response simply keeps people in bondage. This is why we must discern the spirit that is in operation.

Consider the following table on the next page. Notice the fruits or end result that is produced by the different spirits in operation.

| Spirit | Right Spirit | Wrong Spirit |
|---|---|---|
| **Motivation** | Love of God | Pride |
| **Intention** | Glorify God | Honor self |
| **Goal/ Focus** | Lift Jesus Up | Make self God |
| **Results** | Liberty in the Spirit/Fruit of the Spirit | Must control reality, ends in bondage |

Clearly, we must learn how to not only discern the spirit behind others, but the spirit we are operating in. Sadly, most of us unfairly judge others, while justifying ourselves. There is a difference between judging and discerning. Judging is based on the flesh. Such judging will come down to how someone makes a person feel about his or her world. If a person rattles another person's world in any way, it will result in the one who has been offended judging the culprit.

Discerning is wading through the outward influences to determine the spirit or motivation of someone. The ability to discern depends on one's sensitivity to the Holy Ghost, and a balanced understanding of the intent or spirit behind the Word of God. The flesh will never discern, while discernment will not allow the things of the flesh to affect its ability to righteously evaluate the type of spirit behind something.[5]

The motivation of the selfish disposition is pride. This is the essence of self. When a person is not under the right spirit, he or she is operating

---

[5] 1 Corinthians 2:14

according to personal concepts, standards, images, or ideas. These *rulers* make the individual the ultimate authority and judge concerning matters. These rulers also serve as a door through which the spirit of the world, Satan, can come in and reinforce lies, fears, and rebellion.

*Submissive* people who are operating under the wrong spirit become *unmanageable*. An unmanageable spirit can escalate into an impenetrable state where the person becomes *pigheaded*. Initially, this state expresses itself in attitudes. In other words, these people become obnoxious or closed. Both scenarios prevent truth or reasoning from *penetrating* this person's reality. In fact, when a submissive person is closed, it is like hitting an immovable wall. The immovable wall of submissive people is fear. Fear allows this person to ignore or live in denial about what is going on around him or her. Either way, people have a hard time penetrating through the obnoxious bristles or the immovable wall of a submissive person who is out of balance or control.

*Stubborn* people become totally *unreasonable* when they are operating under a wrong spirit. Their unreasonableness makes them *bullheaded*. They will run over you verbally, or take you around the mountain over and over with their endless excuses. In extreme cases, you will hit an immovable wall of skepticism that often hides fear, rejection, betrayal, and anger.

*Self-assured* people become *cruel* and *mule-headed* when they are operating under a wrong spirit. This cruelty comes out of their pride or the need to be right. It serves as a wall that will prevent anything from challenging their reality. They can be verbally or physically abusive during this time, while justifying any action taken in order to survive and come out on top.

*Strong-willed* people become *formidable* when they are operating in a wrong spirit. They become *hard-headed* about what they perceive as being right. In a way, they become unstoppable, regardless of the destruction that may follow them. At this point, these people are often being driven by fear. Their life is totally out of control, and all of their attempts to gain control have fallen to the wayside. Now, fear is about to consume them and they will run, especially in their minds, to figure out how to silence this taunting fear. In fact, these people become their own worst enemy as they teeter on the edge of insanity.

It is noteworthy to understand what opens people up to the wrong spirit. There are three elements that serve as open doors to a wrong spirit. They are:

**Rebellion**
**Control**
**Reality**

Rebellion is a product of pride. Pride will always open people up to a wrong spirit. This is why James 4:7 tells us to, "Submit yourselves therefore to God. Resist the devil, and he will flee from you."

Control can become a form of witchcraft. An example of witchcraft is when someone tries to exert his or her will over another person's will. This is where games come into the picture. People often play games to get their way. Some people are professional about it, but the resentment, treachery, anger, and breakdown of trust and relationships that follow are the byproducts of such control.

Reality is a big issue with most people. God cannot bring truth into a situation that is devoid of reality. He cannot bring instruction when one is in denial of his or her reality. He cannot bring liberty as long as one is trying to adjust personal reality to fantasy. The truth is most people cannot stand their present reality; therefore, they do everything within their means to change it. When reality actually challenges a person's desired reality, fear and anger follow. This state will eventually produce depression.

The final area that must be considered is the heart condition. After all, the issues of life originate in the heart.[6]

# The Heart Condition

People have a hard time coming to terms with their heart. First of all, it is deceitful.[7] This means people cannot trust the intent of the heart because self often sits on the throne of the heart and reigns in utter delusion.

Jesus said of the heart that all sin originates with it. Once again, at the core of sin is self. When self reigns, the flesh is in operation. When the flesh is in operation, it serves as a covering that blinds and perverts a person to the things of God, making it impossible to discern spiritual matters.[8]

The fleshly covering is a veil of unbelief. It actually prevents the things of God from penetrating a person's spirit.[9] In other words, the flesh circumvents the heart. When spiritual matters or truths are perverted and kept from penetrating a person's heart, he or she will remain unchanged in the inner man.

When the right spirit is missing, people will make their Christian life into a religion. They will dress up the works of the flesh in religious garb. They will outwardly try to rehabilitate the old man, as self piously reigns unhindered and unchallenged from the heart. And, as long as self reigns, the heart will remain untouchable by the Spirit. It will remain uncircumcised and far away from God.[10] The main fruit of such a heart will be disobedience.

There is only one reason God's people obey Him in spirit and truth: Because they love Him. Jesus made this clear in John 14:15, "If ye love me, keep my commandments."

---

[6] Proverbs 4:23
[7] Jeremiah 17:9-10
[8] Matthew 15:16-20; 1 Corinthians 2:14
[9] 2 Corinthians 3:14-15; 4:3-6
[10] Matthew 15:3-9; Hebrews 4:12; 10:14-17

The Apostle John reiterated this point in 2 John 6, "And this is love, that we walk after his commandments. This is the commandment, that, as ye have heard from the beginning, ye should walk in it."

Sadly, people trip over the first commandment because they do not choose to seek God with the commitment to love and serve Him with all of their heart.[11] They become religious or obsessed with the "supernatural," while God remains a controllable belief.

Godly love cannot remain indifferent. It must respond to the one who is loved. It cannot ignore cries, pleads, or needs. It cannot justify indifference, abuse, cruelty, or tyranny. It must respond in commitment, uphold in righteousness, and obey that which is honorable in humility and submission.

Many Christians fail to fall in love with God. They may fall in love with their concepts about Him and get caught up with their emotions towards Him. They may become impressed with their images concerning Him, and become confident in their ideas about Him, but they fail to fall in love with the Person of God. And, when that love is missing, so is the reality or manifestation of Christ's attitude and life.

Christianity is a matter of the heart. Everything must be done from a heart that has sanctified or set God apart in devotion and service. This heart must be single in focus, consistent in desire, and unwavering in faith. It must be totally compelled and consumed by the love of God and a love for God.[12]

How do these four natures circumvent their hearts, so that they remain untouched and unchanged by God and His Word? *Submissive* people resort to their mind. This prevents the truth of God from penetrating their hearts as it is carefully processed. By operating in their minds, they can control reality. They comply outwardly to the things of God, while deeming their personal conclusions as being wise. Usually, they are very impressed with their conclusions or knowledge, and see their so-called wisdom as a way of bringing them *honor*. Meanwhile, they become *complacent* towards personal problems and issues around them. This allows them to *ignore* reality as they conclude that everything will eventually turn out okay down the road.

Such a conclusion allows them to become so *self-absorbed* that they end up being clueless to problems in their lives and families, allowing their conclusion to gain momentum. Since they ignore reality, very few issues are resolved. Unresolved issues create a tidal wave that will eventually wreak havoc in their lives. Needless to say, this indifference will cause delusion.

Submissive people need to give the *honor* they secretly desire to others. This will help them to come down from the intellectual pinnacles of their minds, and allow God's truths to penetrate their hearts. As His truth and love penetrate their hearts, they will begin to show proper

---

[11] Mark 12:19-31

[12] Romans 5:5; 2 Corinthians 5:14; Ephesians 6:5-6; 2 Timothy 2:19-22; 1 Peter 3:15

consideration for others. They will become sensitive to others, allowing them to effectively minister to them.

*Stubborn* people circumvent their hearts by keeping reality on an emotional level. They often confuse their deep emotions with their heart; therefore, presuming that those things that are deeply affecting them are a matter of the heart. Therefore, they mistake their emotions as truth. As already stated, emotions are a matter of the flesh, and must come into subjection to the Word of God before they can be properly challenged.

By operating in their emotions, stubborn people create a fantasy that causes them to live in *denial* about their present reality. This fantasy keeps them from facing reality; therefore, truth is never allowed to penetrate their hearts. When reality does challenge them, unbalanced, stubborn people become angry because others have failed to bow down to their illusions to bring forth their desired reality.

This brings us to another important point about stubborn people. Because of their need and their emotional makeup, they desire to receive *adoration*. Therefore, when people fail to bow down to their illusions, they also fail to show the proper adoration towards them. As you can see, this emotional merry-go-round is not only confusing and unrealistic, but it can be insane.

Stubborn people must give up their need to be understood, and give that understanding to others. These people can be very compassionate and giving. However, when they are circumventing their hearts, they often distribute unfeeling criticism to those who fail to bow down to their standards or illusions.

*Self-assured* people circumvent their hearts by changing images. By changing images, reality can be adjusted. Therefore, they never have to deal with the reality of their actions and become accountable to those in their world. Since their images are devoid of emotions, they can be indifferent to others' feelings. They can ignore other people's struggles because perfection is a matter of changing an image and not a matter of a changed heart. Ultimately, these people can become a harsh *judge* of what constitutes reality as they seek *glorification* for their images.

Self-assured people need to get past their images and begin to recognize the humanity of others. Instead of being an ultimate judge of humanity, they need to become identified with it. Instead of trying to lord over others, they need to become a true servant to all. Instead of seeking glorification, they need to lift up Jesus in His glory so others can be drawn to Him.[13]

*Strong-willed* people circumvent their heart by keeping reality a matter of facts. These facts establish concrete ideas. These ideas are considered infallible. Therefore, these ideas make these people *insensitive or hard* to that which does not fit into their controlled worlds.

Since strong-willed people perceive their facts as being infallible, they expect others to pay *homage* to them. This homage is their idea of showing proper recognition for their intelligence, abilities, and actions.

---

[13] John 12:32

These people need to take their need for recognition and start giving it to God in service and to others in ministry. They need to give God permission to shake their ideas in order to make them pliable in His hands.

As you can see, the heart is always circumvented at the point where self is preferred, exalted, and treated as God. This is the hidden agenda behind all unregenerate human nature. Only God deserves honor, adoration, glorification, and homage.

The problem with self being in the position of God is that it is not God. It is contrary to the very nature of God. Its so-called truth is nothing more than perverted reality. And, that which demands service is nothing more than idolatrous flesh. Its insatiable ego wants to be flattered or honored as it reserves the right to prostitute itself with the world without consequences or judgment.

Self strives to be God. And, when self reigns, God will be nothing more than a religious belief. When self reigns, there is no room to love God, because one is in love with self. When self reigns, it desires all worship and adoration. And, when self reigns, there is no room for others to be regarded, considered, or preferred.

What about you? Consider the following table on the next page and see if self is reigning in all of its vainglory, or if God is reigning in all of His majesty.

| Types | Submissive | Stubborn | Self-Assured | Strong-Willed |
|-------|-----------|----------|--------------|---------------|
| Gospel | John | Mark | Luke | Matthew |
| Symbol | Eagle | Ox/Calf | Man | Lion |
| Point of Subjection | Mind | Heart | Soul | Strength |
| Type of Bondage | Bound | Muzzled | Enslaved | Caged |
| Natural Spirit | Unmanageable (Complacent) | Undisciplined (Lazy) | Unyielded (Apathetic) | Unruly (Obtuse) |
| Wrong Spirit | Impenetrable (Pigheaded) | Unreasonable (Bullheaded) | Cruel (Mule-headed) | Formidable (Hardheaded) |
| Type of Self-Exaltation | Self-absorbed | Selfish | Self-centered | Self-serving |
| Types of Games Played | Compliant to get way. | Reforming to get way. | Performing to get way. | Conforming to get way. |
| Agenda | To be honored | To be adored | To be glorified | To be paid homage |
| Substitution of Jesus | Religious Concept | Religious Notion | Religious Image | Controlled Fact |
| Jesus, the Rock | Foundation | Cornerstone | Erected, Anointed Pillar | Rock of Judgment |
| Jesus As Savior | Living, Personal Savior | Powerful Savior | Perfect Savior | Promised Savior |
| Responsibility In Church | Vision/ Perspective | Prophetic Voice | Image of Christ | Authority |

# 14

# A FINAL THOUGHT

My greatest challenge in writing a book is knowing how to start and finish it. This book is no exception. Since my books emphasize the reality of God, I realize there is no good beginning or ending when it comes to His infinite character and ways. He is so faithful to unveil the depths of His character, and to reveal the incredible mercy, grace, and faithfulness He shows to those who desire to know, love, and serve Him.

This book is a revision because He has given me more insight into human nature. In doing so, He has also revealed His Son in greater measure. This is necessary, because without Jesus, there is no balance to man's world.

There is a well-known story about a man who cut up a picture of the world and gave it to his son to put it back together. Surprisingly, the boy accomplished the task quickly. When the father asked the boy how he managed this feat in such a short time, the little boy showed him that there was a picture of Jesus on the other side. He had simply put the world back together by putting together the picture of Jesus.

The *Hidden Manna* information has an incredible history. Back in 1977, the Lord impressed upon me as a new Christian that He had a book for me to write. At the time, I was attending college and felt a real leading to cease my college pursuits and go home. Many questioned my move, but I can see how God wanted to keep my slate clean from the influence of liberal secular education.

In the next seven years, I took many detours in my Christian life, only to end up broken at His feet. It was at that vulnerable time that He began an incredible process in me. This process meant breaking down my preconceived notions about Him and religion. Once my notions were brought down, He could begin to write on my slate the truth about His character, as well as reveal my spiritual state.

It was a bittersweet time for me. He stripped away layers to reveal certain aspects of my selfish disposition, while revealing His love, forgiveness, and commitment to my spiritual well-being. I did not understand the significance of that balance until later when I realized that my life could not be put back together until Jesus was clearly revealed in greater ways.

The truth is man has no identity outside of Christ. The Bible clearly states that our life is in Him and He is in us. Over the years, I have grown to appreciate that little word "in" as it continually stipulates in Scripture my relationship, position, and identity in Christ.

It was not until 1986 that God began to reveal the *Hidden Manna* information. I can see where He gave me a gift of faith to simply believe and pursue the information out of a child-like curiosity and trust. He then gave me a co-laborer in the Gospel, Jeannette, who would also share in testing out and discovering new insights into human nature. I had no idea where it was all leading me, but I sense that it was a valuable tool that could edify others.

In 1995, *Hidden Manna,* the book, finally was published and the first copy sold April 8th. The Lord had impressed upon me that this is the book He wanted me to write. I had my challenges in writing. My English was horrific and caused nightmares for those who tried to edit it. I was also struggling under a barrage of various obstacles that caused me to consider giving up the idea of a book altogether and simply use it as a personal tool in ministry.

As I held my first copy of *Hidden Manna*, it struck me that it represented an 18-year spiritual odyssey. The odyssey began with a zealous ignorance of God, but ended with an incredible revelation of Jesus.[1] Suddenly, it dawned on me how faithful God had been to bring me down a particular course. This whole journey was not about a book. Rather, it was about my own spiritual growth. Even though I had considered some of my experience as a total nightmare, I realized that I had discovered, and was beginning to possess the Pearl of Great Price, Jesus Christ.

When it began to dawn on Jeannette and me how powerful this information was, we wanted the whole world to know about it. Surprisingly, God kept it hidden. This puzzled me. I wrestled with this issue until He revealed to me how people take that which is precious and pure to Him and simply add it to the smorgasbord of information they already have in order to feed their already growing intellectual pride. Or, they would defile, abuse, and use it for their personal gain.

Sadly, I have witnessed people take this information and use it to control and manipulate others. In other cases, I have watched "wannabe" ministers see this information as a means to exalt themselves in His kingdom. Even though this information is simple, it is profound and only those with sincere hearts can properly grasp it. And, even those who have a balanced understanding of it admit they could never do it justice by teaching it.

The *Hidden Manna* information also proved to be controversial. It was often associated with self-help information, the four temperaments, or psychology. I never realized that so many Christians had lost their way and were now seeking means outside of Christ to find their way back to some purpose or meaning. Any time self is promoted, Christ will be missing.

---

[1] Romans 10:2-3

As far as the four temperaments information is concerned, I discovered it had ties with the New Age, while the roots of psychology can be traced back to the occult. It was not unusual to immediately encounter one of two attitudes: I already know the information or you are in error! At times I felt I was walking through a minefield. I never knew when I was going to meet with conceit or skepticism and criticism.

I began to wonder why God would even bother to reveal this information in the midst of these controversies, abuses, and misuses. I even wrestled with God about this predicament. Was I meant to keep it to myself and just use it in ministry? Was it really from God or some terrible joke from Satan who played on my innocence and sincerity? The questions and examinations flooded my soul. Through it all, I was constantly reminded of how the information helped people and remained consistent under my constant examination, as well as the scrutiny of those who bothered to test it. Truth will not change no matter how it is tested. But, the question as to why God would even bother to unveil this information at this time in history when the world as we know it is winding down to a climactic end, continued to challenge the recesses of my mind.

Surprisingly, God seemed to reveal to me the answer to this question. As never before in history, man is searching for his identity and purpose. One wonders why man is so caught up with the concept of self. Is it because he has come to the end of his other pursuits and found them all to be vain? Is it because he has more time to focus on himself?

Whatever the reason, it seems that man is trying to discover the source of his plight by looking inward. He perceives that if he can understand himself, he will come to terms with his world. However, in his search, he avoids seeking out God, and turns to the world's philosophies and doctrines of demons.

Why would man avoid seeking for his Creator? As I studied different philosophies that people pursue, I noticed the absence of one main issue: **Sin**. For example, self-help programs give the impression that man can change his world by simply pulling up his bootstraps and applying certain formulas. The temperament information puts the pressure on people to recognize their temperament, thereby, changing their atmosphere. Psychology explains destructive behavioral patterns according to the past. It often puts the blame of people's destructive patterns and actions on others.

Needless to say, the problem to the plight of man has not changed since man's rebellion in the Garden of Eden. The problem remains the same. It comes down to sin. Sin can only be revealed in the light of a Holy God. Sin is not taken care of by hiding it behind a cloak, ignoring it, justifying it, or denying its very existence. It can only be dealt with in one way—at the foot of Jesus' cross.

The harsh reality is that man needs forgiveness for his sins, healing from its workings in his life, and restoration from its various activities in order to come to terms with the significance of his life and purpose. Man cannot find this forgiveness by shifting the blame, looking inward, or towards some type of relationship and philosophy. He can only find lasting resolutions for his life when he steps outside of self and beyond all relationships and philosophies of the world.

This brings us to *Hidden Manna*. Much of the popular information in regards to the plight of man offered to Christendom is weak, worldly, or heretical. It is meant to appeal to the ignorant, arrogant, and the superficial. It is designed to sell books rather than save souls. It is capable of whetting fleshly appetites, but incapable of satisfying the soul. It offers formulas, but not lasting eternal solutions. It gives the impression of doing spiritual surgery when all it does is put a Band-Aid on a bleeding artery. It uses Christianity as a platform to present and sell ideas that lack both spirit and truth, often merchandising souls in the end.

In spite of this poor, weak, erroneous presentation, God is faithful. He always presents the truth in the midst of error to bring contrast and challenge. Because of people's search for self and the inundation of substandard and heretical information, He simply raised up a standard of righteousness by unveiling the true identity of man. Man's problem has not changed—it is called "sin". His solution remains the same—The Lord Jesus Christ.

Many people have become depressed by the *Hidden Manna* information because it takes the glamour out of human nature to reveal the harsh reality of man's fallen condition. People begin to see their rebellion, pride, and self-exaltation. They start to realize how they strive to become God in order to determine truth and maintain personal control and reality. Some have even whined and complained about how this information does not leave their particular nature in a good light. It cannot be denied. This information unveils the harsh reality of sin. However, this harsh reality was meant to bring people to one conclusion: They need to be delivered from themselves, and there is only One person who can accomplish such a feat. His name is the Lord Jesus Christ.

Man cannot understand or change his world by looking within. For his world to make sense and be put back together, Jesus Christ must become a living reality to him. For his life to take on meaning and purpose, Jesus must be lifted up in his life. For His life to make a difference, he must become an extension of Jesus Christ as he manifests His attitude, life, and examples to others.

*Hidden Manna* does nothing more than bring people back to basic scriptural truths. This information reveals sin, calls for repentance, and lifts up Jesus as the only solution. It calls for self-denial, application of the cross, and obedience to Jesus. It unveils Jesus in the midst of His creation. This is no different than what God's Word has done. Therefore, why write a whole book to bring out these truths when they are clearly outlined in the Word of God?

Sadly, Christianity has been inundated with an endless stockpile of nonsense that has become a detour from these simple truths. This nonsense subtly puts the focus back on man, rather than on God. As long as man is the emphasis, God will never become the solution. The purpose of *Hidden Manna* is to reverse this emphasis by showing people that their endless search for self will bring them to a hopeless abyss.

And, it is when man reaches this abyss of nothingness that he will most likely look upward to the only One who can put his world back together. It is when man finds Christ and allows Him to take His rightful place as King and Lord in his life that he will discover his true identity and purpose.

Although *Hidden Manna* gives valuable insight into the four natures found within humanity, it brings people back to their need for God to find forgiveness, restoration, and to overcome, and to reach their potential in Christ. It unveils Jesus in the midst of humanity, thereby, giving people a vision beyond themselves to see a greater eternal significance for their existence.

I realized that *Hidden Manna* was God's way of making the truth available in the midst of the weak and heretical substitutes. Many people have been blessed and helped by this information. But, to me, the greatest asset is not the insight about human nature, but the revelation of Jesus Christ. He is the Manna hidden within veiled humanity, and He can only be perceived and embraced by those who have the spiritual eyes to see and the ears to hear.

As I come to the end of this book, I realize that it is not my responsibility to make sure God's people are exposed to this information. My job was to write a book in order for Him to make it available to those He chooses to reveal it to. After all, *Hidden Manna* is His information and has been dedicated to Him for His use and glory.

I am both thankful and awed that He has revealed this information to me. It has allowed me to discover how wonderful He is. It has given me a vision beyond self, and set me free to soar in the wonderment and beauty of His love, grace, power, and majesty.

My prayer is that each reader will have the eyes and ears to truly see Jesus in this book. After all is said and done, at the end of every great spiritual odyssey is the glorious reality of the King of kings and the Lord of lords. It is only as Jesus rises as the bright and morning star within man's soul that it becomes obvious that He is man's only great hope in which to discover the promised life and his ordained purpose in light of heaven's eternal purpose and glory.

Book Two

# BRING DOWN
# THE
# SACRED COWS

**(A Candid Look at Marriage and the Family)**

# INTRODUCTION

I asked myself, why write a book about marriage? After all, there is an abundance of books and seminars about this subject. I lay no claim to being an expert on marriage (if there is such a creature).

All I know is that the small flame that was flickering inside me about this subject developed into a raging fire. I do have something to say about marriage. I know that the Holy Spirit within me is grieving for families. The words and thoughts that He has put in my spirit about this subject are not only candid, but also a warning and a call to repentance.

I pray that the Church Jesus died for is big enough, honest enough, and humble enough to get on its knees to honestly rise to such an occasion. Satan is having a heyday with the family, and the tragedy is that he is winning because he has rights to oppress many Christians in their relationships.

Christian marriages are full of idolatrous practices. By this I mean that self, pride, and worldly pursuits are at the core of many Christian relationships. Even though the Church attempts to give the appearance that this sacred institution is indeed distinct from the world, it statistically displays the same problems and failures as the world. This lack of distinction from the world not only implies that the visible Church is no longer the salt of the earth, but that it is also missing the mark in confronting the real issues plaguing marriages. It also apparently lacks the power to overcome.

This book is not about formulas. It is about facing real problems confronting marriage. It is not about bringing romance back into the marriage. It is about bringing God back into the marriage. It is not about helpful insights into our spouse in order to get him or her to respond correctly. It is about how each of us can recognize and stop our own destructive cycles in all of our relationships. This challenging information is not about cosmetic surgery, but about major surgery.

This book is a journey that will examine hearts and attitudes. It will expose and challenge every possible idol in a person's life and marriage. It will answer questions, expose myths, and call individuals to take personal accountability for their lives and actions. It will enable each person to be part of the solution and not the problem.

Bring Down the Sacred Cows is a sequel to my first book Hidden Manna, and has been revised and updated to include additional important insight. It will enable readers to continue their journey to gain greater insight into their nature. This book will take a person even deeper into relationships and attitudes.

I pray this journey will bring every reader beyond the corridors of self into the presence of our precious Lord and Savior, Jesus Christ.

## Part One
# DESTRUCTIVE CYCLES

# 1

# RECOGNIZING THE SACRED COWS

There are many idols in Christianity today. These idols have found their way into the sanctuary of lives, homes, and churches, causing defilement and destruction. Idolatrous practices make people dull of spiritual hearing and discernment. Instead of being sober and vigilant as 1 Peter 5:8 commands them to be, many Christians are complacent towards the issues plaguing their lives, homes, and fellowships. This causes them to serve as doormats to Satan rather than an opposing force against his kingdom.

This spiritual condition has victimized many Christian homes and churches, instead of such victims showing forth the victorious examples of the overcoming life that can be found in Christ. Today the members of the Church are faced with the challenge of trying to put back together the fragments and pieces of broken lives and homes, rather than preaching the Gospel to a dying world. Instead of the Church being a hospital for the lost, hopeless, and blind, it has become a hiding place for disillusioned Christians who resort to game playing rather than confessing and repenting.

It is time to expose and bring down the sacred cows that Christians have erected in their hearts, minds, homes, and churches. These idols are not easily detected because they subtly fit into our lifestyles, needs, and culture. They feed people's flesh and appease their pride. They give individuals a false sense of security and purpose. Ultimately, they bring bondage to people's lives.

Let us now consider some of these idols.

## The "American Dream"

We Americans are in a constant pursuit of the "American Dream." This dream is comprised of a nice house, two cars, and 2.5 children. We equate this dream with happiness, purpose, and success, but it is nothing more than vanity according to Ecclesiastes. I have watched people rob, cheat, and go into great debt to keep up the façade of this illusive dream. In the end, they find themselves in financial bondage and destructive cycles.

This dream has set up many people to pursue materialism, prestige, and power at the expense of righteousness, personal character, and family. It has created the god of self-sufficiency. The core of it is paganism. It is cleverly disguised by "civilized tolerance" towards all lifestyles, along with humanistic religion and education that have no boundaries, no absolutes, and no accountability.

Along with indoctrination, as a culture, we are also being enticed to embrace every evil imagination through entertainment, while being educated into an endless pit of perversion and delusion, lulled into spiritual dullness, and set up to be slaughtered. This is the essence and fruits of the "American Dream."

Years ago, I met a young man who was very disillusioned. He told me how he had worked hard to establish his worldly kingdom. He had grasped the essence of the "American Dream," only to have it ripped away from him through divorce.

The "American Dream" is our culture's idea of the perfect utopia. Man has been in search of this personal utopia ever since Adam and Eve lost it back in the Garden of Eden. This utopia is viewed as a complication-free environment that exists exclusively for man's pleasure. It is in this "so-called" utopia that man establishes his own kingdom, which will revolve around his needs, dreams, and goals.

But like Adam, man continually makes the same deadly mistake. He wants this kingdom without the sovereign rule of God. He wants to be the one who is worshipped and adored. He wants to be independent of God, so that he can control his own world and destiny.

I remember an incident where one woman wanted to be the central figure of her husband's world. She encountered many competitors in her struggle to be adored by him. One such competitor was her husband's son from another marriage. She became jealous of their relationship and tried to discredit his son in devious ways. She played endless games to manipulate her husband to no avail. She was ungrateful, even though she had much to be thankful for. This ingratitude simply came down to her focus that had been exalted. In such cases of idolatry, the need becomes insatiable, and exalts it as being the supreme pursuit in a person's life.

This woman blamed her miserable life on everything but the real problem--her own heart condition. Eventually, she became a bitter woman who defiled her other relationships by being judgmental and skeptical.[1]

Neither men nor women can rule their world without chaos and destruction. It would be the same concept as the sun not being in its rightful place in regards to the earth and its function. The sun, being the center of the earth's existence, maintains a fine balance on earth.

---

[1] Hebrews 12:15

Likewise, without the Son of God reigning in the life of man, life's best eludes him.

Man needs to realize that Adam's utopia hinged on the presence of God in his life. It was fellowship with his Creator that really brought fulfillment to Adam's life, not the physical creation.

Are you in search of utopia? Has your search led you to spiritual, emotional, physical, and financial bankruptcy? Perhaps right now you need to re-establish a right relationship with Christ. He gave up the glories of eternity to ensure that believers would have free access to enter His realm of rule and protection. Just acknowledge, repent of, and confess your need of deliverance from your reign of independence, and invite Jesus to come into your heart as the only Lord of your life.

# Idolatrous Images

In my prayer sessions with Christian couples, I have often referred to a dead marriage as a dead cow. This term was born out of the realization that the Church has done a great disservice to marriage by making it a sacred cow.

This idolatrous position of marriage became evident when I realized that for much of the Church, its main emphasis is to prevent divorce, rather than deal with the heart condition of the people involved. The consistent cry from Church leadership is to keep the marriage relationship together regardless of the devastating consequences. This misdirected emphasis encourages hypocrisy, rather than integrity and accountability. Such an emphasis became obvious when a pastor sent a young Christian man to me for counseling.

The young man had beaten his wife one too many times. She had finally called the police. The law of the state required this man to go to counseling, and the pastor of the Church referred him to me. The main concern of the pastor and this aspiring minister, was to keep this marriage together.

As I sat there meditating on the plight of this young man, the Lord spoke to my heart. He asked me, "Rayola, what is more important to Me, this man's marriage or his soul?" I knew this man's soul was on the line. According to Scripture, the anger he displayed was an open door to Satan and akin to murder.[2] God was making an eternal point to challenge my way of thinking as a means to redirect my emphasis.

I knew that spousal abuse is like alcohol or substance abuse. Before this man could be set free, he had to admit he had a serious problem. The Lord supplied me with the wisdom to minister to him. He did admit he had a problem. The last I heard from him, there had been reconciliation in his marriage and he was attending Bible College to get his credentials for preaching.

We must all acknowledge that God hates divorce, but not because it is being singled out as one of the worst of sins. Rather, divorce is a

---

[2] Matthew 5:21-22; Ephesians 4:26-27

symptom of the reign of man's wicked heart condition.[3] In fact, some denominations treat divorce as if it is the unpardonable sin. Many divorced people find themselves victimized by their local church. They are forced to live in condemnation and isolation from the rest of the church body. The many issues and challenges they face are never addressed, while the church is always ready to accept their financial donations and works.

A comical article titled *"The 1ˢᵗ Church of the Program"* by Robert L. Rees explains the general attitude of the Church towards divorce. The article shows the Church dividing up into various groups for Sunday school. Brother John was teaching the married couples by the Joshua Tree, while Brother Andrew instructed the pre-teens. Brother Bartholomew was overseeing the early teens by a big rock, and Mary Magdalene was entrusted with the singles and teens in a grassy area. The seniors were under Brother Matthew's leadership at the table by the boats. Can you guess who was responsible for those divorced and where their classroom was located? If you managed to guess Judas Iscariot in a lump of trees, you guessed correctly.

Shunning, ignoring, or trying to tip toe around the subject of divorce will not make it go away. It is a harsh reality for many individuals and families. Divorced people are often put aside by different churches. Although they are hurting people, they are rarely ministered to properly.[4]

Spiros Zodhiates explains the real meaning behind the statements made about divorce in Matthew 5:27-32; Mark 10:1-12, and Luke 16:18. According to Zodhiates, Matthew 5 dealt with the pursuit and the sin of lust. It was wrong for a husband who was involved with fornication both mentally and emotionally to put his innocent wife away to feed his own lust. In Mark and Luke, Jesus clearly points out that it is wrong for a husband to dismiss his wife if she is not guilty of adultery. However, He goes on to say that if the man insists on releasing her, he must adhere to Moses' Law and give her a bill of divorcement so she will not be considered an adulteress.[5]

It is important to note that the bill of divorcement is not the same as our present day divorce procedure. Men in the Old Testament had more than one wife and were given the freedom to acquire a divorce, often putting the woman at an unfair disadvantage. Most Scriptures refer to adultery in light of the woman leaving the man, but as you consider all references in regard to this subject, they establish proper conduct on both the parts of men and women. The Apostle Paul's instructions regarding this issue in 1 Corinthians 7 were clearly in agreement with the intent of the Law of Moses. However, in the end, he concluded that they

---

[3] Malachi 2:15-16; Mark 10:4-12

[4] If you would like to understand the issues surrounding the struggles single people encounter due to their status, which might include divorce, see the author's book, *The Manual for the Single Christian Life* in this same volume.

[5] Refer to Deuteronomy 24:1-2

were his judgments. The reason he implied they were of a personal nature was due to the fact that the challenges in marriage vary.

Much of the Church, in its zeal to prevent divorce at any cost, is using "fig leaves" to solve the problems found in couples' relationship. Like Adam and Eve, it may initially cover the shame, but it cannot do away with the consequences of rebellion that has already brought separation and devastation to the relationship. After all, cover-ups never solve problems. Sadly, the institution of marriage has been improperly exalted to cover the problems, making it a *sacred cow*, rather than being challenged to be *sacred before God.*

I have seen many "so-called" Christian marriages that are actually making a mockery out of God's real plan and purpose for this institution. So many couples keep up a religious mask for the sake of the Church and their religious reputations, while their marriages are nothing more than dead cows that are emitting a stench rather than a sweet savor. The marriage, per se, may keep the Church in blissful ignorance, but its stench reaches heaven and breaks the heart of God.

The truth is, marriage is part of the world and the world will pass away. However, the sins that are part of the defilement of this relationship could put a soul in danger of damnation.[6]

Today, many people get married for selfish reasons. They have an image of how marriage will fulfill their needs. They have ideas of how their spouse will treat them. They have standards about how things will be done. They have concepts about how things should go.

Reality hits them like a tornado when they discover the image they married turns out to be an actual person who has his or her own ideas about the relationship. These contrary ideas will cause power struggles between the couple because these "so-called" logical expectations and conflicts are products of selfishness.

Selfishness is pagan in origin. It will defile and abuse what God intended to be sacred. It causes disillusionment and anger because it causes personal expectations to seem so practical and logical. In the minds of these individuals they reason that surely, any "intelligent person" could see the reasoning behind such expectations. Since these expectations are never met, anger takes center stage where it becomes disrespectful and abusive. In the end, the spouse who failed to meet such expectations is considered an "unintelligent" infidel who has clearly failed to see the "obvious logic" behind such expectations!

I remember dealing with a man who was both verbally and physically abusive to his wife. His wife decided to stop the abuse and pursue a divorce. He brought her to see me with the intent of me straightening her out.

As I dealt with their dead cow, I became aware of his arrogance. He demeaned her in every area, including her opinions. Such demeaning is a form of abuse because it makes the spouse or other person a non-person. Since the person is considered a non-person, his or her

---

[6] 1 Corinthians 7:31-34; 1 John 2:17

opinions, beliefs, and rights are non-existent or insignificant to the one who perceives self to be superior.

This woman happened to know her intellectual capacity. She resented her abusive husband's disregard for her ability to think and come to reasonable conclusions without deriding her. I told him that she would not tolerate his constant mocking of her. At one time, he even apologized to her, but eventually he would slide back to his old way of thinking. During one of our sessions, he arrogantly told me his soon to be ex-wife possessed a "small bag," and that in this bag, she had treasures that were in reality worth nothing. These treasures were her opinions.

This man had such a high opinion of his intelligence that he was cruel and critical of anyone who did not line up. The problem with his great perceived intelligence and arrogant attitude was that he was committing idolatry in high places. His intellectual pride may have made him supreme in his own eyes, but the God of the Universe was resisting him. His wife did divorce him. This was not his first marriage, but I pray it will be his last. [7]

These idolatrous images are forever plaguing marriages. They are destructive, and they create a cycle between married couples that will swallow up their relationship in a whirlpool of conflict.

It is time for Christian couples to bring down the sacred cows in their lives and marriages. They must strive to step outside of the destructive cycles, and repent of their personal ungodly attitudes and responses.

The churches must cease to make marriage a sacred cow and call Christians to scriptural accountability and responsibility to make marriage sacred before God. The Body of Christ must take on this challenge. If the Church fails to do so, Christians will come face-to-face with judgment.

From all appearances America is under judgment! The warning signals are blatant. Talk has become a cheap commodity and advice a "sounding brass" and "tinkling cymbal."[7] This is the time for action. The Church must repent of encouraging Christians to cover-up the problems for the sake of appearance, and Christian couples must cease to play the religious game and strive to make their relationship godly. Christian families must get rid of their endless excuses, and turn from their wicked ways to make their homes into holy sanctuaries for the glory of God.

It is now time for every Christian to face the real culprit behind their destructive cycles. Are you ready? Look in the mirror. You will probably meet your main adversary there.

---

[7] James 4:6; Matthew 7:1-6
[7] 1 Corinthians 13:1-3

# 2

# UNDERSTANDING CYCLES

It is not unusual for Christians to give in to hopelessness at different times, as they constantly struggle to live Christian lives. They find themselves temporarily complying outwardly, but inwardly they feel emptiness, guilt, and condemnation because they are simply trying to maintain an outward façade that lacks heart and power.

As well as the torment from within, these struggling individuals often feel no one really cares. To them, it appears that God has turned a deaf ear to their cries. At this critical time, people in the Church can appear to be indifferent or condescending towards these people's struggles, as loneliness and fear begin to swallow them up.

Sound familiar? Obviously, this is not an unusual scenario that can plague Christians at different times. These individuals find themselves trapped in an invisible cycle. This cycle is like a spider web that appears insignificant, but has the strength to ensnare, entangle, and destroy. What is the inspiration behind this destructive cycle? The culprit is known as the disposition of sin or the old man. Romans 6:7, Ephesians 4:17-5:21, and Colossians 3 talk about the old man versus the new man.

The old man and its dictates produce the works of the flesh. Galatians 5:19-21 tells us how sin manifests itself in the flesh,

> Now the works of the flesh are manifest, which are these; Adultery, fornication, uncleanness, lasciviousness, Idolatry, witchcraft, hatred, variance, emulations, wrath, strife, seditions, heresies, Envyings, murders, drunkenness, revellings, and such like: of the which I tell you before, as I have also told you in times past, that they which do such things shall not inherit the kingdom of God.

Be honest. How many of these works of the flesh are apparent in your life and relationships? These acts are nothing more than selfishness, the major sensual idol of all human nature.

According to Romans 6:1-11, the old man was put to death with Christ, allowing a new, resurrected life to come forth. The reason the old man must be put down is because sin is the natural response of this entity. Romans 6:12 states, "Let not sin therefore reign in your mortal body, that ye should obey it in the lusts thereof."

Sin deceives its victims and justifies wrong actions. This deception is exasperated by the sin of pride that persuades man to become independent of God's authority. It serves as a door through which Satan has access into people's lives to oppress them.

Some believe that upon salvation, the separation from the old man occurs automatically. This is true positionally. However, Christians need to understand their position in Christ as sons of God and heirs of salvation.[1] It is because of who we are in Christ, we do have the authority to overcome. However, overcoming is a choice. We must choose to daily put down the dictates of the old man in order for the new man to be worked in us through obedience to the Word of God.

Is self reigning in your life right now? Maybe you have grown to resent this culprit. We are going to examine the invisible cycle that is the product of the old man.

# The Ingredients

There are six ingredients in this cycle that can lead to slavery or oppression if they are not brought under the control of the Holy Spirit. They are *motivation (M), need (N), conclusion (C), desired response (D), judgment or decision (J),* and *reaction (R).* Note the following diagram.

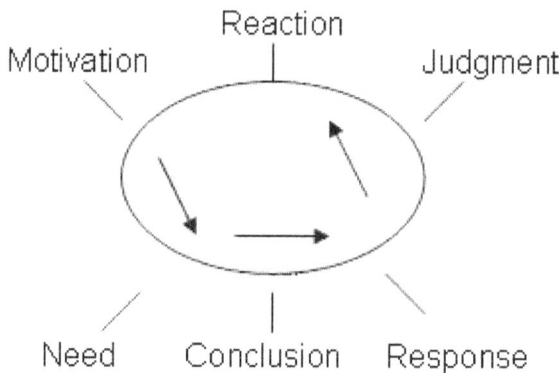

Our cycle always begins with our motivation, resulting in reactions that lead us back to our motivation. Each time we come back to the original point of motivation, our cycle becomes a deeper rut or pit. Bear with me as I explain how each of these ingredients works within the old man.

# Motivation

God looks at the motivation or spirit behind our attitudes and actions.[2] We are motivated either by the love of God or by pride. Pride is self-serving, while the love of God is sacrificial. Any actions not inspired by His sacrificial love, will be counted void or reprobate.

---

[1] John 1:12; Ephesians 1:5-14
[2] Proverbs 16:2

There was a husband who was kind to his wife in order to get his way, but afterwards, he ended up exploding when he did not get the desired results. He lost all the headway he made with his considerate gestures. His explosion exposed his real motivation of pride. He expected something in return for his kind deeds.

Pride is tied to self. It is used to determine a person's worth and value. This value system is based on one of four types of rulers or measuring sticks: *concepts, standards, images,* or *ideas.*

*Concepts* are general notions as to the *way* things should be. These notions are conceived in the mind as an individual puts each adopted idea, detail, or thought in a nice little compartment or box.[3] The contents of these compartments are called upon to make judgment calls about whether something is acceptable, or to bring a complete understanding to a problem or challenge. This individual must make sense of the situation or find out why he or she is in the situation.

*Standards* are criteria established by authority, customs, or general consent. These standards serve as a model of *how* things should be. They can serve as inflexible rulers. Everything and everyone should automatically adhere to them because they are considered to be the known rule or a point of normalcy or requirement by the individual who operates according to them.

*Images* are a vivid or graphic representation or description of the way something *must* be. These images are determined by concepts that inspire standards. Both the concepts and standards produce and reinforce the graphic images that become the final judge as to whether something is either valid or unacceptable.

*Ideas* or *beliefs* serve as immovable lines. They produce a state of mind that determines how something *will* be. Ideas carry much credence. They are considered factual because they are born out of experience. Although everyone has ideas or beliefs, they do not become concrete judgments as they do in the mind of the individual who considers everything in light of these immovable boundaries.

These four types of measuring sticks can be compared to the Law. Like the Law, they may be very scriptural and religious, but they lack the right spirit. They can only make judgments against offenders. Therefore, there is no room for love, grace, or mercy. Fear, broken hearts, wounded spirits, and ruined relationships are the byproducts of these measuring sticks. Although these unseen rulers are natural and "seem so right," few realize their origin is that of pride and selfishness. They allow the old man to judge, as well as reign with a vengeance.[4]

Ask yourself if the old man is alive and well because pride is sitting on the throne as judge. I have learned one thing: God is quick to show a receptive heart its motivation. He is quick to help the person with an open heart recognize his or her pride, and to apply the cross to it. The

---

[3] The definitions of the four rulers were derived from Webster's New Collegiate Dictionary; © 1976 by G. & C. Merriam Co.
[4] 2 Corinthians 3:6; Matthew 7:1-6

Apostle Paul said it best in Galatians 2:20, "I am crucified with Christ: nevertheless I live; yet not I, but Christ liveth in me: and the life which I now live in the flesh I live by the faith of the Son of God, who loved me, and gave himself for me."

# Needs

People have one of three basic needs: *to be loved, to be accepted, and to be recognized or respected*. Having these needs met gives a person a sense of value and belonging. It gives purpose and direction.

Individuals can spend most of their lives trying to fulfill their needs. Conflicting problems develop when people use their measuring sticks of concepts, standards, images, and ideas, to determine whether their need is acceptably met. Because these personal rulers are unrealistic and unyielding, others are not able to meet a person's need on a consistent basis, if at all.

The old man views this inability to meet his need as failure, rejection, incompetence, and lack of respect. The results are frustration, anger, self-pity, and resentment. These mental rulers at this stage become harsh dictators. Unleashed, they quickly escalate to driving and tormenting idols that become insatiable, and will never be satisfied by the actions of mere man.

Perhaps right now you identify with this scenario. You are unhappy because you feel your spouse does not love you. Maybe you feel your mate has never really accepted you the way you are. Moreover, maybe you have never been recognized for your hard work or respected for who you are. Examine yourself and make sure you have not made your need an idol. If you find idolatry, you need to repent and ask God to fill you with His Holy Spirit. Then you will have your need fulfilled.[5]

# Conclusions

People who find their need eluding them must come to some type of conclusion about why they are in such a situation. For instance, if a person is not getting a need met, he or she must try to figure out why and how to satisfy this incredible longing and drive. This is where vain imaginations come into the thought processes of a person. [6]

These idle thoughts fill in the blanks where there is confusion or no answer to a matter. These thoughts always seem "reasonable" and "right." They come into play when there is a lack of communication or unresolved conflict. The results can be devastating.

Time and time again, I have heard spouses falsely accuse their mates of feeling or thinking a certain way. Their unsuspecting mates are quite shocked at these accusations, which totally miss the mark. The

---

[5] Matthew 5:3 & 6
[6] 2 Corinthians 10:3-5

problem with these vain imaginations is that they know no limits to their unfounded accusations or unwarranted presumptions. They ultimately exalt themselves against the real knowledge of God. Since these thoughts operate outside of God, who is truth, they tend to be quite deceptive. Deception in a person's mind finds its origins in the old man who loves the darkness of delusion rather than the light of truth. [7]

Are you operating according to vain imaginations?

# The Desired Response

The next stage of this cycle involves control or manipulation. This control or manipulation begins when an individual's need is not met in the manner that he or she perceives it should be met. Since everyone "supposedly" has a right to happiness, the old man begins to cry foul because the need must be satisfied.

The old man cannot concede defeat, because self-worth is on the line. Somehow, the selfish disposition of sin must get the other person to see it his or her way and respond accordingly. At this point, the struggle begins.

This is where the wills collide in relationships. Emotional games are often played, and conflict arises. Consideration of others is forgotten, and anger often takes center stage. In such an arena, there are no winners, but casualties. Nevertheless, the old man must get the disobedient individual to comply with his or her will. It is a matter of pride.

The battle along with the games end up being a no-win situation no matter what direction they take. If the old man wins over the will of another, the appetite for control becomes insatiable. Disrespect grows towards the "wimp" who is giving in to the whims of this hard, unrealistic taskmaster.

Do you find yourself in such a conflict? If so, the old man is reigning. Obviously, he has not been put down. And, from all appearances, he has no intention of submitting and giving way to the will and righteousness of the Lord of lords.

# Judgments and Reactions

Now that the old man is reigning, he sits in the place of being a judge. He will unmercifully judge the offenses done against him.[8] He will not display any love, and the fruits that will come out in his actions will be contrary to the fruit of the Spirit found in Galatians 5:22-23. He will protect himself at any cost. He must and will survive!

Let me ask you, are you beginning to identify the presence of the old man in your life? Is he reigning without any opposition from you? Open

---

[7] 2 Corinthians 10:4-5; John 3:19-21
[8] James 2:13

up your heart to the Lord right now, and give Him permission to show you how the fallen disposition works in your life.

If you are not sure how the old man works in your life, the next seven chapters will give you valuable insight into how he not only works in your life, but in the lives of others as well. Are you ready to face him and do something about his reign? It is your choice!

# 3

# EXPOSING THE OLD MAN

Understanding and exposing the old man has been an eighteen-year journey for me. This journey started when I asked God a couple of questions. One question went like this, "God, why is it that some people go through extreme situations, while it seems like others hardly go through anything?" Of course, we all know everyone goes through difficulties, but how it affects each individual, differs. The Lord showed me that people go through different processes. Some go through a pearl process. It is the *irritations* that get to them. Some go through a gold process, that of *sifting* or *boiling*. Others go through a diamond process where the *pressure* and *heat* manage to get this type of individual's attention.

I started to see how serious God was about preparing His Body to become the pure Church as described by the Apostle Paul.[1] The preparation does involve a process. At the time of the revelation, I did not realize the process was designed to take all the power away from the old man, so that the character of Jesus, the new man, could be resurrected and worked into the believer's life.

The next question was quite simple, "Is there something that determines why people go through the process they do?" The answer was simple, but profound. It is determined by the way an individual rebels. I never realized that there were different ways in which the old man would respond to God's authority. To be honest, I never thought about my own rebellion. I knew some of my actions and thoughts were sinful, but I had no concept about what constituted my particular rebellious act or opposition to God.

I knew that Jesus had died on the cross for my sins, but I did not understand the deep spiritual unveiling and healing that needed to take place in the inner man. Jesus came as the Great Physician not only to cleanse my sins with His blood, but also to confront my disposition of sin. I had to allow Him to step on the scene and expose its hideous ways. I had to submit to His scalpel, the Word of God, and face my heart and intentions.[2] Was it pleasant? Hardly! It was very painful, but God was faithful.

---

[1] Ephesians 5:25-27
[2] Hebrews 4:12

He used His Word as the mirror to show me how much I actually lined up to the new man.[3] It shocked me to find out how much my selfish disposition was reigning. What was so natural for me turned out to be rebellious to God. My way of dealing with problems made me a "little god." I was trying to solve problems with my own understanding, while subduing the clanging of personal failure and ignoring my many fears. It was all the old man's ways of subtly opposing God's authority in my life.

It is important to point out that at the core of the old man is selfishness. Selfishness is motivated by pride and works within the confines of a delusional attitude. It points to the reign of the self-life. William Law stated that self is nothing else but the creature broken off from God.[2] The delusional attitude can be traced back to the lie embraced in the Garden of Eden by Eve, that man has the capacity to be god of his own world.

Throughout this book, I will make reference to man's pursuit to become God of his world. This is a lie that clearly leads man into delusion. In this delusional state man believes he has the ability to determine what is right and true. As a result, he considers his ways or terms as being clean. In other words, such ways are without deviance; therefore, trustworthy. However, in such a delusion man fails to recognize that his selfishness is toying with, pursuing after, and trying to exalt the person as god in his or her world. It ultimately wants to control reality as a means to get the desired honor, approval, and recognition.

Because of this selfishness, conflict arises in relationships. After all, each person is right in his or her mind. In such a state people will conclude that their perception of right must be upheld, respected, and properly regarded for matters to come out right. However, each person has his or her own take on what is right and proper. Needless to say, this is where conflict arises.

It is hard to face that within our human way of thinking, we desire to be god. This perverted pursuit varies for each person. As we are about to see, there are actually one of four ways in which people perceive or approach a matter in order to resolve it. For example, there are those who create their world in their imagination. In order to bring about their desired world or reality, they cleverly outwardly comply with the present environment in order to work their way of thinking in a situation.

The second group desires to control the whole universe as a means to ensure an environment that will feel right. These individuals will adjust, push, and pull to earn the right to have such an environment on their terms.

The third type of individual wants to be the ultimate authority in his or her world. These individuals try to control people's attitudes and responses according to their perceptions in order to have their world on their terms.

---

[3] James 1:21-25
[2] The Power of the Spirit; © 1971; CLC Ministries International, pg. 30

The final group of people strive to control the activities of their world to bring about the desire results. They do this by trying to control the circumstances. They will comply, adjust, and maneuver their present reality as a means to secure their right to have their world on their terms.

God stated in Isaiah 55:8-9 that man's ways and thoughts are not His ways and thoughts. In fact, man's ways are strange and lead to death or destruction. His thoughts are vain and foolish, while God's ways and thoughts are actually higher or superior to man. God's terms calls man beyond his ideas of right and wrong to that which is excellent. Instead of man insisting on his way, he is challenged to give way to that which is higher to ensure that which would be considered righteous and honorable to God. Yet, man in his delusion fails to see the caliber of God's ways, and ultimately perceives that God will have no other choice but to agree with him in his conclusions.

The journey we are about to take together is the one I have been on for the last two decades. This spiritual journey to discover and subdue the old man led me to an incredible treasure. God helped me discover, in the midst of rebellion and chaos, an order to mankind that proved without a doubt that a Creator exists. This order would uncover what I now refer to as the four distinct natures of mankind.

It is amazing how popular teachings have broken man down into four categories, such as the temperament teaching. One of the things that makes the nature information different from these ideas is it exposes how the selfish disposition works within these four distinct categories.

I have used this information consistently for almost two decades with amazing results. By understanding a person's nature, I can describe what is going on in his or her life. I have actually described the patterns of conflict in relationships accurately to the amazement of the parties involved. I have many times even been accused of having a camera planted in their homes.

Let us now consider these four natures. They are *submissive, stubborn, self-assured,* and *strong-willed*. The names of these natures are not based on a person's character, but on what I refer to as their particular wall of mistrust or rebellion. For example, the *submissive* person will quickly submit to his or her wall. The *stubborn* individual has a stubborn wall. The *self-assured* has two walls to protect his or her identity, while all of the traits of a *strong-willed* person comprise his or her wall. These invisible walls are what each of us uses to protect ourselves, and no doubt, all of us have managed to run into a few during our encounters and conflicts with others.

Let us now consider the old man in light of these different natures and uncover his ways, habits, and cycles. For some of you this will be a review, while for others it will be new insight into humanity. Ask Him to open up your mind to your particular nature so that you can begin to see how the old man operates in and through you.

For a more detailed look at these natures, you can read about them in my book first book, *Hidden Manna* and in the second book, *Revised Hidden Manna*.

# 4

# SUBMISSIVE NATURE

People with a submissive nature often come across as *sweet* and *quiet*. They are considered the most compliant child or one of the nicest individuals. This outward sweetness usually hides a great deal of fear, as well as serves as a means of manipulation. The rebellious wall of a submissive person is *fear*. This wall is quickly erected in situations where the submissive person may not understand or may have to *confront*. In fact, they use different means of manipulation to avoid confrontation, while at the same time striving to get their way.

Due to the sweet exterior and the inward fear, submissive people can send confusing messages to others. Confusion causes problems in their relationships because these people need to be *accepted*, but often feel they are only accepted if they are compliant. This makes them feel as if they must earn acceptance by being good according to the standards of those around them. Such compliance may produce resentment, anger, and rebellion. In fact, these individuals will be compliant in order to build up merits. They actually plan to cash these merits in when they are trying to get their way about a matter. Needless to say, the merit system fails to get the desired results, causing anger and depression for the submissive person.

A submissive person seeks to *understand* the mechanics of something. They have a mind like a computer. It is full of compartments that contain various file cabinets. Within these cabinets are options that can be explored or considered in the right situation. Because of how they process information, they are very *persevering* in their attempts to find the best solution to their problem or challenge.

Submissive people have great confidence in their ability to figure something out. Their attitude is: *"Leave me alone, I will deal with it."* When faced with a challenge, they *withdraw* into their mind and begin to *analyze* possible options. James 4:8 states, "Draw nigh to God, and he will draw nigh to you." This person is actually drawing away from God instead of closer to Him. However, submissive people's great confidence in their ability to reason something out blinds them to the reality that they are in competition or opposition against God.

Submissive people are very *methodical* in their approach to a problem. Their speed of processing information also determines the speed with which they do all of their activities. They will only move as fast as their mind is able to process information. I have seen people of this nature move fast, or have medium or slow speeds. They usually have one consistent pace. In fact, if this person becomes overwhelmed, you will find them parked behind a wall of fear. Each time you try to push them to move or go faster, the wall will be reinforced.

These individuals will seek out the best option, method, program, or diplomatic way to deal with the problem in order to *gain an upper hand*. Sadly, submissive people do not realize that exaltation of their mind is idolatry. Such an unregenerate mind is at enmity with God.[1] It is unable to discern the things of God, which causes a person to walk in the flesh rather than according to the fruit of the Spirit.

The *mind* is where the submissive person's rebellious cycle begins. It leads them down a path of *dramatization* and depression as he or she loses perspective. These people begin to develop ruts in their mind. As different challenges confront them, they stick every bit of information or past conclusions in a compartment to consider or deal with it later. Amazingly, these people can even have a compartment for the things they chose to ignore.

Eventually, all of the compartments become full. When this happens, submissive people cease to be compliant and even-tempered, and become *obnoxious*. Attitudes begin to stick out as they become *unmanageable* in their responses, intense as they hide further behind their wall of fear, and unbearable to live with. By this time, they are out of control and out of perspective. For these individuals, it is like falling off an emotional cliff into a pit; and climbing out of it will take everything in them to come once again into emotional balance. This is why Proverbs 3:5 brings valuable instruction to these people, "Trust in the LORD with all thine heart; and lean not unto thine own understanding."

Emotions are the last reaction that comes out of this person. When this type of person begins to show emotions, you know that the emotional tidal wave is catching up to, and overwhelming them. In fact, their compartments are full of unresolved issues that have been put on the shelf until another day. At this stage of the cycle, they cannot stand the fact their life is out of control, so they have a tendency of withdrawing even deeper into their mind.

The biggest problem with submissive people is that all of this mental exercise often comes down to them avoiding outright *confrontation* or simply facing reality. This avoidance is very self-centered and self-serving making them *self-absorbed*, but it is often considered noble by the person of this nature. These individuals refuse to see that their unwillingness to face problems up front has nothing to do with wisdom, diplomacy, or protecting the other person, but with protecting self from confronting possible conflict or consequences that will make them appear as a failure. This avoidance is a form of control and manipulation that refuses to face the selfishness behind the game that is being played. This *fake nobility* that is displayed often covers up this type of person's greatest initial fear: that of *failure*. These people's unwillingness to

---

[1] Romans 8:5-8

confront problems because of their fear of failure throws them into cycles in their relationships with others including God.

This cycle begins with the submissive person trying to avoid, comply with, or please someone to keep the peace. Such attempts require these people to play the game to avoid confrontation. The natural tendency of people in relationships who are not properly confronted for wrong attitudes or actions is to take advantage of those who appear to be playing their game. Sadly, this game usually unleashes the monster of pride and selfishness in such people rather than subduing it. They become more demanding, abusive, and disrespectful. The submissive person struggles with how to properly deal with the person or issue as the matter escalates, while maintaining his or her sweetness and nobility. As these submissive people struggle, they devise well-planned statements that are meant to stop the other person in his or her tracks; thereby, avoiding confrontation.

Submissive people are good at using *words* as a means of control and manipulating a situation or a person. In some cases, it works, while in other situations, it simply prolongs a matter. In the end, submissive people are left with a lot of *unresolved issues* that will develop into a tidal wave that will eventually threaten to destroy them.

Unresolved issues will eventually bury these individuals. This is where the submissive person will give up and spiral down into depression. These individuals can retreat behind barricades of eating disorders, alcoholism, drug abuse, and imaginary or exaggerated physical problems. These excessive behaviors have three possible sources behind them: 1) they serve as forms of control; 2) they are used as a means of getting attention; and 3) they serve as a form of self-destruction.

Extreme behaviors that are not properly challenged can cause the submissive person to toy with the option of *suicide*. When a submissive person is at this point, he or she is in major depression. It is a sign that the person is out of perspective and needs to be properly confronted. Sadly, this person rarely shares what he or she is thinking about. Suicide; therefore, is often this person's dangerous little secret.

# Pride in Action

A submissive person's form of pride is hard to detect. In fact, his or her pride would be considered a covert pride. Because these people's pride is not obvious, they actually view themselves as superior to others.

Submissive people's arrogance can be observed in relationships. I knew of a submissive woman who displayed steady calmness in most situations. Her husband, who was more expressive about his feelings, would especially vent in traffic. She viewed his actions as unacceptable and felt superior to him. This woman was blinded to her form of pride, a sin that God resists. In fact, it is the covert sins that will sink a person more than outward disobedience.

The pride that motivates a submissive person is *conceit*. Although conceit has a certain air about it and causes *irritations* in others, it is hard to detect in this type of individual because it takes place in the mind; therefore, it is not expressed in obtrusive self-exaltation. In fact, this individual is often considered to have little, if any self-esteem, and will nobly throw the attention elsewhere to avoid being noticed. The reason is that the submissive person wants to be left alone in his or her world. If submissive people do emerge from their self-made world, they will want you to know how smart, humble, sweet, wise, or good they are. Conceit ultimately translates into intellectual pride. It takes pride in what it knows and can do.

These people perceive themselves to be *wise* in all their ways. They will try to reason with others about their way of doing things. If they encounter someone who will not agree or tolerate their reasoning or condescending air, they will nobly give way to the other person and become a suffering martyr. This fake nobility still leaves this individual on top of the game because it appears to be more honorable than the one who refuses to receive wise instruction.

Even though submissive people outwardly give way to someone else's perception, they never give in mentally. They usually maintain their way of thinking, and will go back to the drawing board to devise a cleverer argument for the next encounter. If the issue is not resolved according to their way of thinking, they will end up overanalyzing, causing them to appear unreasonable, foolish, or obsessive. In fact, people who are trying to deal with a submissive person at this state would refer to them as being *pigheaded*.

Conceit's greatest disguise is *false humility*. False humility is nothing more than worldly remorse.[2] Worldly remorse will take some accountability for failure, but it is for the purpose of making these people feel they have properly conceded on a matter, causing them to appear wise and noble in their own eyes. Since they have come to terms with it in their mind, the matter has been resolved; therefore, others need to get off their back and leave them alone.

The reason most submissive people fall short of true repentance is because they mentally deceive themselves. They think that by them simply working a matter out in their mind that it has made it reality or a done deal. However, these people, in their deluded pride, fail to realize that they have not changed their mind due to godly repentance; rather, they have simply added another conclusion to one of their compartments. Since they have not changed their mind, their hearts maintain the same inclinations, and they are still on the same path or course. They have simply complied outwardly as a means to blend into the present terrain until another opportunity avails itself for them to wisely present their case in regard to the situation.

Changed lives are the fruit of true repentance. When those around submissive people do not see the change, they will not give them the

---

[2] 2 Corinthians 7:10

desired acknowledgment. After all, submissive people work hard to bring everything together in their mind. To not accept or recognize such a feat is considered unfair to these individuals. This is when fake nobility turns into self-pity. These people begin to feel sorry for themselves because they have done everything to play the game to get the desired results. In the end, these people cannot understand why others will not recognize their attempts. Once again, these individuals come out on top in their mind as they become a victim.

Like all pride, unchallenged conceit will eventually lead its devoted followers into delusion. This delusion creates a sick little world of depression, obsession, and utter ridiculousness. Ultimately, the submissive person becomes a fool in his or her own conceits.

# Overcoming

Submissive people must come to terms with their traits in order to overcome. They must be surrounded by God's perspective much like the grain of sand is surrounded when being formed as a *pearl*. One of the traits they must honestly *confront* is their sweetness. This trait is not part of the fruit of the Spirit. Rather, it is part of the selfish disposition. This sweetness gives a false sense of goodness to these people. They hide behind it to avoid confrontation. Their unwillingness to confront falls into the sins of omission, where these individuals fail to do right in a matter. This unwillingness is also a subtle form of unbelief because it shows that people who avoid confronting life, do so out of fear and complacency. They must realize that it often serves as a cloak to cover up their true depravity.[3] Such fleshly sweetness is not an expression of Jesus, but a means to receive undeserved acceptance and recognition. Therefore, this trait must give way to the sanctifying work of the Holy Spirit

Certain traits must be disciplined. For the submissive person, he or she must discipline his or her analytical mind. Over analyzing causes this person to *dramatize*. In order to keep their minds balanced, submissive people must withdraw into God, instead of into their minds. Such action allows their earthly wisdom to give way to the true wisdom of heaven.[4] Godly wisdom means one will have God's perspective. And, it is His perspective that ensures balance in a submissive person's life.

There are other traits that must be *mortified* or put to death. The submissive traits that fall into this category are fear and conceit. Fear demands worship from its subject. As long as submissive people give in to it, they will be hindered from reaching their potential in Christ. When submissive people encounter fear, they must step back from the wall of fear, decide to step through it, ask Jesus to take their hand, and leave it behind as they take steps of faith.

Submissive people must realize that their conceit is perverted and made up of earthly wisdom. Once they agree with God's evaluation

---

[3] Galatians 5:22-23; James 4:17; John 15:22
[4] James 3:13-17

about it, they must ask Him to reveal how it works in their life, as well as to give them a hatred for it. Pride can only be overcome by a repulsive hatred towards it. Submissive people must realize that conceit does not make them wise, but sets them up to play the fool.

There are traits that must be *channeled.* Submissive people must learn to withdraw into God. This means they will be putting their confidence in Him, rather than in their minds. This allows the Holy Spirit to properly channel all information, in order to bring forth God's perspective. Once the mind is transformed, the submissive person will gain an understanding about God's way. It is this understanding that establishes the submissive person on the immovable Rock of Ages and brings peace to his or her mind.[5]

# Confrontation

How do you properly confront a submissive person? You must first recognize when he or she is in his or her cycle. There are two indicators that this type of person is in a destructive cycle. The initial sign is bad attitudes. Submissive people do not have strong attitudes per se. Therefore, any sign of an attitude means that they are overwhelmed and their compartments are becoming full.

The second indicator is unbalanced or extreme behavioral patterns. For example, if a submissive person is overly emotional or obnoxious on a consistent basis, there is something amiss in his or her world. Obviously, there are unresolved issues that are filling up his or her compartments.

If the submissive person is very withdrawn, this is a big warning signal. You must not allow him or her to remain in his or her world unchallenged. The submissive person who is very withdrawn is probably in a pit of depression. Depression of this nature can include suicidal thoughts and plans. These people will be tight-lipped about such plans unless asked. However, if you show *acceptance* and firmly challenge them with the facts, they will automatically withdraw and consider what you have presented.

You actually use a person's nature against him or her in confrontation. You do this by using the person's need and way of processing information to get his or her attention. Once you have people's attention, you can effectively speak into their lives. For example, you show a submissive person acceptance to keep his or her wall down. By understanding that all information is analyzed, you must be ready to firmly give submissive people the facts. These facts will challenge the submissive person's perspective. These people might try to deter you from challenging them by being obnoxious or running you around with reason. Do not be sidetracked by either detour. Once the submissive person gains perspective, he or she is most likely to admit when he or she has been out of line.

---

[5] Isaiah 26:3

When giving this nature the facts, avoid being harsh or placating. If you are harsh with this type of individual, you will encounter his or her wall of fear. If you try placating the submissive person, he or she will perceive it as a game and will lose respect for you.

**Note the submissive person's cycle.** It begins with his or her desire to properly understand a situation. This is these people's means to gain an upper hand in a matter. If understanding eludes them, it will ultimately lead to complacency.

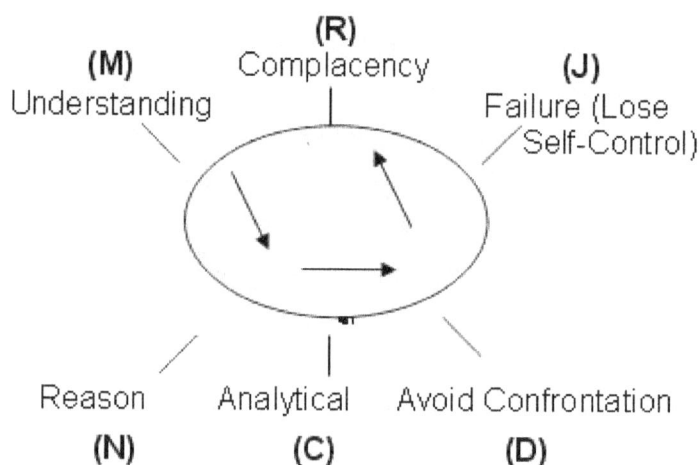

|  | **(R)**<br>Complacency |  |
| --- | --- | --- |
| **(M)**<br>Understanding |  | **(J)**<br>Failure (Lose<br>Self-Control) |
| Reason<br>**(N)** | Analytical<br>**(C)** | Avoid Confrontation<br>**(D)** |

# 5

# STUBBORN NATURE

Stubborn people's biggest struggle is with their *emotions*. Unlike the submissive nature whose emotions come out at the last part of the person's cycle, emotions are the first thing you encounter with the stubborn nature. In fact, these people wear their emotions on their sleeve.

The emotional level of a stubborn person makes them *personable*. This is often a cloak that hides insecurities and doubts while keeping people at a distance. It is also a means for some stubborn people to *con* others. This is a form of control and manipulation that will eventually be exposed for the game it is, causing them to lose credibility.

The emotions of stubborn people run deep, and will cause confusion and conflict in their worlds. These emotions have almost a tormenting force behind them that often cause these people to seek after relief, pleasure, and satisfaction through various avenues. They can become *impulsive* about filling up their world with things or activities that make them feel good, or will suffice their need to bring meaning and purpose to their often-chaotic world. These means are always temporary which sends them on searches at unusual or sporadic times. Needless to say, trying to bring undisciplined emotions under control can prove to be very overwhelming to these people. As a result, they often live in fantasy while unsuccessfully trying to manipulate and adjust their world to their fantasies. If stubborn people run out of fantasies or the means to satisfy their emotions due to harsh reality that remains constant, they will close down their emotions. This will create a zombie who will be expressionless due to utter hopelessness.

Stubborn people need to feel *love*. This love is an emotional love where a person actually enters into the emotional world with them. For the other three natures who do not understand the emotional plight of these people, it can be both frustrating and traumatic. They do not know how to calm the emotional beast that often rises up within stubborn people. This beast can become explosive and abrasive.

This type of nature also feels the need to earn emotional love. There are four reasons for this outlook: 1) Stubborn people feel vulnerable in the area of love because of being gullible; 2) they strive to be indispensable to others to avoid experiencing rejection; 3) they have high standards that demand compliance; and 4) they need proof of love; therefore, they conclude they must earn love. The gullibility of a stubborn person comes down to his or her need to be transparent with others.

This is to ensure that people will simply love him or her for who he or she is.

Stubborn people try to become indispensable to those they love and care about because of their own insecurities and fears. Their greatest fear is *rejection*. They do everything to avoid this fear, only to find rejection haunting them as they are misunderstood, and often taken for granted.

People of this nature have very high *standards*. These standards not only put unrealistic pressure on them as well as others, but they actually box them in. These standards are meant to bring discipline to the stubborn person's emotions and environments, but instead, these people can become hard and unmerciful. These high standards make them very judgmental and skeptical about anything that does not initially line up with their standards or emotions.

The stubborn person requires proof of love. Sadly, this proof may be insatiable and unrealistic. These people can put up a fuss or fight, and expect those who care about them to fight for them, not with them. Even though they want others to fight for them, they either put up resistance to such attempts or they emotionally run people around. Those who are dealing with this type of nature find themselves fighting with this individual, throwing up their hands in utter hopelessness or walking away in frustration.

The emotional stubborn person feels deeply about personal beliefs. These people can be *persistent* in their pursuits. This happens when they get caught up with causes that will rob them of valuable time, take them on detours, or lead to obsessions. It is not unusual for these people to get caught up with the causes of the underdog because they have a deep sense of loyalty and hate unfairness. In the process, such causes can turn into obsessions that often throw common sense and reality out the door. These obsessions imply total indifference and delusion about reality.

These people can display common sense. Their *practical* approach to life, decisions, and situations can cause those of other natures frustration and anger. In most cases, a balanced and realistic stubborn person does see the end results of situations, but due to his or her emotional level, others rarely take this person seriously. Problems, therefore, are not averted and these individuals are proven to once again be correct. This can cause resentment and jealousy with those who did not understand or respect the practical, simple side of these people.

This individual strives hard to maintain or control his or her environment as a means to keep on top of his or her emotions. This need to control the environment as a way to keep emotions intact is often considered controlling and manipulative by others. This will cause more *friction* for the stubborn person who has failed to realize he or she must bring personal emotions under control before his or her world can have order.

Stubborn people are consistent in their emotional patterns. The emotional cycle usually starts when *plans* are *interrupted*. These people try hard to organize their day so they can complete the many demands or responsibilities of their world. For example, a stubborn person may have 20 different activities on his or her list. These people actually can make plans in their mind right down to the last minute as to what they are going to do. Then, when someone adds one more demand; the *pressure* begins to build because this individual no longer feels emotionally on top of it. This becomes obvious as he or she begins to *complain* about all of his or her responsibilities. This is followed by *strong attitudes*.

If the emotional momentum is not properly dealt with, *explosive anger* follows. This anger breeds insult, offense, hurt, and anger in others. The results leave the stubborn person experiencing doubts, insecurities, and *guilt*. Satan starts to support this case of guilt, opening the door of *condemnation*. Condemnation will send this person into hopelessness or *depression*.

Stubborn people feel the depths of depression. They often fear it, and will do everything to avoid this unbearable pit. They actually run from it through activities, relationships, and substance abuse.

These people are often *misunderstood*, causing personal hurts and wounds. Stubborn people perceive themselves as *handling* any situation, and given enough time, they will *prove* it to others. Eventually, reality will collide with their world in the form of interrupted plans or rejection. They stand in confusion as they consider everything they did to get the necessary *approval* from those around them. After all, they have been giving, complimentary, and have even gone out of their way to become indispensable. When they do not receive the necessary acknowledgement or reaction from others, they can feel rejected, used, and abused. This will produce hurt that turns into anger and *complaints*. These complaints can cause others around stubborn people to scramble in an attempt to change their world to keep the monster at bay. To handle these emotions, a stubborn person will stuff them. Now, he or she has unresolved issues that will create frustration, moodiness, and attitudes.

Once the stubborn person has stuffed an unresolved issue, he or she becomes a time bomb as the emotional momentum begins to build up like a volcano. It is only a matter of time before something will cause him or her to explode, leaving others in a state of confusion and chaos.

This is when stubborn people come to the harsh reality that they cannot handle it. They begin to *justify* their reactions at the expense of their environment. For example, if it was not for so or so, or this or that, they would have never exploded. Quickly, they release themselves from personal responsibilities while trying to handle the guilt they feel under the barrage of excuses. These excuses allow them to erect a *stubborn* wall of protection. This wall declares that no one will pass beyond it. It implies the stubborn person is right and will not sway from his or her stand. At this point stubborn people are viewed as being *bullheaded*. Not only do they refuse to be moved, but if challenged, they will also charge and push back all opposition. But, in spite of the justification and wall, the guilt remains intact.

Stubborn people desire to be stopped at the point of justification in order to silence their guilt. Although they can act unreasonably when confronted, the stubborn person does not know how to stop him or herself after a certain emotional point or silence the onslaught of personal excuses. In my experience with these individuals, I have found that their excuses are a means of trying to convince themselves that they are not guilty. If they do not come to truth about their personal involvement in a situation, they can become deluded. This means they create ruts in their minds where excuses become a truth rather than a point of self-justification. When stubborn people are in this type of rut, their bullheadedness becomes apparent as the truth is pushed aside, and they become deluded, defensive, unreasonable, angry, and in some cases bullies.

Due to their *undisciplined emotions*, these people desire proper discipline, but will rebel against any forms of control and manipulation. Although these people can come across as pushy, they will not tolerate being pushed or controlled. Sadly, those who are around them try to control or manipulate them because they are afraid of how they might react in different environments or situations. To stubborn people, such attempts are like putting a red flag in front of a charging bull. Needless to say, they will oblige.

## When Pride Hits the Scene

Pride is the last trait that enters the scene in the stubborn person's cycle, but when it does, it leaves quite a mark or impression. *Selfishness* is the stubborn person's form of pride. It works off of the ego and vanity of the stubborn person.

Stubborn people take pride in what appears to be selfless giving, when in reality, there is usually a selfish motive behind it. The main motive behind this flurry of giving is often to receive the desired love or approval. They *want* people to exalt them in order to feel needed, understood, and important. *Selfishness* rears its ugly head in this nature after attempts of love and approval are not properly returned. This makes the stubborn natured person feel used and unappreciated. This is when selfishness becomes offended.

Offence produces frustration that is verbally expressed by *words* that are followed by strong *attitudes*. These words are complaints or excuses that will escalate the momentum of selfishness. Selfishness begins to blatantly *emphasize* self. This emphasis becomes an appetite that cannot be satisfied. Inability to quiet selfishness and to keep it from exploding causes frustration in those who are trying to contend with it.

Eventually, selfishness will build such a case in its mind that it begins to see the lack of response as treacherous and a form of betrayal. Stubborn people take everything personally, due to the fact that they are at the center of their world; therefore, they perceive that everything is directed at them. They conclude that such betrayal is personal rejection. This will create the disguise of selfishness: that of the martyr syndrome.

As a martyr, the stubborn person becomes a suffering victim with an attitude. This bleeding, wounded victim may display self-pity or sarcasm. The end of this cycle is *depression*.

# Overcoming

Those who are stubborn by nature must go through a *gold* process. This is where God allows friction in their world to sift or separate them from their unending excuses. This friction causes confusion and brings these people to a point of total frustration. God wants stubborn people to realize they cannot handle life on their terms. All of their means of trying to prove their worth is disappointing and depressing. They must realize that they are only justified at the point of the blood of Jesus. This justification can only occur through repentance and faith.[1]

Stubborn people must learn to discipline their emotions and not their environment. This means they must first come under the control of the Holy Spirit. The Holy Spirit creates an attitude of meekness. This meekness produces self-control or temperance.[2]

Self-control is very important for a stubborn person because he or she judges reality according to feelings rather than the Word of God. Once the emotions are lined up with the Word of God, the stubborn person will have stability in his or her reality and world. If the emotions come under control, then this person's impulsive drive, persistence, and loyalties will be channeled in the right way.

It is also important for stubborn people to not take everything personally. They need to keep in mind that the world does not revolve around them. Much of what is happening around them is the evidence of human nature in operation, and not a personal affront against them. They must learn to discern between such matters by getting past touchy feelings and dealing in reality.

Another trait that must be disciplined is the *stubborn* wall. Stubborn people must be careful about where they erect their wall. They need to be stubborn towards and for the things of God, but never in relationship to personal pride or what they consider to be personal standards of righteousness.

Selfishness must be mortified through neglect. It is hard for stubborn people to identify their pride because they are so giving. The test does not lie with outward actions, but inward motives.[3] Their motives constitute selfishness; therefore, stubborn people need to rightfully discern their motives to avoid self-delusion.

Stubborn people must mortify their standards. They are not realistic, and they not only put them into a box, but God as well. God's ways are

---

[1] Luke 13:5; Romans 4:5; 5:18
[2] Galatians 5:22-23
[3] Proverbs 16:2

not the ways erected by the stubborn person's standards. These standards may be high and rigid, but God does not ordain them. Such standards become burdens too great to bear and comprise a yoke too heavy to carry. Stubborn people need to exchange their standards with Jesus' yoke and burden.[4]

Stubborn people must give up their need to be loved by others and allow the love of God to fill up that insatiable vacuum. The desire to find approval from others is a grave snare.[5] Because of this desire, many stubborn people accept ungodly relationships in order to get this need met. It is a dangerous trap.

These people must properly learn to discern between conviction and condemnation to properly confront their guilt. The Holy Spirit convicts in order to bring a person to forgiveness and restoration, while Satan condemns. In condemnation, there is no hope for forgiveness and restoration, just hopelessness and judgment.

# Confrontation

Stubborn people operate according to a consistent cycle. It is easy to observe them and discover this cycle. The key to effectively entering in with stubborn people is one's ability to recognize this cycle and enter in at the right time.

Due to the emotional roller coaster of a stubborn person, it may appear difficult to determine when these people are actually in their cycle or whether they are venting emotions in order to keep things in perspective. If they are venting emotions because the frustration has built up in them, allow them to vent. Avoid getting in their face because you will be causing greater frustration.

To discern if a stubborn person is in his or her cycle, test his or her spirit. There is a decisive attitude behind these people's emotional momentum. In emotional venting, it is outbursts that are allowing the person to work his or her way through the emotional maze, but in the actual cycle this emotional momentum expresses itself in complaining. Complaining is different from the form of explaining or reasoning which takes place in venting. Complaining is the means for this person to work up his or her right to excel in his or her emotional momentum in order to justify undisciplined and questionable actions.

If the stubborn person is working his or her way up the emotional ladder, you must effectively confront him or her at the point of *frustration*. The stubborn person will emotionally run over you past this point. The key is to get him or her to recognize what truly ails him or her. This may be interrupted plans or hurt feelings that have been stuffed. Due to a stubborn person's ability to stuff points of frustrations and hurts, he or she may emotionally run you around, but you need to continue to bring him or her back to reality. Eventually, the source of his or her agitation

---

[4] Isaiah 55:8-9; Matthew 11:28-30
[5] Proverbs 29:25; 1John 4:16-19

will be revealed. Once a stubborn person can get the source out in the open, it can be resolved, stopping the cycle and allowing the stubborn person to emotionally land.

Keep in mind that to enter in with stubborn people means you are emotionally entering in with their emotional struggles. If your motive is to calm this person so you can have peace in your space, the stubborn person will see through it and throw up his or her wall of mistrust. If you are condescending towards these people because of their emotions, or trying to manipulate them to get a desired affect, it will backfire on you. Godly confrontation is always about the other person and not for self-serving reasons. A right attitude in confrontation will ensure that the person's dignity will remain intact.

**Consider the stubborn person's cycle.** It begins with the desire to have a matter proven to him or her in order to ensure he or she emotionally stays on top of a matter. However, this pursuit can end in cynicism and harshness.

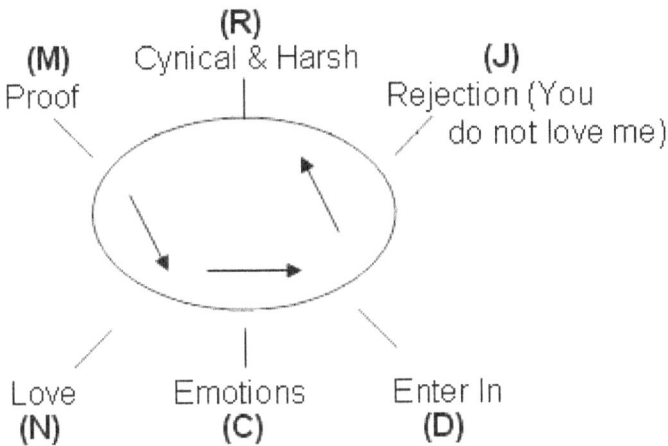

# 6

# SELF-ASSURED NATURE

Self-assured people take pride in the idea that others cannot figure them out. They are *reserved* and will only let people in so far. They are also *unpredictable.* They can change in midstream when it comes to decisions, attitudes, and direction. This often causes confusion, chaos, and frustration for others.

Amazingly, self-assured people are easy to understand. The key to unlocking the mystery and confusion surrounding them comes down to something called *images.* Self-assured people have an image for every responsibility or role in their lives. For example, they will have an image for being a son or daughter, a sibling, friend, spouse, and parent. Each responsibility or demand requires a distinct separate image. These different images are very detailed and demand *perfection.* The reason for this perfection is that these people fear *incompetence.*

These people can only maintain one image at a time. Tremendous frustration and anger arise when their different images begin to collide. You can actually witness the self-assured people mentally scrambling to adjust their image according to the people that surround them. This conflict with images forces them to prioritize their images. The image that takes a back seat is usually that of the spouse.

Needless to say, the changing of image sends a mixed or confusing message to those who are contending with these people. Not only do they see the self-assured person change emphasis and attitude, but his or her course. This *unpredictability* causes confusion, insecurities, and conflict in the relationships of self-assured people.

In observing self-assured people, they use the confusion they create in their world to maintain control over others. They use insecurities to lord over those in vulnerable positions, and use conflict to control their space. In the end, it does not matter what kind of problems or conflicts they cause in their relationships, they will come out on top or *justified* in their own sight.

This brings us to the self-assured person's motivation: pride. These people can display the very epitome of *pride.* High standards comprise their images. They can be very judgmental. They not only personally operate according to images, but they have images for other people such as their parents, spouses, and children. In the mind of a self-assured person, these images dictate how others along with the environment should look and function. When these people encounter any inconsistency, they will become highly judgmental and critical. In most cases, if one thing is out of order, they will zero in on the discrepancy while ignoring that which is right.

Their reactions to such discrepancies are that of *cruelty*. They become very cutting or demeaning in their remarks. After all, the situation is obvious; therefore, there will be no excuse, and judgment will be demanded.

Self-assured people have a *lawyer's mind*. Each discrepancy is added to their list of offenses. This list can be written on various sources such as physical paper, calendars, or simply erected in their minds. These people will use these lists when in a confrontation. When the confrontation is over with, the other person will stand utterly guilty, while the self-assured person has been clearly justified in the courts of their minds.

These people have a *reservoir of anger*. When that reservoir is filled up, they will feel justified in taking actions against the culprit. If integrity and compassion is absent from these people's character, it is at this time that violence, cruelty, and mocking in various proportions will be justified. It is not unusual for these people to shred the guilty culprit into hundreds of condescending pieces with their list of evidence. Even though they leave their victims devastated, they feel vindicated. This justification makes them indifferent to the fruits of their personal actions, while changing their image makes them guiltless of all past wrongs.

Changing image simply means the person will change present reality. The image these people change into is either the "*good guy*" image or the one of a *victim* of others' incompetence or injustice. Both the justification and image keep the self-assured person from ever being called to personal *accountability*. After all, his or her actions are justified, and due to the present image, he or she is not accountable for actions that occurred under another image.

Unless self-assured people have integrity at the point of their images, they can be adept liars, especially to themselves. They will delude themselves by believing that their present image truly represents their character and reality.

As you can see, images are everything to the self-assured person. However, these images are a means of hiding something. What are these images concealing? In fact, when you go to confront self-assured people, they will erect two walls to protect that hidden part of self from being discovered.

The *first* wall is an *emotional wall*. When images begin to fail the situation, mass confusion hits the self-assured person. This confusion implies that this person's world is out of control. This will cause frustration that can express itself in an outburst of wailing or tears of *self-pity*. At the end of this wall is fear of incompetence, which immediately turns into anger. This anger is expressed in the second wall: that of *pride*. The wall of pride proves to be a harsh *unyielding* wall. This is where you discover that this person refuses to be wrong at any point, regardless of how much evidence can be provided as to his or her guilt.

The refusal to be wrong causes this individual to come across as being *mule-headed*. The difference between being bullheaded and mule-headed is that those who are bullheaded push their way through situations. Those who are mule-headed will cause such a fuss that the whole environment around them will be thrown into conflict and chaos, while they appear to remain calm and guiltless as to their personal involvement. Such chaos changes the focus from them, and puts it elsewhere.

It takes everything within a self-assured person to admit he or she is wrong. These people often operate in generalities when it comes to personal discrepancies. This unwillingness to be found or proven wrong causes them to be *indecisive* in making decisions. In fact, they often manipulate others around them to make desired decisions for them. For example, they will present you with self-serving options. As they discuss the options with you, they cleverly push you towards the most preferred choice with their *logic* and strong *attitudes*. In the end, you usually make the decision they desired. The logic behind this game is that if anything goes wrong, guess who will get the blame?

What are these people hiding behind their images? There are two traits they are hiding. The first trait is their incredible pride. This pride expresses itself throughout the self-assured person's many traits. Pride is the essence of self. In the case of this person, it is expressed through being *self-centered*. Therefore, whenever you encounter the pride of any nature, you have come to the end of that person. Unless this pride has been replaced with integrity, there is no character or substance behind it. It is at this point that you discover how deep or shallow a person is. This reality is clearly brought out in the self-assured person who has not developed integrity. Past their images, these individuals can prove to be shallow vacuums that have no substance. They have nothing of importance or significance to offer.

The second trait self-assured people are hiding is their *fierceness*. They are fierce people. This can be expressed and seen through their *anger*. This fierceness is the force behind hiding and protecting both their pride and images. It is the relentless source behind justification. It causes intimidation through strong *attitudes*. These people will always be fierce, but instead of hiding it, they need to switch the fierceness behind their images with integrity, compassion, and sensitivity. Self-assured Christians who do not hide behind images often display their fierceness up front, while being sensitive to others and ready to show compassion at all times.

These people control and manipulate by using their *attitudes*. They can communicate volumes without saying a word. When accused of something that has not been made obvious through word or deed, they can deny it, laugh it off, become angry at the perceived injustice, or mocking. Because of the strength behind these attitudes, people do adjust to them to avoid encountering the self-assured person's fierceness, intimidation, and possible repercussions.

If a self-assured person does make a decision without proper perspective, anger or vengeance often inspires it. These people can be very *persevering* in situations where they plan to make a statement, get their way, or an upper hand in a matter. They often leave a path of destruction without considering the devastation or consequences they have caused.

Once a self-assured person pays the consequences for personal actions, he or she will immediately take on the victim image, and display *self-pity*. Self-pity is the manifestation of fake nobility and worldly repentance. This can be seen in the lives of Esau and Judas Iscariot. Worldly repentance will always express itself in tears, while blaming others or circumstances for personal actions. Such self-pity falls short of true repentance.[1]

# Confrontation

Self-assured people can be quite miserable in their existence. Needless to say, this misery finds company with those who have to live or contend with them. In fact, the more miserable they are, the stronger their attitudes will become and the more difficult they are to contend with. The struggle can become so great within these people that they can appear close to being insane, especially if they are constantly trying to adjust or change images.

Images can cause a lot of confusion and chaos for them as well as the people around them. These people naturally believe that those around them should adjust and bow down to, and worship their images. When their image does not get the desired response, these people will take offence on behalf of their image. Therefore, how can you get past the image to minister to the person?

Depending on whether you are trying to minister to them or confront them will determine the strategy you use. If you are ministering to them, you have to *recognize* their images in order to keep their walls down.

These people desire *recognition* for what they are trying to accomplish through their image. By recognizing the image that is the most important or prevalent at that time, you can discern what they are trying to accomplish in the situation or relationship. This will keep the walls down so you can address their rigid, unrealistic standards, and reason with their emotional side. The goal is to get them past their images to clearly see the fruits of their lives. These people must see the contrast between where they are and what they are striving for. This helps them to realize that their standards are unrealistic and unobtainable. Such contrast is important for them to see that their unrealistic standards cause fear, frustration, and anger.

When in confrontation with a self-assured person, never argue with him or her. These people have a *lawyer's mind,* and they perceive themselves to be *logical*. You will never win an argument with them

---

[1] Matthew 27:3-9; 2 Corinthians 7:10; Hebrew 12:15-17

because they cleverly have built a case against you that will leave you feeling like the guilty party or even a bit insane for having any personal opinions or stands.

Self-assured people use their strong attitudes to draw people into their legalistic trap. The key is to not venture their way regardless of how pouty or moody they become. Leave them alone in their small, self-centered worlds and go about your business. Like the groundhog, they have to raise their heads out of their self-pity and come to you. This means they are coming to you on your terms. When they do, hold the line. In other words, make them responsible for their personal attitudes and actions no matter how much they try to throw the blame on you or others. Emphasize the fact that they are responsible for their own disposition and actions, and one day, they will stand before God and give an account of their attitudes and deeds.

This allows you to put up the contrast and declare that you will not take responsibility for the way they are. Confrontations with self-assured people call for firmness, authority, and brutal honesty. You cannot let them off the hook for one second, and you cannot move from off the line of what is true and right until they realize that you are not budging. It is as though you must gain their respect each time you confront them to be able to effectively speak into their lives.

# Overcoming the Image

Pride is the main trait that the self-assured person must overcome. Since pride is the very essence of who they are, it can require an intense process. This is why their process is related to that of *gold* where it must be *boiled* to separate it from the impurities that are mixed with it. This boiling process is not only intense, but it can be quite drawn out.

Pride dies from neglect.[2] This simply means it must be replaced with integrity, and then ignored when it raises its head to demand obedience. Integrity helps a person discern between reality and the façade that such coverings as images create.

It is important that self-assured people fill up the vacant area behind pride with character that is produced by integrity. As they allow character to be worked in them by the Holy Spirit, their fierceness will be disciplined and channeled. Once channeled, this fierceness can be directed towards the work of God. This will bring forth a powerful leadership in the kingdom of God.

Self-assured people must get rid of their lists. These people not only keep lists against others who have offended them, but against themselves for imperfections in their lives. These lists are the opposite of love and faith. Love proves a person is of God, while faith is the only thing that truly pleases God.[2]

---

[2] Matthew 16:22-26
[2] 1 Corinthians 13:4-8; Hebrews 11:6; 1 John 4:15-21

These people need to ask God to show them each of the lists they have developed against others as well as against themselves. These lists serve as seeds that will breed anger, bitterness, and unforgiveness. These sins will end up breaking a pure heart, and making a person into a judgmental, self-serving skeptic.

The self-assured person needs to discover his or her real potential in Christ. This will bring his or her fierceness and standards under the control of the Holy Spirit. Such a discipline will enable him or her to reach his or her potential in the kingdom of God.

**Note the self-assured cycle.** It begins with the motivation to get you to honor his or her image to remain on top of a situation. In the end these people's cycle ends in anger and unpleasant actions.

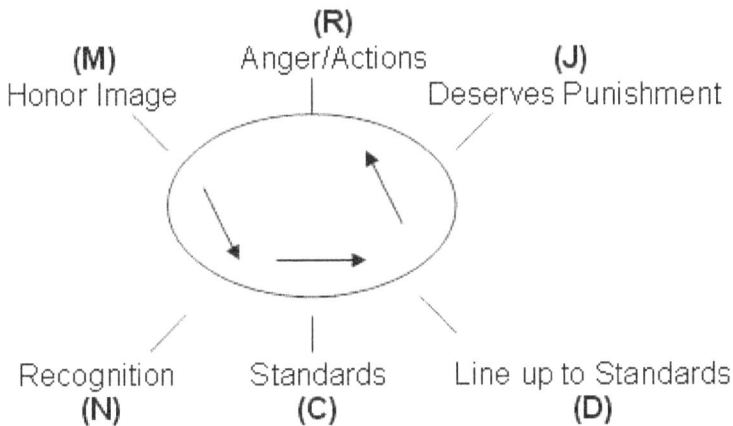

**(R)**
Anger/Actions

**(M)**
Honor Image

**(J)**
Deserves Punishment

Recognition
**(N)**

Standards
**(C)**

Line up to Standards
**(D)**

# 7

# STRONG-WILLED NATURE

The biggest struggle for the strong-willed person is to let go of control of his or her atmosphere or world. In fact, *losing control* is this person's greatest fear. It creates intensity and fear that can completely drive him or her into destructive behavior patterns.

These people operate in *extremes*. Even though strong-willed people give you an impression that all is calm, behind the scenes they can be emotionally compared to bouncing balls. This extreme mode of operation can be seen in their personality and atmospheres as well. For example, they can be very outward or very quiet. They can have an extremely orderly atmosphere or they can live with mountains of clutter. Either way, they are usually cognizant of what is affecting their world.

Strong-willed people are *decisive*. They make decisions that become concrete lines. These lines serve as boundaries in which these people can confidently operate. These boundaries form *ideas* that seem factual. Since this nature perceives themselves as possessing *facts*, they cannot fathom the possibility of being wrong. Everything to them is black or white, and any shades of gray are either ignored or discarded. When these lines or ideas are challenged, they will *make themselves right* in their own eyes regardless of the validity of the challenges.

These people maintain control by lining everything up in their world. They are people of *action*. Although much of what they do can be proved to be nothing more than a bluff, they have a very intense atmosphere around them that causes others to line up or carry out their ideas. In fact, people around them are generally intimidated by the strength that seems to permeate their sphere.

Strong-willed people's ability to get things done makes them appear to be *dynamic*. This dynamic appearance gives the impression that they are fearless. A great deal of this has to do with their sense of infallibility. Due to their factual perception, they believe that there is no way they could be wrong about the decisions they have made. Since they are right, success awaits them. This success is usually just a matter of getting others to see it their way. Their ability to intimidate and bluff their way through situations serves as a powerful means to get others to line up to their way of doing or thinking. In fact, some of these people can bulldoze others over with their intensity, their sense of who they think they are, and their dynamic abilities to take on the impossible.

This brings us to the strong-willed person's need. This individual needs to be recognized for who he or she is. This *recognition* is a form of respect. Without this respect, strong-willed people will display mistrust towards others or lack confidence in their relationship with others. Mistrust will cause the strong-willed person to put up his or her wall.

The wall of mistrust is comprised of all of the traits of the strong-willed person. This wall is immovable, and can make them appear *hardheaded* when trying to reason with them. It also gives this individual a sense of *infallibility*. And, when the wall is erected, it is to maintain control of his or her world. This form of protection hides the tremendous fear that often drives this person to be impulsive or rash. The catalyst that holds this wall together is the strong-willed person's form of pride.

# Immovable Will

Each nature has to beware of their different strengths becoming immovable. When such strengths become immovable, I refer to them as being ironclad. In essence, they make people stiff-necked or unbendable towards any challenge. For submissive people, they can develop an ironclad mind or compartment in their mind that will make them unreachable. For stubborn people, their sense of right and wrong can make their stubborn wall as strong as iron towards a matter, making them unreasonable. Self-assured people's pride becomes the point of reinforcement that can make their form of justification irrefutable, making them emotionally untouchable. For strong-willed people, they can have an ironclad will that will make them insensitive. These people's will is tied up in their need to control and their form of pride. It serves as an immovable barrier that they cannot personally get around no matter what is happening in their world. Amazingly, strong-willed people can be motivated by any of the three forms of pride such as conceit, selfishness, or pride itself. These different forms of pride are what bring distinction among those who are strong-willed. It is obvious what form of pride drives each strong-willed person.

Although strong-willed people appear to be strong, they can prove to be very *fragile*. This becomes apparent when they encounter confusion. Confusion means that reality is colliding with their world. Confusion is unacceptable and will not be tolerated. It is at this point that you can begin to see how the will works in the strong-willed person.

When reality fails to fit within the ideas of strong-will people, they basically will it away by ignoring it as if it was a lie or discarding it as silly, heretical, or deceptive. This ability may maintain personal reality for a season until challenged again, but it causes hardship on those around them. It is the people around them who must pick up the pieces or deal with the consequences of these people's unwillingness to confront challenging reality.

When reality catches up to the strong-willed person, it can cause tremendous self-pity. These people *avoid emotions* because they feel emotions confuse the issue. They often act as if they are afraid or will not tolerate such nonsense. However, when these people lose control, they can be very emotional. In fact, they can be extreme in their emotional responses.

I have been shocked at these people's ability to adjust reality. In a way, they become clueless. This is a form of denial or fantasy. These people have an uncanny ability to actually turn off their minds to anything that will not fit within their concrete lines. It is not unusual for this person to ask the same question numerous times. When this happens, it simply means that he or she had not heard the desired answer. It is as if he or she is waiting for reality to adjust to his or her perception or conclusion to a matter.

Sadly, these people can lose a lot of credibility. People, who do not understand how the strong-willed nature processes reality, will question their intelligence, hearing, and mental functioning. Strong-willed people usually miss viable details that would change their present facts or situation. And, if they don't have integrity, they will bluff their way through situations they do not understand because of their concrete lines and need to control.

# Overcoming

Strong-willed people will be taken through a *diamond* process. The diamond starts out as a piece of coal. It appears as if it has worth, but coal is a piece of material that is ready to be consumed in the fires. On the other hand, the diamond represents a precious gem that will be established in extreme heat. This means the strong-willed person will go through extreme heat and pressure to cease being a piece of coal ready for judgment, and become a diamond, being prepared to reach its potential.

These people often find themselves in extreme situations because they are not sensitive to what is happening in their reality. Because of their immovable lines, they have very limited vision, which leaves them open to fall into Satan's various snares.

The real battle for the strong-willed person begins with his or her will. These people must exchange their ironclad will for the will of the Father. This is very difficult since pride and control is mixed up in it. The will of this person must be submitted before the *lines* can be properly adjusted or disciplined. As long as the will is intact, the lines remain immovable. Once the lines can be adjusted, they can be lined up to God's will and purpose.[1]

These people must mortify their *obsession to control or rule*. This strong desire exalts them as God of their life. This is idolatry that will cause rebellion and set them up for a fall. In order to put to death this obsession, they must give way to the control of the Holy Spirit. This means walking according to the Spirit and not their personal boundaries. The leading of the Holy Ghost will take away the hardness of their lines,

---

[1] Luke 22:42; John 4:34

and will bring tremendous liberty to them as they walk by faith in the Son of God.[2]

Strong-willed people must keep in mind that they are not infallible. They must not take themselves so seriously. This reality will keep them humble enough that others may be able to warn or instruct them. I encourage strong-willed people to surround themselves with godly counselors or advisers whom they respect and trust. [3]

These people must learn to challenge their focus. Their ideas keep them extremely limited from perceiving reality around them. They must discipline their attention to embrace reality. This will help them to properly respond to, and interact with those around them.

In many cases, these people will surround themselves with those who will see it their way, ridding themselves of possible challenge or instruction. Strong-willed people can view any challenge as disrespectful instead of a necessity to maintain checks and balances in their lives and decisions. Beware of such strong-willed people because they harbor fragile egos due to fear, and are untrustworthy because there is no integrity or character.

Strong-willed people need to keep in mind that becoming a diamond is just part of the process. They must not only be completely changed from their lesser state to reach their potential, but they must be cut and polished. This process symbolizes their need to maintain a complete dependency on God to ensure that the remaining extreme traits of their nature will be properly disciplined and channeled for His glory.

# Confronting the Diamond

Strong-willed people demand respect and shun emotions. If respect is missing, they will discard you as an insignificant nuisance. They want the facts, and in their book, emotions confuse the issue. In fact, avoid anything to do with feelings. Even the statement: *"I feel this way about something,"* can be a big turn off to the person of this nature.

The main thing we must determine is what constitutes respect to these people. First of all, fear or intimidation is not considered respect, but a weakness. A person must not only show respect to the strong-willed person, but also have his or her respect. The way you gain respect from this nature is to drop all emotions and signs of weakness.

If you have their respect, *look them in the eyes.* These people like eye contract. In their initial meeting with you, they will size you up on the basis of whether you make eye contract with them. This is hard for other natures that may feel intimidated by them, but is vital if you are going to have any authority to speak into their lives.

Once you have their attention, firmly and decisively give them the facts. Avoid any type of explanations or rhetoric. You will immediately lose them. Keep it to the point and then back off. These people will

---

[2] 2 Corinthians 3:17; Galatians 5:16-18
[3] Proverbs 11:14

make up their mind. Do not take it personally if they fail to respond to your warnings or advice. If these people love God, it will be up to Him to confirm and adjust their lines.

**Notice these people's cycle.** These people start out to gain control, and will do everything to secure and maintain it.

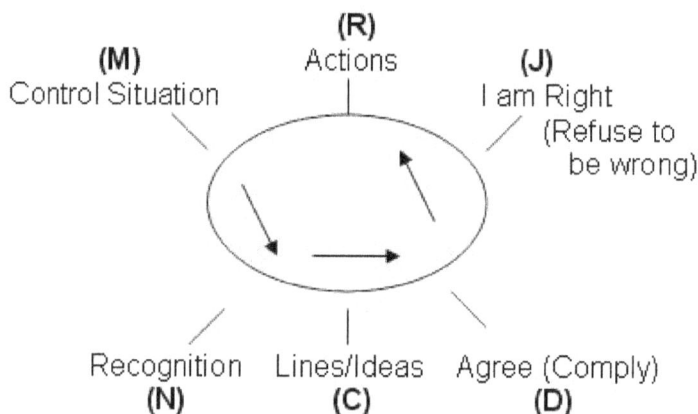

|  | **(R)** |  |
|  | Actions |  |
| **(M)** |  | **(J)** |
| Control Situation |  | I am Right |
|  |  | (Refuse to |
|  |  | be wrong) |

Recognition   Lines/Ideas   Agree (Comply)
**(N)**      **(C)**      **(D)**

# In Review

Let us now compare the differences between these four natures. You will be able to see how distinct they are from each other. The differences are simple, yet they are far reaching when it comes to how each nature responds in crises and in their relationship to God and others. Consider the following table on the next page:

| TRAITS | SUBMISSIVE | STUBBORN | SELF-ASSURED | STRONG-WILLED |
|--------|-----------|----------|--------------|---------------|
| PROCESS | Pearl | Gold/Sifting | Gold/Boiling | Diamond |
| REBELLION | Withdraw | Justify (Front Door) | Justify (Back Door) | Make it Right |
| RESPONSES | Analytical | Impulsive | Unpredictable | Decisive |
| CHARACTER | Sweet | Personable | Reserved | Extreme |
| CONTROL | Words | Words/Attitudes | Attitudes/Actions | Actions |
| APPROACH | Persevere | Persistent | Persistent | Dynamic |
| PERCEPTION | Wise | Practical | Logical | Factual |
| PRIDE | Conceit | Selfishness | Pride | Any of the Three Forms Of Pride |
| WALL | Fear | Stubborn | Emotional Pride | Infallibility |
| NEED | Acceptance | Emotional Love | Recognition for their accomplishments | Recognition for who they are |

# 8

# ESTABLISHING BOUNDARIES

Clearly, marriage has much against it. Most couples start out on a wrong footing. It is not uncommon for men and women to put on masks or play games with each other while dating in order to bring forth a particular reality about the relationship. In the back of the couple's minds, they think they will be able to handle anything that comes their way in their relationship. They perceive that they are an exception to the rule. The exception to the rule is that they have the necessary means to change what they do not like or appreciate about their partner to make him or her into the person they need him or her to be. This is not only immature, but it is an unrealistic fantasy that ends with the old man becoming mean-spirited, resentful, and vengeful.

This brings us to the issue of focus. Most of us understand the significance of focus. We naturally walk or lean in the direction of what we are focusing on. Such focus points to the reality we are trying to manipulate or obtain. Personal reality is tied into affections (how something makes us feel), emphasis (what we value), and attractions (what catches our attention). It will influence our perception, attitudes, and approaches towards any other reality that might intrude or challenge our present or desired focus.

When it comes to marriage relationships that are in crisis, the greatest point couples must discipline in order to change the terrain or environment of their marriage is their focus. The Bible is clear that Jesus needs to be the focus and reality for each of us. In light of setting our affections on Him, the world will fade away. By making Him the great pearl that we must possess, our values will come into line with His heart toward a matter. By setting Him before us, He will have our attention, allowing us to follow Him as His life is developed in us.

The problem with fallen man is that he also resides in a fallen state that keeps him from properly connecting to and addressing the reality around him. In his attempts to reach the goal of his focus, he will come under the influence of his natural or wrong spirit that will put him in a state of mind or prevailing mood. From this false premise it appears as if the person is trying to adjust or control his or her reality according to the state of mind he or she is in.

Changing a relationship or the cycle of the old man involves disciplining the focus. Each nature must address their focus differently in order to make the right investment in others. Due to the *submissive nature's* emphasis on thinking, this individual can end up in a mental rut that will render them into a *self-adsorbed state*. In this state, submissive people can prove to be clueless, indifferent, or hard towards any reality that might intrude into their small, self-absorbed worlds. When reality does intrude, these people become obnoxious because for them they must change gears to adjust. Changing gears when they are at the height of their intensity is like going from drive into total reverse. It can be quite overwhelming to them. To get past this state, submissive people must become flexible enough to change their perspective or premise. This will require them to step outside of their compartment to actually connect with the reality around them.

Once submissive people connect to reality, they must become responsible to do what is right. Being responsible requires them to take heart in what they are doing. These people operate from the mind and rarely connect with their heart. The reason they must put their heart into a matter is to avoid succumbing to fake nobility towards a situation that not only proves inconvenient to them, but results in resentment or becoming a victim in the matter. It is at this point they feel they are personally sacrificing much to keep everything proper for others. Putting their heart into a situation will actually change their attitude towards the matter.

Changing the attitude allows submissive people to change what needs to be recognized as being important. For these people activities that allow them to stay in their self-absorbed state become their emphasis, when what they must learn to value and invest in are the people around them. Such an investment begins with gaining the perspective of the Lord Jesus Christ.

Submissive people must change their focus, but *stubborn people* must determine what their focus must be in order to understand what is really happening in their reality. These people can get caught up with various activities that will rob them of their time and energy, causing tremendous frustration as their world spins out of control. Due to their emotional momentum towards something, these people can become very *selfish* about their reality. After all, to change focus for these people when they are at the height of their momentum is like trying to close a dam that has just been opened to allow all the water out of the reservoir. A *selfish state* can cause these people to focus on petty or insignificant matters to try to control the state of their environment.

By determining their focus, stubborn people will be able to channel their strengths, passions, and zeal effectively by wisely choosing their battles, causes, and responsibilities. Disciplining their momentum by determining their focus will enable stubborn people to emotionally land, allowing them to come to terms with what is really happening in their reality.

Submissive people must get past self, but stubborn people must guard or get a sense of where self is so they can properly focus on that which is important in the scheme of things. It is hard for stubborn people to realize what is really important to the well-being of those around them because of the many demands on their lives. They often find themselves spent out, used up, and often disregarded. At these different points of emotional burn-out, these individuals feel they have left a sense of self or a bit of their life behind, causing insecurity and confusion. Once these people get the right focus and emphasis, their attitude will change and they will realize that what is important is the quality of their relationships and not the things that they can do or offer to those in their world.

Self-assured people operate from a state of *self-centeredness*. Everything in their reality must come into compliance with or center around their images. Because these people often begin with their images, they must initially gain the proper perspective as a means to connect to reality. In order to connect to reality up front, these individuals must discern whether they are operating according to their unrealistic images or harsh standards. Until they deny themselves of the essence of their reality based on images or standards, they are not able to even see what is going on around them.

For the self-assured people to change focus, they must come to a complete stop in their momentum of trying to create the environment that properly honors their images and lines up to their standards. Once self-assured people stop and back away from their images and standards, they can connect to reality, and make the proper commitment to see a matter through. It is only after these people make an honorable commitment to do right in regard to a situation that their attitude towards it will change. At this point their relationships with others will be able to change, allowing them to embrace that which is valuable in the light of that which is realistic, meaningful, and lasting.

Strong-willed people consider matters from a *self-serving state* where everything in their environment must line up to their focus. Because of their intense momentum to bring everything into line with their goal, they strive hard to line everything up to their reality as a means of understanding or controlling what is happening around them.

Each nature strives to understand something in order to somehow control, influence, adjust, or change reality. When their reality is suddenly challenged, submissive people become obnoxious, stubborn become frustrated, self-assured become angry, and the strong-willed can become very hard and harsh.

Submissive people must change their focus, stubborn individuals must determine what it is going to be, and self-assured people must discern it, while strong-willed people's focus must be enlarged. To enlarge their focus, these people's lines must become flexible in order to change their attitude about a matter. Coming to a place where they allow their lines to become flexible can be compared to putting everything into building a road and then discovering that it is not wide enough. Therefore, these people have to go back to the very point they started from, to widen the road to make it feasible for others in the scheme of things. As their attitude is changed by a different perspective towards something, their emphasis or values will be realigned to reconsider what was considered to be insignificant or unimportant, thereby, changing their relationship to it. Realignment of perspective will allow such people to become truthful about the reality around them. As the emphasis changes, the environment will adjust to that which is right before God and right to others.

It is not easy to change the focus. The momentum must be changed, and it cannot be changed unless the goal is redefined based on what must be a person's emphasis to do right by those in their world. This requires a state of humility.

Consider the following table to see how focus works in each nature.

| Nature's Perspective | Submissive | Stubborn | Self-Assured | Strong-Willed |
|---|---|---|---|---|
| Focus | Change it (Reverse) | Determine it (Close the dam) | Discern it (Stop and back away) | Enlarge it Go back to point A. |
| Attitude | Connect to heart | Channel momentum | Change Perspective | Lines must become flexible |
| State | Self-absorbed (Obnoxious) | Selfish (Frustrated) | Self-centered (Angry) | Self-serving (Hard) |
| Reality | Connect *with* it | Understand it | Connect *to* it | Be realistic about it |
| Emphasis | People | Relationships | Commitment to do right | Type of consideration towards others |
| Investment | Change what is viewed as being important | Realize what is important | Embrace what is valuable | Change lines towards what used to seem too insignificant to consider. |

The old man reigns through selfish focuses as it strives to manipulate, adjust, change, and control the reality around it. Couples need to apply integrity towards one another as a means of ensuring reality from the start of their relationship. They need to establish constructive boundaries, not only on an individual level as to their personal focus, attitude, and conduct towards their future mates, but also between each other. To imply acceptance, encourage with silence, or placate to unacceptable or disrespectable behavior, is a form of defrauding the other person. After all, if one does not agree with a particular behavior, but lacks genuine intention to confront it, as well as a willingness to play along with it to get desired results, it is the same as defrauding someone. The Word of God clearly denounces such practices.[1] Couples must be honest on a personal level, as well as with each other. This means instituting behavior patterns in their relationship up front. In other words, do not ignore improper behavior during the courtship time, but honestly confront it as to how it will affect attitudes and trust.

Often, couples ignore irritating or wrong behavior patterns, thinking things will change after marriage. The reality is that behavior patterns often express established attitudes. Therefore, behavior patterns do not change until attitudes change. In most cases, people see no need to change their attitudes towards a matter. The truth is every type of behavior will manifest itself in the marriage relationship. If behavior patterns are not honestly faced up front, they will clearly be reinforced along with the attitude in the marriage relationship. Problems that find their origins in attitudes will often manifest themselves in three of the most commonly troubled areas in marriage: intimacy, children, and finances.

The lack of intimacy comes from the inability to communicate. Communication is vital if a person is going to be able to honestly function and interact in his or her environment. It is necessary to ensure trust and agreement. Sadly, the major emphasis of intimacy is based on the physical arena, rather than the spiritual and emotional aspect of it that is expressed through respect or honor towards each other. Granted, the physical part is a gift of God to marriage, but without the spiritual or emotional part, such an act becomes self-serving, creating frustration, anger, and resentment in the marriage.

The inability to properly interact in the environment of intimacy will often be expressed in lust that will desire to be fed or stimulated in the relationship as vain imaginations are stirred up. Such desires become self-serving as the lust seeks to satisfy itself in the relationship on a physical level, often discarding the other person's emotional and spiritual need.

It also rides on passion in the emotional arena. Such passion is seeking fulfillment as it stirs up expectations of romance and experience. However, it is based on fantasy that will either prove to be disappointing, illusive, or temporary. Such a state will cause frustration and anger. In some of the following chapters in this section, I will be dealing with the issue of emotional and spiritual intimacy in a more explicit way, but it is an issue that must be confronted before people enter into marriage. This type of intimacy will determine the quality of marriage. True intimacy will learn the other person's need, discern his or her spiritual state, and encourage well-being in the relationship.

---

[1] 1 Thessalonians 4:3-7

Due to mistrust, disillusionment, and selfishness, intimacy becomes one of the first casualties in marriage. Walls begin to be established between the couple that isolates them from one another. From this point, speculation, uncertainty, and loneliness begin to grow. If not confronted, the marriage can be consumed by the hopelessness of it all. After all, the couple has become lost in a quagmire of misunderstanding. In most cases the breeding ground for this condition resulted from the masks, the practices, and the games that were fine-tuned and maintained during dating. In the light of marriage, the masks are stripped away, the practices exposed for their selfishness, and the games become harsh and insulting. At this point, spouses feel betrayed or defrauded by their marriage partner. They thought they were marrying this wonderful person, only to find that their prince has turned into a frog, and their princess has turned into a witch.

Children are another point of great contention with married couples. Children often reveal people's level of personal discipline. Wherever parents are lacking in discipline, it will manifest in how they discipline or react to their children. In many couples, there is the spouse who perceives that if he or she shows tremendous love and patience to the children, they will see how wonderful he or she is as a parent and turn out okay. However, children often relate love to fair discipline. Discipline brings important boundaries that clearly establish the parent's authority and much needed order in the home. Without boundaries such children become angry and uncontrollable instead of being well-balanced

The other spectrum of parenting is the parent that believes in discipline, but is often undermined by the other parent who is lenient. If children see this disagreement as to their parents' mode of discipline, they will play one parent against the other. In most cases the lenient parent will display superiority over the parent who agrees with God's evaluation that there must be proper discipline to train a child in the way he or she should go.[1]

Granted, harsh, demeaning discipline is abuse, but real discipline is meant to train a child in acceptable behavior. I will be speaking more on this subject in the children's section of this book. It goes without saying that children should not be abused. However, abuse comes in different ways including neglect. Neglect is not just a matter of neglecting physical needs, but failing to take responsibility to meet a child's spiritual and emotional needs. Spiritual needs are met and reinforced through spiritual examples. Emotional needs involve affection as well as discipline to be balanced and productive.

The final area of conflict between couples is finances. Financial bondage puts major stress on couples. However, how many couples are trying to live the American dream on credit cards? The concept that couples need the best of everything right away has not brought needed discipline or responsibility to young people. They are going into debt without learning how to responsibly earn the right to own such things.

---

[1] Proverbs 22:6

This makes them indifferent to the domino affect that is created by financial irresponsibility. They have no sense of sacrifice, character, and wisdom. The result is that many couples are living in a financial house of cards that will cave in on them at any moment.

In some situations, one of the partners may be responsible with finances, while the other spouse irresponsible. With other couples, one spouse may be a "Scrooge" with money, leaving the other partner feeling like a slave, destitute, and angry. In some cases the "Scrooge" always makes sure that he or she has what he or she wants, while demeaning the mate for his or her financial views or practices. Occasionally, these greedy, self-serving individuals may throw "bones" at their mates to avoid feeling guilty for personal greed and covetousness, but eventually, resentment and conflict will surface.

Obviously, these issues must be honestly addressed and brought to the forefront. The adjustment in marriage in regards to two people coming together into the same space and learning to live in harmony are challenging enough, let alone issues concerning intimacy, raising children, and financial practices.

The Bible deals with all three issues, but many Christians are either ignorant of God's instructions in these matters or they ignore them all together. The challenge is that Christian couples agree with each other at the point of godly instructions and practices. Anything outside of this agreement will point to a relationship that is out of order.

Let us now consider in what way the four different natures need to establish proper boundaries for themselves.

## Submissive Nature

Submissive people refuse to confront. They comply outwardly, while scheming inwardly to figure out a way to gain the upper hand in a situation. They hide behind their so-called "sweetness" to maintain control of their world. The main aspect of this control has nothing to do with their environment, but with how they perceive themselves. They must always gain the upper hand in how they deal with a situation. Their attitude is: after all, look at how sweet I am being in this situation, and notice how terrible the other person is acting. It is nothing more than fake humility, but it is a façade they can personally buy to maintain their high opinion of themselves.

In a certain situation a submissive wife was having problems with her husband. She put up with his ridicule and temper tantrums. She silently watched on the sidelines as her husband lavished himself with "toys" for his pleasure, while shaming her for buying birthday presents for friends.

This wife had even given up material needs in order to merit the right to buy such gifts without the ridicule of her husband, only to discover it did not matter to him. In fact, due to his self-centeredness, he never once recognized her sacrifice. As he became more selfish with his wants and more critical of her, she became irritated. Even though she tried to ignore these irritations, they wore her down. She struggled to figure out a way to reason with him, while avoiding all out confrontation.

Although quite noble in appearance, this continual unwillingness to honestly confront and be forthcoming in what she thought about her husband's selfish behavior towards her, caused her to feel her world was out-of-control. After all, she did not feel sweet or kind towards her husband. She saw him as a selfish little boy who was indifferent to her needs. Since she could not avoid facing her true feelings, she had to admit to herself that she was not at all sweet. It was all a façade that allowed her to be exalted in her own way of thinking.

This inward struggle signified to her that she was a failure. Such a judgment of herself caused her to go into depression. The depression led to complacency as she began to increasingly withdraw into a mental cycle of fear, dramatization, and fantasy.

Eventually, the sweet conviction of the Holy Spirit penetrated through the dark corridors of this woman's soul, illuminating her own selfish act of self-absorption. She discovered her desire to avoid confronting her husband was her means of controlling the reaction of her husband. Such protection was not about doing right by her husband or being right before God, but rather, it was as means to avoid any appearance of failure, thereby, preserving her fragile conceit.

As she began to face the harsh reality of her "sweetness," she realized that her selfish disposition cleverly hid behind the sweet façade in order to reign in arrogance. She had accepted her "lot in life" to become a suffering victim in her plight.

She finally realized that she needed to confront the problem and establish boundaries with her husband. In other words, she would no longer quietly receive his disrespectful comments. Even though he ran her around, she needed to draw lines in regard to her spiritual life and responsibility. This meant she had to get past self and let him know that such disrespect was unacceptable.

The same scenario is not uncommon to submissive men. Husbands placate their wives in order to keep them off their back, or earn what they consider the necessary merits, as a means to do what they consider is important down the line. Many times, placating others just feeds the monster of self in the mate. Although placating may earn some merits, it never earns respect. And, respect is necessary to ensure trust.

Once, when contending with a submissive husband, I challenged him concerning his response towards his wife. He admitted he had hid from her most of their married life. He had two rooms in which he hid. One was a mental room where he was the director of his reality. He would create a reality of dreams and fantasies that all bowed down to him.

The second room was a physical room. In this room he hid in his personal projects. Occasionally he would exit from this room, only to be met with thick silence. There was no communication between this couple. They lived as two complete strangers in the same house, and if there was confrontation, the man's anger surfaced, reinforcing the walls that stood between them.

As I contended with this man, he maintained his right to be angry. His greatest anger was directed at God. After all, he and his wife considered themselves to be Christians. His reasoning was how could God allow this to happen? Clearly, his fruit revealed that his platform was selfishness in the first place. He married an image, only to discover she was actually human.

Submissive people must not only establish boundaries to ensure respect from others, but to determine what they will receive or accept. To establish such boundaries requires these people to look upward to gain God's perspective about such matters.

Submissive people naturally look within to come to terms with reality. Needless to say, stopping with personal conclusions will always fail to interact with reality. Therefore, these individuals must gain a heavenly perspective that comes from above to establish the boundaries that will ensure their spiritual well-being.

# Stubborn Nature

Stubborn people try to discipline their environment to ensure boundaries. In their minds, stable environments will assure them of the security they so desire in their world. However, the environment is not what is out of control in the stubborn person's world, it is their emotions.

Emotions cause stubborn people to try to swing from one emotion to the next. However, when they are insecure, emotions become unbearable tormentors that have no boundaries. In fact, these people will exit into vain imaginations to figure out why they feel the way they do about situations. This will cause them to fill in the blanks of what is missing. These people will see their vivid speculations and vain conclusions as constituting reality.

There was a stubborn wife who was trying to figure out what her husband was thinking. She began to operate in speculation. As she considered all of the different angles from his expressions to his unresponsive actions, she concluded that her speculations had to be true. In confrontation she expounded on her speculations, accusing him of thinking a certain way. He was shocked because she was not even close to what was going on. However, her speculations caused her to falsely accuse him, as well as develop mistrust towards him.

Stubborn people are forever trying to read situations. This is their way of preparing themselves emotionally to come out on top. Often their imagination gets away from them and they overreact. Part of the problem rests with the fact that they are trying to become indispensable to those around them. They perceive that others will not only see their need for them, but be willing to put up with their ever-changing moods.

These people ultimately become their own worst enemy as they sabotage their environment. For example, a stubborn wife overreacted to a statement her husband made. She felt that his statement proved that he had failed to recognize all that she had done in the office where they both worked. Regardless of the presence of others in the waiting room, this woman broke into tears after she had verbally expressed her feelings over his insensitivity to her and her work. His "so-called" insensitivity translated as ingratitude and rejection. She left those who witnessed her outburst feeling uneasy and her husband embarrassed.

Stubborn men have similar problems; however, the main emotion they express is anger. These men are frustrated because culture has stipulated that men are not emotional. These individuals are very emotional, but have not had the freedom to express them. As a result, they become moody, angry, rude, and sarcastic. Although they are good at coning, they are not good at hiding their true feelings.

There was a stubborn man that had many unresolved issues in his life. He had sabotaged his life by not taking responsibility for his state. To avoid responsibility and rejection, he would get his point across by being sarcastic to others. When confronted, he would state that he was simply teasing. Obviously, it was his way of being rude without being called to accountability. Sadly, he died a lonely man because no one could take his rudeness.

Some stubborn men have a terrible time functioning when their work environment does not feed their emotional level. It is not unusual for these men to easily become discontent in their jobs, and pursue other jobs that might feed their emotional state. Sadly, these men can become lazy and unproductive in their life if they fail to challenge their dissatisfaction and channel their energy in a right way.

Since stubborn people are very emotional and selfish, they operate from a fleshly perspective. Due to the lust that can operate within their emotions, these people have a hard time coming to reality. They must "land" to face reality. This means reality will come from below their emotional swings at the basis of God's Word. It is only God's Word that will ground them and bring much needed discipline to their emotions. God's Word will enable these people to establish the proper boundaries. Instead of allowing their emotions to dictate their reality, they will, with the Word of God, establish boundaries to how they perceive and must react to reality around them. It is from this perspective that they will be able to properly discern their thought process and the people in their world.

# Self-Assured Nature

The self-assured person's perspective is very worldly. In other words, it is based on how the world around them sees and reacts to their different images. These different images, along with other's responses will cause confusion for them.

A young self-assured woman admitted she experienced this confusion when her responsibilities grew. For example, she only had a few images that she contended with until she became a student teacher. She could handle being a daughter and even a student. But, now she had to contend with being a teacher, as well as with those in authority over her. Her inability to keep up with all of her images not only caused confusion but anger.

Another challenge for self-assured people comes in the form of communication. These people are forever adjusting their realities by changing their images. In one image they may logic out a matter. The problem is that since it is a "done deal" in their mind, they fail to share their conclusion with those around them. I had a self-assured man admit that he thought he communicated such conclusions to his wife, but in reality, he had not. This assumption on his part caused much conflict between him and his wife as they argued over whether he had truly communicated with her.

Self-assured people have a real struggle with identifying what is real and what is part of their image. A husband confessed to me that when his wife wanted him to do a project, he would consider it and do it in his mind. Once he figured it out in his mind, he perceived that it was done. Needless to say, in reality it remained undone, causing immense frustration for his wife.

Another challenge self-assured people have is finishing a job. Since they operate from images, they emotionally relate all things according to their image. For example, they may be enthusiastic to start a project, but if that project fails to uphold their perfect image and feed their fragile pride, they will quickly lose interest and fail to complete it.

The key for self-assured people is integrity. Integrity is the only way that a self-assured person will discern his or her images from reality. Integrity will establish the boundaries these people need in order to operate in reality, allowing them to properly face the challenges that are before them. After all, their worldly perception is nothing more than vainglory. They consider those things which fail to bow down to their images as being incompetent. At this point they logic that they are justified in becoming judgmental and cruel to those who fail to properly honor their images. Unless they establish integrity to see how useless the false glory of their images is, they will never be able to reflect the true glory of the Son of Man, Jesus Christ, as they decide to express His attitude towards others.[2]

# Strong-Willed Nature

Strong-willed people must understand that real strength and authority comes from outside of their "so-called" controlled atmospheres. There was a strong-willed woman who controlled her atmosphere by alleviating the point of conflict. For example, a heating vent became a point of conflict between her and another individual. Since she liked to keep the vent open to compliment her atmosphere, she took the vent out altogether. In another situation there was a problem over a scale, so she simply removed the scale to stop any more contention.

---

[2] 2 Corinthians 3:18

These people believe that they can control their reality. Often, they simply adjust the lines of truth to reshape their reality. I remember such a situation with a strong-willed man. He had been a preacher, but walked away from his calling. He met a Christian woman to whom he became attracted. As their relationship emotionally grew, he talked about returning to his calling, but he also expressed the desire that they live together. Needless to say, she knew it was wrong. However, he adjusted the truth to convince her that in their hearts they were already married. She accepted his reality, but felt guilty. They eventually married, but it put a black mark on his credibility, and remained a point of shame to her.

I have witnessed these people make unethical practices right in their own minds. Their ability to reshape reality in their small worlds gives them a false sense of infallibility. However, they eventually lose important credibility. For these people to deal in reality they must be challenged to respect the boundaries of others. In other words, people cannot allow strong-willed individuals to establish boundaries for them.

Strong-willed people must recognize strength and authority does not stop with them. In fact, it must be sought outside of their controlled worlds to establish boundaries or lines that show proper understanding. These lines must be pliable towards the Spirit of God in regard for those who enter these people's worlds. If they do not come to terms with the strength and authority of heaven, they become harsh towards that which does not line up to their way of thinking.

As you can see, submissive people look within for reality, stubborn people consider reality in light of their emotions, the self-assured operate their reality within the worldly perception of their images, and the strong-willed insist on that which is outside of their reality to adjust to their personal perception of matters. However, reality is perverted that is processed through that which is from within. The fleshly defiles reality as it fits into its ways, while the worldly perception twists it. Those who insist that reality adjust to personal perceptions will either ignore reality or it becomes refracted and confusing.

It is vital that Christian couples understand the basic practices of Christianity. It is not a matter of our mate seeing it our way; rather, it is a matter of both individuals in the relationship seeing it from God's perspective. However, each person must institute godly boundaries to determine what will be accepted and what will be confronted in their relationship. This will be the only means to find agreement.

In the following chapters we will consider those things that undermine, confuse, and destroy the marriage relationship along with what will establish it. If you are married, or thinking about marriage allow the Holy Spirit to convict, instruct, and change wrong thinking, attitudes, and practices.

# 9

# HARSH REALITY

After considering the four natures, you might feel a little overwhelmed or even depressed! Each nature shows its ability to rebel, be deceived, and miserably fail before God and in their relationships with others. In rebellion, man can easily make himself a god. In deception, he can make self right in his own eyes, regardless of the destruction that has been inflicted upon others. The natural tendency of man is to avoid being accountable, which usually results in some form of personal justification or pity parties. It is a miracle anything is accomplished within the realm of humanity. It is no wonder that a string of victims is left behind, bruised and wounded by the sins of others. The harsh reality is that mankind is in trouble and doomed without the intervention of God.

It is obvious that the old man freely reigns in many Christian homes and churches. We can put on religious masks, but the fruit coming out of our lives will tell on us. We can blame the next guy, but failure to take accountability for personal attitudes and actions will reveal and expose us as the problem. Instead of overcoming the world, the flesh, and the devil, it is obvious many are succumbing to the dictates of the old man, and becoming entangled in the snares of these three main enemies of the soul.

Jeremiah 17:9 tells us that our heart is wicked and deceitful, who can know it? Isaiah 64:6 states that even our best is as filthy rags. Romans 3:10 declares that there is none righteous. The Apostle Paul admitted in Romans 7:18 that there is no good thing in the flesh, and 1 Peter 4:18 tells us that the righteous are scarcely saved. You would think by considering these Scriptures alone that people would get a reality check, but the god of this world has blinded many to their true spiritual condition.[1] They have compromised righteousness, given in to idolatry, substituted religion for truth, and agreed with Satan about their rights to so-called "happiness."

How can we step outside of this cycle to gain spiritual insight and hearing in order to become part of God's plan? Freedom from this cycle can be found in truth. John 8:32 tells us the truth will set us free. The truth will lead us to Jesus Christ.[2]

Jesus must become our mirror. The Word of God must be allowed to penetrate through the excuses, the garbage, and the games right into

---

[1] 2 Corinthians 4:3-4
[2] John 8:36; 14:6

our heart to reveal and expose its condition. We must come face to face with the harsh reality of our own selfish disposition, and take responsibility for the poison that we have spread with our pride, as well as the pollution we have created with our fleshly pursuits and dictates. It is time that we agree with God's Word, and begin to grow up!

We must cease to harden our hearts through disobedience, be quick to flee all idolatry, separate ourselves from all ungodliness and the world, and pursue after righteousness and peace. We must hate sin in our own lives by aggressively confronting it, while approaching others who are in sin or struggling with some type of claim it has on their lives in meekness and humility. We must make our lives and homes a sanctuary for our God.[3]

There were three compartments to the tabernacle. God's glory resided above the mercy seat of the Ark of the Covenant in the Most Holy Place. Priests ministered in the Holy Place where God was upheld in remembrance through the Candlestick, the Table of Shewbread, and the Altar of Incense. The outer court was where the water in the laver cleansed the priest, and sacrifices were offered on behalf of man.

There are three compartments within both man and his earthly home. Within man, there is his spirit, the Most Holy Place, his soul, the Holy Place and his body, the outer court. Within the home is the bedroom, which is to be related to the Most Holy Place. The sanctuary or inner court of the home where the family congregates serves as the Holy Place, and the world is the outer court. Let us consider the following illustration.

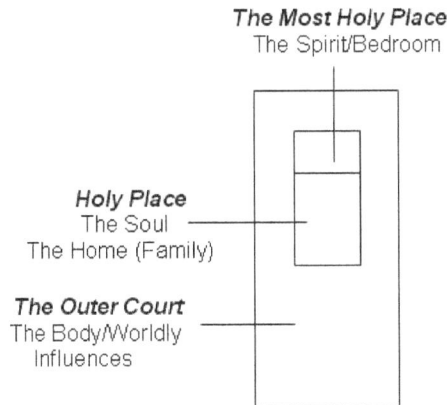

**The Most Holy Place**
The Spirit/Bedroom

**Holy Place**
The Soul
The Home (Family)

**The Outer Court**
The Body/Worldly
Influences

Today, the Most Holy Place is being defiled in various ways, grieving the Holy Spirit. Like the priests of the Old Testament before the temple's destruction by Babylon, man is bringing that which is unholy from the outer court into the inner courts of his life and home.

Minds are becoming garbage dumps as many Christians expose themselves to pornography and other questionable material that would fail the test of Philippians 4:8. The mind, which is part of the soul, is

---

[3] 1 Corinthians 10:14; 2 Corinthians 6:14-18; 2 Timothy 2:19-22

becoming perverted by people coming into agreement with the unholy, and the devastating result is that there *is nothing pure* in the sanctuary of man. As in the days of Noah, the thoughts and imaginations of men's hearts are continually becoming eviler.[4]

Half of the people I minister to are men. Over half of them have a terrible problem with lust, which is often a product of pornography. The defilement that has occurred in their lives is frightening. They cannot distinguish the difference between the pure and the defiled. Everything is perverted and warped. Although it may be hard to face, pornography is one of the fastest growing cancers and addictions in our society and in the Church.

A number of years ago I remember hearing two pastors talking about presenting programs to help those addicted to alcohol and drugs. I asked them if they had any programs dealing with the addiction to pornography. I was met with silence.

Pornography has defiled the most sacred part of the institution of marriage. It has warped people's understanding of real intimacy. It has resulted in unnatural practices invading homes, destroying the innocence of children, and the uprightness of many unsuspecting Christians.

Pornography has affected the Most Holy Place in the marriage, the bedroom, where perverted attitudes and unnatural practices have been brought in. I remember how a Christian individual admitted to me that in the name of her Christian marriage, every perverted practice was being conducted in the bedroom, including bestiality. Another admitted to watching dirty movies in order to be sexually aroused and motivated. Others confessed that various devices, such as ropes, were used in the bedroom.

It appears as if many Christians can no longer discern what is holy from that which is unholy. Some have questioned the intimacy in their own bedroom because they are confused as to whether their acts are considered sacred and acceptable by God. Such spiritual dullness is due to compromising with a bombardment of ungodly exposures in our society. This blatant crime against sexual purity is practiced in the name of marriage, sensual excitement, romance, entertainment, and pleasure. Many of these practices would not have been accepted or even mentioned a couple of decades ago.

One must ask the question, why is this happening? The answer is simple: Men and women have ceased to sacrifice self on the altar of the cross. Instead of cleansing self at the laver from the influences of the world, they have embraced them. Instead of becoming holy priests and godly examples to their family, where both can minister properly to their children the reality of God, their hands are polluted with the stench of the world resting upon their lives, and their hearts have become divided in loyalties.

Hebrews 13:4 states, "Marriage is honourable in all, and the bed undefiled: but whoremongers and adulterers God will judge." Marriage is

---

[4] Genesis 6:8; Titus 1:14-15

to be kept pure. God gave it as a gift to married couples in a state of purity as a means to be used as a blessing, allowing for an intimate bonding to take place in this holy institution. A bedroom defiled means the presence of God will be lifted from the home. This defilement will spread to the Holy Place, affecting what will happen in the sanctuary of the family.

As defilement spreads, it begins to abuse the things of God. A little leaven leavens the whole lump.[5] Nothing is spared from the wicked tentacles of the defilement. The bedroom ceases to be sacred and becomes a place where sensual, fleshly, animal pursuits are encouraged and condoned. Spouses who are to be honored and loved become inferior sex objects to be used or discarded. Children, who are a heritage from God, become insignificant or burdens, as self is exalted to pursue any idol to satisfy the flesh's insatiable appetites of lust for sensual pleasure, success, money, and power.

As a result, the children of many Christian couples no longer regard God. They no longer respect authority, fear eternal consequences, or want anything to do with God. They equate God with the hypocrisy and the game playing they see going on in their parents' lives.

I have met young Christian people who consider sexual pursuits outside of marriage as normal. Few understand that fornication is not a reliable foundation upon which to start any relationship, let alone a lifetime relationship.

I remember talking to a Christian couple who were heading towards a divorce. The lady confessed to me that she and her husband had committed fornication before their marriage. She realized close to their wedding day that she did not like this man, but because of the guilt she felt over their sin of fornication, she married him. When I met with her, it was not just a matter of not liking her husband any longer, she resented him. His very person made her feel repulsed.

The problem with unrighteous actions or living is that it will come back to blackmail you. Sins committed in darkness will surface. The end result is that many Christians find themselves playing the outward game of piety and love towards their mates, so no one suspects them of the inward darkness that continues to plague them.

You might be saying, "Rayola, it is not as bad as you state. You must be dramatizing the condition of marriage." Am I? How does our Holy God look at our practices in the Most Holy Places of our lives, as well as our involvement with the different pursuits of the world? If our Lord will spew out those who are lukewarm, what will He do with those who are in blatant sin and defiling that which is to be considered and treated as sacred? Let us not deceive ourselves. We are in trouble. Maybe it is not obvious on the outside, but something is terribly wrong. The family is disintegrating from within, and our society is being consumed with darkness. Our nation is decaying from within and coming under judgment, while the church is proving to be ineffective, and our society is

---

[5] 1 Corinthians 5:6-7

close to collapse because of crime, divorces, and the lack of family stability.[6]

It is time to come back to center, God's center.  We must understand how God looks at our lives, homes, and activities. We must honestly face the harsh truth of our own miserable plight, repent, cry out for mercy, and begin to live a life that agrees with God in love, holiness, and obedience, which produces righteous fruits.

---

[6] Galatians 6:7-8; Revelation 3:15-16

# 10

# THE INVASION OF PERVERSION

We are being conditioned by worldly influences to embrace perversion. It is vital to recognize the unholy practices in our lives in order to come back to godliness. Recently, I talked to a single Christian woman who asked me how she could ever find a pure Christian man in the perverted world of today. My sympathy went out to her as it does to all godly single Christians. Regardless of gender, it is hard to find a Christian mate who has not been warped by the perversion that has invaded our society. This is not only true in America, but all over the world.

This perversion has a lot to do with truth. Truth and purity have been perverted to fit people's perception about what constitutes reality. Since reality is unpleasant and boring for most, many try to create a different reality that will appeal to their desires in regards to life. The reality that is often erected entices the flesh, heightens vain imaginations, and appeals to the ego.

Sadly, this perversion has invaded not only relationships between men and women, but people's perception of sexuality, marriage, and healthy relationships. Many people have adopted the liberal Hollywood mentality about these issues. They are looking for the perfect man or woman who fits this perception. They believe if they find the right person, then all of their hopes about life will be fulfilled.

The sad reality about these perceptions is that they are nothing more than self-serving concepts or unrealistic images that have no substance or purpose. The people who pursue them discover that these ideas comprise the proverbial carrot that proves to be illusive. Deferred hope of this nature creates anger, despair, and depression.

In contending with these people, you discover that they harbor unrealistic expectations because of these standards. In their minds, these concepts not only constitute reality, but also offer the happiness and attention they desire. When you consider why these people value these ideas, it comes down to the fact that these expectations exalt them as god of their worlds.

We are once again reminded that the most underlying desire of people is to be God. This means they desire to be served, honored, adored, and recognized by others, especially those in their lives. It places them on the throne where their desires are constantly considered, their needs met, and their happiness a priority.

When they consider love and marriage, they see both as a platform for them to make this reality true. Little do they realize that their spouse probably has similar expectations. When the spouse fails to meet their expectations, they will resort to games.

It is amazing to watch the different natures play games with the people in their lives. These games are deceptive, but they are appealing because they allow people to play them in the name of happiness and security. For example, *submissive* people play with other people's minds. They observe the way people think and speak. Once they can discover patterns or key words, they give the appearance of complying with the other person's reality. This is all a game because their real motive is to get the other person to comply with their personal way of thinking without confrontation. By appealing to the person's mental patterns or by saying the right things, they are trying to flatter a person into thinking that they are adjusting to his or her world. This is just a clever way to get a person to respond or comply without realizing it. It is also a way of developing necessary points for credit.

The submissive person will use such credit in gaining an upper hand in matters that are vital or considered important. Since they have the necessary points, it will prove to others that they have a right to do it their way in particular situations without confrontation and opposition. After all, they have nobly given way here and there in other matters, even though it was for self-serving purposes. What submissive people fail to realize is that every nature believes there should be compliance to their particular reality, and perceive such compliance as reasonable service, love, and recognition. Therefore, their self-serving compliance eventually will cause confusion and anger in the stubborn person, while it produces mocking from the self-assured, and is translated as hypocrisy or weakness by the strong-willed person.

*Stubborn* people play games with people's emotions. They have various means of doing it with such devices as conning, guilt, and pressure. They con you by appealing to your good or just side. If conning doesn't work, they try reasoning with you in the area of guilt. Since these people are often driven by guilt, they assume everyone can be moved by it. This may be applicable in some cases, but most people resent such tactics. They can also put extreme pressure on a person to get him or her to see how something should be done. They may get results, but the backlash is not always constructive. Submissive people choose to ignore such attempts. Self-assured people will turn the games back on the stubborn person, often causing insecurity and guilt. Strong-willed people will throw them a bone just to get them off their back, but nothing ever really gets accomplished as the stubborn person's frustration grows.

*Self-assured* people cleverly change the perspective a person may have about them in order to show how right and logical they are. For example, a person who may be contending with a self-assured person over attitudes or actions will encounter a list of things he or she has done wrong in the past. This confuses the issues and makes the one who was on the offence on the defense. As the person's discrepancies are pointed out by the self-assured person, his or her perception about being right and having the right to confront these issues is now made to appear as being wrong. Since the person is wrong, he or she must now agree with the self-assured person's evaluation of reality and adjust accordingly. This tactic will close down the submissive person, cause confusion, anger, and bitterness in the stubborn nature, and cause strong-willed people to adjust their personal game plan accordingly to gain back the control.

*Strong-willed* people play games with the mind, emotions, and images. They will quickly adjust their tactics according to the situation. They are good at mentally figuring out what to say to throw people off. They can be quick at appealing to the good side of a person in order to get him or her to react according to personal preference. They know how to adjust their present presentation to receive the desired response. These attempts are simply their way of reshaping the person and the activities to fit into their reality. These means are nothing more than throwing a bone at someone. If this diplomatic tactic does not work, then they will bluff or intimidate a person to fit into their reality. This causes a submissive person to erect an immovable wall. Once the stubborn person sees it as control, they will charge in total defiance or they will emotionally close down. The self-assured person will patiently wait to discover the weakness in the strong-willed person's armor to send well-aimed arrows.

Games are not only deceitful, but also destructive. They pervert one's perception, relationships, and reality. They set people up for failure, relationships up for destruction, and life becomes an arena where disillusionment, conflict, and defeat plague those who are within its space.

There is nothing kept sacred from the destructive tentacles of perversion, regardless of which form it may come. It will bring everything into question as to what is pure and acceptable. It harbors treachery and disloyalty. It is fleshly in pursuit, evil in nature, and destructive in practice. Perversion is nothing but defilement. Defilement desensitizes a person towards that which is holy, while indoctrinating them to embrace the profane.

It is important to understand how this perversion works. I have seen unholy practices ignored and overlooked in churches, as Christians commit fornication without showing any real conviction. In fact, my friend heard two men talking about finding vulnerable women at single groups in churches. I have realized that many of these single groups in churches are prime areas for predators, and serve as a breeding ground for fornication.

Perversion has been invading the hearts and minds of people for some time. It is coming from all directions, but its main goal is to change people's perception about what is right and what is wrong, resulting in people calling good, evil and evil, good.[1] Sadly, it has become an acceptable mentality. This mentality condones lust and fornication at every level, from the mind to immoral practices. Ultimately, it will set each

---

[1] Isaiah 5:20

society up to fall into its destructive traps, while it robs of its ability to stand from within.

This same mentality can be clearly seen in the Church, and is deemed as the natural extension of what is normal for men and women in regards to how they view each other. This is fallacy. Jesus represents the normal man, and there is no indication that He expressed any perversion or unholy attitude or conduct towards any individual, including the opposite sex.

Since Jesus is the truest example of what is acceptable to Christians, He reveals that these attitudes are not a natural extension of man, but a preferred expression and practice of the selfish disposition. This unholy mentality has been cleverly excused away by the depravity that plagues man, the very depravity that he refuses to face and take responsibility for. Sadly, some leaders in the Church are guilty of not exposing this lie and properly challenging this mentality and its attitudes.

How does this perverted mentality work? I already alluded to it. It works from the point of vain, evil imaginations. These imaginations are stirred up by a bombardment of images that have been erected in the mind of the person by some outside source such as Hollywood, music, books, videos, and magazines. Few people realize that each society's concept of beauty and success has been determined by the culture that has been or is being established by those in high places. It is nothing more than propaganda.

The images that the American culture promotes, promise satisfaction and/or happiness. Once these images are in place, the mind toys with the possibilities as to how these images will indeed bring satisfaction and fulfill all desires for happiness. Needless to say, the possibilities of these images begin to stir up incredible ecstasies in the mind. This creates obsessions that drive the person to pursue relentlessly these images in order to experience the satisfaction or happiness they seem to promise. Of course, the reality of these images falls short of the expectations, but they seem so real that people continue to pursue them.

This pursuit is nothing less than idolatrous. People are bowing down to these images as they entice people to pursue the possibilities of satisfaction and fulfillment of happiness. These possibilities are unrealistic, but the emotions, feelings, and attractions attached to them are real and powerful. They create superstition, darkness, and delusion, but people insist they are real and obtainable; therefore, they cling more tightly to them.

These images are obvious between men and women. Men have an idea of the perfect mate produced by the images of pornography, Hollywood, and magazines. This unrealistic image feeds their ego as it stirs the imagination as to how this image would make them feel and look to others if they could personally possess it.

Women have an idea of how the perfect man will treat her. Amazingly, the images that often affirm the manhood of men stir up their sexual desires, while the ideas of women in regard to the perfect man is a matter of how the man will make her feel about herself, which points to vanity. Does the man value her by chasing after her? Does this man uphold her by protecting her from outside sources, and will he maintain her respect by honoring her? No wonder men harbor the philosophy of chasing, conquering, and challenging when it comes to pursuing women. On the other hand, women who operate in integrity towards men will challenge the man in his attitudes toward her, avoid being conquered, and will monitor and control the extent of the chase to ensure proper boundaries.

Sadly, these attitudes in men and women become a vicious game that can rob both of self-respect. The main key to this game is the idea of need. Men need to conquer and women need to be loved or honored. This is why men give "so-called" love to get sex, and women give sex to get love.

Sex outside of marriage does not signify victory for the man or love for the woman. If the man conquers, the woman may become a notch in his belt, but he leaves a part of himself behind. If the woman is conquered, she feels she has lost her dignity. This does one of two things: She feels like a prostitute, therefore, acts like one. Alternatively, she develops games where she ultimately will make each man she encounters pay in some way for using her dishonorably.[2]

Amazingly, men want to marry a virgin and women want to marry a pure man who knows how to be a lover. Talk about blatant hypocrisy on both. How can men expect to marry virgins when they are so busy trying to conquer each woman they come in contact with? How can women expect men to make them feel special when they have tasted the forbidden fruit of other women? Talk about fantasy!

Sadly, this mentality is brought into the marriage. Because of this mentality, the relationship is kept on a fleshly plane as people see it as a legalized way to express their perverted imaginations through lust, as well as their pursuit to experience passions and their expectations to be constantly stirred up by romance. This is all fleshly and temporary. Marriage is earthly in nature, but if it remains earth-bound in focus, it will never embrace the heavenly.

Perversion comes in two forms: pornography and fantasy. Pornography stirs up the appetites, while fantasy inspires vain imaginations. Pornography conditions a person to pursue certain images in order to experience pleasure and satisfaction. Fantasy creates certain images in the mind that offer happiness and fulfillment.

The problem with these images is that they cause comparisons. People are forever comparing prospective pursuits with images. Will this person or situation give me the desired satisfaction or fulfillment? Such examinations are all surface, and never get down to the person's character. Since images have no substance, the reality is clearly missing, giving way to games, insensitivity, and indifference.

These perverted games not only change the perception of the relationship between men and women, but they warp the concept of

---

[2] 1 Corinthians 6:13-20

marriage. One of the biggest breeding grounds for fornication is the practice of dating. Perverted games are prevalent as the man and woman put his or her best foot forward to get the desired results. Supposedly, dating is for the purpose of people getting to know one another, but people rarely discover the character of an individual. Instead, what they encounter is an attractive image that stirs up their imaginations and lust. People fall in love with the image without ever discovering the character of the person.

When they marry this person, they are still caught up on the image rather than the person. When reality and drudgery hit the marriage, those fleshly attractive elements fall to the wayside as disillusionment, discontentment, and anger set in.

This brings us back to the idolatry these images create. Man often sees himself as the savior of a woman. After all, he is saving her from being an old maid, lonely, and undesirable. Since he is the savior, he deserves to be worshiped and served. His home is the castle, and his wife now has the responsibility of making him happy in all of his desires.

The woman wants to be saved. She perceives that if she is valuable enough to be saved, the man will automatically love and adore her as his queen. In fact, he will honor and cherish her in every way possible to ensure her happiness and security. What does this tell you about the idolatry that is prevalent in marriages? Simply, that both the man and the woman are vying for the position of God in their relationship. When the man is not properly exalted, he becomes discontented. And, when the woman is not cherished and adored, she becomes disillusioned.

There was a woman who admitted that when she saw the hatred in her husband's eyes towards her, she was shocked. She asked herself how could a man who vowed to love and cherish her, stand before her with absolute hatred. She had not really changed except she was not putting up with his self-centered ways. She knew if she questioned him, he would give her various reasons for his discontentment, anger, and hatred towards her. Underneath, she knew that she had failed to live up to the images he had for her. She had failed to be the perfect companion, friend, lover, wife, and servant. She also knew she could never make him happy no matter what she did.

Sadly, many marriages are nothing more than two immature, selfish adults playing house. The reality of marriage is that it is not a temporary game, but a relationship that takes investment. The strength and endurance of this relationship are often forged in adversity. Its commitment is tested in ongoing drudgery. The marriage relationships can only mature as each person takes personal responsibility for attitudes, personal behavior, and actions.

Today, marriage has become a platform to exploit every point of selfishness, regardless of how it affects others. It is no longer about two people becoming one. Rather, it is about one person being exalted over another. Marriage has been reduced to a battle of the wills as people exert their rights to maintain personal rights and identity. This exploitation has made people parasites in their marriage, rather than honorable partners.

Sex that was intended as a gift to marriage has been defiled as it supposedly confirms the worth of a man, and becomes a tool for women. It is a platform for every infidel and pervert to mock God and destroy the moral fiber of this nation. No wonder sex is also the very avenue by which deadly transmitted diseases find their way into one population after another.

The Bible is clear about marriage and sex. But even religious people harbor warped perceptions that defile its instructions. Their realities are not in line with the Bible. Instead, the Word of God is being adjusted to worldly practices. This simply means such people are maintaining a perverted reality. Their interpretations often maintain and condone cultural attitudes, prejudices, anger, and hatred. Prejudice is often hidden behind Scripture, anger concealed behind the cloak of self-righteousness, and hatred behind religious rhetoric. Regardless of the religious façade, these defiled perceptions cause people to handle truth in unrighteousness. Ultimately, everything becomes defiled.[3]

The challenge to return to truth is not directed at the unsaved, but to the Church. Christians are to be an example of what it means to be holy in a world that has been defiled in every way.[4] Believers are to reveal the purpose of marriage and how to maintain integrity within its godly boundaries. Therefore, saints need to seriously examine their attitudes about this relationship, to ensure that it lines up to the intent or spirit of God's Word.

Christians must seek to understand God's design for the home, the bedroom, and their children. It is only in light of God's mirror that real change begins. Are you ready to face the mirror of God?

---

[3] Romans 1:18; Titus 1:14-15
[4] 1 Peter 1:15-16; Hebrews 12:14

# Part Two

## *GODLY MARRIAGE*

# 11
# THE MIND OF GOD
# CONCERNING MARRIAGE

What was in the mind of God when He took woman out of the side of man and established what we now call marriage? I believe this is the most important question the Church must answer concerning this relationship.

You can find various books on how to bring romance back to your marriage. Women can read about what their husbands need, and men can find out what their wives require to make them happy. From all appearances, these attempts are still trying to appeal to the fleshly appetites rather than deal with the spiritual implications that are really undermining the real intent of marriage.

I am sure some of these books written by experts have been of some help, but according to statistics, the percentage must be small. In spite of all such attempts, godly marriages are on the verge of becoming extinct. I use the word "extinct" because how many godly marriages exist today? Even with the Christian marriages that have managed to stay together, how many are godly, and how many are simply a religious façade? The real figures would probably throw Christendom into major panic.

Today we are trying to put a bandage on a ruptured artery. No amount of psychological formulas will right the wrong that plagues marriage. It will take major surgery beginning with heart surgery to completely change ungodly and selfish attitudes.

In most cases, marriage has simply become the latest "fig leaf" that covers every type of lust, perversion, and selfishness. This has not enhanced the sacredness of marriage; rather, it has made it a stench before heaven. As a result, godly marriages are becoming extinct.

Some may ask the question, if you take away sensual pleasures, the emphasis on needs, romance, or emotional fulfillment, what is left? Don't get me wrong, some of these things are not bad, but many people have put the wrong emphasis on them. Most of these pursuits are fleshly, self-centered, and influenced by worldly mindsets.

Again, what was in the mind of God when He established marriage? Was it to satisfy men and women's appetites, and give them a license to explore wicked imaginations by practicing them under this sacred covering? I think the answer to this question is obvious. Holiness is required in every area of a Christian's conduct, and that means even in the marriage relationship.[1]

The success and solution to a godly marriage does not hinge on sensual arousal, romance, or understanding our spouse's needs, but on Christ being the center of our lives and homes. In summation, He must be Lord of the marriage. Regardless of the various attempts made to inspire men to be the head of their families, instruct wives to be in submission, and demand children to be obedient, the attitude, authority, and honor will be missing without the Lordship of Jesus in the home. Through example, Jesus established the right attitude, served as the source of authority, and revealed how honor works. Without Him being in His rightful position in people's lives, marriage will have no real substance in which the couple is able to stand. Obviously, the real purpose behind a godly marriage can only be understood in light of Christ on the cross.

The relationship of marriage is earthly and temporary, but God had an eternal perspective in mind when He ordained the first marriage in the Garden of Eden.[2] The eternal purpose behind marriage actually remained a mystery until the establishment of the new Church of Jesus Christ. The Apostle Paul confirmed this when he made this statement in Ephesians 5:32, "This is a great mystery: but I speak concerning Christ and the church."

The first marriage was to serve as a foreshadow of the eternal relationship Jesus would establish between Himself and His Body, the Church. God put Adam to sleep in order to bring forth Eve. Jesus was put in the grave in order for His Church to come forth by faith in His death, burial and resurrection. Eve was an extension of Adam just as the Church is to be the extension of Christ. Ruth Specter Lascelle pointed out that man came from the earth, but woman from the side of man. This meant that woman was once removed from the earth, and was meant to pull man upward and heavenward.[3] As you consider the relationship of the Church to Jesus, she is meant to point the unsaved upward and heavenward to her God, Lord and Bridegroom.

God ordained that husband and wife would become complete by becoming one in this relationship. Jesus made this statement about His relationship with His followers in John 17:22, "And the glory which thou gavest me I have given them; that they may be one, even as we are one." The Body of believers will not be whole until they are one in purpose and direction with Jesus.

---

[1] Hebrews 12:14; 1 Peter 1:15-16
[2] 1 Corinthians 7:31-33
[3] *Jewish Faith and the New Covenant;* page 100

In order to secure the Church as His bride, Jesus gave up the glories of heaven, took on the form of a servant, and became a sacrifice for everyone who would accept His invitation. He redeemed His future bride with His blood. The Apostle Paul confirms this in 1 Corinthians 6:18-20 when he made this statement,

> Flee fornication. Every sin that a man doeth is without the body; but he that committeth fornication sinneth against his own body. What? Know ye not that your body is the temple of the Holy Ghost which is in you, which ye have of God, and ye are not your own? For ye are bought with a price: therefore glorify God in your body, and in your spirit, which are God's.

We do not have a right to discard our holy calling in any area of our life. Jesus is coming back for a bride who is without spot and wrinkle.[4] His bride will be pure in heart and thoughts, upright in actions, and free from idolatrous and lustful pursuits.

The questions Christian couples must ask are, "Does our marriage fulfill the eternal purpose by representing Jesus Christ in Spirit and in truth?" "Does our marriage represent to a lost world, the commitment and sacrificial love of Jesus for His Church?" "Can the world see something unique, sweet and pure about our marriage?" "What category would our marriage fit in: the five foolish virgins who did not have enough oil, or the five wise virgins who had enough oil to sustain them until the bridegroom came for them?"[5]

We must cease to grieve the Holy Spirit with unholy living and alliances. He is the One who gives us sustaining power to overcome. He reveals Jesus to us and transforms our minds.[6] He prepares and keeps us undefiled for our bridegroom. Are you in submission to His work in your life? Do you desire to hear, see and dwell with your future bridegroom more than remaining in this world? Do you desire to become one with Him? We need to get back to the center of the Lordship of Jesus Christ in our life before God. This is what it will take for our lives, marriages and homes to be restored.

---

[4] Ephesians 5:26-27
[5] Matthew 25:1-13
[6] Romans 12:2

# 12

# COMING BACK TO THE CENTER

Philippians 2:5-8 gives us the example of what it means to come back to the center of real godliness. These scriptures reveal the heart, attitude, and actions of Jesus Christ.

We are told to have the mind of Jesus. The mind represents our prevailing tendencies, moods, and inclinations. We must understand all three of these areas as displayed by Christ if we are going to comply and develop His very attitude. To grasp Christ's tendency towards His Body, the Church, we must first discern the meaning behind Jesus making Himself of no reputation. He literally emptied Himself of His glory and became void of His authority and power as God.

To empty Himself of His glory meant that Jesus actually gave up His sovereign rule as God to become a servant. He gave up His identification as Creator to become a man. What an incredible feat. Jesus, the Creator, gave up His glory to become part of His very creation. He became poor so we could be made rich.[1]

What does this example mean for Christian couples? It is simple; they must individually empty themselves of personal rights and fleshly pursuits, and be willing to acquire a new identity together for the sake of a godly marriage. This identity will be totally contrary to the essence of their very humanity.

You might be shaking your head right now in opposition to this thought. Everything in you might be resisting such a notion. In fact, you may be ready to run away from the challenge. Perhaps your church has not presented Christianity in such a light. Like the world, it has given you the impression that it is all right to heap upon yourself the best the world has to offer. You need to know that worldly philosophy is contrary, not only to the example we have in Christ, but to the Word of God.[2]

Consider what most people look to when coming to their terms with their identity or position in marriage. They look to their partner to give them a sense of identity. Consider the following example.

Husband ◄——————————————► Wife

---

[1] 2 Corinthians 8:9
[2] Colossians 2:8

Bear in mind that there is not much substance to this type of relationship. Ultimately, it will become lacking and empty instead of fulfilling.

God has provided an instrument that will help you empty yourself, but you must make a choice. Jesus made the choice to become less in order for you and me to become more. Can we be any less committed in our Christian life? After all, we cannot afford to lose the battle for our homes. Take courage and make the right decision. In fact, give this decision precedence over all desires, allowing it to become a determination or a tendency that will become a habit.

What decision must you make if you are to become of no reputation? Matthew 16:24 tells you what your decision must be up front. You must decide to deny yourself. According to *Strong's Concordance*, "deny" means to disown. You must disown self with all of its rights and demands.

The biggest destructive culprit in marriage is self. It is arrogant and unteachable. It demands its way, claims superiority, and will discard anyone or anything that will not worship it accordingly. Fear, insecurities and anger surround it. It wears a mask to hide its cruel face, and it plays wicked games to control and manipulate. This pagan god is often unmerciful, inconsiderate, rebellious, and contrary. It refuses to be wrong; therefore, it will not submit. It cannot be reasoned with, and the results are contention and strife.

Consider the following diagram when you disown yourself in light of Jesus taking His rightful place as Lord. You must take your eyes off of your mate to properly deny yourself. This will relieve your mate of the responsibility of giving you identity and your life meaning and purpose.

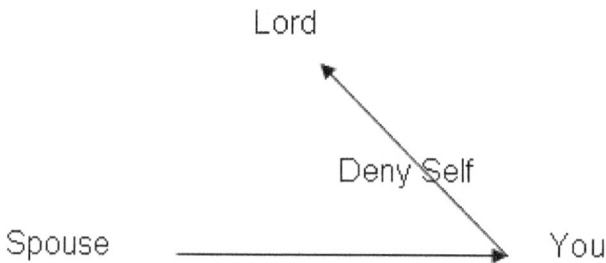

Lord

Deny Self

Spouse          ⟶   You

We could write volumes about the ruthless tyrant of self that plagues all mankind with its insatiable pursuits, masks, and games. But, as you can see, it is to your benefit to disown this hideous taskmaster. To deny self entails a great personal battle initially, but down the line you will discover what it means to be set free from the insidious tentacles of this vicious dictator.

After we make the decision to deny self, we must follow Jesus' next example; we must make an exchange. Jesus exchanged His sovereign rule for the position of a servant. Talk about taking a step down! His step transcended every conceivable dimension.

You need to realize that to make this exchange is not a step down, but a step up. Granted, we need to exchange self for the position of a servant. What many of us fail to realize is that we are already servants to sin. Servitude in the kingdom of God offers the greatest form of liberty, that of choice. I am choosing whom I am going to serve. Needless to say, servitude of this nature appears to be a step down in light of the American mindset. But, according to Jesus, being such a servant makes you chief in the kingdom of God.[3]

A servant has a lord and must come into submission. Submission is a form of agreement. Before such agreement can occur, there must be a giving way to that which is great to produce an agreement that will ensure the integrity of a matter. "Great" in this text points to that which is worthy and honorable. Agreement means that parties are coming into agreement in regards to purpose and direction to accomplish a greater purpose. For example, the agreement found in the Godhead, resulted in the provision of salvation being offered to mankind. Such agreement requires that the parties involved get beyond personal goals to accomplish tasks that would be beneficial to others. This type of submission sets the type of mood that produces greatness in the kingdom of God. Matthew 11:29 tells us Jesus was gentle and humble in heart. Psalm 18:35b states, "…thy gentleness has made me great."

Godly submission creates strength in a relationship. When there is agreement, the bonds cannot be easily broken. We see this strength in Jesus in regards to His relationship with the Father.[4] He was in total submission to the Father's will. In other words, He was in complete agreement with the Father.

Godly submission results in subordination. Subordination expresses itself in obedience to the One who is the overseer. Because there is agreement and subordination, the will of the one in authority will be carried out in a right spirit and attitude. This obedience comes from the heart of a committed servant who loves his or her lord. This is why Ephesians 5:21 instructs, "Submitting yourselves one to another in the fear of God."

It is important for Christians to understand that Christ is not calling us to fill a role, but for us to understand positionally who we are in Him. A role implies an assigned or assumed pattern of behavior. A role is something you actually critique or judge because it is based on personal performance determined by scripts written or designed by others, such as our culture or religious organizations. Roles have no regard for personal talents or abilities. There is usually an unseen director with assumed expectations establishing the script as you go. All scripts require conformity.

A husband had a rigid script for his working wife by which to perform. She knew her moral and ethical duties, but was surprised to find out her husband's script required her to take care of any whim he had conjured

---

[3] Matthew 20:27; Romans 6:20; Philippians 2:1-8
[4] Ecclesiastes 4:11-12

up in his mind concerning her duty. Besides caring for the house, she was expected to do the yard work, and take care of camping details along with any other desires that would arise. She began to realize he was always rewriting the script for his benefit without any regard for her. It was also apparent that he solely claimed rights to determine her responsibilities, while establishing his personal obligations that pretty well served his causes and preferences.

Positions, on the other hand, carry moral and mental responsibilities. These responsibilities serve as guidelines. These assigned positions involve a person assuming the obligation to carry out the responsibilities of the position. The beauty of positions is that people can respond to their responsibilities in compliance with their particular personality. They are not under the scrutiny of a director.

Godly positions do not call for conformity, but have the power to transform. For example, Jesus calls His sheep to follow Him.[5] Upon His invitation, Jesus turns around and leads. Jesus is not a director of His sheep, but a leader. He leads them to places where they can find rest and nourishment for spiritual growth and well-being. There is a big difference!

In marriage, there are positions instead of roles. These positions are superior to roles for they properly deal in reality. They allow the person to operate according to personality. They carry realistic and sure responsibilities. Let us consider these godly positions in light of their scriptural responsibilities.

# Unveiling Christ in Marriage

Few Christians will argue that men and women have distinct responsibilities in marriage. These different positions and responsibilities are outlined in Ephesians 5:22-33.

The challenge confronting Christian marriages is finding the real intent of marriage when it has been shrouded in a cloud of confusion. This confusion is a product of man defining these different positions in light of his own self-serving perceptions. The purpose of marriage has been lost  many people fail to see God's heart in it. A "golden calf" of philosophies, formulas, and traditions has been erected in its place. This "golden calf" has taken the very life out of this institution. It may stand in all of its beauty immovable, but it lacks heart.  Therefore, we must bring the "sacred cow" down and exalt Christ in His rightful place if we are to understand marriage according to His ordained design.

Christ left us with a living example of marriage. Let us consider marriage in light of His heart and purpose for it.

Philippians 2:8 tells us that after Christ became man, he humbled Himself.  Humility comes out of godly submission.  We see that humility is required for all Christians in the verse leading to the subject of marriage in Ephesians 5:21, "Submitting yourselves one to another..."

---

[5] John 10:3-5; Romans 12:2

Therefore, it should not surprise us that the first responsibility in marriage is to submit. We see submission setting the prevailing mood for the family unit.

To understand mood, one must understand how it affects our attitudes. Mood is the same as our temperament. A mood actually reflects the environment of our emotional state. Attitude is a manifestation of our disposition. Temperament greatly affects our disposition, while our disposition can reinforce our moods. Therefore, moods set the tone of our attitude towards something.

Jesus gives us insight into attitude and temperament in Matthew 11:28, "Take my yoke upon you, and learn of me; for I am meek and lowly in heart:. and ye shall find rest unto your souls." This Scripture is about coming to the place of rest with God, so we can find rest in our lives. The key here is Jesus' attitude and prevailing mood. His attitude is that of meekness, but His prevailing mood is that of lowliness. Such a mood points to humility that will result in submission. It is such a mood that will bring us to a place of rest with God and others.

The problem with most people is something called unbelief. They do not believe what God says is true for their particular situation. They justify self-serving moods and give way to tyrannical attitudes towards others. If they do refer to the Bible, they display a legalistic or worldly interpretation of it. There is no love, and they are devoid of an attitude of submission, a mood of humility, and honorable actions. Such an inward environment points to a wrong spirit.

This brings us to the prevailing mood that must be present in godly marriages. Ephesians 5:22 states, "Wives, submit yourselves unto your own husbands, as unto the Lord." The first mention of Jesus in the marriage stipulates that He is to be the Lord in godly marriage. 1 Corinthians 8:6 reminds us that, "But to us there is but one God, the Father, of whom are all things, and we in him; and one Lord Jesus Christ, by whom are all things, and we by him."

Wives are to submit to their husbands, but in light of being in subordination to the Lordship of Jesus. It is within the righteous boundaries of the Lordship of Jesus, that women will find protection and integrity in their relationship with men. Jesus serves as the real protector and provider of a woman's needs and spiritual well-being.

Once again, submission points to agreement. A wife must come into agreement with her husband, but it will always be in light of Jesus Christ. The Apostle Paul clearly distinguishes whom all servants of God must serve in 1 Corinthians 7:22-23, "For he that is called in the Lord, being a servant, is the Lord's freeman: likewise also he that is called, being free, is Christ's servant. Ye are bought with a price; be not ye the servants of men." (Emphasis added.) If a husband steps outside of Jesus' authority, and demands that his wife do something contrary to her Lord's character and heart, she must remain in subordination to Jesus Christ. This is quite evident in the cases of Abigail in 1 Samuel 25 and Sapphira in Acts 5. No one can serve two masters at the same time. Any attempt on a woman's part to try to juggle loyalties of this type will cause anger and resentment in her.[6]

Subordination to Jesus points to sanctification or being set apart for God's glory. The Apostle Paul talked about how an unbelieving spouse can be sanctified by his or her partner.[7] When a mate is doing right, it ultimately forces the issue of righteousness in a relationship. Sometimes, it serves as a mirror to the spouse, or a sword in a relationship that will force the mate to make a decision about Jesus or the marriage.

Now that we understand a woman's responsibility, what is her position in marriage? Her responsibility actually stipulates her position. Submission is the main obligation of a servant. Like her Lord in relationship to His Father, a wife must become a servant in the marriage. This may make her position appear to be insignificant, but in sight of God's plan, she has been placed in a position of exaltation in the marriage, not one of subordination. It is the woman who maintains spiritual liberty for the family because she is choosing to serve the Lord for the benefit of her whole family. This sets the correct attitude in the family, one of submission for the purpose of honoring the Lord. The position of abasement ensures that the wife will be in the position of being honored by her husband. Keep in mind, a servant is chief in the kingdom of God.[8]

In God's kingdom, there is not one member who is superior or inferior. We are told in 1 Corinthians 12:22-24 that the weaker parts of the Body are indispensable. The parts we think are less honorable need to be treated with special honor, while the parts that are not presentable need to be treated with special modesty. We see this same principle in marriage when man was instructed to treat his wife with respect as the weaker partner. Being a servant puts a woman in a position that makes her more vulnerable. The husband has the scriptural responsibility to close the gap by showing proper honor, by exalting or preferring her to his personal needs, agendas, and desires. Wives may be in a position of servitude, but when husbands show the proper honor by preferring their wives to their own agendas, they will find themselves serving their wives in a proper way. The proper preference must be present in every Christian relationship to ensure godliness and integrity. If the husband does not show this proper respect, God will not answer his prayers. [9]

Ephesians 5:23 tells us that the husband's position in the marriage is that of headship. According to *Vine's Expository Dictionary of Biblical Words*, this position implies leadership by example. Jesus left His Body, the Church, with two examples: servitude and sacrifice.[10] He was not a tyrant or dictator. He was a gentle, loving leader. This example was the

---

[6] Matthew 6:24

[7] Luke 18:14: James 4:6, 10; 1 Corinthians 7:10-14

[8] Matthew 20:25-27

[9] Romans 12:10, 16; 1 Peter 3:7

[10] John 13:4-15; 1 Peter 2:21

secret behind the power and authority of Jesus' leadership. 1 John 4:19 confirms this, "We love him, because he first loved us." Jesus' example created the environment in which one under the right spirit would naturally reciprocate or respond to Him.

The Apostle Peter upholds this meek, loving leadership in 1 Peter 5:2-4,

> Feed the flock of God which is among you, taking the oversight thereof, not by constraint, but willingly; not for filthy lucre, but of a ready mind; Neither as being lords over God's heritage, but being ensamples to the flock. And when the chief Shepherd shall appear, ye shall receive a crown of glory that fadeth not away.

This brings us to the responsibility of a husband in marriage. Ephesians 5:25 states, "Husbands love your wives, just as Christ loved the church." Godly headship lacks power without benevolent love.[11] Benevolent love points to good will and kindness.[12] Such love is more than just a moral obligation to do right by someone, it is an actual privilege to show such consideration to the one you regard with charity and honor. Such charity and honor points to serving those you have a moral obligation to. This is why so many Christian men are failing their families.

I have often felt sorry for Christian men. They are trying to fit into roles determined by culture and religious traditions, instead of allowing the Holy Ghost to transform them so they can take on the attitude of Jesus and adhere to His example. Instead of being meek, they are trying to be fearless and macho in appearance. Instead of being loving, they are trying to rule their family with an iron fist to prove their manhood. Instead of being submissive, they are trying to be strong and immovable. These roles have isolated many men. It has caused some to feel that their only worth and responsibility in their family is to bring home the money so that their wives and children can live the "so-called" American Dream. For some, life has become complicated and devoid of real purpose and meaning. They do not know where to turn. These men cannot afford to be afraid, admit uncertainty, or be vulnerable. Much of this comes down to the sin of pride, but sadly, this stiff-necked attitude has been conditioned and promoted by the culture and sadly some of the Church. This attitude is the opposite of benevolent love, and prevents a person from being vulnerable and possessing a servant's heart.

Although the Apostle Paul is advocating an order in family structure, he is telling the wife and husband to respond to each other in the same way. Benevolent love always ends in submission, and submission is an outward act of godly love. Both of these responses end in servitude and show honor or preference to the other.[13] In fact, these two inseparable godly companions come out of the very heart of Jesus, and were reinforced by the examples He left us.

---

[11] 1 Corinthians 7:3
[12] Strong's Exhaustive Concordance of the Bible, *#2133*
[13] Romans 12:9-10

Jesus' example shows couples how to prevent the same failings that occurred in the Garden of Eden. If a woman is in submission to Jesus, her Lord, the serpent will not deceive her because her vision will be single. Unlike Adam, who failed to lead Eve away from temptation and seduction, man must meet the responsibility to lead his family into godly paths by examples that are inspired by benevolent love.[14]

This is a beautiful picture of marriage in line with Spirit and truth. Although positions may vary in how they express themselves in marriage for the couple, the responsibilities of love and submission are a complete picture of Jesus' prevailing mood and attitude towards the Church. This brings us to Jesus' next step. The final stage of coming back to center is the step of becoming the sacrifice in relationships.[15]

---

[14] Genesis 3:6

[15] For more information on the subject of marriage, see my study, *Women's Place in the Kingdom of God,* chapters 2-4, located in the fifth volume of the foundation series.

# 13

# SACRIFICE AND EXALTATION

As I stated in the previous chapter, God has provided an instrument to deal with self. It is the cross. We see that after Christ took on the form of a servant in the flesh, He humbled Himself. According to *Strong's Concordance,* He abased or brought Himself low. This was a heart response that would produce the necessary attitude or inclination to go on to the next steps of obedience and sacrifice. Once again, His lowliness of heart comes into focus, pointing to the temperament of His inward environment.

Philippians 2:8b tells us, "…he humbled himself and became obedient to death, even death on a cross." This action was contrary to Adam's response in the garden. He was disobedient and sacrificed Eve whom he blamed for his actions. The results were opposite. Death came through Adam and life came through Jesus.[1] The type of sacrifice Jesus made implies that self did not reign. It was the ultimate act of submission and the evidence of benevolent love towards the Father, on behalf of mankind.

Mathew 16:24 reminds us of our cross, "Then Jesus said to his disciples, If anyone would come after me, he must deny himself, and take up his cross, and follow me." It was not enough for Jesus to empty Himself; He had to go to the cross out of obedience and die. It is not enough that we deny ourselves of our vainglory; we must become obedient to the work of our personal cross in our lives.

The cross represents death to self. It is symbolic of pain and suffering. Scriptures are clear that if I want to live, I must die. If I want to reign with Him and share in His glory, I must suffer with Him. Suffering involves self-denial, and death means dying to one's right to live his or her life according to his or her terms.[2] In fact, the greatest obstacle with most married couples is that they want their spouse to adjust to their life according to their terms. This causes conflict as the spouse begins to resent being a servant rather than a partner. The typical battle comes down to spouses demanding their rights with each other, instead of doing what is right according to God. Such fruits reveal that godly submission and love are clearly missing.

Some of you may ask, "Are you trying to tell me Christianity is not a feel-good religion?" Nothing in Scripture gives such an impression. The

---

[1] Genesis 3:12; Romans 5:9-12
[2] Matthew 16:25; Romans 8:17; Philippians 3:10-11; 2 Timothy 2:11-12

way of Christ is that of self-denial and the way of a cross. It is the narrow path that leads to a life that does not always feel good, but it will prove to be rewarding in the end. Obviously, none of us can truly follow Jesus up this path until we deny ourselves and pick up our cross.[3]

Disciple means disciplined student or follower of Jesus. The cross is what disciplines followers of Jesus. Its adversity is what molds and shapes each of us as believers. Its relentless course is what makes us upright. Its harsh judgments are what try the heart, and its revelations of Jesus are what change the heart.

A Christian couple must come to terms with the personal application of the cross. Without the cross, there will be no victory in the marriage. Self will continue to reign with a vengeance. The flesh will continue to respond without reservation because there is no means of disciplining it effectively. The world will outweigh the unpleasantness of religious games that must be played to keep others from seeing the hypocrisy.

Jesus left us with an example of sacrifice. He would have been disobedient if He had not died on the cross. This is true for every Christian and every married couple. If they do not become a sacrifice, they are in blatant disobedience to our Lord.

Let us now consider how the cross is applied in our marriage relationship. We will finish the diagram we started with in the last chapter.

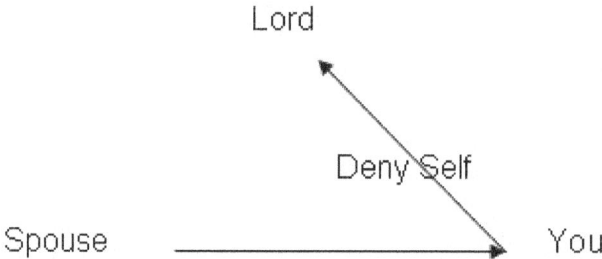

Lord

Deny Self

Spouse                                                You

You must first deny self before you can follow your Lord into a sacrificial life. Once you come into submission to the Lord, you can then follow Him by way of the cross. The cross not only ensures a right attitude, but it ensures that you will do right by your spouse instead of giving way to personal rights. Consider where the cross is applied.

---

[3] Matthew 7:13-14

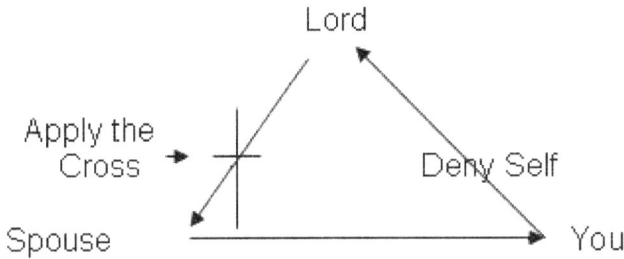

Lord

Apply the Cross

Spouse

Deny Self

You

Position can only be established when self is out of the way. Identity can only be realized when there is submission to the Lord and the cross has been applied to our way of thinking, doing, and being. It is at this point that the life of Christ will flow through us to our spouse. Such a life will display benevolence or good-will towards our mate.

This brings us to the sacrificial life that will be prevalent in a godly marriage. There were two types of sacrifices in the Old Testament. There were the necessary or mandatory sacrifices of the sin and trespass offerings, which were the offerings made for man's sins. I refer to these two sacrifices as being the dead sacrifices. There were also the sweet-savor or voluntary sacrifices that showed consecration (burnt offering), purity (meal offering), and intent (peace offering). I refer to these sacrifices as perpetual, ongoing, or living sacrifices that ultimately reach heaven in honor and glory of God. We see the contrast between these two types of offerings in Genesis 22. Abraham took Isaac up to Mount Moriah to offer him as a burnt offering. As he was about to offer up Isaac, God pointed out a ram to him. The ram was offered up as the dead sacrifice, while Isaac went on to serve as a perpetual living sacrifice for the glory of God.

In the case of Jesus and His Body, Jesus became the dead sacrifice, allowing His Church to become the perpetual living sacrifice, emitting a fragrance for the glory of God. This is confirmed in 2 Corinthians 2:14-16,

> Now thanks be to God, which always causeth us to triumph
> in Christ, and maketh manifest the savour of his knowledge
> by us in every place. For we are unto God a sweet savour
> of Christ, in them that are saved, and in them that perish:
> To the one we are the savour of death unto death; and to
> the other, the savour of life unto life. And who is sufficient
> for these things?

We see these sacrifices being advocated in marriage. We are told who must serve as the mandatory or dead sacrifice in Ephesians 5:25, "Husbands, love your wives, even as Christ also loved the church, and gave himself for it." The husband serves as the mandatory sacrifice. Such an offering allows the opportunity for his wife and family to be presented to the Lord in holiness and purity through the personal example of love and sacrifice. This is a tall order for the husband. His family cannot be purified unless he leads them into a growing

211

relationship with the Savior and Lord through personal example. Such a sacrifice cannot be prepared unless he willingly visits the laver, God's Word, daily to ensure personal cleansing. God's Word will change the prevailing tendency of the husband, causing him to know how to love Jesus and honor his wife. His prevailing mood will be that of humility, and his inclination will become godliness and sacrifice.

The husband who becomes a mandatory or dead sacrifice will give way to the perpetual living sacrifice. Giving way for the husband is translated through honor. Honor encourages the necessary freedom for the wife to become a perpetual living sacrifice. As a perpetual living sacrifice, the wife must do everything for the benefit of her family and the glory of her Lord. The wife is ultimately to serve as the godly fragrance of the family. This fragrance will reach the throne of her Lord.

Sacrifice does represent death and suffering. Dead people have no rights. They have nothing to lose and everything to gain. They cannot be blackmailed by the defilement of the flesh or bribed by the perversion of the world. This is why sacrifice is so necessary for Christian couples. They must lose personal rights in order to gain their true identity in Christ.

These two sacrifices represent the complete ministry of Jesus on behalf of man. Jesus, as the mandatory sacrifice, prepared the way for His Body, the living sacrifice so that He could be glorified through His Body. Once again, we get a glimpse of Jesus in marriage.

Can people see the ministry of Christ in your marriage? What kind of fragrance is coming from your family? Is it a pleasant odor to our Lord or is it a stench?

# Who is Being Lifted Up?

Godly sacrifice leads to exaltation. Jesus confirmed this in Luke 18:14b, "for every one that exalteth himself shall be abased; and he that humbleth himself shall be exalted."

The Apostle Peter made a similar statement in his first letter, "Humble yourselves therefore under the mighty hand of God, that he may exalt you in due time" (1 Peter 5:6).

And, in Philippians 2:9 we read, "Wherefore God also hath highly exalted him, and given him a name which is above every name."

Exaltation is the next step after sacrifice, but how does exaltation work in the marriage relationship? The first letter to the Corinthians gives us an insight into this exaltation. It stated, "But I would have you know, that the head of every man is Christ; and the head of the woman is man; and the head of Christ is God" (1 Corinthians 11:3).

Exaltation points to honor. As stated previously, both husband and wife are instructed to honor each other. Submission gives way to something that is worthy and honorable for the benefit of all involved; while love surrenders all for the sake of what is right and honorable. Submission comes into agreement with *what is right*, while love gives all in order to maintain and *uphold what is right*. You can see this principle in the physical relationship between a husband and his wife. The wife must submit herself to physically become one with her mate, while the husband must physically offer himself up to become one with his wife. In a sense, they are both giving up personal rights and identity to become the sacrifice that will ensure the well-being of each other. As a result, they are honoring the other above personal preference, and becoming one in identity.

The implication of exaltation or honor can be clearly seen in light of the examples set before us. God is the head of Christ, but according *to* Philippians 2:9-11 He will exalt Jesus above all creation. Christ is the head of man, yet as a servant in John 13, He abased Himself in order to exalt His disciples when He washed their feet.  Man is head of the woman. Based on the examples of both God and Christ, what must man do?  He must exalt her.  If a man exalts his godly wife, who will be lifted up? The answer is simple, her Lord. Jesus will be lifted up, and if He is lifted up, He will draw all men to Himself.[4]  In fact, He would have the liberty to draw the married couple's children to Himself.

Consider the center of a godly marriage in light of the following diagram.

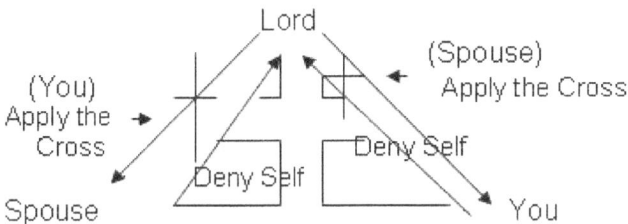

As you can see from the diagram, godly relationships have substance. When people deny self, look to the Lord, and become crucified to their ways, they cease to carry the marriage relationship. In fact, the relationship is upheld by their Lord, as He is lifted up and glorified in their midst and in their home. Note the existence of the cross in the midst of the relationship signifying sacrifice. Clearly, the vertical relationship (with Jesus) is exalting the horizontal relationship between the husband and wife, bringing communion and agreement in a godly manner.

A man must properly honor his wife so that she can give way to Christ. If Christ is Lord of the wife, He will rightfully be head of the husband, serving as his example. This is the way marriage was intended to work in the framework that was established by God through His Son, Jesus Christ.

The tragedy is that few Christians understand this concept. Husbands rarely exalt their wives in a godly fashion, and wives do not have the heart, understanding, or freedom to give way to their husband in submission to Christ. In such a relationship, honor is not practiced,

---

[4] John 12:32

love is conditional, submission is mocked, and sacrifice is unheard of. The results are death and destruction to the family.

Time is running out for Christians to turn this death sentence around. Repentance and the application of the cross is a must. Self-denial is necessary to ensure real life, and sacrifice must occur to ensure obedience and the exaltation of Christ.

What about you? How far will you go to stop the destruction of your family? Perhaps a good question is, do you even care? If you don't care, you have left your first love. You need to do what James 4:7-10 instructed,

> Submit yourselves, therefore, to God. Resist the devil, and he will flee from you. Draw nigh to God, and he will come near to you. Cleanse your hands, ye sinners; and purify your hearts, ye double-minded. Be afflicted, and, mourn, and weep: Let your laughter be turned to mourning, and your joy to heaviness. Humble yourselves in the sight of the Lord, and he shall lift you up.

# 14

# BECOMING ONE

It is in the heart of God that a married couple becomes one. Jesus confirmed this in Matthew 19:4-6,

> And he answered and said unto them, Have ye not read, that he which made them at the beginning made them male and female. And said, For this cause shall a man leave father and mother, and shall cleave to his wife: and they twain shall be one flesh? Wherefore they are no more twain, but one flesh. What therefore God hath joined together, let not man put asunder.

It is important for married couples to understand what this oneness implies. If Christian couples do not come to such a state of agreement, their marriage relationship will never fulfill its potential or purpose. To become one, a couple must become one in spirit and truth. In essence they will become likeminded about matters.

As we follow the progression of marriage, we can see where married couples must go through a process mentally, emotionally, and spiritually to come to a place of agreement. In fact, marriage entails a vow, a covenant, and a testimony. When people are married, they make a vow to consecrate themselves to one another in faithfulness. Such a vow is a mental agreement, where the couple recognizes that without placing this relationship in a right place emotionally and spiritually, it will never stand distinct or important. This particular idea of distinction is the same as sanctifying the Lord in our hearts.[1] Without setting Him apart in importance and worship, we will prove to be fickle and unpredictable in our devotion and service to Him,

The second aspect of the Christian marriage is the covenant that is associated with a relationship that has been sanctified by God. This covenant establishes moral and godly responsibilities that the couple must individually adhere to in order to establish a secure, healthy environment in their relationship. We have already discussed the spiritual aspects of submission and love in the marriage. These are the responsibilities that have been laid out for the Christian couple to ensure integrity and good will in their bond. The purpose of covenant is to not only establish a certain environment, but to ensure the right intent and attitude in regard to the relationship established towards one another. Such responsibility produces stable and realistic emotions. Without the

---

[1] 1 Peter 3:15

emotional commitment to that which is honorable and right, there will be no real place of accountability.

At this time it is vital to point out the reasons why so many problems in Christians' marriages remain unresolved. One of the main reasons for unresolved problems is because there is no real place of accountability. Without such accountability present, people will adhere to their own ideas about marriage and their responsibilities towards it. Since they see their ways as always being clean, they cannot imagine how they can be responsible for any destruction occurring in their marriage. Yet, if the couple can be called to a common point of accountability, there will be no debate or escape from facing one's personal part in the destructive cycle that is engulfing their relationship.

The second biggest problem in marriage is that there is no place of agreement. You cannot have a place of agreement unless you have a common point of accountability. For Christians their common point of accountability is the Word of God, but their place of agreement is the Lord. The point of accountability prepares people to humble themselves before each other, while the place of agreement requires them to submit to that which is worthy or greater in order to come into agreement to ensure that which is beneficial.

The final aspect of Christian marriage is that it is to serve as a testimony to others. A vow can be fulfilled, but a covenant is ongoing. Marriage has the capacity to be ongoing in the form of a testimony. Godly couples who come into complete oneness leave a tremendous heritage in regards to godliness, as well as serve as an ongoing testimony of Christ to their children and others who have witnessed and benefitted from their relationship. Godly marriage has a sweet taste to it, as well as a beautiful fragrance that reaches the throne of God. Since such a relationship represents that which is excellent in God's kingdom, godly marriage leaves a lasting impact that can affect the following generations.

The example and power of oneness can be clearly found and observed in the Godhead. For example, Jesus said in John 10:30, "I and my Father are one." To be one implies that there is oneness in agreement, authority, and purpose. The Word shows us that the three persons of the Godhead are in total agreement. They have one purpose—to bring mankind to salvation. They have the same authority but distinct responsibilities. Jesus always pointed to the authority of the Father. The Holy Spirit was and is the One who leads people to the revelation of Jesus. The Father pointed to the Son for salvation and sent the Spirit to build the Church upon the foundation of Christ.[2]

There is no competition or division between these three Persons. They are in submission to one another, showing preference towards one another as they exalt each other. Clearly in their example, submission points to coming into agreement with one another for a common goal

---

[2] Matthew 16:16-17; John 5:19-23, 26-30; 14:16-18, 26; 16:7-13; 1 Corinthians 3:11; 12:11-14

and purpose to ensure the betterment of a situation. Keep in mind, for this submission to occur, personal agendas must be put aside and priorities readjusted in order to change the focus. Ultimately, submission gives way to oneness that leads to the exaltation of those involved in the relationship. This is the secret of becoming one.

Self-exaltation and competition cause divisions and conflict. Matthew 12:25b tells us, "Every kingdom divided against itself is brought to desolation; and every city or house divided against itself shall not stand." Therefore, we do not have to go very far to understand why so many families are being destroyed.

Being one is a must for Christian couples. They must become one in spirit, purpose, and direction. There are three elements in becoming one. They are identification, agreement, and fellowship (intimacy). To become one, couples must give up personal identity in order to take on a new identity that is representative of the Spirit and attitude of Christ. Taking on a new identification involves entering in with the person for the purpose of ministry or doing right by the individual. Jesus gave up the glory of heaven to become identified with us. To call ourselves Christians means we have become identified with Jesus in His death, burial, and resurrection to be made in the righteousness of God. This ensures a new life that possesses resurrection power. However, before one can acquire a new identity, the person must deny the old man and crucify the flesh that serves as a source of the old man's existence.

Becoming one was the purpose of marriage in the first place. Eve was taken out of Adam's side, leaving him incomplete. God completed Adam again by bringing Eve to him and instructing them to become one. This is why Paul reminds men that they are to love their wives as their own body.[3]

To become one can be related to another scriptural concept of, *"being equally yoked."*[4] To be equally yoked points to spiritual agreement. In marriage there is a concept that there is more importance accredited to the role of husband than the wife. Obviously, "equal" means that those who are yoked together are equally important to maintain the balance and function of the task ahead. Balance comes when people recognize their particular responsibility and when they are equally carrying their weight. As those who are yoked together come into agreement about the purpose or goal of their task, they will be able to define their path, bringing into focus their destination. As Amos 3:3 points out, "Can two walk together, except they be agreed?"

There are some misconceptions about the term *unequally yoked.* This became evident when I was contending with a young married woman. This woman had grown up in a Christian family. In her teenage years, she became rebellious and started dating a man who was in the drug scene. Her parents were greatly opposed to the relationship, so she moved into this man's house where they lived together for a time before

---

[3] Genesis 2:21-24; Ephesians 5:28-29
[4] 2 Corinthians 6:14

finally marrying. They had a child, and much to her displeasure she found that some of his former lifestyle followed them into parenthood. This concerned her because she wanted their child to be spared from any introduction to possible destructive lifestyles.

As I confronted some of the more visible issues plaguing their marriage, I sensed that this young woman had no regret about the type of shaky foundation her marriage was founded upon. One day the subject of her pre-marital relationship with her husband came up. I asked her how could she have become involved with a man to whom she was unequally yoked. She looked at me with a puzzled expression. I then asked her what the term meant to her. She told me she had been taught that this term referred to people marrying those of different races.

The term "unequally yoked" is found in 2 Corinthians 6:14. The context in this reference has to do with agreement between people of different spirits. This is poignantly brought home in 2 Corinthians 6:15-16, "And what concord hath Christ with Belial? or what part hath he that believeth with an infidel?"

In the Old Testament, this principle is mentioned repeatedly. God called for a total separation of Israel from foreign influences. Naturally, these influences included intermarriage with people of different faiths and influences. The Israelites were to drive out the godless nations of the land. This action was to prevent these idolatrous people from becoming snares to Israel by encouraging the people to worship other gods. Idolatry would ultimately defile God's people, resulting in judgment.[5]

The importance of this separation was upheld and carried out in the days of Ezra and Nehemiah. Israel had come back to the land of Judah to build a temple and a new life. To the shock of these two leaders, certain Levite men had married foreign wives and had brought them and their children to the land that was set apart for an undefiled nation. This caused Ezra to visibly mourn, resulting in Israel mourning and repenting. However, Nehemiah took more drastic actions. He rebuked these men, called curses down on them and pulled out their hair. In the end, the Levites had to actually send their wives and children back to their own countries.[6] What a heartbreak!

Believers who marry unbelievers usually meet with the same type of heartache. Jesus admitted He did not come to bring peace, but a sword that would cause division or separation. There is always a battle going on between light and darkness. This is true in marriages where believers have married unbelievers. I have seen how unevenly yoked marriages erode the resolve of believers, causing some of them to fall into compromise, idolatry, and spiritual bankruptcy.[7]

It would be wonderful if every Christian obeyed 2 Corinthians 6:14. They would spare themselves of a lot of unnecessary heartache. The sad part is Christians allow feelings and lusts to win over scriptural

---

[5] Joshua 24:14-24; Judges 2:1-3
[6] Ezra 9 & 10; Nehemiah 13:23-25
[7] Matthew 10:34-39

instruction. Many think they are an exception and not the rule, and that their relationship will beat the odds. They end up putting God to a foolish test, and eventually find themselves living a nightmare.

The harsh reality always hits home when these people find out that God's Word is true. Light cannot effectively mix with darkness. The godly instructions they chose to ignore in the first place now require them to take responsibility for their actions. Christian spouses must become godly examples to their mates regardless of the situation. Godly conduct is the means of not only sanctifying the family, but also possibly opening up an unbelieving spouse to the Lord, so that he or she can be brought to salvation. But, in spite of this wrong mixture and its many challenges, Christians are encouraged to stay in this relationship unless there is the breaking of the vow, covenant, or the unbelieving partner wants to leave.[8]

There is another widely accepted misconception about being unequally yoked. Many believe that to be evenly yoked with someone only requires the individual to be a Christian. This is not true! Many committed Christians have fallen for this fallacy and have paid dearly.

The term "equally yoked" is based on teams of oxen and horses. These teams were carefully matched. Each animal had to be *equally* submitted, committed, and fitted. This entailed matching the size, strength, and disposition of the animals.

Each animal had to be equally committed to pull their weight to ensure one did not become overburdened by doing the work for two. Each animal had to be equally in subjection to guarantee there was no division that would hinder the job from being done in an orderly manner. Each beast had to be fitted according to responsibilities and work habits. Yokes and harnesses were even designed to keep them equal in position and stride. All these measures were taken to ensure that a capable and qualified team was established to do the best job.

Only God can establish a godly team. Jesus made this quite clear in Matthew 19:6b, "What therefore God hath joined together, let not man put asunder." God brought Eve to Adam, and He likewise needs to bring prospective mates to each Christian.

Problems occur when Christians get anxious about their mates. Many do not realize that God must prepare both parties spiritually, mentally, and emotionally to complement each other. He must ensure personal godliness in both people to establish the maturity and attitude in which to entrust another person's spiritual well-being. Sadly, many Christians fantasize about marrying a godly person, but fail to become godly. They remain spiritually immature. Such immaturity is nothing more than selfishness.

God's timing to bring the right spouse is perfect, but in their impatience, many Christians begin to look for this person on their own. Satan, who is always quick to accommodate the impatient person, sends in a counterfeit.

---

[8] 1 Corinthians 7:1-16

One of the most interesting courtships I have read about involved the one between James and Elizabeth Elliot. To my recollection their sweet, non-committal relationship spanned five years before they felt God ordained their marriage. They had spent only a couple of happy years together when James laid down his life on the mission field.

We could look at the circumstances surrounding the Elliot's and call it shamefully unfair. They could have had more years of married life together if they had not waited. But, God's timing is perfect and always in line with eternity. God does not look at situations in the same way we do. He has an overall view of everything, while we have a very limited view. The Elliot's wanted God to ordain their marriage. It had to be His will and His timing. By faith, they accepted His plan for their lives. Only in eternity will God unveil the full reasons behind His purpose and timing.

Another important ingredient to ensure oneness is like-mindedness. Romans 15:5-6 states, "Now the God of patience and consolation grant you to be likeminded one toward another according to Christ Jesus: That ye may with one mind and one mouth glorify God, even the Father of our Lord Jesus Christ." According to *Strong's Exhaustive Concordance*, like-mindedness in this Scripture has two meanings. One meaning points to having all of your affections in the same place. Affections have a lot to do with priorities, dispositions, and desires.

On one occasion, I spoke with a counselor who was ministering to a couple I had been working with. This counselor referred to the couple as being equally yoked because both were born again. I agreed, but reminded the counselor that division was occurring because of the different level of commitments they were displaying in their Christian lives.

Levels of commitment determine how much regenerating and sanctifying work the Holy Spirit is able to do. The work of the Holy Spirit makes a new wineskin that is distinctively different from the old wineskin.[9] This means the carnality of our flesh and mind is being transformed, changing our priorities and desires to line up with the character of Jesus Christ. The goal of this transformation is to make Jesus. Lord of the person's life. Therefore, it should not be a surprise to find nestled within the confines of Romans 15:5 the key to ensure like-mindedness between individuals, "...according to Christ Jesus."

Once Jesus is Lord, the main thrust of a person's affections will be directed at Him. This will result in obedience to the command found in Colossians 3:1-2, "If ye then be risen with Christ, seek those things which are above, where Christ sitteth on the right hand of God. Set your affection on things above, not on things on the earth."

In a Christian's life, carnality resents sharing affections with anyone, including Jesus Christ. It will become jealous, critical, and judgmental of others whose lives are totally dedicated to Christ. It will deride any evidence of spiritual maturity. It will not listen to wise instructions or warnings. The tragic result of carnality is an unrepentant, cynical

---

[9] Matthew 9:14-17

response to the Lordship of Christ, and a hard heart towards the person of Jesus.

Spirituality and carnality in the lives of Christian couples rarely mix in a marriage relationship. Like gold in its separation process, the dross (carnality) will float to the surface, while the pure gold (spirituality) will remain in the heat for greater refinement. The separation ends in battle lines being drawn as each individual decides whether Jesus is going to truly be Lord of his or her life.

Another definition of like-mindedness is having the same mind. The mind represents beliefs and callings. Admittedly, it is hard for two Christians with different theologies to come into genuine agreement unless they possess maturity and the same agenda and call.

To have the same agenda or call means both partners will be moving in the same direction. Often, I have come into agreement with Christians who may hold different beliefs from myself, but our agenda is the same: *Christ crucified.*[10] Our goal is to see the salvation of souls. We are not interested in converting people to some kind of belief system, but to the person of Jesus. After all, personal beliefs never saved anyone; only an encounter with Jesus brings salvation.

It is vital that people who have a call on their lives understand that their future partner needs to have the same vision. This is necessary if they are to go in the same direction. If individuals are going in two different directions spiritually, the result will be strife and contention. This division can stifle a person's call, causing God's kingdom to take a back seat. Initially, God's call on our lives may seem elusive. Daily obedience to the vision God gives us is a prerequisite for fulfillment of the call. Obedience determines the direction we are to take on a daily basis. We can see this in the life of Jesus.

Like-mindedness also implies one spirit. The Apostle Paul confirmed this in Philippians 2:2, "Fulfil ye my joy, that ye be likeminded, having the same love, being of one accord, of one mind." Here we see the call for similarity in spirit or motivation and purpose. However, we see this spirit and purpose is motivated by love.

The love Paul is talking about is not fleshly, lustful, and self-serving, but selfless and sacrificial. It abounds more and more because of the knowledge and depth of Christ in our lives. This love is submissive in attitude, humble in spirit, and obedient in response.[11]

Love brings us to the final element of being one, that of fellowship or intimacy. The intimacy I am talking about for married couples is not found in the physical arena. Granted, it will be manifested in the physical realm. The intimacy I am talking about is that ability to reason together. Most couples are fighting, instead of reasoning together to seek the heart and mind of God. The inability to reason together means there is a breakdown in communication.

---

[10] 1 Corinthians 2:2
[11] Philippians 1:8-11; 1 Corinthians 13

There can be no real communication unless there is agreement. In other words, there must be a point of agreement before each person will be able to humble him or herself to seek that which is worthy or excellent. However, there cannot be agreement, unless there is identification. Identification means we have become identified to the individual for the purpose of doing right by him or her or ministering to the person. Such identification will not happen without submission and honor.

Without communication, the walls between couples grow. Walls cause vulnerability and weaknesses in the relationship. This produces speculation, mistrust, and loneliness. It is important for each of us to realize that the level of intimacy in the marriage will determine the prevailing temperament in this relationship. The temperament will express itself in the attitudes that the individuals display towards each other.

Obviously, many couples experience problems because they are not equally yoked. Some operate totally from the flesh. This allows another spirit to motivate their lives. Some desire God's will, but succumb to hopelessness as the struggle between the Lordship of Christ and their spouse escalates.

Right now, you may be in such a marriage. Keep your eyes on Christ. Let Him have His way in your life and marriage regardless of what is going on. Begin to press forward towards the high calling you have in Jesus. Be faithful to Him and His Word, and He will be faithful to keep you and deliver you through all types of situations.

Right now you may be looking for a mate. Stop! Give God permission to bring your future partner to you. Meanwhile, be faithful to your God and the vision He has given you. Give Him permission to prepare you for your future spouse. Establish the elements of oneness by becoming one with Jesus, so they will come natural to you in your marriage. Never settle for second best, but do not expect your future partner to settle for second best in you either.

Pray and wait. Waiting is the biggest test. It is hard on the flesh, and challenging to the pride. Keep in mind, a lifetime partner is a serious matter best left in the capable hands of God. Think about it.

# 15

# GODLY ATTITUDES

What is your attitude towards marriage? Attitudes are the manifestation of our disposition. The harsh reality about our disposition is that it is selfish to the core. The main desire of selfishness is to be god of its world. It wants all that is in its environment to revolve around it. This self-serving disposition wants to determine reality, be adored, and worshipped.

Due to this disposition, people must give up their personal identity to ensure a proper disposition. For married couples this means giving up their personal identity in order to establish a new identity with each other. Sadly, most people marry to have their spouse reaffirm or confirm their identity. They have no intention of giving it up. Needless to say, this causes a tremendous amount of disillusionment and conflict.

The unrealistic attitude most people possess about marriage is the biggest hindrance when it comes to them realizing that marriage is not a fantasy, but a relationship in which the different challenges of life are constantly intruding. The first casualty in this fantasy is the emotional hype. Every couple must land from their fairytale ideas of marriage and begin to live in a real world of responsibilities, drudgery, differences, and transitions.

The next casualty is the expectations people have towards marriage. The images and masks come off to reveal the real person. Weaknesses, irritating habits, and different mannerisms come to the forefront. Strengths often become a form of control and manipulation. One of the first shocks that couples must endure is that at times they actually will not like each other.

When reality finally strips away all the fantasy, there is not much left. It is at this point couples make one of two decisions, 1) My spouse is a joke and I have made a big mistake, or 2) it is time to grow up and begin to work on this relationship. In the first case, people often become disillusioned about marriage, and deem it as the culprit or failure. In the second situation, the person learns that marriage is not a give and take relationship; rather, it requires our best in the challenging times and our all in the daily drudgeries and responsibilities.

To properly confront marriage, it is vital that people start out with a realistic view of both it and their partner. A realistic view does not mean people will be prepared for what they may experience in this relationship, but it does mean they will not be shocked. There is no way one can understand either the good or the challenging aspects of living with another individual in this type of relationship until they experience it.

Disillusionment towards marriage will cause us to become mean spirited towards our spouse as we struggle to tolerate or get through each day with a stranger that we may not trust or respect. As we become mean spirited, we become unreasonable. For Christians, this means they become unreceptive towards the truth of God. It is at this point that people justify ungodly attitudes and actions.

Being mean spirited just means we are motivated by another spirit and are operating according to our selfish disposition. At this point we want our way. The ability to reason with us in such a frame is missing as we give way to personal logic that makes us right in our own eyes. For each nature this unreasonableness is expressed in different ways.

As previously pointed out, the submissive person comes across as pigheaded. No amount of reasoning can penetrate his or her mind to bring proper instruction or challenge. Stubborn people become bullheaded. They will not be moved, and when push comes to shove, they will push their way past any reasoning or warnings. For the self-assured, they become mule-headed. This means they cannot be budged, but they will also cause tremendous chaos in their environment to change the focus from their mulish ways to others. Strong-willed people prove to be hardheaded. Nothing will get through their wall, but at the same time there will be harshness when you push up against their wall to challenge their present reality.

It is also important to start out with the right type of attitude towards marriage. Wrong attitudes are usually expressed in conflict or when people become disillusioned. For the submissive person a wrong attitude will make him or her unmanageable when he or she sense failure, stubborn people will prove to be undisciplined when they become vulnerable, the self-assured unyielding when exposed, and the strong-willed will be unruly when proven to be wrong.

For Christians, there is no excuse for not possessing godly attitudes when it comes to marriage regardless of their nature. The Apostle Paul set the tone for the type of attitude believers should have towards this institution by referring to marriage as a gift in 1 Corinthians 7:7. According to *Strong's Concordance,* "gift" means spiritual endowment or qualification. Like the gift of salvation, these gifts are free and are meant to complement our lives before God.

Marriage was a special gift given by God. It was meant to bless a man and a woman in a covenant, and to represent Him in a special way. Today this gift from God is receiving a bad rap due to the attitudes that a percentage of society has towards it. We are watching our society becoming more and more insane about this institution.

Encouraged alternative lifestyles mock this institution and perversion of every sort is abusing it. Some Christians are using it to cover up lust, while society at large is rejecting its sacredness. There is a relentless move to change or redefine the moral and legal laws of this nation to whitewash evilness, and slander the Creator and His purpose behind this institution. This blatant attack against marriage is producing delusion and destruction.

God's plan and purpose for marriage has not changed and it will never deviate from the original pattern. Regardless of man's attempt to modify or abolish the established laws of God, the design of marriage will remain unaltered as it was established in the Garden of Eden. God put one man and one woman together. He will not change this design because men or women want to give in to every wicked imagination, whim, and drive without being challenged by what has been established as righteousness by God.

It is time to agree with God and His Word. We must repent of all compromises and disrespect we have shown to God, His Word, marriage, and our spouse. We must begin to separate ourselves from those things which are unholy. We must call upon the name of the Lord and invite Him back into our lives and homes as Lord and only Savior.

The presence of God in our midst will make a difference. It is His presence that sanctifies and changes hearts. God's presence will establish godly attitudes and give us an eternal perspective.

# Investing in the Eternal

How should you look at your spouse? What kind of spiritual investment must you make in the life of your partner? Sometimes it is hard to think objectively when we consider our mates. We are too close and too familiar with them. We know their shortcomings, hypocrisies, and sins. At times, this familiarity makes it hard to respect them and cynicism results.

Marriage is a temporary relationship. Jesus assured us there would be no marriages in heaven because we would be like the angels.[1] For some of you, the idea of not having to put up with your spouse for eternity is a great relief. But, what must you emphasize in your everyday relationship with your mate? It is simple; you must see him or her as an eternal investment.

Perhaps you are married to an unbeliever. The destination of his or her soul represents the eternal perspective. Your spouse is a mission field to which you must be faithful. At best, your mate represents your nearest friendly neighbor, and at worst, he or she could be your worst enemy. The Word tells us we are to love both our neighbor and our enemy.[2] According to Mark 12:31, we are to treat this neighbor in the same way that we would want to be treated.

Romans 12:17, 20-21 give us this insight into our enemy, "Recompense to no man evil for evil. Provide things honest in the sight of all men...Therefore if thine enemy hunger, feed him; if he thirst, give him drink: for in so doing thou shalt heap coals of fire on his head. Be not overcome of evil, but overcome evil with good."

---

[1] Matthew 22:30
[2] Matthew 5:43-44

The reason for treating a spouse in an upright manner can be found in 1 Corinthians 7:14, "For the unbelieving husband is sanctified by the wife, and the unbelieving wife is sanctified by the husband: else were your children unclean; but now are they holy." There is always hope that the unbelieving spouse will come to the saving knowledge of Jesus Christ through example.

Perhaps your spouse is a believer. When spouses are believers, they often fall short of godly conduct. Failing to practice what they preach can make these spouses appear as the biggest hypocrite in your life. We are all hypocrites in our own way. We all fall short of our Lord's glory.[3] If you find yourself in this type of situation, you need to give the other person a break. Keep in mind that you will be spending eternity with this person, not as your spouse, but as a brother or sister in the Lord. You also have scriptural responsibilities to them.

Romans 12:10 tells each of us, "Be kindly affectioned one to another with brotherly love; in honour preferring one another." Regardless of how you feel about your spouse, you must honor or prefer him or her above yourself. In order to be obedient to this instruction, you must first deny self.

Honoring others above self is what rests at the core of all godly relationships. Honor involves humility of self and exaltation of others. As servants to their Lord, Christians must realize it is not about them, but about the spiritual welfare of those for whom Christ died. To recognize this reality, believers must get past self in order to prefer others to themselves. As long as everything is about self, people will fall through the cracks and disappear into the abyss.

It is obvious that as believers we cannot get away from our absolute need to apply the cross to our own life. It is necessary to apply the cross to avoid superior attitudes towards spouses who are failing to meet personal expectations. Honorable preference towards others squelches prideful, unyielding attitudes.

Once we get past ourselves, we can actually live in harmony. This harmony brings us into obedience to Romans 12:16, "Be of the same mind one toward another. Mind not high things, but condescend to men of low estate. Be not wise in your own conceits."

When you consider the instructions found in Romans 12 and the condition of Christian homes and churches, it is easy to see that Christians who are in crisis need to get back to basic Christianity. We have strayed away from obedience to the Word. James 1:22-24 makes this point,

> But be ye doers of the word, and not hearers only, deceiving your own selves. For if any be a hearer of the word, and not a doer, he is like unto a man beholding his natural face in a glass: For he beholdeth himself, and goeth his way, and straightway forgetteth what manner of man he was.

---

[3] Romans 3:23

If individuals excuse themselves from being obedient, the results will be devastating. They will actually lose sense of their identity as saints.

It is not surprising to me that counseling offices are full of discontented couples. We have moved away from the simplicity of Christ and His heart concerning our lives.

Relationships are vital and must be worked out here on earth. The reason we need to work out our relationships with others is because they affect our relationship with God. God has given us instructions concerning our heart, attitude, and responses toward others. Non-compliance to these principles means disobedience. God cannot bless rebellion.

God has wisely set these rules down to work godly attitudes in us. He actually uses others in our life as sharpening iron.[4] This iron is to work selfishness out of us by sharpening and refining. Every time we demand our own way, we stop or hinder this valuable process.

Is your attitude and your actions towards your spouse godly? If not, you need to take responsibility for your disposition and repent. Repentance will set you free to make the right investment in your partner.

# Communication

Clearly, in the initial stages of falling in love with our future partner, we cannot say or share enough with them. The communication is pleasant and full. We open ourselves up to them because we do not fear rejection or disapproval. We have confidence in a relationship that appears to be sure and immovable.

Then marriage comes, and one of the first areas challenged is communication. Many couples become silent strangers in their own homes. Real communication becomes rare, and if there is any conversing, it is either superficial or confrontational.

There are a couple of reasons communication breaks down. One reason is that many people fail to establish true intimacy. We have already considered this subject in a previous chapter. However, intimacy is something that must be worked into a marriage. When trust is being replaced with walls of mistrust, the intimacy will be lacking. Lack of intimacy is what causes the greatest frustration in many relationships. Without it there is no satisfaction. If satisfaction is missing, it creates loneliness in the marriage that often mocks the person. It is in this state of vulnerability that people fall into traps through temptation.

Another reason for a lack of communication is because people use words to tear down rather than lovingly challenge to build up. Ephesians 4:29, 31-32 tells us,

> Let no corrupt communication proceed out of your mouth, but that which is good to the use of edifying, that it may minister grace unto the hearers...Let all bitterness, and wrath, and anger, and clamour,

---

[4] Proverbs 27:17

and evil speaking, be put away from you, with all malice: And be ye kind one to another, tenderhearted, forgiving one another, even as God for Christ's sake hath forgiven you.

We have no right to demean or belittle anyone, but many couples use words as a means to strike out because of hurt, or to put a person in his or her place to control a situation. This ungodly method erects walls and brings bondage.

We need to discipline our tongue regardless of what is going on. James 1:26 states, "If any man among you seem to be religious, and bridleth not his tongue, but deceiveth his own heart, this man's religion is vain."

James goes on to give us these clear illustrations about the tongue in James 3:6 and 10,

And the tongue is a fire, a world of iniquity: so is the tongue among our members, that it defileth the whole body, and setteth on fire the course of nature; and it is set on fire of hell…Out of the same mouth proceedeth blessing and cursing. My brethren, these things ought not so to be.

Satan does not have to be too active when there is an uncontrollable tongue on the scene. This small member of humanity has done more to tear down relationships than any other means. Couples need to control this wicked device, but many give way to it, causing hurt, and destroying respect and trust. When will we learn? When will we obey God's instructions? So much hurt would be avoided if only Christian couples would comply with the instructions in God's Word.

Another problem in communication is responding out of assumptions. Many people have an unrealistic, immature idea of love. They assume if their partner really loved them, they would be able to read between the lines and sense what their desires or needs are. I have not met one person who could really read the mind of his or her spouse.

Cycles begin as the insulted partner interprets the lack of understanding or response from his or her spouse as a sign of not being loved. Misunderstandings, hurt, anger, and conflicts are the byproducts of these assumptions.

Each nature has a different way of assuming. For example, *submissive* people will usually fail to give details about how they feel regarding something. They will quietly hope the spouse is sensitive enough to sense their reluctance or their lack of comfort with a situation. Needless to say, submissive people are left behind to contend with their fear or their feeling of being insignificant to their mates.

*Stubborn* people assume you should know how they feel. They become very hurt when their spouse not only fails to respond, but reveals that they do not have a clue as to what is going on. To stubborn people, this translates that their mate does not love them.

*Self-assured* people think about pending plans. They think about them so much that they begin to assume or believe that they have communicated these thoughts to their spouse. When these people are met with no response from their spouse, they become angry and begin to accuse and condemn their mate for irresponsibility. Because the spouse was never verbally informed and had no idea what the self-assured mate had planned, the fight is on.

*Strong-willed* people are so factual that they believe their conclusions should be obvious to those around them. They perceive that their spouse should know what is on the agenda and do it. They do not stop to think that it is not obvious to their spouse, or to others as well, and that there needs to be communication.

Real communication is not criticism or assumptions. *Webster's New Collegiate Dictionary* defines communication as an actual process by which information is exchanged between individuals through a common system of symbols, signs, and behavior in order to exchange ideas. Real communication involves interaction and ends in understanding.

Jesus Christ was God's means of communicating to man. He never assumed anything about man's understanding. We see Him carrying out the process of real communication in symbols, signs, and behavior. He taught with parables, reinforced them with miracles, and upheld them with examples. He was patient and persistent. Although He reproved His disciples for their unbelief, He continued to teach them truths in meekness.

Communication is a necessary tool that must not be abused. Christian couples must begin to communicate in a godly manner. They need to seek agreement to ensure intimacy, as well as ask God to put a guard on their lips like David in Psalm 141:3. They must avoid making assumptions.

Without godly communication, couples often resort to games of control and manipulation. These games are not only a form of control, but they lack integrity. Ultimately, they will end in mistrust, destroying the inner core of the relationship.

# Games People Play

The games people play are at best deceptive and at worst destructive. In summation, they are false ways because they encourage a false reality. Since God is light and operates in truth, such games are deceptive and unacceptable. Psalm 119:104 says, "Through thy precepts I get understanding: therefore I hate every false way." Sadly, many develop these games to control situations or people. It is not unusual for people to play sexual, emotional, and mental games to gain control as a means to get their way with their spouse.

Each of these natures has their own way of playing the game to get their partners to fall into line with demands. For instance, *submissive* people will withdraw in a noticeable way, hoping someone will come after them and show them they are important. In some cases, they play games by dramatizing illnesses or physical problems to get attention.

*Stubborn* people in their frustration and anger will push their spouse away to gain control. They are like a porcupine, bristling in every direction. But in reality, they are actually asking their spouse to enter in with them and fight for them to prove their love and commitment. There are times spouses should fight for their stubborn mates, but they must never allow these outbursts to become a constant means to gain attention.

*Self-assured* people often use silence in the form of pouting and self-pity to get a person to recognize them and their plight. An attitude of anger will also be evident which may cause nervous spouses to try to appease them.

*Strong-willed* people will try to maintain control by using intimidation to get their spouse to agree with them. They will also throw a bone to keep their mates off their back as they continue on the same path, or they will choose to ignore the situation altogether. They will wait for another time to present their case and hopefully change the other's mind. Even though they may be trying to understand, their lines will keep them bound to their already formed decisions or ideas.

People also use their strengths to control their spouses. This causes real irritation because it is the strengths of their mate that usually attracted them in the first place. At first, these strengths seem to complement personal weaknesses. When strengths overlap a person's weaknesses and vise versa, couples will feel they have an unbeatable combination. However, this possible combination begins to unravel as individuals begin to recognize that these strengths are often used as a means of control. Suddenly, these strengths become culprits in the battle of the wills.

The games of control and manipulation people play have no rules, and are unfair to all concerned. They lack integrity and are without mercy. They are void of respect and the fear of God. They are motivated by pride, and therefore, lack submission and meekness.

As Christians, we must recognize the games we play and cease from playing them. These games are often played out of habit, and are part of the destructive cycle. It is not easy to break these habits, but we must if we are to be victorious. At the core of the game playing is the selfish disposition. It is reigning, and God resists such prideful nonsense. Spouses will eventually become wise to the games and become resentful. A person who plays such games eventually loses credibility and respect.

Are you a game player? You need to cease and repent. You are playing a dangerous game of Russian roulette with your relationship, and eventually, you will lose.

# 16

# RESTORATION

There are many reasons for the failure of Christian marriages. We could never exhaust the excuses for these failures. Over 97% of the spiritual validity for such failure could be a matter of debate in the sanctuaries of our churches. But I believe in my heart that until Christians and the Church confront the idolatry, bring down the various sacred cows, distinguish the difference between the old man and the new creation, ensure real salvation, a growing relationship with Jesus, and submission to His Lordship, we will continue to see Satan win in the family.

It is God's will to restore all ailing marriages, but Christians need to quit being just pew warmers in church and bystanders to the problems confronting their homes, and become part of the solution. Each Christian must take personal responsibility for his or her personal attitudes and actions.

I realize this is easier said than done. In ministering to couples in troubled marriages, I have seen one consistent ingredient: These tormented individuals are basically lost. They are in an identity crisis because they have no idea who they are in Christ.

They have sought their identity in relationships, people, religious activities, jobs, worldly pursuits, and even in their manhood or womanhood. They have sought after direction for their life because they are discontent and miserable. I encourage these lost individuals to seek to know the person and character of Jesus Christ. Genesis 1:1 states "In the beginning God created the heavens and the earth."

Jesus said this in Revelation 1:8, "I am the Alpha and the Omega, the beginning and the ending, saith the Lord, which is, and which was, and which is to come, the Almighty." Obviously, everything begins and ends with our Creator. Mankind usually begins with self to find self, but we must start at the point of who our God is and end with Him being pre-eminent in our lives if we are to find our true identity.[1] It is only within the boundaries of the "Alpha and Omega" that our identity will be revealed, our manhood or womanhood understood, our authority received, our position illuminated, and our ministry established.

With this in mind, I explain to these confused individuals that they will never understand who they are until they first come to know their Lord intimately. After all, our identity is in Christ, and as we begin to know Jesus, we will begin to get a sense of who we are. Once we start

---

[1] Colossians 1:15-18

knowing who we are, our potential will be realized, our gifts brought forth, and our confidence developed and rooted in the true source and Vine of our lives.[2]

Restoration is not only God's desire; it must be our choice. We must choose to let God be our solution and seek Him and His direction. We must deny self and pursue His righteousness. We must become responsible for our actions and be quick to minister the life of Jesus to those around us.

Each of the natures has different areas in life to become accountable and responsible for. For example, *submissive* people need to become responsible to confront others. They must take accountability for conceit and dramatization. They must seek God's perspective.

*Stubborn* individuals must take responsibility for their emotions, tongues, and imaginations. They need to discipline these three areas. Before they can bring order in these areas, they must become accountable for their selfishness, and their harsh and unyielding standards. These sacred cows will not let anyone off the hook, so they must be identified and put down.

*Self-assured* people must take responsibility for their pride, anger, and cruelty, and do away with them. The only way they can put these responses down is to be accountable for incorrectly accepting assumptions over truth, and become compassionate in order to avoid being an unreasonable judge.

*Strong-willed* individuals must become flexible. They must take responsibility for the havoc their persistent control causes others. They must put down this control by realizing that it is often in competition with God and His best.

Christians must become servants in their marriages and Christian examples to their children. Ministering the life of Christ is not an option, but a responsibility. This is the only way this destructive trend that is separating families will be turned around.

We even see a trend in the church of separating families. Families are broken up and go in every direction when they come to church. Each family member goes to his or her separate little niche. Yet, the Church is supposedly concerned about the survival of the family unit. The purpose of the whole Body of Christ is for edification of all members of the Church in love and unity.[3] How can our young people learn to pray and minister if they are not allowed to come alongside those who minister? When do the older godly men and women teach the younger men and women about self-respect, chastity, and inward strength or beauty? Where do divorced, troubled, lonely, or lost people find caring Christians who will actually minister to their hurts and needs, and be available to them in practical ways?

I believe the end of the article, *"The 1ˢᵗ Church of the Program,"* by Robert L. Rees identified the real problem with the majority of Christians

---

[2] John 15:1-8; Ephesians 3:16-18
[3] Ephesians 4:16

and the Church. In the midst of all the activity of directing each person to his or her proper class: that of married couples, pre-teens, teens, singles, and the divorced, there was one more speaker to be heard who was called Master. This speaker, Jesus, raised His hands to speak. Mr. Rees's article concluded, "But the sheep had all dispersed to their scheduled classes. No one was there at His feet." [4]

How we need to come back to the foundation of Christianity, Jesus Christ. God needs to send the fresh wind of the Holy Spirit to impart the balm of Gilead to the family. But before He can do this, Christians must bow their stiff, independent necks, and submit their self-sufficient hearts at the feet of Jesus. They need to yield their carnal minds to the Holy Spirit to be transformed, as Jesus is unveiled in greater glory. They need to become humble in order to allow Him to minister to them so they, in turn, can minister properly to their spouse and children. This is not only the secret for spiritual survival for the family, but also for revival of the soul.

When was the last time you sat at the feet of Jesus?

---

[4] For review on this article see chapter 1.

## 17

## THE BREAKDOWN

One of my favorite shows on TV was *The Dog Whisperer*. It is amazing how one man, Cesar Millan, can take an out-of-control dog and change its behavior in a matter of minutes. The one consistent theme you can observe through the whole program is that an out-of-control dog signifies an environment that is out of order.

As you consider each incident, you realize that the environment is not out of order because the dog is out of control. Rather, the dog is out of control because it is running the household in some way. Clearly, it amazes most people that a two-pound dog is actually calling the shots in a home, but it is a reality that cannot be ignored. When Millan hits the scene, he knows in most cases it will take a matter of minutes to bring the dog into order. However, the real challenge posed to him is not the dog but the owners.

As people who know us will testify, we have an six-pound Chihuahua mix that pretty well calls the shots in our home at times. Thanks to Millan's show, we have been given some valuable tools in which to remedy our dog's behavior. We had to recognize the problem rests with how we look at our dog. After all, she is a dog. The affection and pleasure we take in her personality feeds our selfishness, but as a dog, she is not getting her needs met—that of exercise and discipline. The reality is she has taken the position as the head of the pack because we have conceded to her. As a result, her behavior has adjusted accordingly. To change her behavior, we had to first change our attitude.

As we consider the world we live in, there is only one correct conclusion: it is out of order. We can always look at those individuals who are out of order, and declare they are the source of the problem. However, chaos originates with people's way of thinking and attitudes. Therefore, the lack of order can be traced to wrong thinking.

As you trace an out-of-order society, it will lead you to the one place that screams chaos, and that is the home. If order is lacking in the home, it will spill over into our society. Each point that is out of order will cause confusion, escalating into destructive consequences.

Consider the behavior of those who make up gangs. Obviously, these people are out of order. They are clearly thinking wrongly, but where did such thinking begin? What kind of breeding ground produced the behavior that reinforced their wrong thinking? In most cases you will find that their homes are out of order. These young people have become lost in their way of thinking and in their mode of behavior.

Homes that are out of order can start with an abusive or indifferent parent. It can be identified because there are no set rules in the home, or responsibilities that would give a person a sense of direction, accountability, or discipline. In fact, a person needs to feel as if he or she belongs. Such people can only function properly when there is security. These individuals must also experience affection in a constructive way.

Although we can consider some of the reasons homes are out of order, I have discovered another major reason that homes do not represent a place of security. In many cases, children are calling the shots in the home. Such children are obvious in their behavior, due to the fact they are rebellious and contrary towards authority. However, the responsibility for children's behavior does not rest with the child, but with the parents. Parents either perceive their young children as being incapable of understanding right and wrong, or they see them as someone who can be reasoned with. Both perceptions are wrong.

Young children are not stupid, but they still lack the ability to reason out matters. We as adults must, first of all, cease from seeing our children in the wrong light. We must learn how to communicate to our children. Granted, infants and young children cannot be reasoned with, but you still can communicate with them. It is in proper communication that our child develops the ability to reason between right and wrong.

To properly communicate to a child, you must recognize what a child is capable of responding to. Young children initially communicate through behavior. A parent's response to their behavior will either reinforce that behavior or the behavior will be negated and challenged to change.

For example, a baby cries to get attention. However, different cries will tell a parent if the child needs something or whether he or she is demanding attention. If parents refuse to placate a baby when he or she is demanding attention, the child will change his or her behavior. If a child sees that a behavior will receive rewards such as candy or attention, then that behavior will be associated with the response.

Once a child associates a certain behavior to a certain response, the child will either use the behavior or change or adjust the behavior. If behavior encourages selfish attitudes and actions, then the child will be reinforced in his or her behavior to obtain his or her selfish demands. If those demands are not met, then the child's bad behavior will escalate until the child gets his or her way, or he or she realizes it will not work. By associating certain behavior to unproductive responses, the child will choose to change such conduct in the future.

Most parents figure children will out grow bad behavior. However, the truth is that bad behavior will be expressed in other ways, such as pouting, being moody, whining, and complaining. Bad behavior never really goes away until a child changes his or her attitude towards a matter. Children do not volunteer to change self-serving attitudes as long as their behavior gets the desired results. Therefore, bad behavior only changes when the child learns that it is not beneficial to act in such a way.

In most cases parents do not start out to encourage bad behavior in their children. They believe that they have good intentions towards their children, and that they are showing them love by giving them what they want. However, in reality placating or showing indifference to bad behavior are not signs of love to these children, but one of tolerance. If parents are being tolerant due to personal comfort or convenience, children become dissatisfied, insecure, and uncertain about their place in the family and in their small worlds. Since their environment is out of order, these children's worlds will seem disjointed. They are not old enough to wear the pants, nor are they capable of making sound decisions that would ensure a healthy environment or lifestyle for themselves. All they know how to do is to be selfish because foolishness is bound in their heart.[1] They have no self-discipline or integrity in which to judge a matter. They are dependent on those who oversee their well-being to put down the proper boundaries that will ensure their well-being.

The real issue behind parents who do not properly confront bad behavior with their children is their own selfishness. Many parents are complacent and inconsistent when it comes to dealing with their children's behavior. Although they have been given the authority to oversee their children's well-being, they relinquish that authority when they try to keep their children's selfish monster at bay. They console themselves that they are being loving, as their children become more frustrated in their uncertain worlds. In reality, these parents are dropping the ball as far as raising their children. Sadly, it is our children who pick up the slack and begin to run the show.

Placating selfishness is not training a child in the way he or she should go. It simply causes chaos in the home and the child's life. The more a child becomes insecure about his or her parents' love and his or her place in the scheme of things the more the child's bad behavior escalates.

Children need boundaries in order to be trained (disciplined). They need to be under authority in order to be guided and they need to be placed in the proper order to feel secure in their place in the family and home.

Obviously, homes are out of order because parents are failing to take their rightful position in the home. This failure has to do with their way of thinking in regards to God, their parental responsibilities, and their children's needs. Since selfishness is the major platform that these parents are operating from, they see children on the basis of what they will do for them, rather than meeting the need of their children to ensure healthy relationships and environments.

It is vital that homes come back into order. This will begin with parents having a godly marriage and adjusting their thinking to God's

---

[1] Proverbs 22:15

perspective about all matters including their children. Parents must take their rightful place of authority, and begin to influence and channel the behavior of their children in such a way, that the children will develop a right attitude about authority, God, and life.

In the following chapters, parents will be challenged to line their attitude and way of thinking up to Scriptural instructions and practices in regards to their children. Clearly, parenting is the hardest job and can only be done in light of God's wisdom. However, it must be done, and it must be done in light of God if our homes are going to serve as a sanctuary to our spouses and children, and if the following generations are going to be saved.

# 18

# CHILDREN,
# HERITAGE OF THE LORD

A good examination of our spiritual condition and attitude towards God can be found in how we treat the things of God. For example, salvation is a free gift of God, but Hebrews 2:3 states, "How shall we escape, if we neglect such a great salvation?" Once we receive a gift from God, it becomes a priceless responsibility that must not be abused or neglected. Any abuse or neglect of the things of God will bring judgment.

Psalms 127:3 tells us, "Lo, children are an heritage of the Lord." This Scripture points out that all children belong to the Lord and are part of His estate. He has entrusted parents with these priceless gems. The questions are, how are we in America and the Church treating God's priceless estate, and what does it say about our attitude towards Him?

The one word that describes the spiritual condition of America and the Church is *pagan.* Don't get me wrong; we are civilized in our paganism. Nevertheless, we have become pagan. According to *Webster's New Collegiate Dictionary,* one of the definitions of pagan is "one who delights in sensual pleasures and material goods." Is this not a description of much of America today and, in some cases, the Church?

Like the pagan nations of the Old Testament, we are sacrificing our children to various gods, such as selfishness, insatiable appetites, perversion, convenience, materialism, pleasures, and humanistic and New Age philosophies. These sacrifices are done in the name of rights, education, success, and happiness. These ungodly sacrifices and pursuits are promoted and condoned by the mindset that everyone should do whatever feels good regardless of who it hurts.

In the midst of our feel-good and "civilized" paganism, we are losing our children. Our children are turning from sanity to those things that feed their lusts, dull their conscience, and shut out reality. They are, in essence, selling their souls to the god of this world by embracing New Age philosophies, witchcraft, drugs, demonic music, and various immoral and ungodly practices.

From all appearances, we are a society bent on destruction. The generation that could turn it around seems to be running as fast as they can from God. Much of this upcoming generation lacks integrity, character, purpose, and most of all, Jesus Christ. At best, this generation is indoctrinated by humanistic philosophy that puts self at the center of a small, insipid world that is void of compassion, respect, and common decency. At worst, it is creating a generation that lacks imagination, is emotionally dead, and thinks more about death than life. We wonder why violent youth crimes are up, suicide has become a preferred solution, and godliness is mocked.

This last generation serves as a mirror that should make the most righteous tremble and weep, and the most ungodly fall on their face and ask God for mercy. The mirror's reflection is a product of each generation getting further and further away from God in spirit and truth.

The generation that lived through the Great Depression began to pursue after money to secure happiness and create security. Like Solomon, the next generation saw the vanity and futility of such worldly pursuits. It went after the right to have and display individual expression that would appear to have substance and reality.

The following generation found itself shrouded in conflict, confusion, and anger. The hippie generation came out in total rebellion with a Marxism revolutionary view, flaunting sexual immorality, and falling headlong into the drug scene. This rebellion was overshadowed by the Viet Nam conflict. Divisions took place in hearts, families, and the entire nation as many questioned and mocked the validity of this war where blood was spilled, lives destroyed, and where America's best offered up the ultimate sacrifice, their lives.

The 1970's found America putting Band-Aids on the scars caused by the previous conflicts. The Viet Nam struggle was far from over as those who survived were fighting a greater battle on the home front.

There was even a greater war lost in the highest court in America. Using AGI figures through 2005, estimating 1,206,200 abortions for 2006, 2007, and 2008, and factoring in the possible 3% undercount AGI estimates for its own figures, the total number of abortions performed in the U.S. since 1973 equals 50,757,903. There remains an on-going conflict over abortion. Abortion is a legalized way of sacrificing our children. In God's eyes, we are offering up our children to Satan, the god of this world.[1] All of those who have failed to repent and continue to participate in this atrocity will stand before God with the blood of God's heritage on their hands.

The casualties of this silent war are not only unborn babies, but also women and men who realize all the excuses and logic cannot drown out their conscience. Their conscience tells them that a child's life has been eliminated for the sake of wickedness. Their excuses, which seemed logical to them at the time, haunt them as they begin to wonder why they resorted to a seemingly senseless act. Perhaps the life of this child was taken to cover up fornication and preserve reputation? Maybe selfishness was the motive behind the sacrifice. Or, maybe it was terminated because of pleasure. The fact is, babies are being offered up to the many different gods of America.

This regression in our society has led us to this place in history. Our children are referred to as latchkey children. After being dumb down by a

---

[1] 2 Corinthians 4:3-4

socialistic, godless, public education system, they come home to an empty house because most parents are busy trying to make ends meet or supposedly secure the American dream for the sake of the family. The ungodly television is their babysitter and Hollywood their psychologist. They lack imagination because they have all forms of entertainment at their fingertips that neither challenges them nor enlarges their capacity to think, reason, gain understanding, and acquire wisdom. Their childhood innocence is assaulted by images of sexual immorality and violence. They are alone, confused, and often afraid.

Children have the same basic needs as their parents. They need to be *loved, accepted,* and *recognized.* Since many are not getting these needs met at home, they look elsewhere. They look to gangs, sex, drugs, and their peers to have a sense of belonging. In fact, our children are being set up to blindly follow another Hitler, or, I should say, the anti-Christ.

Hitler understood the needs of young people and he devised a way to fulfill them. Discipline was a form of love; belonging to the organization brought acceptance; and being with the elite that would rule the world fulfilled the need for recognition.

Most parents will cry out, "I am doing the best I can." I have no doubt you are, but what is the best as far as your children are concerned? How do you treat your children? Some parents treat their children as if they are unplanned accidents or burdens. They act as if the child is an inconvenience. Maybe your children's conception was unplanned, but they must never feel they are burdens. They did not ask to be born. Since they are here, every parent needs to make his or her offspring feel like a pleasant blessing or a priceless gift from God.

Perhaps the motive for having children was selfish or self-serving. Some parents have a child to confirm their manhood or womanhood. Their plan is that the child will bring a special value to their life or be an extension of them. Children can add value as well as heartache, but a child is an individual, not a puppet. They were created to be conformed to the image of God, and not to be shaped into the image their father or mother has designed for them.

I heard of one woman who wanted children so they could be her slaves. What a sick motive. We are to make an investment in our children, not the other way around.

Sadly, I have often watched many young children display more maturity and responsibility than their parents. When parents refuse to grow up and be responsible adults, their children often lose some form of innocence at a very young age.

Many people blame the problems in dealing with children on the "generation gap." Every generation is influenced by what it has been exposed to in society. Obviously, God and Christian values have not influenced the upcoming generation.

Children's relationship with their parents has a far-reaching effect, even into their teenage years. First of all, their perception of God is based on how they view their parents. For example, if they have a harsh father, they will perceive God to be harsh.

Parents determine their children's level of respect for authority. If a child does not learn to respect the authority of his or her parents, he or she will not respect the authority of others, including God. I have been around so many children who have no regard for authority or other people's property. They mock authority, are rude, and appear to lack manners. In one incident, I was involved with two children who showed a blatant disrespect towards adults. Later, I learned that one of their parents told them that they did not need to honor other adults. Obviously, the parent who told them this nonsense did not have a godly love for these two children. Rebellion reigned in these children's hearts.

The Bible is very explicit about younger people adhering to the authority of older people. What this parent did not realize is that she was undermining her own authority, and encouraging rebellion in her children. This rebellion will either come out in their teenage years or when they are young adults.

Environment also has an effect on children. What kind of environment have you established for your children? Is your home a battleground, or is it a holy sanctuary? Do your children feel the need to look elsewhere, such as to peers and other sources to find love, peace, and joy because it is missing in their home?

Another area that affects children's attitudes towards God is their encounters with the religious realm. If they witness hypocrisy, games, and rigid rules without love, their view of God will be superficial. They will either be driven away from a relationship with God or they will refine the religious games to get by without being called to accountability. They may also adopt self-righteousness instead of humility and compassion.

Young people need to realize that God is calling us into a relationship, not a religion. They need to see parents who are honest, upright in dealings, and submissive in attitude and example. In other words, they need to see the real thing in their parent's lives.

Check out your motive and attitude towards your children. Wrong motives are hidden under the delusion of pride and wrong attitudes under excuses.

Our children belong to God. Parents need to raise their children in light of this truth. There will be no excuse for any abuse or neglect of these gems because the Word of God gives parents clear instruction concerning the raising of their children.

In the end, every parent will stand before the Lord and be held accountable for how he or she treated His priceless inheritance. Can you be confident of the outcome, or is there fear rising up in your heart because you know deep down that you have in some way neglected or squandered this precious gift of God?

# 19

# TRUE DISCIPLINE

According to *Webster's New Collegiate Dictionary,* "discipline" means teaching, which can be associated to that of a disciple or disciplined follower. It is also training that corrects, molds, or perfects the mental faculties or moral character. It implies punishment and results in self-control. These definitions agree with the Word of God's references to discipline.

It is important for parents to understand true discipline according to God's instructions. As stated, discipline of children along with intimacy and financial practices are the major points of conflict among married couples. It is not unusual to find parents whose philosophies about discipline are opposite. Both may act as if they have the perfect understanding of discipline, and will often argue and debate about these methods in front of the children.

Children who can quickly fine-tune games to get their way will see a wonderful opportunity to pit one parent against the other. It turns out to be a free for all. No one wins, including the child.

Proverbs 13:24 tells us, "He that spareth his rod hateth his son: but he that loveth him chasteneth him betimes." Lack of discipline means you do not really love your child. This lack of discipline will make your child feel like he or she does not belong. Hebrews 12:8 confirms this, "But if ye be without chastisement, whereof all are partakers, then are ye bastards, and not sons."

Discipline must always be done in godly love and be for the sake of the child. Many times, the parents simply react to a situation that is causing them irritations, rather than respond to rebellious unacceptable behavioral patterns that will lead the child to destruction. Proverbs 19:18 instructs parents with this warning, "Chasten thy son while there is hope, and let not thy soul spare for his crying."

It is quite easy for parents to be a willing party to the spiritual death of their child. Lenient discipline is as dangerous as harsh and unloving discipline. Love will not ignore iniquity, but on the other hand it will not provoke a child.[1] Provoke means to cause "anger and rage". There are many children who are full of anger. Unfair and unloving demands and discipline have provoked them to this dangerous disposition.

Parents often demean their children in order to get them to conform to unrealistic demands. This is also a type of provoking; however, this

---

[1] Ephesians 6:4

verbal deriding may not only be a cause for anger, but it also may break a child's spirit, causing him or her to become hopeless.[2]

Another point of provoking is when parents fail to recognize their children's nature. To improperly discipline a child will provoke them as well. For example, if you try to confront a stubborn child like you would a strong-willed child, you will provoke anger and rebellion in that child. It is vital that parents properly recognize their child's nature to ensure effective discipline.

There must be balance in discipline. To accomplish this balance, parents must understand what true discipline is, and allow God to align their attitudes. True discipline is not based on a parent getting his or her way or getting the child to cry "uncle" in defeat in order for him or her to quietly submit. Godly discipline goes past the outward defiance to the heart of the matter. The problem with most parents is that they never get past the defiance to challenge the heart attitude because their "sacred cow" of self is in the way.

It is important that parents understand that their child will rebel. A child is a person with a selfish disposition. Children are born with the inclination to rebel. They are full of folly. After all, it is in their disposition to rebel against authority, while flexing their immature muscles of independence at different times in their lives.

Many parents get insulted when their child rebels. They expect to simply say something and have their child comply. In some cases, you may see such compliance, but in most cases, a child will eventually test the parent's authority.

If parents are honest, they should not be surprised at a child's rebellion. Adults are no different when it comes to God's authority. They are just more diplomatic about their rebellion. They have learned to play the games, wear the masks, and delude themselves. Children learn games early, but they do not delude themselves. They know what they are after. They want their own way, and they are willing to test those in authority to obtain it.

Parents, keep in mind, discipline is not a means to get a child to simply comply and agree with you. It is designed to establish acceptable behavior and attitude. Parents need to let children know what correct behavior is, and engrain in a child's mind that there will be consequences when he or she gives way to unacceptable behavior and the attitudes that inspire it.

Again, consequences are not for the purpose of getting children to respond correctly, but to establish within their heart the knowledge that they will reap what they sow. If they insist on making bad decisions, they will pay the consequences. They must accept these consequences with graciousness, and not complain because it is a matter of choice. If they do not like the consequences, they need to make the right decisions. This will hopefully bring a healthy fear that produces wisdom and brings about self-control and responsibility. Children who are disciplined fit the

[2] Proverbs 17:22

criteria found in Proverbs 29:15 and 17, "The rod and reproof give wisdom: but a child left to himself bringeth his mother to shame.... Correct thy son, and he shall give thee rest; yea, he shall give delight unto thy soul."

The first order of business in confronting a child's rebellion is to get self out of the way. We have found many parents who react to their children based on their own nature. Let us first consider parents' unacceptable reactions to their children before we tackle the subject of children's rebellion.

*Submissive* parents can either become too complacent or very obnoxious in the area of discipline. Submissive people hate confrontation, and discipline is a form of confrontation. They want to come across as a sweet or reasonable parent who will try to come out as the "good guy". In some cases, they feel superior towards the parent who is more abrasive in his or her discipline. Thus, the submissive parent wants to come out looking good instead of caring about what is best for the child. Therefore, it is normal for submissive parents to have a hard time following through with any constructive discipline. They often ignore their child's rebellion, or try to reason with him or her through fake humility or conceit. This combination is expressed in an "ooey-gooey," unrealistic love. This approach will drive a strong-willed child to anger, a stubborn child to frustration, a self-assured child to mockery, and a submissive child into his or her obnoxious state.

On the other hand, submissive parents can also become obnoxious or unreasonable in their form of discipline. They can end up throwing more tantrums than their child. They can appear harsh and unrealistic in their demands. They are susceptible to lecturing their children, rather then communicating with them. This type of reaction will provoke greater rebellion in a child's heart or close him or her down. Usually, a submissive parent who operates with these two extreme forms of discipline will come face to face with a child out of control. It is during this time that a submissive parent can conclude, "What's the use," and give up.

Submissive parents need to confront in godly love and firmness. This love has a commitment to do right by the child. Firmness implies that you do have authority and you will carry out the consequences. In order to do this, submissive parents must get past self, their good reputation, and their fear to confront, and deal with the child according to his or her nature.

*Stubborn* parents take their child's rebellion personally. They feel a child is questioning their authority because they do not love nor respect them. Their attitude is, "How could you do this to me?" This reaction comes from selfishness and will cause them to become angry. If they are not careful, this anger can become uncontrollable, causing them to overreact verbally and physically.

This anger will push sorely against a child, provoking him or her. It will cause a strong-willed child to defy the stubborn parent; the stubborn child will see it as control and challenge the parent; a self-assured child will usually ignore the outrage and add it to their list of offences; and the submissive child will either withdraw or become obnoxious.

A good rule of thumb is to never confront a child while angry. Stubborn parents must put down their selfishness and their emotions, and confront with fairness and consistency. Instead of being out of control and losing all headway and respect with their child, they must show themselves as being disciplined in their attitudes and actions if they plan to make a point.

Most *self-assured* parents try to portray themselves as being the best parents in the world. All of their reactions towards their children are based on the "good guy" image they want their children to perceive. They often leave discipline up to the other parent in order to maintain their image, which is quite unfair. This type of parent can end up being apathetic towards their children's behavior.

If self-assured parents do respond to their child, it is because the child has questioned or tarnished their image. This will insult them and their attitude will be, "How dare you." Anger can be the final result, and consequently, they can easily verbally demean a child, provoking the child to anger and causing him or her to become hopeless.

These people can be very critical and unyielding towards any discrepancies in their children. Since they are unpredictable, it can cause a stubborn child to become confused and upset. Their strong attitudes can cause a submissive child to become fearful and withdrawn. A strong-willed child will react or choose to ignore them. A self-assured child will usually take note and adopt the same harsh attitudes and demands, even if he or she disagrees.

Self-assured parents need to forget their image when confronting their children. They need to consider what is best for the child and carry through with consistency and fairness. They need to avoid anger and harsh demands and show meekness and integrity in dealing with the problems.

*Strong-willed* parents usually assume a child will comply. They have an attitude of, "You will comply or else." The "or else" can be pretty harsh on a submissive and a stubborn child because the intensity behind it can break a child's spirit. It will encourage a facade of compliance in a self-assured child and provoke rebellion in a strong-willed child.

On the other hand, I have watched strong-willed parents ignore their children, leaving the discipline to the other parent. Again, this is unfair. Discipline needs to be the job of both parents. Strong-willed parents have the authority to make a point, but they need to take time to really evaluate the situation to avoid undue harshness. They must have flexibility in their conclusions and consideration for feelings. They can then act in love after all of this has been taken into account to ensure fairness.

The reason right attitudes and responses are necessary is to keep a child from playing games of deception. Children play such games to get along with their parents and survive their childhood. They quickly learn how to put on a compliant mask, even though rebellion reigns in their heart and anger seethes below the surface.[3]

Godly discipline not only keeps the parent upright, but also forces a child to be honest. Children must learn to be honest with themselves if they are to overcome. They must learn to respect people and their property. They must learn meekness over aggression, compassion over personal gain, and sensitivity over mockery, anger, and unforgiveness.

How are you doing in disciplining your children? Is the "sacred cow" of self in the way? Are you provoking your children or pushing them into hell with your leniency and apathy? Are you being faithful with God's heritage by being obedient to the Word concerning your children? Ask the Lord to illuminate these answers for you.

# The Three Cs

There are three Cs in godly discipline. They are simple to remember: *confront, challenge, and channel.* Confronting a child means you are trying to alert them to possible dangers. This form of advice falls into the same category as *admonition.* Ephesians 6:4 gives this instruction, "And, ye fathers, provoke not your children to wrath: but bring them up in the nurture and admonition of the Lord." (Emphasis added.)

Admonition is a caution and warning. Many times, all a parent can do is caution and warn his or her child as to consequences. This does not mean lecturing the child, for lecturing is the quickest way to cause your child to go deaf to your concerns. Warning a child means giving the facts and letting the youngster make the decision. Children will make a decision regardless of all of your attempts.

Admonition is the most effective after parents have first met their children's need up front. If children need acceptance and understanding as to their plight, give it to them. Perhaps you need to enter in emotionally and address their feelings and confusion; take time to do so. Maybe, the child needs you to recognize his or her attempts to overcome the behavior pattern or pending problem about which you are confronting them; be quick about recognizing what the child is trying to do. On the other hand, maybe you need to recognize your child's abilities to overcome; do not fail to do so. Caution and warning, while honoring a child's need will not be mistaken for control, but will be seen as genuine concern. This will always take the bitterness out of the pill of this type of discipline.

In challenging your child, you are attempting to *nurture* or develop him or her. Nurture in this context means to cultivate or refine something. Cultivate means to break up and prepare for planting. Obviously, in nurturing your child, you will be tearing up the turf. Take note, this is different than tearing down, which is an improper use of authority. To

---

[3] For more information about relationships between parents and children see the book, *Parents are People Too* in this same volume.

tear properly at wrong attitudes and behavior, you must learn how to challenge your child according to his or her nature.

A farmer who cultivates the soil does not change the soil, but the character or ability of the soil in order to develop the landscape. The type of soil that is present cannot be changed, but it can be cultivated. By knowing the condition of the soil, the farmer is able to replenish it with necessary nutrients.

You cannot change your children's nature, but by understanding their nature, you can challenge their rebellion, cultivate their lives with integrity, and replenish their souls with the reality of God. You can help them to develop their character, as well as encourage their growth in a right way. This is why this nature information is so important. It gives people a valuable tool and the right ingredients with which to work to change their relationships with their spouse and children.

After we have nurtured a child to receive the right instruction, our next responsibility is to *train* the youngster. Train implies that we channel our child's behavior. Channel does not mean change. This form of discipline serves as the means of working constructive, lasting discipline in children's lives, while allowing them their identity. Proverbs 22:6 states, "Train up a child in the way he should go: and when he is old, he will not depart from it."

This discipline occurs by establishing boundaries. These established boundaries are created by way of instruction, which is wrought through example, teaching, and discipline. These boundaries actually shape and mold a child's way of thinking and responding. Boundaries of this nature become security for most children even though they kick and scream. They are consistent, but not stifling. They are fair and will not give room to pity parties. They are honest; therefore, they can be trusted.

As you can see, God's scriptural instructions in raising children are very simple. They are full of godly wisdom and common sense. All we need to do now is properly apply them. We must stay away from basing these instructions on our understanding, but we must allow the Holy Spirit to illuminate God's presentation of them according to spirit and truth.

How about you? Have you put these three scriptural truths into practice? In the next chapter, you will learn how to determine your child's nature. This will give you special insight into changing your child's heart and mind in a godly manner, instead of trying to subdue your child into some form of outward compliance without a heart change.

# 20

# DISCOVERING YOUR CHILD'S NATURE

True discipline means you are making the right investment. Parents who are considered successful in their parenting endeavors discipline according to the child. They actually make distinct investments in each one of their children. I watched a mother with eight children accomplish such a feat.

This particular mother was busy taking care of the younger children when one of her older sons came in from school. His face was long and he seemed disturbed. Even though the other children were walking in from school and her younger ones were demanding attention, she zeroed in on him. She asked him what was going on. She did not take her attention off of him until the problem was resolved.

Parents have made many assumptions about their children. I remember when the *Hidden Manna* information was in its infancy, I was teaching a Women's Bible Study. The women were being gracious enough to test this information out on their families.

One of the mothers assumed she understood her children until she began to observe their rebellion. To her surprise, she was incorrect about her previous conclusions. Her discovery caused her to rethink how she confronted them, and she changed her response.

Many parents react rather than respond properly to their child. Reaction points to opposition, which means the child is in control, pushing the parent's buttons. Response implies the parent is in control of the situation, and ready to interact with the child in a constructive way.

By understanding your children's natures, you can respond to them in an effective way. It is quite easy to determine their nature. The next time you give your child a responsibility, watch how he or she responds to your instruction. I refer to this instruction as a parent's line of authority.

*Submissive* children are usually the most compliant up front. They will obey because it is their desire to please and keep the peace. Problems arise when parents take this obedience for granted and do not acknowledge it. This child will begin to feel the love or acceptance they receive from their parents is conditional, especially when other siblings are not compliant and manage to slide by. If they ever come to this conclusion, they can withdraw into their own little worlds or become obnoxious and literally fall over their parents' line of authority. The outright rebellion of this child usually happens in their teenage years. This catches parents off-guard and leaves them in a state of shock.

*Stubborn* children will try the line of authority. In other words, they will try to slowly nudge across the line or adjust it according to their game plan. This adjustment of the line can be quite trying for a parent who is trying to maintain consistency.

One of the ways stubborn children manage to get away with moving the line is by conning their parents. They have a way of being so sweet and loving, while they have their hand in the forbidden cookie jar. It is hard for a parent to be consistent with such an adorable con.

Not all stubborn children are cons; some are independent smart-mouths. This type of child will be quite independent in actions and will have a comment for every occasion. Such children often appear argumentative, blunt, and rude. They can display loud outbursts over anything that may challenge their fragile world or change their patterns or environment. This child can be hard for parents to take and will test every bit of patience they possess.

I remember how my stubborn friend fell in the latter category in her childhood. She confessed she was known for countering with "Yeah, but." She managed to drive her parents' friends away with her undisciplined, open rudeness. She remembers her childhood being plagued with a lot of spankings. She admitted that they did bring some discipline into her life.

*Self-assured* children usually come across as reserved or shy. They can be sweet and easy-going, especially at a young, tender age. You need to be aware that these reserved children are observing behavior patterns of those around them. They are trying to adopt some kind of image or identity. This is why it is very important to shield them from exposure to the wrong behavior of others as promoted in movies, and the like. These children can actually develop images that are destructive and then act them out.

This truth became very obvious to a self-assured friend who was working at a day-care school. She encountered a disorderly little boy. None of the workers could control or reason with him. She observed that he was self-assured, and she began to approach him based on his nature. The young boy eventually confessed to her that he was a bad boy. She reassured him that he was not a bad boy, but that he made bad choices. She told him that underneath he wanted to be a good boy and that all he had to do was begin to do good things. The boy's entire attitude changed. Apparently, this young boy had adopted the image of a bad boy and was simply acting it out.

The self-assured child has what we call a façade of obedience. This façade is a means of trying to adjust the parent's line of authority, but it is not as obvious as with a stubborn child. This deception is what usually gives this child away. For example, you might tell your self-assured child to pick up his or her room. This child is usually aware that he or she is to put toys, clothes, etc. in their proper places. Upon inspection, the parent finds the room in order until he or she looks in the closet or under the bed, where all the articles are hidden away instead of being in their rightful place.

Self-assured children must decide to make the necessary commitment to do things right. This will develop integrity in this type of child. If these children do not establish this integrity, they will slide by in all those things they consider to be unpleasant. I have watched parents' frustration escalate over their self-assured children who refused to crack a schoolbook because they knew they could get by without much effort.

These children can be powerful leaders. The type of leadership will be determined by their images. People of this nature can be bullies or potential gang leaders. They often influence the type of character and moral leadership of those around them.

*Strong-willed* children can be your most well-behaved child or your greatest challenge. These children actually make a decision as to whether they are going to obey or disobey. If they decide to obey, they are a blessing. But, if they decide to disobey, they will test you by drawing their own line and demanding that you comply.

A father shared with me how his strong-willed son made a decision that was contrary to the father's rules. The father told the son if he disobeyed, he would have to pay the consequences. The son told the father up front that he would pay the consequences because he was going to carry out his decision.

Consider your children. What nature are they? If you are not sure, observe them closely. Eventually, their type of rebellion will tell on them.

# 21

# MAKING THE
# RIGHT INVESTMENT

Now that you understand your children's natures, it is vital that you make the right investment in their lives. You must begin the long process of properly training them if you are going to bring out the best in them.

We get an insight into this training in Deuteronomy 6. In reference to God's Law, we see these instructions, "And thou shalt teach them diligently unto thy children, and shalt talk of them when thou sittest in thine house, and when thou walkest by the way, and when thou liest down, and when thou risest up" (Deuteronomy 6:7). The reason for this intense emphasis of God's Law was to create a healthy fear in young people towards authority so they could experience a quality, prolonged life.[1]

The reality of Jesus Christ should lie at the center of all training. Children who are missing God in their life will have no guidelines or purpose. They will be prone to indoctrination into worldly lies because they have no solid foundation. They will be like a cork on the ocean, swinging from one philosophy to another trying to find meaning and substance. They will lack identity because they will not have any sure reason for their existence.

Ensuring children know the true God should be the foremost concern of every parent, and the main pursuit and goal when instructing children. This instruction can only take root and be reinforced when the parents are living and breathing the reality of God in their own lives.

By making God a reality to a child, he or she will choose life over death. This choice will determine the route children take in their lives. Even though they may take detours, they will always know where to come back to when they are ready.

God, in the midst of homes and at the center of hearts, will bring wisdom to parents and truth to a child. This wisdom will enable parents to fight the good fight for their children. The truth will serve as a valuable guideline to children as they mature and face temptations.

With God taking His rightful place in our homes, not only can we confront our children according to their nature, but also in wisdom and with authority. If you have a *submissive* child, you must show him or her *acceptance*. This acceptance must be communicated outside of the obedience and good deeds this child may be displaying. Somehow you

---

[1] Deuteronomy 6:2

have to let these children know that regardless of their type of behavior, good or bad, you accept them just the way they are. They do not have to work to gain your acceptance. This will give submissive children a sense of being loved and appreciated just for who they are.

In confrontation, your response must be *balanced*. You cannot be too lenient with them, but on the other hand, you must not be too harsh. You must be firm, and get to the bottom of the matter.

Your investment in this type of child must be *complete*. In other words, make sure the submissive child has everything in proper perspective. Never leave him or her to his or her own imaginations or evaluations. Pursue this child until you have the full picture of what is going on.

This is why your approach to a submissive child must be that of a *marathon* runner. This child will not volunteer information about what is going on in his or her mind. You must question the child until you draw the matter or struggle out into the light. This can be a long process, but it is well worth it.

Good investments bring good dividends. If you properly accept the challenge of submissive children, they will work *sensitivity* in you, which is valuable when it comes to the Holy Spirit. A parent must be sensitive to a submissive child to properly confront him or her. The parent must also determine if the child is withdrawing for the purpose of getting space or rebelling. Remember, rebellion comes down to a person doing it his or her way. A submissive child tries to figure everything out. You cannot afford to ignore these children or let them remain in their own worlds because it can lead to outward rebellion and disaster.

I remember how a sixteen-year-old submissive girl tried to commit suicide. Her actions shocked her parents because there was no warning. After attending the seminar, her mother began to go after her to discover the reason for her drastic action. Her mother found out that Satan had been lying to her about her mental stability. The young lady also confessed that she yielded herself to a compromising situation. Once everything was brought to the light, the young woman was restored.

*Stubborn* children need to know that they are *loved*. This love is actually reaffirmed by fair and consistent discipline. This is often surprising to parents who watch this type of child fight against any authority. The truth is, fair discipline brings a sense of security to this child, which gives him or her a sense of being loved.

In drawing your line of authority for this child, ask yourself two questions. Is this line too hard for me to constantly maintain because this child will continually test it? Will it be unfair to this child because he or she will be quick to recognize such a discrepancy and yell, "Foul"? Your response to this type of child must be *consistent* every time. If you draw a line of responsibility, maintain the line and make sure you follow through on all warnings.

The investment that this type of child requires is *long-term* because he or she will continue to try you. In fact, your experience with this child will seem like a *wrestling match*. You may throw the child out of the ring, only to find out that he or she is coming from another direction to try to tackle you.

Stubborn children are easy to deal with if you recognize their patterns and challenge them before they hit all-out rebellion. My mother shared how she had to give my stubborn brother a spanking every three months in the first six years of his life. It seems he would work up to a point in the area of his rebellion, and my mother would quickly nip it before it got out of hand. After each spanking, my brother seemed content and was obedient.

Parents also need to put aside a specific time for this child. These children love to tell parents about the happenings of the day. Their excitement, imagination, and enthusiasm can be great. They need to be able to express themselves.

A parent can channel and encourage this expression by setting the rules and allowing the stubborn child to know that he or she has so many minutes each day at a designated time to share about daily activities. Make sure you automatically put time aside, and sit down with your bundle of excitement. Commit your total attention to the child. If you do this consistently each day, you will find that it will eliminate a lot of trying moments.

As you can see, if you accept the challenge of a stubborn child, *consistency* will be developed in you. Consistency is a form of discipline, which can be a valuable asset in every area of your life.

*Self-assured* children need you to recognize their images. A friend was relating how this information helped her understand and effectively confront her self-assured teenage daughter. What she found interesting was that her daughter was always changing images. One minute she was addressing the image of the good daughter, only to find her daughter had changed to the image of a good student. She had to learn to adjust to the image in order to communicate with her.

This is why parents must respond with awareness of and *sensitivity* to their self-assured children. Parents must discern what is going on with their images, and be willing to confront these children about destructive images or unacceptable patterns of behavior. This is a challenge and involves a *long-term* commitment.

The long-term commitment will also involve a *wrestling match.* Parents will wrestle with the different images of these young individuals as long as they are contending with this child. They must insist on integrity to images by calling this youngster to take responsibility for ungodly attitudes and actions.

Usually, a parent has to get downright tough to bring this child to a point of accountability. This child will either twist or ignore his or her parents' inquiries. Self-assured children can be sneaky and have a tendency to twist the truth concerning their actions in order to protect their image and avoid admitting when they are wrong.

A mother shared with me how her self-assured son cheated in a card game. She actually caught him in the act twice. She kept challenging his honesty and each time he denied it. She asked the Lord to convict his heart over his deception. She watched as the Holy Spirit began to work on him. Before the night was over, he tearfully came to her and confessed his deception.

Parents of self-assured children need to seek God for wisdom about what may be going on with their child. In fact, if you notice that your self-assured child is deceptive, ask God to show you what your child is up to and call him or her to accountability. The youngster may deny it, but ask the Lord to convict him or her and bring the child to a point of accountability. It does not hurt to occasionally remind self-assured children that God is aware of their actions and every deed is being recorded. They may get away with it down here, but not when they stand before God. Liars will not make it into the kingdom of God.[2]

Self-assured children will work *discernment* or sound judgment in parents. This is important in testing the spirits and is helpful in determining what is behind self-assured children's actions.[3] Satan can pressure these children, and parents need to discern the spirit that could be influencing them.

*Strong-willed* children need you to *recognize* that they are *"strong-willed."* If at any point in time you forget this fact, they will remind you that they are who they are. These children are very decisive in their actions. Therefore, parents need to be *decisive* in their responses to these children. Rebellious strong-willed children do not respect parents who are wishy-washy, syrupy, or emotional in their responses. They will challenge the parent even more.

Your investment in this child will be *extreme* because it will involve an all-out confrontation. It is a lot like a *boxing match*. It can be rough, and in some cases can come close to a knock-out fight.

I recall the desperation of a stubborn mother who was contending with her strong-willed son who was only four years old. She admitted that she almost hated the kid because he was so rebellious. My advice was simple: Give him choices. Strong-willed children make decisions as a means of controlling their small space; therefore, parents must channel these children's decisions by giving them a couple of choices. I told her the next time she wanted him to do something, she needed to get eye-level with him and give him choices, and wait for his decision.

She quickly put this into practice. She had to take a trip that would take over an hour to get to her destination. She got on her knees and looked her four-year-old in the eyes. She told him that if he was a good boy, there would be benefits awaiting him. But, if he chose to be a bad boy, he needed to make the decision right then because she was planning to deal with him on the spot. The little boy thought for a second and told her he was going to be a good boy.

During their journey, he began to act up. She pulled the car off the road and looked straight into his eyes. She reminded him of his decision

---

[2] Revelation 21:8
[3] 1 John 4:1

to be a good boy. It sparked his recollection, and he settled down. She told me he was perfect the rest of the day.

These children must have some say. By giving them a couple of choices, and allowing them to make a decision, gives them some control over their lives. It is important that you present only a couple of choices at a time to avoid causing them confusion. These children hate confusion, and will often express their dislike for this state with rebellion.

Strong-willed children bring *character* to your life. This character is translated into strength that comes from learning how to stand and withstand when these children challenge your character, word, and authority.

Consider the difference between these natures in children in the following table.

| Nature | Submissive | Stubborn | Self-Assured | Strong-Willed |
|---|---|---|---|---|
| Need | Acceptance | Love/ Discipline | Recognition (Image) | Recognize (Who they are) |
| Response | Balanced | Consistency | Sensitivity | Decisive |
| Investment | Complete | Long Term | Long Term | Extreme |
| Approach | Marathon Runner | Wrestling Match | Wrestling Match | Boxing Match |
| Quality | Sensitivity | Consistency | Sound Judgment | Character |

Parents, you can take heart. You can understand your children and effectively confront them. Your investment in them will require your best and all the commitment you can muster, especially on the bad days. However, there is a God who can help you. Look to Him and ask for wisdom, patience, and a sense of humor.

God has given parents simple rules to apply. He understands these little inheritances, and He sees the potential for them to become priceless heirlooms in His kingdom. Rising to the occasion and seeing your child in light of God is vitally important. Be willing to make the investment no matter what the cost. The final blessings are that of spiritual character.

# 22
# A FINAL THOUGHT

It is hard to put into words the sorrow I have experienced over the condition of Christian homes. I have been trying to be instrumental in helping to pick up the pieces of shattered lives and homes long enough to understand the core of the problem and recognize the path of restoration.

The family has the highest calling in the kingdom of God. Husbands and wives should represent the sacrificial, loving ministry of Christ. Children should be cherished heirlooms that are being prepared to one day be presented to the King of kings as servants and lovers of God.

The real tragedy surrounding the failure of the family is that we are betraying Jesus Christ. We may not be a Peter who verbally denied Christ. Nevertheless, we betray Him in action and attitude.

There is no reason for our miserable failures. God has given us all the tools to overcome. He has given us the Holy Spirit to teach us, a Book to guide us, and eternity to inspire us.

Obviously, believers must catch a hold of Jesus' heart and become obedient children before Him. After all, He has entrusted His people with salvation, marriage, and children. If His followers fail to be trustworthy in any of these areas, He will be unable to entrust them with more. If God is not entrusting the Church with more because believers have not been faithful with what is right in front of them, how will they make a difference in a lost world?

Christians often console themselves in the midst of staggering statistics because people are still being converted, but to what? Conversion without repentance or change is of no use to God and His kingdom. There must be change of heart and mind. A standard of holiness needs to be raised up so Christians can fairly discern where they are in their lives before Christ.

Believers need to get back to the cross of Christ and true repentance. They need to repent of all their idols. In fact, sacred cows stand between the cross of Christ and some Christians. These idols need to be brought down before the cross. Once these sacred cows are down, Jesus will be lifted up, and He will draw spouses and children to Himself.

At the cross of Christ, real restoration begins. Will you not humble yourself before the cross, repent and ask Jesus to come back into your life and home as Lord? Accept the challenge, and forever change the course of your life and the spiritual environment of your family.

Book Three

# MANUAL FOR THE
# SINGLE CHRISTIAN LIFE

Copyright © 2007 by Rayola Kelley

# INTRODUCTION

It is a challenge to be single in a world that appears to fear being solitary. After all, how many people are searching for that perfect "soul mate?" Sadly, the issue of being single in the Christian realm poses similar challenges and defeats as such people face attitudes influenced by a combination of the world and religion. Such a challenge ought not to be present in the Church since the Word of God deals with the issue of being single. However, the reality is that single people have a hard time trying to fit in, as well as find their proper place in this world.

In the present age of political correctness and confusion these lone figures still must appear to possess some kind of sexual reputation or identity that shows they are in compliance to the world's liberal philosophies to feel accepted. Due to the influence of the ungodly moral climate that is engulfing the thinking of many people, single people, even in the Church realm, can be plagued by the suspicion and anxiety of others who are unable to discern their real state or desire. Depending on their age, Christian single people can be shoved aside into some kind of group, often giving the impression that they are being thrown some sort of religious bone to pacify them or satisfy religious obligations. However, such an attempt makes the Church appear inept in tackling the issues that confront these people.

It is hard to be single in a world that is conditioned to consider people's identity and worth based on status or relationships such as that found within marriage. The issue surrounding single people is often narrowed down to their sexual identity or the moral challenges that go along with being single. However, some of the greatest challenges facing single people come from the pressure of what is considered to be the "status quo" around them. After all, they do not fit in with what is considered normalcy. Since they do not fit the status quo, people become uncomfortable, and begin to put pressure on single people to comply with something that will bring order to the narrowness of these people's worldview or philosophy. Such pressure is selfish, and has no regard for the single person.

Some Christians are called to be single, but they do not always feel they have the liberty of being so. They encounter suspicion and uncertainty as they strive to find their place within the Body of Christ. Granted, eventually they can gain the respect from others who choose to know them, but in most cases, they have to fight hard to overcome the suspicions of many who do not know how to discern.

This manual is not only for the struggling, single Christian, but it is also for those who live, work, and worship with such an individual. It is time for the Church to understand the real issues that plague single people. It is time that the Church as a whole confronts its own attitudes about these individuals. Single people need guidance, wisdom, and support to find their proper place in the kingdom of God. They do not need suspicion, matchmaking, or to be stuck in some group separated from the rest of the local church. Likewise, single Christians also need to understand the real challenges and issues of being single so that they can make the right decisions in regard to their life before God.

# Establishing Your Place In Christ

## 1

## ARE YOU A CHRISTIAN?

Before we can expound on what it means to be a Christian in the single realm, we must define what a Christian is. Christians are subject to a higher form of lifestyle. Their conduct must be impeccable in regards as to how they live their lives. Clearly, the life that must govern Christians does not apply to those who live according to the world.

There are many single people in the religious realm that refer to themselves as Christians, but in reality some of these poor souls may not be sealed with the Holy Ghost.[1] They are Christians in name only, and not in lifestyle. It is important to point out that lifestyle, and not names or terms, is what really sets a Christian apart. This lifestyle is not just a matter of conduct, but of attitude. As we will see later in the manual, attitude has to do with what people expose themselves to and choose to embrace.

Obviously, if you are single, but not a Christian, you can live any old way you want to live in this present world. However, it must be noted that the repercussions or consequences of such a life will reverberate through the corridors of eternity. But, if you are a Christian, then you must be living a life that distinguishes you from the rest of the world. It is a life that will bring contrast, rather than a life that fades into the crowd. It is a life that will speak volumes without saying a word. It is a life that will not fit into people's comfort zones, normalcy, or what is considered to be acceptable to those who belong to this present age.

This brings us to the point of considering what makes a Christian. Does it mean a person is religious or goes to some type of church? Does being a Christian mean you are moral and living in such a way that you are referred to as being a goody-two-shoes? Although the Christian life clearly will embrace excellent moral practices, such points of identification or qualities alone do not distinguish a person as being a believer.

There is only one point of identification that clearly distinguishes a person as a Christian. That identification is Jesus Christ. Being a Christian means I have agreed with the Bible about my spiritual plight,

---

[1] Ephesians 1:13-14

that I am a sinner doomed to separation from God for eternity. Such a separation is judgment for not receiving the provision of Jesus Christ. By receiving Jesus in my heart as my personal Lord and Savior, I will be born again from above. This new birth means I have received a new spirit and heart. This new spirit and heart point to a new disposition or creation that will be responsive towards the God of heaven. Obviously, the evidence of this new disposition in operation will identify me as being a Christian.[2] Consider how this disposition will express itself.

*New life:* New life will be brought forth by the indwelling presence and work of the Holy Ghost. The Word of God describes this new life as being the very life of Jesus. The key to this new life is we must daily put on Jesus. As the Holy Spirit works the divine life of the Son of God in us, we must work it out through application in our way of doing, being, and thinking through obedience to His Word. As we walk out this life on a daily basis, we will be transformed in our minds. In other words, it will change how we regard God and life.[3]

*New attitude:* As the life of Jesus is worked in us, we will develop the attitude that is associated with His character. The Apostle Paul tells us to let the mind or attitude of Christ be in us.[4] Jesus' attitude is described in Matthew 11:29 and Philippians 2:6-8. Clearly, Jesus' disposition is lowly (humble), and it is expressed in an attitude of meekness.

Meekness expresses itself in submission. For Jesus, this submission came in the form of subjection to the will of the Father. Meekness simply implies that all of one's focus, strength, and affections are under the control of the one the person is in subjection to.

In meekness one will submit to that which is worthy for the benefit of a greater purpose. For Jesus the greater purpose was the redemption of mankind. In other words, the true character of meekness does not submit to that which is lacking in quality such as the flesh and the world. Rather, meekness displays the greatest type of strength, because all of its strength will be disciplined and channeled for that which is greater and righteous.

Many people may be under control, but they lack meekness. In other words, they are controlled by factors greater than they, but they are not channeling their strength for that which is greater and worthy of their consideration. They are simply giving in to a matter because they lack strength to subdue it, rather than giving way to that which is greater in order to channel their strength.

As we will see, this meekness is an important characteristic to possess as a single person. Too many times single people are subject to influences that lack authority or power because they are not under the leading of the Holy Ghost. They find themselves giving in to temptations and lusts because they have failed to give way to the work of God in their

---

[2] Ezekiel 36:26-27; John 3:3, 5; Romans 6:23; 10:9-10; 2 Corinthians 5:17
[3] Romans 12:2; 13:14; 1 Corinthians 3:16-17; Galatians 2:20; Philippians 2:12
[4] Philippians 2:5

lives. This is why Paul tells us to put on the Lord Jesus Christ so we will not give room for the works of the flesh to operate.[5]

*New countenance:* The real distinction in a Christian will be a new countenance. Some people think that Christianity is reflecting their best. In other words, they are reflecting their "so-called" goodness, their sweetness, or their religious piousness. However, if others get past such attractions, they will be disappointed.

John 12:32 tells us that Jesus was lifted above all the attractions of man's best and the world to draw men to Himself. If people come to Jesus, they will never be disappointed. If they put their faith in Him, they will never be ashamed. The reason for this is because Jesus has the means to save them.

Christians must avoid the trap of trying to reflect the best of religion or self. True distinction in God's kingdom will not reflect a person's religious attempts to present him or herself in the best light; rather, it comes when he or she reflects the life of Jesus. People should be able to see Jesus Christ in a Christian's attitude and lifestyle. It is the glory of Jesus in a person that clearly distinguishes a person as a Christian.

The evidence of His glory in each of our lives will be determined by our openness to the Spirit and our level of maturity. The Apostle Paul talks about going on from glory to glory. To serve as an unhindered reflection of Jesus does not happen overnight. It takes a person continually growing in the knowledge of Jesus to possess greater measures of His life, attitude, and countenance.[6]

It is vital that a person resolves whether or not he or she is a Christian. Some people struggle with whether they are saved, but the Bible clearly states that if a person is saved, he or she has a witness in his or her spirit. That witness is the Holy Spirit, who not only testifies that a person is saved, but serves as the believer's seal or down payment until his or her redemption is realized in full.[7]

If you have identified that witness in your life, but there is something amiss, examine to see if there is any sin, attitude, or practice that may be grieving or quenching the work of the Spirit in your life. Allow the sweet conviction of the Holy Spirit to bring your attention to the matter. Once He does, repent of your ways and attitudes and ask for cleansing, reviving, and restoration.[8]

If you realize that your spiritual experiences have been nothing more than an intellectual acceptance or a religious assumption, you need to resolve the issue of your salvation right now. The Apostle Paul stated that today is the day of salvation. However, you must open your heart to receive Jesus, and confess with your mouth your sins that need to be forgiven, as well as confess Jesus as the Lord of your life.[9]

---

[5] Romans 8:12-14; 13:14
[6] Matthew 5:14-16; John 1:4; 2 Corinthians 3:18; 2 Peter 1:3-9
[7] Ephesians 1:13-14; 1 John 5:4-13
[8] Psalm 51:10-11; 139:23-24; John 16:7-11; Ephesians 4:30; 1 Thessalonians 5:19
[9] John 1:12; Romans 10:9-10; 1 Corinthians 15:3-4; 2 Corinthians 6:2; 1 John 1:9

Since there are questions throughout this manual, I would suggest you designate a separate notebook for your answers. Your first challenge is to write a short testimony of your salvation experience or your prayer of salvation in this notebook. If you are not sure about what a testimony entails, see the book *The Power of our Testimonies* in the Volume 6  or contact us through our website for information or encouragement.

# 2

# THE SACRIFICE

Jesus took the route of sacrifice in order to obtain salvation for each of us. The Apostle Paul declared that Jesus became the sin offering for us so that we could be made in the righteousness of God.[1] It is pretty incredible to realize that Jesus, who is the essence of righteousness, became sin. He did not taste sin; rather, He took our sin upon Himself, and experienced the desolation of it. The desolation of sin involved Him tasting physical death and experiencing the emptiness of the grave.

Christianity involves its own route. We must experience salvation before we can embrace the Christian life. The problem with many Christians is that they tack Jesus on to their life and devotion. Many have Him in a nice compartment, boxed in by standards, limited to an image, or controlled within the arena of ideas. However, the Christian life is not another addition to one's life; it must become a person's very life.

When Christianity becomes a life, rather than a religious practice or code, it has the potential to revolutionize a person's perception towards God, his or her attitude about life, and his or her very inward being or state. Once again, as believers, we must recognize that this life is the life of Jesus. He is the sole source behind it, while the Word of God serves as the means to reveal His life to us, and the Holy Spirit is the power behind establishing this new life in us.

Once salvation is established, we must offer the necessary sacrifices. There are a couple of important sacrifices that we must offer. One is the sacrifice of praise. We must recognize what our wonderful Lord did to secure our redemption. As part of a glorious priesthood, we must not be sparing in offering this sacrifice. Praise must be a glorious reality in our hearts so that it will always be close to our lips.[2]

Other types of sacrifices are doing good and sharing the life of Christ. The Word is clear that we are God's workmanship created in Christ Jesus unto good works. These works were actually ordained by God. We are told in the second book of Timothy that we must be sanctified and fit for the master's use, ensuring that we are prepared unto every good work. We are reminded in Titus that we have been redeemed from all iniquity, purified to be special, and zealous of good works.[3] It vital to note, that as Christians, we are not here to live only for ourselves. We are here to live unto God. Such a life will express itself in

---

[1] 2 Corinthians 5:21
[2] Hebrews 13:15-16; 1 Peter 2:5, 9; Titus 2:14
[3] Ephesians 2:10; 2 Timothy 2:21; Titus 2:14

praise, and show itself in good works that will bring glory to the One who has the ultimate say over our lives.

The other sacrifice is sharing the life of Christ with others. People need to see the life of Jesus in us. To God, it will serve as an acceptable fragrance that will reach His throne. To Christians, it will revive their spirits in edification, but for those who are unsaved it will speak of death, as the light and truth serves as a contrast to the hopeless darkness reigning in their lives.[4]

The reality of this sacrifice is that it is meant to produce the life of Christ in others. Christ's life in us is to be spilled over to others and poured out as a sacrifice for the benefit of others. It is a life that cannot be hidden, for it is glorious. It is a life that cannot be hindered, for it possesses the very power of heaven. It is a life that compels those who possess it to share it.

Sharing Christ is why every Christian remains in this world. If salvation was the end of our journey, God would take us out of here. However, salvation is the beginning of a journey of not only discovering the depths of this new life in us, but also planting the seeds of it wherever we go in order to see this life reproduced in others.

This brings us to the final sacrifice, that of our bodies. We see where we must offer the sacrifice of praise, but we need the use of our lips and hearts to offer such an offering. We must offer the sacrifice of good works, but we will need the use of our hands and feet. We are told to offer the sacrifice of our testimony, but we must possess a will and mind to do so. Hence, enters the instruction to offer our bodies as a living sacrifice. Consider the Apostle Paul's words, "I beseech you therefore, brethren, by the mercies of God, that ye present your bodies a living sacrifice, holy, acceptable unto God, which is your reasonable service" (Romans 12:1).

It is out of the mercy of God that we are able to offer the sacrifice of our bodies. We experience this mercy, because we have been marked for death. And, it is because of His Son's sacrifice on the cross that we can offer the sacrifice of our bodies.

We must present our bodies as a living sacrifice. In other words, such a sacrifice points to becoming a perpetual or ongoing sacrifice. It remains living so it can always come to a point of death, which is expressed in consecration. For example, the sacrifice of our bodies point to consecration or total abandonment of the life we know, desire, or prefer. The whole purpose of this sacrifice is to be prepared in holiness in order to become acceptable to God. However, note that such a sacrifice is our reasonable service.

Scripture states that we do not belong to ourselves; therefore, our bodies belong to God to do as He will with them.[5] Our lives must give way to the life of Christ to ensure that it will be offered up in praise, established in good works, and distributed as bread and life to the

---

[4] 2 Corinthians 2:15-16
[5] 1 Corinthians 6:20; 7:23

spiritually hungry and thirsty. Obviously, we must have only one focus, Jesus; we must have one goal, to glorify God, and we must have one destination, heaven.

At this point you may wonder why I am spending time on the subject of sacrifice. It is simple: God will require a sacrifice from each of us in order to place us in His Body. Most Christians fail to discover their place in Christ because they do not recognize the need to offer the sacrifice of their bodies to Him. Yet, every Christian must determine to offer such a sacrifice.

For the single Christian, he or she has a tremendous opportunity to offer a very important sacrifice up front. As we are about to see, this sacrifice is actually a gift from God. It is in light of God requiring Abraham to offer up Isaac that we can begin to see that even the gifts God gives us, such as His eternal life, must always be offered back to Him for the purpose of sanctification and fulfilling His promise and plan in each of our lives.

As single people, we need to now come to terms with the gift we must initially offer up through our bodies of service to Him. The Apostle Paul gives us insight into two of these gifts in 1 Corinthians 7:6-7, "But I speak this by permission, and not by commandment. For I would that all men were even as I myself. But every man hath his proper gift of God, one after this manner, and another after that." What is the Apostle Paul talking about? He is talking about the gift of being single or the gift of marriage.

God has imparted one of these gifts to every believer. For singles to find their place in the Kingdom of God, they must come to terms with what gift God has given them. Most assume that every person is meant to be married. But, according to this chapter in 1 Corinthians, some are ordained to remain single.

When I was a young single person, I presumed that I was to be married. After a disastrous marriage, I had to go back to the drawing board to find out what went wrong. After all, marriage is honorable and acceptable. It took some years before I realized that God had given me the gift of being single.

We assume much about our Christian life. I initially strove to find God's will for my life in the area of marriage, but I started from the wrong premise. Instead of starting from the premise of whether God's will for my life was to remain single or be married, I started from the presumption that I was to be married. Although I am not proud of my failed marriage, I have learned the importance of starting at the right basis to ensure that I end up in the right place.

Single Christians need to start from the right premise. They must avoid any assumption about their marital status, and start from the basis that their bodies belong to God. In the kingdom of God, it is not what we do for God that counts in eternity, rather it is what we allow God to do in us. He wants to bring forth the life of His Son through our bodies for service.

The question is, are we willing to initially offer our bodies to Him in this important matter? Clearly, this is where one can begin to understand how a gift can require a sacrifice. Let's say you want to be married, and yet the prospect that God may call you to the single life will cause an unwillingness to offer up your body in light of the future. Am I willing to sacrifice something (marriage) that has always been so close to my heart?

On the other hand, you may like your independence, and see no need to consider this subject until years down the road. God may have other plans. He may want to confront your independence, and He may use another individual to challenge your self-reliance in the near future. Once again, the possible sacrifice is being brought to the forefront. Am I willing to offer up the liberty that my single life offers to come into line with God's plan for my life?

It is important to point out that whatever sacrifice God requires from you concerning this matter, it is in line with who He has made you to be. Granted, you may want to be married, but in reality, you cannot properly balance your life in God and your relationship with a spouse without confusion or idolatry. As a result, you will be greatly hindered from serving Him.

Perhaps you want to remain single, but your independence or self-sufficiency will hinder you from ever coming into dependency upon God. Keep in mind, that as long as certain people do not have anyone to answer to, they can have the idea in their self-sufficiency that they are in control of their reality. Service in the kingdom of God requires genuine humility, while spiritual growth comes through adversity. God may use marriage to humble such a person.

I hope you are now realizing that God knows the particular state that will bring you to the place of sanctification, maturity, and growth in Him. Whether He uses a spouse to compliment your life or sharpen you, as iron sharpens iron, or whether He uses the liberty of the single life to bring you into places of unhindered service before Him, your body should be used for His purpose and glory.[6] As you can see, there are sacrifices required with each gift. If you are entrusted with the gift of marriage, you must offer up your right to yourself and ask God to prepare you for your future partner.

One of the major challenges with marriage is that it is a relationship of the world.[7] In other words, it can be very fleshly and influenced by the world. Therefore, Christians must ensure that the relationship does not remain worldly, but that it reaches its spiritual potential. In order to ensure this takes place, one must make sure that God picks his or her spouse. The problem with many Christian marriages is that people pursue the image they have of a mate, rather than allowing God to prepare them for the right partner.

---

[6] Proverbs 27:17
[7] 1 Corinthians 7:32-33

When God ordains a marriage, there is always preparation, and then at the right time, He will bring the future partner. Remember, a future partner will also be sharing in one's service to God. A mate will not only compliment the person in his or her life before God, but such a mate will challenge him or her as well. If each person remains true to God and humble before one another, the couple will be made into a powerful team that will honor God in example and service.

Personally speaking, if your gift is being single, then any ideas and desires concerning the prospect of the normal life (marriage and family) must be offered on the altar of consecration before God. You must realize that the Lord will serve as your partner in all that you do. Granted, He may bring team members along side of you who will share in your vision, but He will step into the place of your spouse.

The Apostle Paul preferred that all Christians would be content in an unmarried state, due to the liberty to serve God without any distractions. However, he recognized that some could only properly function within the state of marriage.

It is vital that single Christians resolve this issue before they make any decisions about their service before God. After all, serving God in a single status or married status will radically define the capacity in which a person will serve Him.

If you do not know God's will concerning your marital status at this time, you need to humble yourself and seek His face. Remember, offer your body as a living sacrifice and give Him permission to purge anything that would keep Him from having His way in your life. Be sure to start from the right premise, and resolve in your heart that God's plan for you is perfect, regardless of whether it lines up to your personal dreams, plans, and desires. Trust Him with your life and your future. Know He will work out the details.

**In your notebook**, write what you sense your *gift* is in the area of being single and married, as well as the sacrifice you will have to offer to receive the gift from God that will prepare you to walk out the life He is calling you to.

There is another aspect single Christians must keep in mind, whether they are waiting on God for their future mate or whether they are waiting for God to establish them in their single life. Single people rarely fit in most of their environments. Such a reality can cause an identity crisis.

# 3

# THE CRISES

One of the challenges that single people must confront is that they do not fit within society as a whole, neither are they usually regarded as "equal" in most of the religious world. As most single people are aware, they are the "odd man out." In fact, they can cause those around them to be uncomfortable and insecure. There are various reasons for this, which I will briefly discuss. The reason for addressing this issue is because at the core of this challenge lie attitudes. These attitudes have been established by the conditioning of the society we live in.

Conditioning is based on what we as a society perceive to be "normal" or "acceptable". For example, we perceive that what is normal is to be married and have children. When someone fails to fit into that which is considered normal, speculation begins as to why that individual is "abnormal." Needless to say, this speculation can end in suspicion, gossip, and slander.

Hence, enters the struggle for single people. It is important to realize that if these unspoken rules as to what stipulates normalcy in society were not in place, most people would not be concerned with whether a person was single or married. However, they are firmly in place in how we view life and the emphasis we put on life. These attitudes put pressure on single people to somehow comply so that order will once again reign according to the acceptable perception.

Obviously, there is a fragile balance in people's reality that many are not forced to face until their perception is challenged by that which does not fit. How do single people challenge the reality of those around them, especially in the Church that Jesus died for?

The first challenge has to do with identity. Sadly, most people seek their identity in relationships such as marriage or they seek it in their children. Keep in mind identity stipulates purpose and a reason for being here. However, this identity is not established on an individual basis, but according to the conditioning of our society. Most societies or cultures determine a person's place based on gender. Therefore, much of a person's identity is based on the collective masses perceiving life on the basis of their conditioning. Such identity strips individuals of the liberty to simply discover who they are outside of the unspoken rules of their society or culture.

Another challenge the single person poses to others is that he or she serves as a mirror. Through the years, I have had people admit to me that if they had the opportunities that I did when growing up, they would have never married or had a family. In other words, it was expected in past generations that a woman should marry and a man should settle down and have a family. Some women found themselves corralled into lifestyles that they were not comfortable with, but felt they had no choice in the matter because it was expected of them. Men, on the other hand had to prove they were responsible by getting married and having a family.

Single people sometimes can call into question the state of married people. For instance, an insecure married person can see a single person as a threat or point of temptation to his or her spouse. I have especially noticed this in women. One must ask if the insecurity is justifiable or if it is because the wife is not sure of her place in her spouse's life?

In some cases, single people uncap resentment that an unhappily married person may feel in regard to his or her present situation. Often marriage is the proverbial carrot that is put before people as a means to find and secure happiness in this present world. However, marriage can present the opposite picture. Good marriages do not just happen; rather, they are often forged through transitions, upheavals, challenges, and adversities. The relationship will be refined through the fire, defined through tribulation, and brought forth through sacrifice. It takes integrity, devotion, and commitment on the part of both individuals to make a good marriage.

For other people, they may have felt they had to marry to fit the mold of what was taught in reference to their lot in life. In a way, they were forced into this place by the pressure of those around them to produce the picture of normalcy. Single people who know their place in Christ will display a contentment that will bring a contrast to those around them, a contrast that will reveal the environment of other people's state of affairs.

Single people that encounter the insecurities and jealousies of others find themselves not only under suspicion, but isolated. They can also find themselves being pressured to conform to the ways of the world in order to make others comfortable. As the saying goes, "misery loves company". It is not unusual to see that those who are often unfulfilled in their married lives strive to see single people married. This can be seen in family situations where a parent is trying to fulfill his or her unfulfilled fantasy through the child's life.

Much of the struggle of single people has nothing to do with who they are or what is right for them; rather, it has to do with what other people are comfortable with. Single people find themselves being pressured to comply to what is acceptable, so others have a common ground with them. Or, they are pushed into a certain situation to silence speculations so that order can come to the personal world of others whose relationships are already out of order due to fear and speculation.

This brings us down to identity. It is important to point out that no one is born with an identity. Granted, we each have a need for identity to be established, and we have the means in which to bring it forth. However, it is the people around us that give us our initial identity. As a result, we are told what we should be content without ever discovering who we are meant to be. Obviously, we need to find out who we are meant to be to know what we want our lives to say.

Therefore, who needs to determine our identity? The first question we must ask is what is identity? Identity is that distinguishable characteristic that identifies you on an individual level. Such an identity will speak of your purpose, worth, and function. Each source has it way of identifying us. For example, our family identifies us with a name, while society begins this identification process at the point of gender. Education begins this identity at the place of one's intellectual abilities. The business world starts this identity at abilities. However, what really distinguishes a person? It is something called personality.

Personality states that each of us are unique individuals. We may have similar looks, opinions, talents, etc, but we are unique and our personality is going to distinguish us from others. Personality is actually the reflection of the inward disposition or state of a person. The inward state is affected by the decisions we make and the influences around it. This disposition is manifested through our attitudes or prevailing moods.

Usually, personality is rarely considered. Family tells us to comply with its rules regardless of the person we are designed to become. Society tells us to conform to the place our gender puts us in as a means to maintain the scheme of things, regardless of our dreams. Education instructs us to perform on an academic level, in spite of our desire to explore outside of "acceptable boxes", while the business world demands we produce, regardless of the quality behind the product.

When personality is discarded, ignored, or controlled, a person is devoid of the means to find out who he or she is. On the other hand, God is after our personality. He wants to bring it out by refining it with the attitude of His Son. He wants to channel it by His Spirit, and He wants to establish it with His Word. Since He is our Creator, He knows how to bring forth our individual personality. However, it is important to point out that our personality is meant to reflect Jesus Christ. As we are transformed by the life of Christ in us, we will be conformed to His image. In other words, we are fashioned or formed to be like Him. Our personality will reflect Him in our attitude, approach, and conduct.[1]

To ensure our personality comes out, we must first bring order to our world. Order is only established when Jesus takes His rightful place as Lord and King of our life. Once we come into God's order, He will have the liberty to reveal our place in His Body. This will define our position in Christ. Position reveals in what way we will reflect Jesus to the Body and reflect Him in the world. As we allow God to have His way, we will begin to reflect Jesus from the vantage point of our potential in His kingdom. As our personality reflects Jesus, people will be attracted to His life in us.

The key to personality is that it is not only the means to reflect who we are, but it is the point of attraction. More often than not, the attraction is according to the façade and image that we have been conditioned to present. However, these attractions are directed at fakery, and will fade

---

[1] Romans 8:29; 2 Corinthians 3:18; Galatians 2:20; Philippians 2:5

when tested or challenged by life. Sadly, many people marry an image, rather than a person who has needs, struggles, and weaknesses.

The greatest struggle for anyone in God's kingdom is to ensure that no one defines him or her but God. Once people discover their identity in Christ, then they must maintain it. The problem is that Satan is always striving to destroy the image of Christ wherever its light penetrates into the darkness of this world. He does not care how he does it. Whether he uses the world to drown it out; the conditioning of family and culture to cause one to give way to pressures of compliance; education to humanize it; entertainment to desensitize its impact, sin to defile it; friends to wrongly influence it; or the world to cause it to compromise, he will try to undermine or destroy the image of Christ.

Consider who or what has defined you the most. Examine how this influence is affecting how you look at your present life. Do you have a true sense of the person you are, or whether you have simply complied to get along with those around you? Write your conclusions in your notebook to consider or meditate on as you continue this personal journey of discovery.

It is important to understand and remember what these identity crises are and how they affect each of us. Keep in mind that no one is born with an identity. Rather, their identity is greatly determined, and often influenced, and manipulated by the environment around them.

# 4

# THE SEXUAL CRISIS

There are three types of identity crises a person can encounter throughout his or her life. It is not unusual that each crisis will serve as a breeding ground for the next crisis as people struggle to come to terms with their place and purpose in life.

The first crisis has already been mentioned. It begins early in life. In fact, every aspect of life is defined according to this one arena—that of gender. You are named based on gender, and as you grow, society begins to condition you to fit a particular role in life. For example, a woman's place is to be married and bear children. Supposedly, this will secure her worth and purpose in society. A man must prove his manhood. Usually, he initially proves it by his ability to conquer the opposite sex, subdue some kind of personal kingdom in regard to a home, and prove his worth in the working arena.

This conditioning procedure not only causes people to conform in order to fit roles, but it often conditions attitudes about the different issues confronting life and relationships. As my friend and co-laborer in the Gospel, Jeannette, stated, such influences condition us in the area of pride and prejudices. We will pride ourselves according to whether we fulfill the roles allotted us, and we will attach prejudices against that which does not fit nicely according to our perceptions.

Pride feeds off of our prejudices and prejudices are justified and reinforced by pride. The harsh reality is that they both have been conditioned in us by the attitudes of those around us. Hence, enters the tremendous influences of our culture, not only upon us, but our families as well.

Each culture has its own way of defining a person's worth, purpose, and place that he or she will fit into according to his or her gender. People can argue that our sense of self comes down to hormones and personal likes or dislikes, and not culture. However, if you observe different cultures around the world, you will discover that attitudes towards people's gender, as far as the role they must play and the value they will hold in society, are indeed conditioned by our way of thinking that has been influenced by our culture.

This conditioning can be clearly identified when individuals decide to step outside of the roles established for them in opposition to, or in search of discovering who they are outside the confines of prejudicial and limited definitions. Such people are considered rebels that can cause unrest to those who encounter them outside of acceptable roles.

As you observe these so-called "rebels," you will realize that they are often opposing the way they have been conditioned by family, religion, and/or society. Such "rebels" rebel because they recognize that such conditioning has no real regard for who they are. As they struggle with the concept that is based on gender alone, they begin to see how their entire life has been laid out for them without any regard for them as a person; thus, they lose all sense of identity and purpose. In a way, they hit a void that seems unfair, indifferent, and cruel.

All that an identity crisis simply means is that a person has lost his or her way concerning knowing the purpose and meaning of his or her life. In fact, lost people have come to the end of a matter to find out that nothing makes sense in their lives. Such people conclude that life appears to be stupid, ridiculous, and foolish.

However, what these "rebels" fail to see is that the conditioning is already in place in the form of a worldview. A worldview comes down to a person's value system. This value system will determine how we look at the issues of life. Ultimately, we will judge all matters, as well as define the worth of something, according to this ingrained view of life.

When people rebel against their conditioning, they will ignore, justify, or betray their worldview, but they will not change it. Regardless, of how extreme their opposition may be against the conditioning around them, they cannot get around this unseen ruler. Eventually, their worldview will unmercifully judge them, causing despair, disillusionment, and depression. Such an inward environment will cause people to feel even more lost as they struggle with who they are.

Does gender alone define each of us? Is our place in society determined strictly by our sex? Regardless of how some may oppose this unseen conditioning, they are nevertheless constantly being haunted by it.

Even if people manage to wade through this conditioning, and earn a place in society apart from it, they can find themselves becoming angry and embittered at the injustice of it all. Ultimately, they want to rage against all of it. They want to scream, fight, and destroy that which dictates and demands them to conform through compromise or game playing with something that has no regard to their person.

Sadly, what most people fail to realize is that in all their opposition against the conditioning, there appears to be no reliable source that is able to establish a person's real identity. All that remains is darkness invading their soul. Although they may be rebelling against what has been established by different influences of the world and culture, they have no real guidelines to discover who they are outside of the roles that have been established for them.

It is a harsh reality that no person defines who he or she is. The key in determining who we become rests with what we allow to influence our way of thinking. Such an influence will set up the boundaries by which we regard life and ourselves. For the Christian, the influence is obvious. It must be the Spirit and the Word of God. The Holy Spirit will ensure a right environment and the Word of God will establish the right premise within which we will regard the issues of life.

As Christians, we must understand how we are being conditioned so that we can test attitudes and conduct in light of the Word of God. We are first of all conditioned by the *world* we live in. The world establishes images and ideas as to how we should dress, act, and conduct ourselves as far as gender. In a way it becomes the *standard of what is to be considered good, beautiful, or attractive.* In other words, I must be a certain way to attract the type of life that I have been conditioned to desire or submit to. Clearly, this attraction appeals to ego or vanity and lacks any real substance. However, many automatically adopt the idea as a standard of gaining acceptance, winning love, and earning recognition.

Secondly, we are conditioned by *culture.* Culture determines what is *acceptable.* It often puts pressure on people to not only conform, but to comply with its philosophies concerning life.[1] It conditions us as far as the type of lifestyle we are to live. This lifestyle will establish our worth. We prove this worth by complying with the practices of our culture. In most cases the practices of culture are nothing more than paganism and idolatry, but since we are conditioned, we see such practices as normal and trustworthy, as far as determining our reality and attitudes.

Thirdly, our *family* and *religion* condition us. Families, along with religious influences, determine our *moral code* in which to test the matters of life. This code can be tied up in various aspects of our way of looking at life. It may be tied up in our name, lineage, heritage, belief, or inheritance. In some cases, people actually find the past enslaving them to some kind of code that is indifferent, unrealistic, and arrogant. However, we see such codes as a means of *perfecting* ourselves. No wonder the Apostle Paul talked about our minds being transformed so that we could know the good, acceptable, and perfect will of God.[2]

Finally, *friends* will have a big impact on our lives. In many cases, especially in the area of young people, friends play the advocate against that which influences us the most, such as our families or religion. As a result, they will influence us towards *lifestyle, preference,* and *attitude.* In some cases, the lifestyle is influenced by rebellion. In rebellion, people are simply going against the grain of a matter, rather than coming to terms with who they are. In a way, these people are still allowing their past conditioning to define them. After all, going against the grain of what is considered right, is not discovering that which will bring meaning to life. Ultimately, such influences can prove to be just as empty in possessing the answers to life.

As Christians, we must beware of how we have been conditioned. Such conditioning is what will define us. Its enslaving tentacles may judge or condemn any attempts to discover our identity outside of what has been established for us by the world, our culture, and those who are

---

[1] Colossians 2:8
[2] Romans 12:2

directly involved in our way of thinking. And, to think most of this conditioning started at the base of our gender!

It is vital that Christians properly discern this conditioning in their personal lives. The reason it must be discerned is because it influences people in different areas. The first area is that of *attractions*.

Much of our taste has been conditioned in us. Such conditioning has been reinforced by experience. In other words, we have experienced certain aspects of life that have become a standard to our tastes and preferences in light of fleshly desires. Although we conclude our attractions are a matter of choice, we fail to realize that our taste for different aspects of life is based on what we have been exposed to in our particular culture. Granted, we can lay claim to some attractions, but when you consider other cultures, one must conclude that attractions or matters of taste and preferences, have been greatly established by the environment people grow up in.

For example, if you grew up in another culture, you would prefer foods and practices of that particular culture. Although a different culture would give you different choices, your preference would often be for that which you were accustomed to.

The attractions that have been adopted will determine the emphasis or direction of our *affections*. A person's particular emphasis can be to have a nice family and home, which is considered normal to many cultures. However, such affections will be directed towards the things of the world. A worldly focus will drown out the things of God, as affections are wrapped up in expectations as to how such a life would make a person feel or look to others.

We must discern our attractions in order to discipline our affections. The Apostle Paul instructed us to set our affection on things above.[3] In other words, fix our affections on Jesus. We need to make sure there are no divided loyalties in our affections.

Most of the time, people are attracted to the idea or image that a person or society portrays about a matter, rather than the real thing. In fact, as a society, we Americans are bombarded by images that have no substance. Our affections simply get caught up with the propaganda associated with these images. Sadly, the feelings that originate from the basis of images seem like reality, even though such images are nothing more than illusions.

Our affections cannot discern a matter. For this reason, we must discern a matter to discipline the focus and intensity of our affections. Affection in turn decides our *desires*. It is at the point of desires that our perception can be perverted towards what is right. Perversion is adding to or taking away from, that which God has deemed to be true and righteous.

It is important to realize there are various things that can attract us. A person's spirit can be attractive. We can be fascinated with a person's

---

[3] Colossians 3:2

personality, abilities, talents, or even their countenance. As you can see, not all attractions are based on the opposite sex or physical appearance.

However, these attractions can become confusing, idolatrous, or obsessive if they are not kept in the right perspective. Affections are disciplined as people discern the source of their attraction. Why am I attracted to this person? Is it a healthy attraction, or perverted and dangerous, or simply a fascination that has no merit? This is why all affections must be directed heavenward to keep all of our desires in check. The only real vantage point from which discernment can operate is from a heavenly perspective that is based on and confirmed by the Word of God.

Desires in turn will determine our *preference.* Preferences are influenced by agendas and priorities. What do we really prefer? It takes integrity to be honest about the environment in which desires operate. Are my desires worldly and self-serving, or do they have a touch of the heavenly behind their inspiration? Jesus tells us that most people prefer darkness because their deeds are evil. Evil deeds simply mean these individuals are giving in to the desires of their flesh, which will bring them under the spirit of the world. [4]

Fleshly desires have no limit in exploring all matters according to vain imaginations. The possibilities in which the flesh can partake of the tree of knowledge, as it tastes of the forbidden fruit of the world, is limited only by the death and destruction it brings. There is no greater arena in which these forbidden fruits can be tasted and experienced to the extent of its evilness than in the sexual arena.

It is easy to get caught up in the sexual arena and lose sight of all that is holy, satisfying and eternal. It is easy to lose all sense of what is right or wrong as our attitudes adjust to the world and our practices are compromised to bow down to fleshly experiences. Ultimately, we become confused as our preferences become perverted.

For example, many people have come to me who are confused by their sexual preferences. Due to their past experiences, such as sexual encounters that have not been properly brought to the light, or affections that have not been properly disciplined, people find their attractions to be confusing. They may feel strongly towards a person or friend of the same sex. This attraction immediately causes confusion, especially when they have not felt such an attraction towards the opposite sex before. Sadly, they presume that since the attraction is there, it must be defining them in the sexual arena.

Such confusion in the sexual arena can cause people to go into the extreme. For example, to prove that they are not strange, some will go to the extreme to prove that they are normal. This brings them into tremendous moral deviation, but at least it subdues their confusion. On the other hand, others will give way to these affections, allowing them to define their preference while trying to drown out or console their conscience with the conclusion that this is who they must be. There is

---

[4] John 3:18-21; Galatians 5:16-21; Ephesians 2:2

the third scenario where such confusion causes shame for the individual and he or she simply closes down and keeps it in darkness.

What many people do not understand is that affections and attractions are not meant to define us. They have no preference, personality or distinction as to gender, race etc. In other words, we determine the type of audience or platform we give to our affections and attractions. We are the ones who must discern, discipline and define their focus and direction. This is why the Apostle Paul instructs us to direct our affections heavenward and to flee the drawing power of youthful lusts (attractions).[5]

The escalation of this sexual confusion is in part due to the breakdown that has been occurring in this nation for at least the last four decades. Back in the 1960s a sexual revolution took place in America. This revolution consisted of a revolt against all moral decency. It was as if mankind thumbed its nose at the concept of purity. This revolt was not just against moral responsibility, but against the attitudes it promoted. For example, where there is a sense of moral accountability, there is also a sense of patriotism towards what is right and liberating, and the willingness to sacrifice.

The sexual revolution found its greatest breeding ground in the division brought on by the Viet Nam War. To a generation being influenced by liberal, socialistic education, who had been completely removed from the sacrifice of WWII and was slightly on the radar during the Korean Conflict, the idea of sacrifice and liberty did not make sense. The moral values seemed obsolete, especially in light of liberal education, free love, and drugs. It was at this time that America suffered a national identity crisis that it has never recovered from.

Sadly, the repercussion has desensitized many in the Church. For example, many Christians think nothing of premarital sex or living together. Although there may be some twinge of conscience, it has been accepted as a normal lifestyle. However, God sees it as fornication, and has not changed His mind just because many people have become more liberal in their views and lifestyles.[6]

If we, as Christians, are to stand distinct in this world, we must come out from its influence and agree with God's evaluation about a matter. This means we must discern our attitudes about matters that involve the issue of righteousness. We must step out of the mode of being conditioned by the influences of the world and become transformed by the Holy Spirit in our way of thinking, being, and doing.[7]

We must insist on integrity and heavenly wisdom in our way of thinking, demand righteousness in our way of being, and exercise our way of doing unto godliness.[8] We must cease from trying to fit Christ into our worldly ways and practices, and separate from them so that Christ

---

[5] Colossians 3:2; 2 Timothy 2:22
[6] 1 Corinthians 3:16-17; 6:18-20
[7] Romans 12:2
[8] John 3:18-21; 1 Timothy 4:8; Titus 2:12; John 3:18-21

can fit us into His kingdom. It is important that we recognize that God will have no part of the world, and the world will oppose all that is of God.

Examine your attitudes and practices. Ask the Lord to expose how the following issues and questions may be affecting your attitudes, focus, and life.[9] Write the conclusions in your notebook.

1) Preferences

2) Attractions

3) Affections

4) Desires

5) How much of the world is influencing your present attitudes?

6) How much of your culture is affecting your lifestyle and how you look at life?

---

[9] If you would like to read more about the subject of attractions, see the presentation, "A Matter of Attractions" in the book, *The Challenge of it,* in "*The Christian Life Series.*"

# 5

# AT A LOSS

We are discussing the identity crisis we can find ourselves in during our lives. A crisis leaves us vulnerable. In such a state, other sources can begin to define who we are, ultimately determining who we become. It is always important to keep in mind that we are not born with an identity; rather, we are born with the means to establish an identity.

The main key in developing an identity is who are we allowing to define us as a person. The point of identity comes down to whom or what is influencing us in our way of thinking. The Apostle Paul tells us that our mind must be transformed.[1] In other words, how we look at a matter must be changed. When you consider what needs to be transformed, you will discover that it is our worldview.

As previously stated, our worldview is made up of our moral code. Needless to say, these values can be liberal or conservative, depending on who or what has influenced us over the years. We have already pointed out how family, religion, culture, the world, and friends can influence us. However, it is important to understand the concept of influence.

Influence means having the power or the capacity to cause an effect in an indirect or intangible way.[2] Such an influence will become our authority in how we perceive matters. It will affect our attitudes, establish the direction of our moral practices, and become the avenue that determines the person we become. In other words, what we will reflect to the world.

This brings us back to the power behind our worldview. We must once again establish that this view will not only define who people are, but who we are. For example, we know a thief is someone who steals but how do we know this? It is because of our worldview. Our moral code identifies a person who steals as being a thief. This is because our moral code has been established by influences such as parents and religion, and is often reinforced by our culture.

The worldview is made up of conscience, influences, and perception. Much of what influences us will either condition or indoctrinate us with the goal of influencing or changing our reality about a matter. This will determine our perception or frame of reference. Such conditioning or indoctrination affects our subconscious. Conditioning or indoctrination can make the subconscious indifferent to reality. It causes judgmentalism in regards to others, but will be indifferent to the fruit coming out of one's

---

[1] Romans 12:2
[2] Webster's New Collegiate Dictionary

personal life. In other words, people will not even be aware of how such conditioning or indoctrination is affecting them, but indirectly such influences have the power to dull their conscience and desensitize their perception concerning their own personal life and practices. Ultimately, at this point anyone can write over the slate that has already been established. Obviously, this will influence a person's attitude and who he or she perceives him or herself to be.

The problem is that as the subconscious become subdued, the conscience will become confused or seared. The mind will be unable to perceive anything outside of the indoctrination. However, to properly discern, the conscience must be sensitive to the things of God. The subconscious must be aware of what is happening in the inward environment to ensure the integrity of the conscience. Therefore, perception will judge the essence or worth of a person based on the discernment of the conscience and the examination of the subconscious.

Obviously, our personal worldview will define us. Conflict arises when a person's subconscious believes that personal deviant actions are justifiable in a particular situation. As a result, such a person will give in to his or her flesh. After the initial thrill dies down and reality sets in, then the conscience will kick in as one's perception begins to evaluate and judge the deviance according to its view of a matter. In the end, a person's worldview will condemn him or her.

Let me bring this down to laymen's terms. The biggest compromise for most people usually happens in the area of sex. All sins against God reveal that we are getting off center and beginning to deviate away from that which is true, moral, and acceptable to our holy God. However, when it comes to the sin of fornication, which is all illicit sex outside of the institution of marriage that was clearly established in the beginning by God, it also points to a sin against the body.

The Apostle Paul made this statement in 1 Corinthians 6:17-20,

But he that is joined unto the Lord is one spirit. Flee fornication. Every sin that a man doeth is without the body; but he that committeth fornication sinneth against his own body. What? know ye not that your body is the temple of the Holy Ghost which is in you, which ye have of God, and ye are not your own? For ye are bought with a price: therefore glorify God in your body, and in your spirit, which are God's.

What is Paul talking about? If you read 1 Corinthians 6:15-16, you will realize it is about unholy alliances. When a person has a sexual relationship with another, he or she becomes one with that individual in a spiritual agreement. It is important to realize that God gave the gift of sexual intimacy to marriage to establish an example of oneness that takes place in the physical (body), emotional (soul), and spiritual (spirit) arenas. This is why harlotry or idolatry is also considered fornication. It points to unholy agreement in the spiritual realm.

As Christians, we belong to God, and our agreement with Him is at the point of the Spirit. In fact, our bodies serve as the temple of the Holy

Spirit, and God will destroy those who defile this temple at any level: body, soul, or spirit.[3]

Agreement will determine what will influence us in our attitude or way of thinking. Unholy alliances will affect how we regard and handle the issues of life that surround that particular matter. Once an arena is defiled, then a person's attitude and way of thinking towards the matter will be perverted. From that point on, everything will be tainted unless that person repents and is once again cleansed from all unrighteousness.[4]

Meanwhile, the defilement begins to break down the moral fiber of a person's resolve. Let me give you an example. I have dealt with many young women who have given in to premarital sex. The affect upon them is devastating. They feel as if they are now "damaged goods" because someone has immorally and dishonorably tasted of the fruit of their life. It is from this vantage point that these young women view their worth. After all, their worldview may define them as a tramp, and the culture's attitude is that they are nothing more than a piece of garbage to be used and later discarded because they have prostituted themselves.

In many cases these women stop growing emotionally. As I have struggled with understanding this issue, I have somewhat come to the conclusion why many women stop experiencing emotional growth after this experience. I believe it is due to how our culture presents sexuality. For example, Hollywood depicts this familiarity to be the pinnacle experience in our emotional makeup and human pursuits. In reality it is not a pinnacle, but a door that will open a Pandora's Box of confusion, guilt, and uncertainty. In the right premise, it will hopefully open a door to intimacy that will allow married individuals to develop a deeper relationship with the one they are becoming one with in body, soul, and spirit.

Needless to say, this experience rarely proves to be a pinnacle in a person's life. It often leaves a person feeling confused, guilty, empty, and dirty. Since much value is put on people's sexuality as a point of identification, these people become lost in it all. In their mind, there is nowhere else to go emotionally. They have experienced the peak of their "so-called" identity and it has proven to be anything but satisfying. It is from such vantage points that people make terrible decisions.

For women, they might conclude that since they are "damaged goods," there is now no need to be concerned about moral restriction because they are hopelessly lost. Such women continue to spiral down in hopelessness as they become numb to being used up and sacrificed in this way. Some women see it as a means to make men pay for defiling them in the first place. Clearly, we can see how this defilement greatly influences people's perceptions and attitudes.

What about men when it comes to attitudes toward their sexual identity? The men that have been honest with me admit that their peers,

---

[3] 1 Corinthians 3:16-17
[4] Titus 1:15-16; Hebrews 10:21-23; 1 John 1:9

as well as society, put much emphasis on them performing in this area. They must conquer the woman and taste her forbidden fruit to prove their manhood. The attitudes that are encouraged in this arena prove to be devastating to some men. It tells them that their worth is strictly found in the physical arena. Therefore, men are confused about what it means to love a woman. If their concept of love does not graduate from the physical arena to embrace the emotional and spiritual aspects, then they will never understand what real love is as far as God's perspective of it is concerned. At such a point sex will be nothing more than a physical activity that has no real worth or moral responsibility.

However, this physical activity brings people into agreement. When the moral accountability is absent in this act, man is reduced to a brute creature like the animals. When the emotional arena is lacking in this pursuit, then this act is nothing more than fraudulent because it lacks genuine intention and purpose.[5] If the spiritual aspect is missing, it becomes a point where the agreement not only taints people's perception of themselves and the opposite sex, but it robs them of dignity and self-respect as their sense of worth is sacrificed for the sake of temporary lust. In the end, it all seems hypocritical and empty.

This brings us back to the second type of identity crisis. As you can see, everything around us can influence us, thereby, defining us. However, such identification reveals itself to be indifferent to the person we can be. After all, such identification is generic and not personal.

Therefore, who can bring identity to me without stripping me of my potential? There is only one entity, who can properly define me in light of my personality, abilities, and potential, and that is my Creator. God is aware of every detail of each person's makeup and being. He will not go against the grain as to who He designed each of us to be in His kingdom and in His Body according to His eternal plan.

Obviously, the reason so many people are lost is because they are allowing everything and everybody to define them except their Lord and Savior. People will characterize us according to who they want us to be. Family will often identify us according to their ideas of how we should fit into the family unit or represent them. Religion will pigeonhole us according to religious codes, and the world will classify us according to philosophies and cultures. These influences will write on our different slates, but in the process how lost do we become as we realize that our true identity is missing in the midst of all these endless, fickle concepts as to how we should be, and what we must become for the sake of others and the environments around us?

When people come to the end of this continual vacuum of identities, either they will go into rebellion and utter despair or they will realize they cannot leave such a matter in the hands of others, including religion and even the world. Personally, I got tired of *complying* with others' idea of me to gain acceptance, *conforming* to some religious code that was powerless to change me to gain some type of recognition, *reforming* so I

---

[5] 1 Thessalonians 4:3-7

could come across as genuine to gain respect, and *performing* so others would accept, value, or admire me. It was all utterly useless and senseless. In the end, I found myself miserably lost and unsure of my place in this world.

How do we find identity in Christ? It comes down to finding our position in Christ. It is from this point that we can come to a place of rest, peace, and life in Him. So many believers are beginning from the wrong vantage point of self, the world, family, religion, friends, or personal strengths to find their position in Christ. However, to find one's position in Christ, he or she must start from the point of Jesus. This often means starting from the perspective of His Word to seek Him out in order to understand one's personal identity in Him.

Much of this identity will be realized because He indwells the believer. It is His life in me that allows me to realize my true identity, bringing satisfaction and purpose to my life. After all, my life will be defined according to His life working in me and will be brought forth by the Holy Spirit. It is from the vantage point of His life within me that I will discover my position in His kingdom.

Until I discovered my position in Jesus, I was lost in the maze of identities that were constantly being thrust upon me. There was no peace or satisfaction in any of it. I struggled with the various issues of life because I could not discern what belonged to me as far as my perception of likes and dislikes. But, what a blissful time it was when I finally came home to my Lord and Savior, and was given the way to discover His identity, purpose, and plan for my life.

The question is have you come home to find your identity in Christ and have His life established in you? Consider who or what has influenced your present identity. Be honest. Are you satisfied or miserable? Are you confused or standing sure in who God made you to be?

Prayerfully consider how the following influences are affecting your personal identity and write down your conclusions.

1) Gender

2) Family

3) Friends

4) The World

5) Culture

6) Religion

7) Jesus & His Word:

8) Others

# 6

# LOSING ONE'S WAY

As we have seen, the different means that identify us create a greater identity crisis. When our gender is used as a point of identity, we become robbed of our right to discover who we really are. When those around us try to identify us, we become lost among all of the identities that demand our submission and adherence. Sadly, these different means of identity have no real regard for the person that we are, can be, and are meant to be.

The third identity crisis does not occur because individuals have given way to the various identities around them. The last identity crisis is a product of one losing his or her way because of trying to establish his or her identity through personal pursuits.

For example, a man came to me who was in what most would consider a "midlife crisis". He was in a compromising situation that could destroy every aspect of his life. As we discussed his situation, he admitted that in his younger years he felt he had a call on his life, but he ignored it and pursued the world. After succeeding in business and finances, he found himself plagued by emptiness. After all, business and money cannot bring meaning to life. He began to question the reason and purpose for his life. He had worked hard, and had created an appearance of having everything a man could want. However, he was empty and viewed his life as a complete waste. This threw him into an identity crisis.

Women can hit this crisis once all their children leave home. After all, they put every ounce of time and energy into raising their children. Once the children are no longer a focus, some women find they have no vision or purpose. This type of scenario creates the third type of crisis.

The reason that people hit this third identity crisis is because they have put value in that which is temporary, rather than in that which is eternal. Granted, they may have raised their children in a godly manner, but they failed to establish their own personal life in Christ. They may have attended church and paid their tithes, but these are all outward investments. Ultimately, they failed to establish their inner life on the immovable Rock, Jesus Christ.

The third type of crisis occurs because people get away from the center of life. The center of life is God. Everything must come back to center, be regarded in light of the center, and always align itself to the center, or the person becomes lost in the maze of demands. As people begin to run the race of family, success, money, fun, pleasure, and the best money can buy, they often lose sight of what is important and eternal.

The most meaningful aspect of our life is our relationship with God. Everything of value, purpose, and meaning will flow from this center. Finding our place in His kingdom, being placed in His Body, and being prepared to realize our calling in light of His eternal plan is what fulfills and satisfies us in our lives and relationships with others. It is all so simple. However, we miss it because of the demands, attractions, and meaningless pursuits of this present world. Our world becomes lopsided with demands, top-heavy with vanity, upside-down with failures and despair, and unbearable with its many burdens. Suddenly, we find our present life has no meaning or purpose. In fact, we discover we have become lost in the vanity of it all.

It is easy to lose our way in this world. Our focus can be taken off of God by the glitter of the world. Our affections can become entangled with the false idea of happiness. Our hope can become tied up with the idea of worldly success. Ultimately, our heart will be divided by perverted loyalties.

It is vital that every believer discovers his or her position in Christ to avoid each identity crisis. Granted, crises will come even in the Christian life. However, the crisis will come along the line of our faith, and not always in light of our purpose and direction.[1] After each test of our faith, our purpose will remain sure in Christ, and our direction will be directed beyond the present world to taste the glorious reality of His unhindered presence for eternity.

Clearly, Jesus is the only one who can establish my identity. Through His Spirit He will develop my personality to reflect His glory. His Word will challenge and change my way of thinking. In the end, I will find satisfaction because I will discover His life and place in His plan for my life.

This is why Christians must always start from the right premise if their life is going to count for God. He must reveal their gift (being single or married) to ensure that His people discover their potential according to His design. However, each of us must allow God to be God if we are going to properly discern influences and discover personal identity. Otherwise, we will fall prey to the various identity crises, and possibly fail to find our life in Jesus.

The Christian's life is summarized in the type of attitude we developed about the matters of life. If our attitude is not right about God, our attitude towards life will prove to be burdensome, miserable, and wicked.

Let us now consider the picture that has been developed thus far in the following table. Prayerfully examine the following table to see if you are struggling in regard to your identity in Christ.

---

[1] 1 Peter 1:6-9

| Gift | Discover Potential | Discern Influences in My Life. | Identity Crises | Finding Identity in Christ. |
|---|---|---|---|---|
| Sacrifice (Consecration Premise to discover gift.) | Allow only God to define me. | The world (Culture, philosophies, education, entertainment.) (Who I should be to fit.) | Sexual (Identified according to gender without regard to person.) | Heavenly position according to His kingdom. (Finding out who I am.) |
| Being Single (Sacrifice the hope or dream of experiencing normal life to establish identity in Christ.) | Personality (Allow the life of Christ to be established in me to reflect Jesus.) | Family And Friends (Who I must be for the sake of others.) | Personal (Identified according to roles and expectations designed by others.) | Place in the Body according to the working of the Spirit in light of God's plan. (Find out what I am intended to be in His kingdom.) |
| Being Married (Sacrifice personal identity to discover a new identity with spouse.) | Position (Allow the Spirit to establish me In God's kingdom.) | Religion (Who I must become to be recognized and acceptable.) | Mid-life (Lost one's way because of a worldly value system and pursuits that have no lasting purpose.) | Discover my life in Christ according to my calling and purpose in the harvest field. (Finding out what my true potential is in His kingdom.) |

The one lesson I discovered about my life is that I had to take it back from all the different influences. The reason I needed to take it back was not to lay personal claim to it, but to offer it to God in total consecration. I realized that I was in bondage to the pride and prejudice of the world, culture, family, and society. To be under the influences of such bondage simply defiled the things of God. Such things could never properly define them.

When God called my co-laborer, Jeannette, and me to be missionaries to the Church in America I argued with His reasoning. It appeared as if people were "churched out" with self-righteous requirements, sick of the hypocrisy, and had enough religion to last them a lifetime. My perspective was somewhat correct, but I failed to see that in spite of the religious atmosphere that was in operation, Jesus was missing from much of the picture. Granted, His name was being mentioned or tacked on in many arenas, but He was missing from most of the religious activities. Many people claimed they were Christians, but few possessed a testimony that clearly identified them to the Lord of lords and King of kings. It appeared as if they simply played church.

In asking myself where the real sheep of Jesus were, I was reminded in Scripture that when the Church became weak with compromise, sick from sin, defiled by heresy, preyed upon by wolves, and used by hireling shepherds to promote personal kingdoms, the sheep scattered because they could not hear the voice of their shepherd in the midst of the counterfeits.[2]

There are many attractions, distractions, and detours we can take as Christians. However, they lead us to crisis, frustrations, disillusionments, and hopelessness. I cannot tell you how many detours I have taken. Although the lessons I learned from these detours have been priceless, I realize I could have learned some lessons in a more constructive way, and avoid wasting precious time and distress from tasting the bitter dregs of sin, compromise, and failure.

As you consider the information in this manual, I pray you will realize how important it is for every aspect of your life to be established in and on Christ. We must always come back to center if we are going to avoid losing our way in this present world. We must avoid assuming that the different matters about life are insignificant and unimportant to God. We must step beyond what others consider to be acceptable boundaries in order to discern each attitude, decision, and action in light of the Spirit, heart, and intent of God. We must make sure that our position and identity in Christ are firmly established.

Once we become established in Christ, we can begin to prepare ourselves to embrace the life He has for us. This life is not meant to heap upon ourselves; rather, it is meant to offer it back to God. Its fullness is meant to break us so that it can be poured out and hopefully spilled out to others for His glory.

Where are you in your Christian life? This information is meant to shake, challenge, and tear down any prejudice, wrong perception, and attitude in order to establish the reader in righteousness. Righteousness involves preparing oneself to not only discern a matter when confronted, but to do right in it.

Obviously, it is not enough to know your position. You must learn to withstand all that would rob you of your testimony, stand for what is right when challenged to compromise, and withstand all that would undermine your faith and life in Jesus. It is about preparation. We must be prepared in the life of Jesus to withstand, prepared in His truth to stand, and

---

[2] Jeremiah 23:1-4; Ezekiel 34: John 10:4-10

prepared to withstand all matters with Jesus' attitude, authority, and power.

Consider and honestly answer the following questions, and don't forget to record it in your notebook for future considerations.

1) What are you seeking at this time to bring purpose to your life?

2) In what way is your pursuit bringing meaning to your life? In the end, will this pursuit prove to be worldly and temporary, or spiritual and eternal? Explain your answer.

3) Is your pursuit truly bringing satisfaction to your life, or are you beginning to question the purpose of it?

4) Does your pursuit always bring you back to center (God) or are you finding yourself drifting away from God?

5) Do you need to reconsider your pursuits?

# PREPARATION

## 7

## THE PREPARATION BEGINS

The Christian life is full of disciplines. In other words, every aspect of the Christian's life must be marked by godly disciplines. These disciplines prepare us to walk out our life in God whether married or single. Notice, they are necessary for preparation. Nothing gets accomplished in a believer's life without discipline that ultimately leads to sacrifice. As God clothed in humanity, Jesus experienced every type of discipline. He gave up and gave way to every aspect of humanity and servitude in light of the Father's will.

As our example, we can do no less than our Lord. First, we must offer up our bodies, and then we must deny ourselves our right to have life on our terms. From this premise, we apply the cross to mark our spiritual growth with death to all that would hinder our progression in Christ. It is from this point that we can follow Jesus into the life He has ordained for each of us before the foundation of the world. And, what a glorious life it is!

Each discipline serves as another point of enlargement, testing, and endurance on the battlefield of life—and life can certainly prove to be a battle. The battle has to do with who will ultimately serve as our God, Lord, and Master. This is the bottom line to all of the battles that we contend with in the flesh, wrestle with in regard to our pride, and fight to overcome Satan's various devices.

As I have dealt with the issue of why many people fail to discover the life God has for them, I have come to realize that at the core of their defeat is their unwillingness to grow up or come to full age in this extraordinary life. This often reminds me of the illustration in Ecclesiastes where servants ride horses, while princes walk.[1]

In relationship to the world, much of the leadership, even in some churches, seems upside down. Those who are true leaders are lowly servants while those who need to learn what it means to be servants are in leadership positions. But this also seems true when it comes to relationships among people. When you see young men strutting their manhood while the older generation act like immature, spoiled adolescences in their relationships with others instead of leading by

---

[1] Ecclesiastes 10:6-7

example, you realize how upside down our society has become. Such people have refused to grow up while maintaining their fantasy or delusion about life, while being set up for failure. Perhaps such individuals have striven to maintain an outward appearance of a "normal" life while manipulating others, including God to adjust to their world by submitting to their terms.

Truly, this is a tragedy. People refuse to grow up in order to take their rightful place in society and become responsible and productive. As a result, people are simply "playing house" (or playing at the game of life) while the number of people who are establishing productive homes or living mature and upright lives are obviously dwindling in numbers.

In the 1970s an actual game called "Life" proved to be popular. You cast your lot and left all of your moves up to the possible chances that life might offer you as you tried to reach the finish line with something to show for your adventure. In this game you had actual choices. You could choose college to acquire a profession and hopefully prove to be successful. Along the way you could get married, have children, and buy a home, but at the end of the game it was not unusual to have nothing to show for the route you traveled in the game of chance. However, in real life, it is not a matter of possible chances, but of personal choices that one makes in regard to life.

One of the first choices a person must make is to grow up. But, what does it mean to become mature? Instead of being self-centered, maturity is marked by the distinction of a person becoming a source of blessing and benefit to others. In light of Christianity, it means making an eternal difference in the scheme of things. After all, the Christian life is not self-serving; rather, it is the life of Christ flowing through each believer and being spilled out into other people's lives.

There are a couple of platforms that encourage maturity. These platforms must come together to produce what we call integrity. Each platform serves as a discipline. The first discipline will determine our premise.

Our premise in regard to life must be the willingness to face life for what it is. Most people hate their present reality. Usually, this hatred is towards the fact that they cannot control it. Sadly, they will not take responsibility for the attitude they have about it. They refuse to face unpleasant matters head on. They take the pleasant situations of life, and declare that this is the essence of life—that all matters must be pleasant before they will accept any type of reality about life.

However, life will not be adjusted, nor will it always prove to be pleasant. The reality of life is it can be good or bad. It can be joyful or sad. It can bring happiness or sorrow our way. Life is life. Life is a current that continues to move whether people decide to get in its flow to experience the gift of it, or spend time trying to detour, adjust, avoid, or change its current.

Life will never adjust. It will push aside or find its way around every obstacle that it may encounter. It cannot be avoided, and ultimately, it will change the terrain of each person. As a result, maturity hinges on us taking our life back by facing it head on, not by avoiding it.

As we face daily challenges, occasional losses, and the threat of constant change, these events will force us to grow up or become embittered by it all. If we choose to go the way of maturity, we will become enlarged as we consider the vastness of the world around us. This vastness not only challenges our faith in our God to ponder how big He is, it helps us to realize how small we are in the scheme of things.

Smallness of this nature helps us gain a realistic perspective about life. After all, we often consider ourselves big in the scheme of things when we perceive we are in control of the reality that affects our lives. However, we will fail to realize that the only control we have is to determine how we will respond towards the reality that not only intrudes into our life, but also tests our character and challenges our devotion to a matter.

This brings us to the next stage of maturity. The reason we must face life for what it is, is to take responsibility for who we become. The difference between maturity and immaturity comes down to responsibility. We cannot control the current of life, but we can determine how it will affect us. The main reason people refuse to grow up is to avoid taking responsibility for the quality of their life.

People fear what life will expose about them. They resent what it will require from them. They rage against it because it will not bow down to their fragile egos. Ultimately, they are brought to the point of making a decision about how they are going to handle the matters that confront them. The harsh reality is that these individuals want to avoid making decisions because they want to come out on top. Although many of these decisions are nothing more than making small steps forward in maturity, people who do not want to grow up refuse to make them. They will play the game to force others to make such decisions in order to hide their own immaturity. Their attempts to hide their irresponsibility may prove they are clever, foolish, or ridiculous, but in the long run, their true character will be exposed.

Such people want to feel noble about failure, honorable about irresponsibility, and superior in their arrogance and foolishness. Therefore, they play games at the expense of others, or they come out as a poor victim or even appear noble in their immaturity. After all, they know how to play certain people, while maintaining a false perception of themselves as being clever, superior, and justified in their wicked practices.

A person's foolishness will avoid taking any responsibility for the quality of life. By skirting around decision-making, people who operate in foolishness always avoid taking personal accountability. They do not mind taking credit for successes, but they refuse to take accountability for personal failures. However, maturity is developed in people as they take responsibility for the quality and direction of their personal well-being. These people also take accountability for their failure to finish the course. It is in this arena that people learn the valuable lessons of life.

Failure to finish the course has nothing to do with inability, but with the fear of not coming out as number one or being on top. We each would like to maintain a perspective that we could be number one at whatever we pursue, but in reality, we all have our limitations and weakness that can prevent us from making the grade. However, we can make it look like it is not our fault, and that we are noble victims as we accept the indiscretion. It all seems noble and honorable, but in reality, it is the biggest form of justifiable self-delusion.

The decisions people make will determine if they live life or play some game called life. The perspective they develop concerning the matters of life will establish whether they merely play at life (such as playing church or house), or whether they actually experience life in each area.

This brings us to the other unrealistic, irresponsible aspect surrounding decisions. Most people want to make one big decision, and then arrive at their desired destination or pinnacle. The major decisions that result in successes are made up of many small decisions. Each little decision begins to discipline or bend a person in a certain direction.

It is important to point out that we all start with being bent towards wickedness. Due to our fallen condition, our preference is darkness.[2] That is why we play games to cover up the darkness of or own souls.

To change our tendency or preference, we must begin to make those decisions that will begin to change the angle of our slant in regards to life. This means we must make the right decisions. Each right decision will change our slant or tendency towards the ways of righteousness. Therefore, when we must make the right decision according to a major issue, we will naturally go towards righteousness. Sadly, most immature people believe they are prepared to make the right decisions for their life, when in reality they are still bent towards the preference of darkness. Their main struggle will not be doing right, but how to cover up the wrong they desire to do. When they have such a slant towards life, they are prepared to play the games of life, but never to become responsible for the outcome of their own life.

Being in ministry has constantly brought out this contrast. There are those who, through pure determination, have made the right decisions in life. As a result, they are able to make the tough decisions in a way that is pleasing to God. On the other hand, there are always those who refuse to make the right decisions. They run around the outskirts, playing the religious games, but always failing to enter into what is real and lasting. They give lip service, but there is no real heart devotion.[3] They still prefer to maintain some aspects of their self-life. Perhaps they prefer the world, their idea of control, or their own way of thinking, being, or doing. They may wear their best religious cloaks, be clever in their ways, and act noble and pious in their sin, but they will never give way to a life

---

[2] John 3:18-21
[3] Matthew 15:6-9

of total consecration to God. They want life on their terms, not on God's terms.

Eventually, these individuals will make the decision to go with their preferences, but, unfortunately, it will be at other people's expense. After all, they refuse to be at fault, take accountability, or be responsible. If they belong to God, He will take them around the mountain. They will be purged by the bitterness of their own wickedness, and experience the emptiness of their own wasteful pursuits. They will, nevertheless, be brought to a decision.

This decision will be simple. It is the premise of every right decision and action. The decision is to love the truth. It takes deciding to love the truth to do right regardless of the situation. In light of this understanding, we can see why truth makes a person free.[4] Love of truth prepares us to make the decision to do right. Love for truth causes us to continually lean towards the ways of righteousness. Being in love with truth ensures that we will ultimately possess Jesus, Truth personified.

Truth is a great discipline of one's ways. When one walks according to the truth, he or she can be assured of walking in the ways of righteousness.

Obviously, to be prepared for the life God has designated for us, there must be the process of maturing in the ways of God. We must become responsible to have a right attitude towards each challenge of life, and accountable for how we handle the issues of life. This leaves the reader with these final questions. Record the answer for your edification and meditation.

1) Are you growing up in Christ, or are you growing away from Him? Explain your answer.

2) Are you leaning towards the natural preference of the darkness of the self-life or towards your life in Christ? Explain how you have correctly discerned this answer.

3) Write down some of your recent decisions in regards to your life. Explain whether they are in light of personal preferences or in light of your life in Christ.

In order to honestly answer questions in regard to spiritual matters about our life and attitude towards God, we must have another discipline, that of integrity.

---

[4] John 8:31-32; 2 Thessalonians 2:10-12

# 8

# INTEGRITY

Maturing in Christ is a process. To ensure that the process is successful, one must develop integrity. Integrity is considered to be a form of honesty. Granted, integrity possesses honesty. However, honesty can operate differently in certain arenas. For example, people might be honest about their feelings, opinions, and practices, but not necessarily honest about the reality around them. Such honesty does not constitute actual truth.

Integrity implies that one is operating from the type of honesty that is honorable in its evaluation and practices. It allows one to be receptive to truth no matter how challenging it may be. By being receptive to truth, a person is able to connect to reality. Such connection takes place because one is being honest about his or her personal spiritual environment.

It takes integrity to be honest about the fruits that are coming out of one's life. The problem is that few people connect to their environment to test their fruits. They may consider their spiritual environment in light of their activities, religious veneer, or cloak, but they will not rightly test their fruit. By considering themselves in light of the exterior, they can deceive themselves as to their interior state of affairs.

Self-delusion is the greatest challenge among religious people, even in the Christian realm. Anyone can create a false reality, but they cannot maintain it. This false reality simply hides the fact that these people do not really have the goods. Granted, they may have an appearance of righteousness, but they lack the power or substance behind their appearance to effectively walk out the Christian life. Eventually, their religious veneer will be stripped away by their inconsistencies and hypocrisies.

It is absolutely essential that Christians come to terms with integrity. It takes integrity to maintain a consecrated life before God. A consecrated life is maintained by devotion. Devotion points to the heart. King David walked according to the integrity of his heart.[1] His integrity kept him honorable in his walk, humble before God, and open for instruction. The key to a heart that possesses integrity such as King David's is that it is not divided in loyalties, but totally committed to God. Obviously, such a heart is able to take detours, but ultimately it will always come back to God in humility and repentance.

---

[1] 1 Kings 9:4

Sadly, when people lack integrity, they can delude themselves about being honorable towards God and others. They will resort to worldly sorrow, while failing to truly repent. They maintain their pride behind a façade of self-pity. They shed tears because they have been caught in their deviation, not because they have offended or hurt someone. Ultimately, they will stand justified in their mind towards their actions, but not before God.

When people lack integrity, they will play games to maintain their personal reality about themselves. This reality has to do with fear, pride, and control. People fear that reality will expose their arrogance, preventing their pride from coming out on top. Or, they will discover that they are not God; therefore, they are incapable of controlling any aspect of their life or the reality that surrounds them.

These games represent a false way. The psalmist in Psalm 119:104 made this statement, "Through thy precepts I get understanding: therefore I hate every false way." Once again, integrity will not stand for any false way. As we consider this Scripture, we realize that false ways are the result of people failing to possess the real light (understanding) of God's ways.

In Psalm 119:128, we read these words, "Therefore I esteem all thy precepts concerning all things to be right; and I hate every false way." In this Scripture verse, we see where God's way of doing is esteemed as true and right above all other practices and realities. Due to this exaltation, every false way will be rejected.

The goal of Christians should be to live a consecrated life unto God. However, to possess and maintain this life, they must develop integrity towards their personal life before God. It is not enough to walk around with the title of "Christian." One must be possessed by the life of God in them. It is not enough to tack Christ on to religion; He must be the source behind all a person does, establishing Christianity as a way of life.

When integrity is lacking towards others, it will be lacking in one's life in regards to God. The problem is that people can easily deceive themselves about their life before God because He is unseen. They can convince themselves that their sentiment or emotional zeal towards God is evidence of their devotion, when in reality it is nothing more than being caught up with their idea of God. As a result, they can play a game with themselves and others.

Consider some of the games people play. These games are actually different forms of control and manipulation. There is the game where people transpose their own moral deviation upon others. For example, they are not trustworthy; therefore, they perceive those they are involved with as being untrustworthy. With this type of person, you will encounter jealousies and insecurities. For example, if a spouse possesses this deviation, he or she will try to control through environment. In other words, these possessive individuals must know where their spouse is all of the time. They will check in on their mate when least expected, attempt to control finances to ensure that the spouse remains dependent on them, and at times check out associations. Their jealousies make them unpredictable and ridiculous.

These individuals can come across as time bombs ready to go off at any moment in speculation, anger, and fits of jealousy. Even though these people are tormented by their jealousy, they cannot let it go. Although truth will often prove their insecurities as unwarranted, they are still subject to their own speculation and moral deviation. They strive to maintain their outward image of being honorable, while holding on to their moral deviation or right to be jealous and manipulative.

Another game is the emotional game. This is where people know how to push other's emotional buttons in order to gain the upper hand over them. They actually use these people's emotions against them as a means to control them and come out on top. After all, emotions represent weakness; therefore, these individuals see people who display emotions as weak, vulnerable, and easily controlled by strong attitudes. These people are not interested in the truth. All they care about is maintaining their arrogance while manipulating the weaker person to perform according to their own reality.

The next game is the intellectual game. These people see themselves as elite in their knowledge in regard to others. They know how to debate issues, cause confusion about what is true and important, and come out on top. These people do not care about truth; rather, what they care about is maintaining their own conceited reality.

The dichotomy in such games is that people become angry with you when you refuse to play the game, causing their character and games to be exposed. On the other hand, they do not respect those who innocently or cleverly play their games. In fact, these game-players often develop a mocking spirit towards what is true, show disrespect towards everyone regardless of how they respond, and often live a life of misery and isolation.

It is easy to play games with others. However, such games represent a false way, and for those who have integrity they will not submit or partake of such wicked games. The problem is that people have fine-tuned their games so well, that they fail to see them as the wretched games that they are. In fact, playing them is a habit. They perceive them as reality even though the fruit of such games points to wickedness, rather than righteousness.

The only way to develop integrity is to refuse to play such games. Refusing to play the game demands that relationships be honorable and pure. This should be the goal of every Christian, regardless of the relationship. It is up to us to demand that each relationship be honorable.

Granted, holding such an upright line will make you unpopular with those who assume you will play according to their reality. You will ultimately challenge the deception that plagues many people in their fantasies and delusions about themselves.

Developing integrity involves a process of testing every aspect of your attitude and practice. Without this integrity, as Christians, we will not be able to discern good and evil, right or wrong.[2] Obviously, the main reason many Christians do not have discernment is because they lack the integrity or substance to be able to properly discern.

Keep in mind, integrity is about humbly and honestly testing one's personal fruits. To do this, one must test his or her spirit or motivation behind matters. Even though we attempt to look good in all matters, the motivation behind most of our pursuits is self-serving. Therefore, the spirit is wrong. When the spirit is wrong, a person's disposition or inward environment will be wrong. Wrong environments are incapable of producing godly fruits that exemplify the attitude of Jesus and the sanctifying work of the Spirit.

Next, we must consider our attitude. Spirit is influenced by agendas. However, attitude is inspired by emphasis. If the emphasis is self-serving, pride will manifest itself in works of the flesh such as being touchy, rude, controlling, angry, and unreasonable. Attitude will affect the outward environment as people respond to the prevailing mood that is invading the environment.

The final test is our approach to a matter. Approach will determine if we are going to oppose a matter or come into agreement with it. Behind approach are priorities. Agenda will determine the direction of a person's values. Emphasis will establish the source of his or her affections, while priorities will influence the person's pursuits. As you can see, the inward environment will decide how each of us operates in the environment around us. It will allow us to live in denial as to the reality around us, which prevents us from connecting with it.

Most people think that examining themselves requires introspection on their part. However, testing the fruit has nothing to do with introspection, but being honest about how our attitude is affecting our environment. Is our approach godly or self-serving? These are the matters that make up our fruits, ultimately revealing the spirit motivating us.

Consider the following table. Note that Christians must possess godly character to be honest about their spiritual condition.

| Disposition | Attitude | Approach |
|---|---|---|
| Spirit | Influence | Point of Agreement |
| Agenda | Emphasis | Priorities |

---

[2] Hebrews 5:12-14

For Christians, the examination should be quite simple if we are not hiding behind some religious cloak, religious image, or unrealistic Christian façade. We should be able to clearly discern our fruits to determine our inward environment. Is it an environment where the Spirit of God has freedom to work? Is it where righteousness will be the natural preference and godliness the expression? If we are to walk in truth, we must walk in integrity about our spiritual condition.

Do you have such integrity? It is vital if you are to maintain a consecrated life before God. After all, if one aspect of your character deviates away from the mark of God, the results will be inconsistency, failure, and defeat. Obviously, we each must demand spiritual maturity from our own walk.

Consider each area of character and honestly examine if it lines up to God's plan of preparing you to fulfill His call in your life. Write down the findings of your examination. Keep in mind that if any of the areas fails to line up to the right Spirit in the right attitude with the intent of approaching a matter in a pure, honorable way, the inconsistency will serve as the very point where you will be persuaded to compromise your life in Christ with the flesh and the world.

1) Plans

2) Calling

3) Spirit motivating you

4) Attitude behind your goals:

5) Approach to each matter

6) Is the inward disposition lining up to what you know is right in your life before God? Explain your answer.

# 9

# THE ISSUE OF PURITY

One of the greatest means of preparation comes by way of purity. The big fad a few years ago was abstinence in sexual behavior. I totally agree with this practice among single people. However, outward abstinence does not deal with the attitudes that truly defile man, corrupting everything he does. This defilement is taking place in man's inner chambers. Defilement simply means people are taking something that is pure, and corrupting or debasing it, making it unclean and unacceptable. Ultimately, such defilement will pervert matters. In other words, it will add to a matter with fleshly designs or it will take away from its importance, impact, or integrity.

This brings us to what constitutes purity before God. Purity is actually a state in which a person lives a pure life. When you consider this state, it actually points to a place of holiness, and it entails more than just a practice of refraining from that which results in immoral acts such as fornication. It is a disposition and an attitude that demands uprightness in every area. If the right attitude exists, one will flee that which would strip him or her of an upright standing before God.

It is not unusual for people to refrain from outward immorality, but remain unclean inwardly. Jesus referred to such people as being white sepulchers, outwardly beautiful, but within full of dead men's bones and uncleanness. He also stated that the source of this defilement is the heart.[1] The Apostle Paul addressed the result of such impurity in Titus 1:15-16, "Unto the pure all things are pure: but unto them that are defiled and unbelieving is nothing pure; but even their mind and conscience is defiled. They profess that they know God; but in works they deny him, being abominable, and disobedient, and unto every good work reprobate."

As you can see, if the source is unclean, then it will pervert and taint everything the person is involved with. The problem with most religious teaching is that it advocates the appearance of purity, but it does not teach or demand inward purity. Obviously, if people abstain from immoral practices, but they are inwardly unclean, they are still defiled in God eyes, and incapable of being pure and pleasing to Him.

If you consider what the Apostle Paul stated in Titus 1:15-16, you will begin to see how impurity invades and destroys the totality of a person. The first point of impurity is unbelief. People who operate from the premise of defilement do so because they do not believe what the Word

---

[1] Matthew 15:10-20; 23:27

of God says. The Word tells us to separate from that which is unclean. The reason for this separation is as children of God we must not come into agreement with any unholy alliances. When people come into agreement with the unholy, they will bring themselves under a perverted spirit. It is hard for people to realize that there is a spirit of the world in operation behind every attraction and function of this present age.[2]

Today one of the greatest invasions of darkness that is occurring in our society comes through pornography. Yet, how many Christians are exposing themselves to this unholy environment? Each time we expose ourselves to the unholy, we come into agreement with the spirit behind the environment that is being created by unholy activities. Wrong spirits will desensitize people towards the fact that they are clearly standing at enmity with God. In other words, the ability to discern between good and bad becomes clouded as one loses a sense of right and wrong.

Unbelief is a form of darkness. It affects how we look at matters. Genuine faith chooses to believe the Word, but unbelief takes the Word and strips it of authority by justifying away personal responsibility. Good examples of the arguments that are presently going on are: "The Word is not for today"; "It is out of touch and out of date with the mentality of today's present age"; and "I know what the Word says, but there are circumstances that make me an exception to it".[3]

There are many points of justification and qualification as to why people do not believe the Word of God. Such points of justification and qualification are points of perversion that will add fire to a person's right to compromise or minimize the authority of the Word in their lives. However, the real reason is because such people's hearts have become hard towards the truth of God's Word. Somewhere along the way they failed to believe the Word and obey it. No doubt the debate that raged between the Spirit and the flesh during this critical time was shaking their very foundation, but clearly they gave way to the darkness of the flesh, causing their heart to become hardened towards the truth.[4] From that point on the heart became harder each time these individuals gave way to the darkness of their unbelief, while their perverted reality became more acceptable to their conscience. Eventually, the invading darkness of unbelief will cause these people's hearts to become completely hardened towards the truth.

These very same people may profess they know God, but their works deny Him. Although, these people may throw a bone towards God, much of their attitude and activities will be centered on doing things for their own benefit. They only do good deeds when it exalts or benefits them. As long as they feel good about a matter, they will have a pleasant attitude, but as soon as it becomes a source of any inconvenience, out come the complaints and the nasty attitudes. These people are touchy

---

[2] 1 Corinthians 6:13-20; 2 Corinthians 6:14-18; Ephesians 2:1-2

[3] If you would like to know the eternal, unchanging power of God's Word, see *My Words are Spirit and Life* in Volume 1 of the foundational series

[4] Hebrews 3:8-19

and prove to be unreasonable when it comes to facing the darkness of their own soul. They often play games of control and manipulation. In the end, they prove to be very untrustworthy.

Sadly, these people not only muddy their own waters, but they will muddy the pure waters that may be flowing through the life of others. In many cases they are attracted to the waters that run through a pure life. After all, perversion can make one feel unclean. Such a person desires change, but such change is not going to occur in the outward environment until there is a complete cleansing of the inward environment.

It takes integrity to ensure purity. For those who have purity, they must guard it. For example, it is not unusual for those who are in perversion to seek out those who are pure. After all, in their perverted perception, they either believe a pure person will make them pure or they believe they deserve a person who is pure. However, the book of Haggai refutes such logic. That which is holy and clean cannot make something that is defiled, holy. And, if the holy touches the unclean, it becomes unclean.[5]

It is hard for people who are unholy to realize all they can do is taint and pervert that which is holy. Such individuals do not see the necessity of maintaining purity in a world that comes from the very premise of defilement and perversion in its way of thinking and doing. In a way, there is a double standard in such people's thinking.

A man who was himself very immoral confirmed this. He considered his mate to be "damaged goods" because (before their marriage) she had been involved in fornication with him as well as other men. This man's philosophy was clearly of the world. From God's perspective, this woman along with the rest of humanity is "damage goods" because of unholy agreements and alliances with the evil mentality and sinful practices of this present world. Because of the tainted view of this man, he perceived that fornication was not only expected of him, but an acceptable attitude and practice. As a result, he believed that he had the right to possess and defile what was pure, but a woman must keep herself pure regardless of the pursuits and games of such predators as him. However, in God's sight the man was as much a fornicator as his mate.

Obviously, the premise that a person operates from will determine if something is pure or impure. I cannot tell you how many Christians I have dealt with that are under the influence of pornography, but they perceive themselves as worthy ministers of the Gospel. They console themselves that they are serving God regardless of their defiled environments. Clearly, such people do not know their God. God could care less about little sacrifices offered to Him in the name of ministry. If such sacrifices are coming from that which is regarded as unholy, they will be considered defiled and unacceptable to Him.

---

[5] Haggai 2:11-14

It is important that we understand the premises that will defile something. We already know that the premise of the world is contrary to God in spirit, thinking, attitude, and doing. In fact, the Apostle Paul stated that we must not be conformed to this present world, but we must be transformed by the renewing of our minds.[6]

Another premise of defilement is self. Sometimes I separate the concept of self from the works of the flesh. Flesh entices self, while self gives way to the flesh. The word, "self" involves one's idea of life and his or her right to experience it according to his or her perception. Everything that comes from this premise is selfish, and represents the spirit of the natural man in operation. The natural spirit of man cannot rightly discern spiritual matters.[7] Ultimately, self will pervert all that pertains to God.

We have already made reference to the works of the flesh. Every time a person gives in to the works of the flesh, they are giving way to a form of paganism. In this premise, all matters become sensual. In the religious realm emotions or sentiment replace the moving of the Spirit, and experiences become a sick substitute for God. A good example of this is the fleshly, carnal, and soulish worship that is taking place in some churches. People are literally getting caught up in the flesh, thinking it is worship. Such worship becomes a source of idolatry.

Idolatry is found at the core of each of these premises. The world demands our alliance, self desires adoration, and the flesh strives for our compliance and servitude. In the end, the world determines our worldview, self determines our reality, and the flesh becomes our authority.

As Christians, we must demand that we establish and maintain a pure state. Whether we remain single or married, that purity must be present. After all, the Spirit of God cannot move where the waters are defiled. If a marriage is to ensure God's ordination and blessing, the parties involved must be pure before Him.

Obviously, there is much that will influence our thinking and determine what we will ultimately come into agreement or fellowship with. We must take responsibility for this aspect of our life. We must control what influences us. For example, we must be careful what we expose ourselves to. We must not justify any unclean alliances, and flee all youthful temptations that will encourage us to compromise with the unholy.[8] We must discern the spirit around us and the environment it is encouraging.

We must guard our attitude to keep our discernment on the cutting edge. In other words, we must be sober and vigilant concerning what is affecting our inward and outward environments. Keep in mind, once we let our guard down, Satan can come in like a lion to devour us.[9]

---

[6] Romans 12:2; James 4:4
[7] 1 Corinthians 2:13-14
[8] 2 Timothy 2:19-22
[9] 1 Peter 5:8

This is what happened in the Garden of Eden. Many people get caught up in the blame game. For example, it was the woman's fault that Adam gave way to his own rebellion. However, if people put aside the silly debate about who is at fault, and consider it in light of how sin enters into an environment, the text would become a point of great instruction and edification, rather than one of debate and finger pointing.

Adam had dominion over creation. He also had the responsibility of dressing and keeping the garden. Remember there were no thistles or thorns in this garden.[10] It possessed a perfect environment. This perfect environment was due to the fact that Adam had liberty to walk and commune with his Creator. As you study the meaning of these two words, you will realize that Adam had the responsibility of maintaining the quality of the garden. In other words, he was to maintain and protect it from any intrusion that would rob it of its perfect environment.

Hence, enters a threat to this garden through Satan in the form of a serpent.[11] Satan's very presence not only threatened the quality of the garden, but also became a point of darkness. Adam had the authority to demand Satan to leave, but he did not. Whether Adam did not think Satan was a threat to the harmony in this garden, or whether he thought that he could handle it would be a matter of speculation. However, Adam failed his first responsibility. When you consider failure in this area, it points to a flippant attitude towards that which is pure and holy. As a result, Adam failed to serve as a protector to that which was entrusted to him.

The second mistake was made when Eve tried to reason with Satan. You cannot reason with darkness. Darkness will never become light; it will only seduce you to compromise and come into agreement with its deceptive reality. After all, there is no truth in darkness. It can only confuse truth, bring false accusation against God's character by putting doubt on His Word, and lead one into transgression and death.[12]

Adam and Eve revealed to us how sin can find its way into our midst. We fail to maintain a right attitude towards that which is pure or impure. Once our attitude is compromised, we are open to reason with darkness in order to get it to come into agreement with the light, usually for self-serving purposes. Since darkness is incapable of taking on the nature of light, all it can do is bring us into agreement with its deceptive reality.

Once we come into agreement with darkness, our disposition will begin to change as it takes on the darkness we have now exposed ourselves to. At this point darkness becomes the false, deceitful light we walk according to.[13] From this perspective a wrong spirit establishes our agendas, as our priorities become defiled and perverted. From this point, we are unable to approach any matter from the state of purity. Therefore, it will be defiled.

---

[10] Genesis 1:28; 2:15
[11] Genesis 3:1
[12] Genesis 3:1-6; John 8:44; 2 Corinthians 11:3; 1 Timothy 2:14
[13] Matthew 6:22-23

Perhaps, as you read this you can see how you are struggling with the issue of purity. Maybe you sense you cannot trust any aspect about your thoughts, feelings, and activities. After all, you have been walking in agreement with the filth of the world, the perversion of self, and the idolatrous works of the flesh. You have lived according to the darkness of your unbelief towards God. Your light has been your worldly understanding. Your point of inspiration has been self and you have been subject to the flesh. Now you struggle with what is true and right.

If you are at this place, take courage because you are open and ready to be cleansed to ensure a state of purity. There are three ways in which you can be assured of cleansing in your life to ensure purity before God.

The first thing you must do is go to God's washing machine. The thought God possesses a washing machine probably shocks many. But God has provided such a tool. It is called His Word. God's Word is able to cleanse us in our way of thinking and living, but we must apply it as truth. As you know, it is not enough to have a washing machine; you must use it to clean your clothes. Likewise, we must apply the truths of the Word of God by faith to every aspect of our lives. We must reckon His Word as life and truth, and walk according to its warnings, instructions and commands.

As we obey the Word by faith, it will begin to wash us of the filth of the world. It will start to change our mind as we see more and more into the very character of our holy God. As our mind becomes more Christ-like, our disposition will take on His character and reflect His glory in this dark world.[14]

The second point of cleansing is the blood of Jesus. Positionally, we are placed in a place of sanctification. Sanctification means we have been set apart for God's use. However, to benefit from the cleansing of the blood of Jesus, we must walk in His light. This means we must walk according to who He is. He is holy; therefore, we must come to a holy state.[15] This involves consecrating ourselves.

As a reminder, consecration involves separating ourselves from the unholy and separating ourselves unto the holy to walk in it. The problem most Christians have is they want to be made holy without exposing themselves to a holy environment. It cannot happen. Environment represents spirit. Spirit determines what will influence us as far as our point of agreement.

This brings us to the last source of cleansing, which is the Holy Spirit. He is the One who sanctifies or sets us apart unto God. He renews or regenerates us. However, to be cleansed by the Spirit, we must walk after the Spirit to secure a holy life before God. This means we will walk in uprightness before God. Once we walk after the Spirit, we can come under His leadership. It is at this point the Holy Spirit will lead

---

[14] John 17:17; Romans 10:17; 2 Corinthians 3:18; Ephesians 5:26; Philippians 2:5; James 1:21-25

[15] 1 Corinthians 1:30; 1 Peter 1:15-16; 1 John 1:7

us into a life that is fit for the Master's use. We will serve as sanctified vessels, where the Living Water has free access to flow out to others. We will be instruments that will declare the heart of God. We will also become a source of blessing to those who are open to the abiding reality of God's presence.[16]

Purity is not an option. We must come to this state to ensure holiness in our lives. Hebrews 12:14 tells us that without holiness we will not see the Lord. Jesus tells us who will see God in Matthew 5:8, "Blessed are the pure in heart: for they shall see God."

Prayerfully examine the following areas in regard to purity. Explain your conclusions in your notebook.

1) Is there any defilement going on in your life due to unholy agreements? If so, what are they, and what do you plan to do to remedy your present state?

2) Is your heart pure before God, so you can truly see Him? If not, what are you going to do to change the condition of your heart?

3) Do your influences ensure a state of holiness in your life? Explain your answer.

4) Do your thoughts maintain a pure state? Explain your answer.

5) Are your practices displaying a disposition of righteousness or are they a façade that covers up what is really going on in your life? Explain your answer.

Based on your answers have you come to a state of purity? This is the only state that will allow the Lord to have His way in your life. And, if the Lord is having His way in your life, you can be assured of being prepared for the life He has for you.

---

[16] Romans 6:13; 8:1-5, 10, 13-14, 2 Corinthians 13:14; Galatians 5:16-18; 2 Timothy 2:21; Titus 3:5; 1 Peter 1:2

# 10

# SEEKING GOD

Securing and maintaining a state of purity is a major discipline in our lives. It involves being honest about motivation, honorable in regards to our attitude, and just or righteous in our conduct. The state of purity is necessary if we are going to see God. This brings us to the next discipline, seeking God in all matters.

The reason we consecrate ourselves is to find God's will for our lives. The goal is to ensure that our lives will count for something as far as His glorious kingdom. Otherwise, we will become lost in the demands and activities of life. Knowing God's will, will help discipline our focus.

As you study the concept of finding, you will realize that to find something or someone, you must personally seek what you are looking for. In seeking God, you will realize He is not far from you, but He is obscure to you because of the flesh. Therefore, each of us must mortify the old man within us to find God. This means becoming dead to the influence of the flesh and the world, while neglecting the tendencies and claims of the pride in our life. As we put to death the old man, we must discipline our affections to direct our focus towards that which is holy and eternal.

The main purpose for seeking God is not for one's will to be realized, but for one to see, know, and commune with God as a means to discover God's will. We seek to see our God in His glory, to know Him according to His perfect ways, and to commune with Him to establish a growing relationship.

Christians fail to understand, God may find us in regards to our salvation, but we must seek Him to find our life in Him. Amos 5:6a makes this statement, "Seek the LORD, and ye shall live."

To experience life, we must find life. Only God provides such life; therefore, we must seek Him to realize the purpose and fulfillment of our existence. However, we must discipline where we look for Him. As the angel declared about Jesus after His resurrection, "Why seek ye the living among the dead" (Luke 24:5b)? People seek life in so many different places, but it is either in that which is dead or among that which is incapable of giving life. Jesus is not dead. He lives this very moment. He sits in heaven as our High Priest, and reigns as King. If we are to seek Him, it must be in the heavenlies. We must seek Him beyond self, the world, and others.

Jeremiah 29:13 gives us this promise, "And ye shall seek me, and find me, when ye shall search for me with all your heart." We have already discussed that our hearts must be pure before we can see God.

Once again, we are reminded of the necessity to have the right inward environment. Those that are corrupted and profane will not find God. These people may even profess Him and strive to enter into that narrow place of life, but will fail to do so.[1] Only those who are humble and pure in disposition before God will be able to see Him.

It is important to point out that we must be prepared in our hearts to seek God. Obviously, this is where discipline must be applied. King Jehoshaphat had found God's disapproval in his unholy alliance with King Ahab, but God found some good things within his character that spared him from judgment. He had taken away the idols out of the land and prepared his heart to seek God.[2]

Obviously, King Jehoshaphat had sought the Lord about many issues, but had failed to seek Him on the matter of his unholy alliances. He probably felt it was the right thing to do, but God had already divided the kingdom of Israel due to the sins of Solomon. What God has separated—man must not try to put back together.

To properly seek the Lord, we must do it before we make any decisions. The psalmist made this wise statement, "O God, thou art my God; early will I seek thee..." (Psalm 63:1a). The reason we must seek Him early is to maintain a correct focus. If our focus is not correct when we start out our day, we will end up taking detours away from what we need to accomplish in our spiritual lives.

Focus is made up of agendas, emphasis, and priorities. Sometimes these matters collide because they are not in agreement. For example, our agenda may be right, but our emphasis could be fleshly. Our emphasis could be on target, but our agendas could be self-serving and our priorities influenced by the world. Such a conflict will cause a divided heart and a double-mind.

Divided hearts are idolatrous, while a double-mind implies that a person lacks stability in focus. This is why as Christians we must have integrity to test such matters, and purity to properly approach inconsistencies in our lives with the intent of lining them up in the ways of righteousness.

As we consider our agendas, we will realize that they will determine the spirit in operation. We may perceive ourselves as focusing on Christ, but our heart's affections might be divided between self-serving agendas and a desire to be right before God. The more I understand how agendas work, the more I have come to realize wrong ones will defile our intentions towards God, and delude us to the mixture that is in operation.

One area that agendas affect is our prayers. If we pray from the premise of self-serving prayers with the idea of seeking God about a matter, our self-serving agendas will ultimately be upheld. Although we will feel that our conclusions are being confirmed in prayer, in reality we have simply set ourselves up for self-delusion.

---

[1] Luke 13:24
[2] 2 Chronicles 19:3

Keep in mind, God cannot work in just any environment. Therefore, wrong agendas create a perverted environment, causing confusion for the person as he or she attempts to seek God out about a matter.

The one agenda we must maintain in all matters is that our attitude and conduct ultimately must bring God glory. God must be exalted, and not conclusions that have been inspired by self-serving agendas.

The next area that determines focus is our emphasis. Agendas are tied up with our will. Emphasis has a lot to do with our affections. This is why attitudes are expressed in this arena. When you combine the desires of emphasis and the momentum of affections, you produce an attitude towards a matter. When people have lousy attitudes towards life, it is because their desires are directed towards the world and their affections are set on pleasing self.

The main emphasis of every Christian should be to please God. This is why we must set our affection on things above.[3] Without the commitment and momentum of affections directed heavenward, our desires will prove to be fleshly. If our desires are fleshly, then our momentum will prove to be undisciplined because our affections have not been set in the proper place, bringing necessary boundaries.

In order to please God, we must first seek the kingdom of God and His righteousness in all matters. By defining desires according to what is right, we will change and discipline the tendency to justify wrong attitudes and activities in our life. The ways of righteousness are what will clearly define our desires and align our affections. Righteousness operates within the boundaries of spirit and truth. This is why we are told to first seek God's righteousness in a matter. Righteousness will ensure a right environment, thereby, allowing God to work though His Spirit to bring revelation and life to His truths.[4]

It is at the point of emphasis that we will know what it means to *walk after* the Spirit and to be *led* by Him. To walk after the Spirit, means we are walking by faith in what we know to be right before God. Walking after the Spirit will bring us under His guidance. From this premise, we will begin to be *led* by the Spirit in all we do in regards to our life in Christ. Once we come to the point of being led by the Spirit we will begin to *walk in* the Spirit. It is in the Spirit that our life in Christ will be clearly established. As a result, we will not fulfill the lust of the flesh.[5]

Obviously, the Holy Spirit will lead us into a complete life in Christ. After all, walking after the Spirit means that I am seeking out my life in God. Being led by the Spirit means the life of God will be brought forth in me. Walking in the Spirit implies that the life of Christ is being established within me.

Since emphasis has to do with realizing the life of Christ in us, we must realize that emphasis will determine the authority of our testimony. Agenda affects our prayer life because it is a matter or realizing one's

---

[3] Colossians 3:2
[4] Matthew 6:33; John 16:13; Romans 8:1-5
[5] Romans 8:1, 14; Galatians 5:16

will. The Apostle John emphasized this fact when he instructed us to pray according to God's will.[6] Since emphasis determines the validity of our authority, we must reason that if it does not line up to all that is pleasing to God, we will not have the authority or power to overcome. Consider the Apostle John's words in Revelation 12:11, "And they overcame him by the blood of the Lamb, and by the word of their testimony; and they loved not their lives unto the death."

When you consider agendas and emphasis, you will realize that emphasis may be influenced by agendas, but ultimately agendas will give way to the momentum of emphasis. This brings us to priorities. Priorities will determine how we approach a matter. Needless to say, our priorities will be influenced by agendas and will be defined by emphasis. In other words, if my agenda is to do my will, and my emphasis is to please my personal desires, my priorities will simply adjust according to the emphasis that is being upheld. From the premise of my selfish attitude, I will approach a matter based on how it will cater to my self-serving desires and serve my purpose. Ultimately, everything I do will appease my affections.

As Christians, we should have only one priority, and that is to obey God. Obedience to God means nothing if our agenda is not to glorify God and our emphasis is not to please Him. Clearly without these two areas properly lined up, all obedience will be a matter of duty and not one of love and reasonable service. The writer of Hebrews showed the importance of godly obedience, "Though he were a Son, yet learned he obedience by the things which he suffered; And being made perfect, he became the author of eternal salvation unto all them that <u>obey</u> him" (Hebrews 5:8-9). [Emphasis added.]

We learn obedience through self-denial. Self-denial involves obeying what is right regardless of what it may cost us. The reality of the Christian life is that it will cost us to know God. It will cost you and me to seek God and find Him.

To obey God means you are obeying His Word.[7] You are not just obeying it in practice, but you are maintaining the spirit or intent of it by having an upright emphasis or attitude towards God, His character, and His ways. It is in this environment that minds are transformed, lives are changed, and believers are conformed to the very image of Christ. In other words, they will be reflecting the very glory of the Lord through their countenance. Hence, we are reminded of the words of Matthew, "Let your light so shine before men, that they may see your good works, and glorify your Father, which is in heaven" (Matthew 5:16).

We can see that seeking God from the premise of setting, establishing, and maintaining a right focus is vital in our preparation. Many people are not prepared to follow God into the life He has for them, because their focus has not been disciplined. It is easy to lose your way through this world, but if you know how to discipline your focus, you can

---

[6] 1 John 5:14
[7] James 1:22-25

always find your way home. Otherwise, you will find yourself taking one detour after another. You will encounter confusion and instability along the way. Your prayers will prove to be ineffective because your emphasis is not that of righteousness. The flesh will constantly toy with your desires as your testimony loses its credibility. Your affections will be tossed to and fro as your loyalties remain divided. And, your priorities will prove to be unstable, lacking the power to finish the course.

Preparing for our life in God, whether as a single or married person, must be a priority. We must realize that unless the inward man is prepared to meet God, the individual will not see or commune with his or her Creator.

Consider the following table:

| Agendas | Emphasis | Priorities |
|---------|----------|------------|
| Will Area | Desires/ Affections | Approach |
| Glorify God | Please God (Righteousness) | Obedience |

As you consider this picture, examine each area in your life. Ask the Lord to turn the light on to your agendas, emphasis, and priorities. Seek out His perspective in each situation. Write your findings, as well as explain in what way your agendas need to change, your emphasis redefined, and your priorities realigned.

1) Agendas: (Do they need to change?)

2) Emphasis: (Does it need to be redefined?)

3) Priorities: (Do they need to be realigned?)

4) Explain what you have learned thus far.

# 11

# THE PURPOSE OF PREPARATION

As we consider the preparation that clearly must take place in a Christian's life, we realize why this walk is able to revolutionize a person. There is not one area of the inner man of the committed Christian that will not be marked by self-denial, the cross, and the life of Jesus.

This is why we must examine the fruits of our inner man. They must be distinguished by the work of the Spirit, the attitude of Christ, and godly conduct that exalts God as the person's source. It must manifest the life of Jesus as a means to serve as a light in this dark world.

We have been examining the different areas that must be transformed, changed, and established by the life of Christ. We know that we must be prepared to walk out the life of Jesus in our daily lives. However, what does it mean to be prepared to live this life? It means we are prepared to face reality and stand in truth regardless of how formidable and uncomfortable our surroundings might be.

As you study the end days, you will conclude that the greatest point of exhortation is to be ready to withstand the harsh reality of these times, and to stand on the Rock in the midst of great darkness, possible persecution, and widespread destruction. As Jesus stated, "But he that shall endure unto the end, the same shall be saved" (Matthew 24:13).

Jesus also said, "In your patience possess ye your souls" (Luke 21:19). We must be sober about the days we live in, and we must be watchful and on guard. It is easy for the world to dull our senses. It is not unusual for the saints to become weary with the battles that they must not only confront on a spiritual level, but in the physical, emotional, and mental arenas as well. It will take much diligence on our part to possess our souls. It will take patience.

However, we are told in Romans 5:3-5, "And not only so, but we glory in tribulations also; knowing that tribulation worketh patience; And patience, experience; and experience, hope; And hope maketh not ashamed; because the love of God is shed abroad in our hearts by the Holy Ghost which is given unto us." Patience comes out of tribulation, but it becomes a point of experiencing the reality of God. Such experience will establish us in our hope, knowing in the end we will not be ashamed of standing on and maintaining such confidence in our Lord.

Most people avoid reality. They desire to control it in order to have power over how it will personally impact them. Such people can remain indifferent to the plights of others as they become experts, judges, or act as consciences to those who appear to be too weak or foolish to be able to control the reality that is affecting them.

Other people live in delusion about reality, denying its power and ability to impact them. They hide from it by creating an unrealistic world for themselves, or run from it through such means as drugs, alcohol, or some form of fantasy such as pornography. Although these people are simply running from the reality of their own existence, that of depression, they will not face what is plaguing them. They are haunted by the idea that reality will never really adjust to their terms or ways.

For many people, they live in a depressing reality because they will not take responsibility for their attitudes in regard to God and the gift of life that He has entrusted to each of us. Their greatest battle is that they are judging the quality of their life from the premise of the self-life. From this premise, self sits on the throne as God, while the flesh reigns according to the pride of the self-life. Obviously, this self-life must be dethroned and the reign of the flesh crucified.

It is vital to understand how to dethrone the self-life. By dethroning the self-life, one will actually bring discipline and balance to the inner man. The only way that the self-life can be dethroned is through judgment. This judgment also serves as a form of discipline.

Judgment means separation. Obviously, we must separate from the influences of the self-life. There are three types of judgments that are in operation. There are the past, present, and future judgments. To be an overcoming believer, we must experience the first two judgments in order to avoid the future judgment. It is important to point out that everyone will experience at least two of these judgments.

The past judgment is that of the cross of Jesus. The cross judges the influence, working, and activity of sin upon a person's life. Jesus' death on the cross redeems those who believe upon His character and work, back from the dictates of sin. It destroys sin's influence over those who apply by faith the personal cross to its reign and dictates. Needless to say, sin is what operates in and through the flesh.

Everyone will experience the second judgment: the judgment on the self-life. God is forever trying to confront the self-life in each of us. This confrontation comes through two sources of judgment: that of chastisement and consequences. Every time God puts His finger on the self-life, He is pointing out the part of the self-life that is no longer acceptable to Him. Keep in mind, God's ways and thoughts are higher. When God puts His finger on an agenda, emphasis, approach, behavior, thought process, or some type of influence such as culture, He is declaring that you or I need to judge it as unacceptable in our life, come into agreement with His evaluation about the matter, and separate from it.

Each time God puts His finger on a particular area of the self-life in the Christian, He is calling him or her to separate from that particular attitude, tendency, practice, or behavior to come higher in His ways and thoughts. After all, the self-life serves as excess baggage that will hinder each of us in our Christian life. Hence, enters the instruction of Hebrews 12:1, "Wherefore seeing we also are compassed about with so great a cloud of witnesses, let us lay aside every weight, and the sin which doth so easily beset us, and let us run with patience the race that is set before us."

Chastisement for the believer means that God's hand is heavy on him or her until he or she learns the valuable lessons, and changes his or her way of thinking, being, or doing. However, consequences mean that a person is simply reaping the judgment of his or her own deeds. Such judgment will bring a person to a point of decision. Either he or she will repent of his or her wicked ways and line up to the righteous ways of God, or, he or she will decide to give way to the preference of the self-life and begin to taste the bitterness of his or her fruit.

If such an individual does not repent, then he or she will taste the final judgment: that of eternal separation from God. Needless to say, we all want to avoid the last judgment, but sadly people refuse to let the self-life be properly judged by God and His Word. People maintain this life so they can hold on to their personal agendas, maintain their emphasis, and justify their deviant approaches to the matters of life.

Since the self-life must be properly judged, it is important that we understand what constitutes this life. But, in order to confront and properly judge it, we must deal in reality. After all, reality tests and exposes the influence and power of this life in each of us. Because of its deception and arrogance, we can convince ourselves that we are in control of our reality and life. However, life has a way of exposing this notion to be a fallacy.

Keep in mind that when self is reigning, we are forever trying to change and adjust our reality to bow down to our self-life. Therefore, we must honestly face reality to recognize how the self-life is opposing the ways of God in our lives. However, this life is clever. It does not mind God being a part of a person's reality, but it will not allow Him to reign. As a result, God is expected to adjust to the self-life in each of us. After all, He should understand how we feel, our strong desires and the needs of our humanity, regardless of how it undermines, disregards, or defies His character and Word.

The first part of the self-life we must consider is that of *self-sufficiency*. Self-sufficiency represents our personal strength. This strength serves as our point of reliance. Since we have this incredible strength, it is easy to perceive that we can actually force or manipulate reality to agree with us.

Life has a way of exposing the vulnerability of people's strength. Eventually, it will wear them down, as it robs them of their resolve to see their agendas come forth. As resolve gives way to despair, people become hopeless. It is in this state that individuals will be forced to face reality, give up on life in resentment, or go into delusion.

For Christians we must choose to face life in order to maintain a realistic point of reliance. This point of reliance must be Jesus Christ. Facing life allows us to come to truth in regards to the character, teachings, and examples of the Son of God. Truth operates from the premise and vantage point of God. It is from this vantage point that we can honestly face our limitations, as we put our faith in His character and strength.

As humans, we are plagued by limitations. We cannot control life, change reality, or others. We can push and shove to get our way, but such attempts will cause conflict and end up mocking us. In spite of this truth, we refuse to face our limitations, because we may have to admit our incapability, defeat, and failure to control life.

The Apostle Paul put our limitations in perspective in light of God's grace. After all, faith gives us access to experience God's grace in times of weakness. In fact, God strength is made perfect in our weakness. This is why Paul made this declaration, "...I rather glory in my infirmities, that the power of Christ may rest upon me. Therefore, I take pleasure in infirmities, in reproaches, in necessities, in persecutions, in distresses for Christ' sake: for when I am weak, then am I strong" (2 Corinthians 9c-10).

We must face our limitations in character and strength in order to recognize our need for God's mercy and grace. We must humble ourselves to ask for mercy, and become thankful enough to receive His grace. However, people who operate from the premise of self-sufficiency will never see their need for God's mercy and grace.

We must face the truth that we cannot make our personal agendas a reality, regardless of our strength. Eventually, such strength will fail us, as will anything that is attached to the arm of the flesh. Those who rely on the arm of flesh stand cursed.[1] In light of this truth, the Apostle Paul made this statement, "Not that we are sufficient of ourselves to think anything as of ourselves; but our sufficiency is of God" (2 Corinthians 3:5).

The second area of the self-life involves our different notions about life. We all operate within rulers in which we judge all matters of life. In this arena we not only serve as judge, but the final authority as to what constitutes truth and reality. Although such conclusions collide with the "so-called" truth and reality of others including God, in our arrogance we maintain we are right, that our way is true, and our conclusions constitute the reality of a situation.

There are four rulers people operate within: concepts, standards, images, and ideas. Although these rulers are different in how they perceive or process an issue, they all come out with the same conclusion to a matter, that there is no way the person could be wrong. After all, whatever premise he or she operates within, points to superiority over those who do not hold the same opinion. The Apostle Paul gave these warnings in Romans 12:3 and Galatians 6:3.

> For I say, through the grace given unto me, to every man that is among you, not to think of himself more highly than he ought to think; but to think soberly, according as God hath dealt to every man the measure of faith...For if a man think himself to be something, when he is nothing, he deceiveth himself.

---

[1] Jeremiah 17:5

These rulers not only judge God, His Word, and ways, but they establish their own particular notions where God is concerned. In the end, these rulers actually create a god to their own image or liking. They will admire their god, worship the notion of this god, and defend this god. However, this god will fail them, and when it does, these people end up raging against the true God of heaven.

The cross must be applied to these rulers to bring the proper discipline to them. This will strip them of their power, as well as bring them into subjection to the Jesus of the Bible. The conclusions of these rulers must be considered mere opinions that have to be regarded as fleshly in nature, blinded by pride, and insignificant in light of God's ways and thoughts. In fact, the spirit or intent behind them must be tested, and they must be brought under the scrutiny of the Word of God to be purified by the washing of the Word or purged and burned up by fire.

Abilities make up the final aspect of the self-life. Agendas will influence the direction of personal strength as people resolve to see a matter through. Notions will determine the type of emphasis they put on a situation, and abilities will be channeled through their priorities as a means of expressing their importance and purpose.

People see abilities differently. Some people may perceive their greatest ability is to reason out a matter. Others may see themselves as having the ability of dealing in the practical. There are people who take pride in their ability to figure their way around a situation, while others possess the ability to get things done. These abilities usually manifest themselves through talents. As you can see, the greatest ability for most people is to be able to express themselves in order to get things done. Some of these abilities are disciplined by integrity, while others are used in wicked ways. Obviously, the motivation behind abilities will determine how people approach something.

It takes integrity to discipline natural abilities, but one must also be willing to lay such abilities on the altar. These abilities need to be offered up to God for His use. His fire needs to come down on the altar and purge them. Those that are left, God has designated for His use and purpose.

Every aspect of the self-life must be properly judged as a means of preparation for a consecrated life. Whether single or married, these preparations are necessary in order to maintain an upright life before God.

Consider the following table on the next page.

| Personal Strength | Notions | Abilities |
|---|---|---|
| Agendas | Emphasis | Priorities |
| Change point of reliance. | Apply the cross. | Put them on the altar. |

Prayerfully ask the Lord to shine a light on any aspect of your self-life that must be judged. Explain in your notebook what you have discovered about each of the following areas in relationship to your own life.

1) Self-sufficiency
2) Notions
3) Abilities
4) What have you learned about your inner man?

# 12

# ORDAINED MARRIAGE

These last five chapters establish how people prepare themselves for the life God is calling them to. Whether a person has a gift of marriage or a gift of being single, he or she must be prepared to enter into union or agreement. This union could be with Christ in total consecration of communion and service to God, or union in Christ with a spouse to prepare to serve God.

The Christian life is all about being prepared to come into agreement. Daily, we must always come into agreement with the Spirit of God in preparation to line up to truth. This agreement could be at the point of Scripture or righteousness. However, true unity in Christ always comes along the lines of Spirit and truth. Such agreement is going to determine who or what will influence our way of thinking.

Single people who have the gift of marriage must realize that they are obligated to be prepared emotionally, mentally, and spiritually for their partner. Likewise, their partner must be prepared for them. Preparation means God must define position, calling, and ministry for each person in order to establish a place of agreement. Agreement implies people are likeminded, heading in the same direction in the matters of God and life.[1]

When God brings a couple together in marriage, it will be at the point of a covenant. A godly covenant must be maintained in integrity and intent. It finds its power in communion. Such spiritual communion finds its agreement in the spirit, and not from the premise of the flesh. In fact, the outward attraction, which is nothing more than lust, must be put in proper perspective to keep the relationship pure and acceptable before God.

The question that most single people, who have been called into the institution of marriage, must ask is where can they find their mate? The truth is single Christians must not seek out their mate. Rather, they must give God permission to bring their mate to them. God brought Eve to Adam after He had specially prepared Eve to become a helpmate.[2] As the Bible clearly states, "...What therefore God hath joined together, let not man put asunder" (Matthew 19:6b).

Obviously, God must put a couple together. Sadly, most couples put themselves together because of fleshly attraction. However, such attraction does not necessarily mean that the couple is evenly yoked on a spiritual basis. These couples assume God put them together because

---

[1] Romans 15:5-6; Philippians 2:1-5
[2] Genesis 2:18-22

it appeared so right to them. In reality, God may have not been in it. This is why many such relationships fall to the wayside. Clearly, marriage is hard enough even when God ordains it. Each individual in this relationship must maintain personal integrity and purity, as well as keep his or her relationship honorable before God.

This brings us to the necessity to ensure the integrity of this relationship among Christian couples. Christian marriages are to represent Christ and the Church. Husbands must become honorable in attitude and conduct towards their wives. To honor a person above self is the way godly love expresses itself. Wives are to come into a place of servitude before the Lord. This honorable position allows them to submit to Jesus' example of servitude in regards to their husbands and families. Godly submission only gives way to that which is worthy. Honoring somebody is the truest example of godly love since the person will prefer the welfare of the other person over his or her own needs.[3]

Obviously, godly marriages must start from the premise of the eternal, rather than from the basis of the flesh. Its vantage point must be the fulfillment of what God intended when He first established marriage. It must represent the union between Christ and the Church. As a result, godly marriages must serve as the visible fulfillment of why God established this incredible bond in the first place.

Since God established the first marriage, He is the only one capable of establishing godly marriage. He knows who will properly compliment, challenge, and encourage each person in his or her relationship with Him to become more effective in His kingdom. Any emphasis outside of this focus will be fleshly and worldly.

The next consideration is how does a person know when God is bringing the right mate to him or her? It is not exactly a matter of knowing, but of discerning. Satan often sends in a counterfeit. This counterfeit may present the perfect picture of what a person has perceived his or her future mate to be. However, it is only a picture or image. It is simply a point of surface or outward attraction and not one of spiritual agreement.

This brings us to concepts, standards, images, or ideas. We all think we know what we have need of as far as a partner is concerned, but few of us really understand what we need. Our ideas of the perfect partner represent our wants that are often based on unrealistic notions. These notions are based on the flesh or what we think will please our eyes, excite our tastes, arouse our feelings, sound right to the ears, and serve as a special aroma to our way of thinking. However, such notions are prideful and self-serving. They are fleshly and lack substance.

These notions make people vulnerable and set them up to accept the counterfeit. Therefore, the first procedure a person in this state must do is to get rid of personal agendas, as far as having a say about his or her mate. These people must deny themselves of their right to have this aspect of life on their terms. Once agendas are denied, then they must

---

[3] Romans 12:10; Ephesians 5:21-33; 1 Peter 3:7

continue to be about their Father's business. If a likely candidate enters the scene, they must step back and discern the spirit, attitude, and conduct of the person.

This is where controlled environments are important. I am not talking about dating. Dating is a cultural practice, and simply serves as a breeding ground for defrauding, betraying, and committing fornication. People defraud others when they give false impressions concerning their intentions towards them. This is what usually occurs in dating. In the dating game, most people are after compromise, not purity. They will say whatever it takes to break a person's resolve to get aspects of their pride and flesh fed.

These people betray the emotions of others by playing them like a fiddle to make a conquest. Sadly, the goal in most dating is geared towards fornication, not establishing a godly relationship. Such fruit clearly stipulates that dating is fleshly and worldly.

When you remove the idea of dating, many people question how they will ever discover their future mate. If God is going to bring your mate to you, He will identify that person to you in the spirit. Ultimately, it will be confirmed. The responsibility of each person is to discern the different aspects of his or her prospective mate's character.

Let us now begin the process of breaking down the different areas that must be tested. Keep in mind, each single Christian must be able to pass these tests to verify their testimony, character, and life in Christ. This does not mean each person will not display occasional challenges due to his or her humanity. Beware of someone who appears to be the perfect mate! Most likely it is a game or façade. The person may not have any real substance behind his or her image. But, if the person possesses godly character, he or she will have a consistency that is obvious in his or her disposition, attitude, approach, and conduct. After all, we do not wander far from who we are. We will always come back to the type of person that is being formed in us.

It is important at this point to state that possible problems must not be downplayed. In many cases, people did see problems in their future mate, but chose to believe that it would be taken care of in marriage, or deemed that the attitude or conduct was insignificant. Do not ignore such points, especially if they have something to do with the person's character.

*Environment:* You must always consider the type of environment you meet a person in. Allow me to state, even though you meet a person in a casual or acceptable arena such as church, it does not guarantee that the person is the one God has ordained. Many people seek out "proper" environments to find the "proper" mate for themselves. The key about environment is that by discerning the person in his or her environment, you can see if the person's character is consistent with the environment. People will prove to be genuine or hypocritical in their different environments.

In some cases, the environment, such as church, may not distinguish good or bad about the person, but environments have a lot to do with common ground. What kind of environment serves as a place of agreement? Where there is a common ground, one has the liberty to discern the next area.

*Disposition:* The next area of discernment is disposition. In other words what spirit motivates the person? Remember spirit will determine if there is agreement. In fact, it is not unusual for people to be attracted to a person's spirit. Both the right and wrong spirit can actual draw you into a person's personality. Keep this in mind. The spirit in operation determines the reality people operate and maintain.

For example, the person can have a seductive spirit that is powerful. It may set off alarms in your own spirit, but you sense yourself being caught up in some uncontrollable whirlwind. This whirlwind is the person's personal reality, but it is sinister, and it is trying to entrap you into his or her reality to hide the fact that he or she is a fake.

You can also find yourself attracted to the right spirit, but you must be aware that this does not stipulate the person is the one God has chosen for you. You are simply caught up with the sincerity of the person's spirit, which can be quite refreshing, but it also can prove to be quite fleshly. Once again, you must stand back and discern your point of attraction. Such attraction implies that flesh is being stirred up for one reason or another. You must properly discern the premise it is operating from.

*Attitudes:* You must discern a person's attitudes. You do this by observing how he or she reacts or interacts with others. This can include family members, the church family, in play, or work. Does this individual show a healthy consideration to others? If he or she is inconsiderate with other people, he or she will not be considerate with you. Do these individuals show respect to those in authority? If they fail to show proper respect, they will not know how to honor or properly come into submission to what is right. Do they know how to play fair? People who are overly competitive can prove to have fragile egos. If they do not come out on top, they will sulk and make you pay. Are they secure or comfortable "in their own skin"? In other words, do they have a sense of who they are? If they do not, they will look to you to confirm their identity. Are they kind to those who are less fortunate? If they are not, they will not know how to show kindness when there is lack of agreement or conflict with you.

*Conduct:* How do these people handle themselves in adverse situations? There is nothing that exposes a person's character or level of maturity more than how they handle themselves when they are being confronted by that which opposes their agendas, fails to honor their emphasis, or tempts them to compromise what they know is true. People who cannot handle opposition prove to be unteachable. People, who must be honored at all times, will prove to be harsh and cruel. Those who give way to temptation or play games are divided in their loyalties and are self-serving, proving to be untrustworthy.

*Company:* The Word of God tells us bad company corrupts good morals. It also states deep calls to deep.[4] This simply means people are attracted to those who have the same spirit, maintain the same attitudes towards life, and possess like moral values. The company individuals keep, will tell much about their level of maturity and character. After all, there are points of agreement in such relationships. Therefore, it is easy to get valuable insight into someone's spirit. In fact, the people we attract could very well serve as mirrors to our own disposition.

*Responsibility:* The final point of discernment comes down to whether a person is truly responsible. People, who fail to be responsible for their burdens, decisions, financial practices, and to do right regardless of the circumstances, will fail to be responsible towards other obligations, whether it be marriage or children. If people are irresponsible with their burdens in life, they often prove to be users. In other words, they will simply find ways in which they can use you, as well as others to serve their purpose. If they refuse to take accountability for their decisions, they will blame all matters on you, proving to be an unteachable fool about the matters of life. If they fail to possess good work ethics in order to pay their bills, they will always know the bitter and shameful taste of being in debt, as well as losing valuable credibility with others. If people fail to do right regardless of the situation, they will not see any need to do right by you. In fact, such people will not have any regard towards you when it fails to serve their purpose.

Another area of character that is a good indicator about a person's level of integrity is if they value their word. Do they mean what the say, say what they mean or do they cleverly use words to con and manipulate reality? People who are not true to their word cannot be trusted.

Character in these different areas will express itself in personal disciplines. Personal disciplines enable a person to be honorable and diligent in all he or she does. These individuals will prove to be trustworthy and reliable. They will not betray you, nor will they take their covenants and responsibilities lightly. They will not be perfect, but they will prove to be mature in how they look at and approach life.

As you can see, it is easy to discern those around you. If God brings your partner, you may not have the attraction, but you will have the respect or friendship. In other words, there will be a pure foundation upon which to establish a right relationship. It is also important to point out that couples need to learn to be friends first, and then they can develop an intimacy in their marriage.

The problem in most marriages is that the attraction is sexual or fleshly, but not spiritual. Such attractions wear off quickly, taking the passion with it. However, if there is substance to the relationship, it can mature in a deep way, allowing for an intimacy that will also grow into maturity.

It is vital that Christian couples start from the right premise in order to develop a godly relationship. God so much wants to use couples to

---

[4] Psalm 42:7: 1 Corinthians 15:33

exemplify the reality of Christ and the Church. He so much wants to bless homes. However, the right environment is missing in many homes, preventing God from sanctifying the marriage and blessing the family.

If you have the gift of marriage, you need to know that you must withstand destructive temptations by discerning in these areas for your personal welfare. You cannot expect God to entrust you with a person of impeccable, godly character, if you lack such character. If you lack character, you will not only defile that person's testimony, but you might cause despair in his or her spiritual life. God will not ordain such a relationship.[5]

Examine your own character by honestly evaluating the following areas of your character. Write down your conclusions.

1) Disposition: (Discern your spirit—natural man, spirit of the world, or Holy Spirit)

2) Attitudes: (Consider your relationships.)

3) Conduct: (Handle yourself.)

4) Company you keep:

5) Responsibilities:

6) If you have a gift of marriage, are you ready for your mate? Explain your answer.

---

[5] Matthew 9:16-17

# 13

# STANDING ALONE

The idea of being single usually does not appeal to people. However, Paul encouraged such a state for those who wanted to truly serve God.[1] To be a single Christian consecrated to service to God is to be undivided in vision, purpose, and goals. Although Jesus sent people out in two's, it was for the purpose of protection and contrast. When we are flying solo, we can sometimes lose perspective. We can become self-sufficient and independent because there is no contrast or challenge to rock our world. As a result, we can become narrow-minded, self-centered, and unrealistic. Therefore, God will bring some source to challenge those who are single to keep their perspective realistic about life and others.

Even in the best of circumstances, it can prove hard to come to terms with the concept of being alone. After all, God created us to discover the different aspects of life in relationships. We all want to be special to someone and to belong to a group, unit, or family. Therefore, the idea of being alone for some can prove to be the greatest fear and torment.

Out of my six decades of life, I was married only five years. As I look back at my life, I realize that I have never really been alone, Granted, I have experienced loneliness, but it was not because I was alone. I have occasionally felt betrayed and sacrificed by those for whom I cared, but I have never been alone. I know about the isolation of depression, but I was not alone in my torment. I know the forlorn feeling of desolation as I have stood among the debris of personal sin and failure, but I was not alone.

Are there people who are really alone in this world? We would have to define what being alone means. Does being alone mean that no one really cares? In rare cases this could be true, except there is a God in heaven that cares. Is a person alone when others are not present? Just because a person stands solitary in his or her space does not mean he or she is alone. Since there is life flowing through our veins, there is activity such as thoughts, feelings, and other functions that remind us that the activity of life is in us, as well as surrounds us in some way. The

---

[1] 1 Corinthians 7:7

presence of life stipulates we are not really alone. We may stand alone, but we are never just alone.

The only place that could constitute being alone is the grave. Obviously, this is the sincerest example of being alone. There is no life, no hope, function, or presence in the grave except a dead body. Yet, how many people feel alone? How many people feel they are facing the world without there being any regard or consideration for their existence?

This brings us to a very important subject. If a person is single and traveling life in the single lane, does this mean he or she is alone? Once again, we are reminded that a person's perception about this matter is based on his or her attitude towards life. For Christians, we are never alone if we believe what the Bible says. We not only have the life of Christ in us, we have the constant companionship of the Holy Spirit, and the ever abiding, watchful care of the Father. Whether we physically stand alone in our present situation, we clearly are never alone. This is our hope and promise. We need to stand in the place of expectancy, and cling by faith to the reality of our God and not to what we see or feel.

Being single does not mean one is alone. Years ago, a Christian woman came up to me one day to talk to me about my single status. She had a brother who was in his late twenties, but was single and had no future prospect. I remember how she commented to me how hard it must be to be single person because you do not really fit. Most people my age were married and had children, meaning I had nothing in common with the people in my age group. I had to agree with her. My closest friend was over a decade older than me, and her son was a teenager.

As this woman frankly spoke to me about the challenges of being single, I could tell she had a real concern and desire to understand the plight of the single person. It is true that at a certain age bracket, single people have a hard time making friends that display the maturity and experience that allows for common ground to be established in other areas. At certain ages it seems that people are consumed by the demands of their family. However, when children are older and priorities have been somewhat redefined, these very same people can find common ground outside of the family realm.

Through the years, I have been able to recognize the difference between being single at 28 and being single now. Presently it appears as if my age and experience allow me the right to cross over the many barriers of age, gender, and so forth, and find places of fellowship with people of all ages. Because of my many experiences, I am able to relate to people in every stage of life.

However, the critical age bracket for most single people ranges from 19-39. This is when these people feel pressure from the standards and practices of society to somehow fit in. Such pressure can be immense for someone who is struggling with his or her place and identity in this world. It can cause an identity crisis. Sadly, in many cases, people simply give in to the pressure, to only end up disillusioned by all of it.

The first section of this book dealt with the identity crises that people can find themselves in. The second section of this book dealt with the preparation that is necessary to find our life in Christ. In fact, it is about being able to survive this critical time of our single status until society begins to take us seriously about the person we are becoming instead of suspicious about our intentions.

In this section of the book, the different aspects of being single will be considered and honestly confronted. If God is calling a person to serve Him in a single status, he or she must come to terms with being single and the different temptations that can confront him or her.

The reason for following this particular pattern in this book is because single people must be comfortable being their own person if they are going to discern and overcome the pressures and temptations that are common. If they do not know their particular gift as far as marriage or being single, as well as their position in Christ, they will be quicker to fall into the traps and temptations that await them.

When people are comfortable with their present place, they are not easily confused about a matter. After all, their vision is sure and single; therefore, they stand assured in their particular situation.

People who are doubtful about their present status can quickly become confused. In their situation, they will begin to doubt their place, question their status, and second-guess their decisions. Such confusion will cause dissatisfaction.

Dissatisfaction means there is a lack of contentment. The Apostle Paul made this statement about contentment, "But godliness with contentment is great gain" (1 Timothy 6:6). People must learn how to be content regardless of their status.[2] Learning such contentment has to do with not only changing behavior, but also changing the attitude behind it. Contentment is a state. And, each believer must find that contentment in the living Christ. This contentment in God's kingdom can only be realized if a person is truly godly in his or her life.

Obviously, no matter the state, Christians must learn to be content in their particular situation. Therefore, single people must learn to be content being single in God's kingdom to prevent them from looking elsewhere for their life. They must become comfortable with who they are in His Body and plan, knowing they belong to His family, have been endowed with an eternal purpose, and have been identified with a heavenly calling and inheritance.

Another challenge for the single Christian is to maintain checks and balances. Single people without proper challenges can become set in their ways instead of set on the ways of God. If their perspective is not challenged, they will develop their own particular reality that will become self-righteous and judgmental towards that which fails high, religious standards.

I have met a couple of single people who spent their life serving God. Such a concept is commendable. But these people had become so rigid in their way of doing and thinking, that they could not imagine how they could be wrong about any issue. However, when the attitude of

[2] Philippians 4:11

meekness is missing, there is a wrong spirit in operation. Meekness does not make one tolerant towards others in sin, but keeps a person pliable or teachable under the hands of God. Instead of a person insisting on his or her way, the person will simply stand upright for the truths and ways of God, giving the Holy Spirit liberty to convict others.

Since single people can become independently set in their ways, they must develop checks and balances that will keep them reliant on God and meek before others. For me God gave me co-laborers in the Gospel to challenge my reality. As I have looked back over the years, I am so thankful that God's provision turned out to be the very checks and balances I needed to keep me on track in my life.

These co-laborers have brought necessary discipline in my life. Granted, this discipline has not always been fun, but it has kept me from going into some form of delusion, as it has challenged and reminded me to consider the reality that truly exists around me. The main reality is that I am not the only duck in the pond.

These checks and balances also remind me of various responsibilities. When you are in full-time ministry, you can lose touch with what is going on. You can become obsessed with the idea of ministry while failing to truly minister to God's sheep. This obsession often translates into becoming so spiritually minded you possess no earthly good. In fact, you can become indifferent to the real problems that may be besetting others. You can become complacent about ordinary responsibilities. Such a state robs a person of effectiveness, and makes him or her worthless in the practical applications of Christianity.

The greatest challenge for most people is to operate in reality. This is true for Christians. We have a tendency to think if we don't like our reality, we will have God change it. It is never that simple. Reality is meant to confront, challenge, and expose our character. Our confidence does not rest in God changing our reality, but Him using present reality to challenge or change us; therefore, we can trust Him in our present situation.

If you have the gift of being single, you need to consider whether you have consecrated yourself to God, and therefore are being prepared to serve God in your status. You need to come to terms with your position, as well as ask God to bring necessary checks and balances to your life that will keep you pliable and realistic about what is going on around you. Take the opportunity to answer the questions on the following page, as well as prayerfully consider the matters we have discussed in this chapter, and summarize your findings.

1) Are you comfortable with the person you are becoming?

2) Are you content with your present life in Christ?

3) What types of checks and balances has He put in your life, or needs to be put into your life to keep you in tune to the reality around you?

# 14

# VULNERBILITY

The one aspect that people have a hard time confronting and acknowledging is the fact that if they are part of the human race, they are vulnerable. Our pride often keeps us from properly recognizing and facing our vulnerability. After all, vulnerability implies we have needs, weaknesses, and flaws that make us susceptible to others, circumstances, and challenges.

As Christians, it is vital that we confront vulnerable areas. For example, we do have the need to be part of some type of unit, whether it is a family, group, or organization. We not only have this need, but we want to feel needed or important in some way. Needless to say, such a need has opened people up to pursue relationships, causes, or things that fall short of benefiting their well-being.

We all have weaknesses. These weaknesses exist in our way of thinking, doing, and being. They are not always obvious to us. In fact, we may not even know they exist. However, the enemy of our soul seems to have no problem in locating them. And, when least expected or when we are weary, we find these weaknesses being exposed in a time of temptation. The unexpected revelation leaves us in shock, and weariness can leave us too depressed to properly confront such temptation.

Flaws indicate weaknesses in our character. We all have these flaws. Once again, we may or may not be aware of them. However, wherever there are flaws, you will also find points where possible compromise can take place in your Christian life. Flaws often find their source in our pride and their platform in our prejudices. They disguise themselves behind various cloaks from religion to self-sufficiency. In some cases, people try to overcompensate for their flaws to keep people from recognizing that they are present in their character.

The importance of recognizing these areas is to avoid temptation. One of the main aspects of life people must take responsibility for is what they allow themselves to be exposed to. Life with its circumstances will come and go, but we still can determine what we expose ourselves to in regards to environment and influences. For example, we need to stay away from such environments as dens of iniquity and darkness, or that which will expose us to the ways of wickedness.

We also determine what will influence our way of thinking. We need to be discreet about what we expose ourselves to such as entertainment, literature, music, and art. We all know environments serve as the expression of the spirit behind them, and likewise, there is a spirit behind such things as the different forms of entertainment. When we expose ourselves to those things that are profane, we come under the influence of a wrong spirit.

As a single person, I must be careful as to what I watch, because it can stir up my lust. I have to be mindful as to what I read, because it can cause me to become sentimental about that which is imaginary and useless. I have to be aware of what I listen to as it may pervert my reality. These are the things I must discern. It is up to me to guard my disposition, attitude, approach, and conduct. I must not lose my edge when it comes to spiritual matters. This is why the Word of God instructs me to separate from unholy allegiances, flee youthful lusts, keep myself from idols, hate that which is evil and follow after godly virtues.[1]

Guarding one's spiritual life requires constant vigilance. We must be sober about what influences our spirit, discerning about our motivation, diligent in the matters of righteousness, and consistent in our conduct. Our testimony of Christ must not be contradicted by our practices. Our creeds must not prove to be hypocritical by our lack of commitment and devotion to God. Our ways must not mock righteousness. Our tongue must not betray our character. We must hold the line of righteousness in regard to our personal well-being before God.

Spiritual maturity hinges on our level of responsibility that we take for our personal life. As Christians, we must be responsible for what affects our life, and what kind of impact it will have. We must take accountability for what is not right in our life, as well as display the necessary character of humility to right the matter. We must be wise enough to learn the lessons and open enough to be enlarged in our faith to take greater steps of obedience.

This brings us to our source of reliance. The biggest inconsistencies found in the Christian life can be traced back to a lack of faith. Faith is established in the fiery ovens of trials and temptations.[2]

In fact, the fire not only reveals the source of our reliance, but it also proves how strong it is. I have put faith in man, creeds, abilities, personal strengths, and religion, to only be disappointed. Each false point of reliance simply set me up to see the vanity in my idolatry.

Establishing my life by faith in Christ proved to be a process. I discovered much of the process had to do with revealing my presumptions and assumptions. For example, I had presumptions about God. I presumed various things about His character and work. As a result, I put Him to a foolish test many times.[3] Each test confirmed how longsuffering God can be towards His foolish people. Peter summarized presumptions in this way, "But chiefly them that walk after the flesh in the lust of uncleanness, and despise government. Presumptuous are they; self-willed, they are not afraid to speak evil of dignities." (1 Peter 2:10).

---

[1] 2 Corinthians 6:14-18; 2 Timothy 2:22; 1 John 5:21
[2] 1 Peter 1:5-9
[3] Matthew 4:6-7

Presumptions are made up of standards or ideas. They show that people who give way to them are walking after the flesh. They will manifest in some type of perversion, and will refuse to submit to any rule. Ultimately, they will arrogantly demand their own will be carried out and speak evil of that which does not serve their purposes.

Presumptions are in relationship to God, but assumptions are in regard to life. We possess so many assumptions because we think we know about a matter, when in reality, we do not. Those who have influenced us the most have conditioned in us the assumptions that we possess. Since we assume that these influential people were knowledgeable about what they were advocating, we believe such matters to be true. However, presumptions and assumptions represent misdirected faith that will not stand when the storms of life challenge us in our understanding and reality.

Each false source of confidence within me had to be exposed and brought down before the feet of my Lord. I had to realize that each false point of reliance represented a false way in my life, causing me to be vulnerable. In fact, my faith continues to be established on the only true foundation of Jesus Christ. No doubt this process will continue until I meet Christ in His glory.

Meanwhile, my faith must be enlarged so that I can receive in greater measure from my Lord.[4] This is true for every Christian. We receive according to the measure of our faith. Unless, we are enlarged in our perception of God, we end up limiting God. We limit Him by putting our own presumptions on Him. "God, you must do it this way."

As we expect God to do it our way, God approaches the matter according to His character and His plan. It is important to realize that wherever we put a stipulation on God that is where we will walk in unbelief towards Him. After all, we do not trust Him with the details of a situation. We do not believe that it will serve our best interest. We do not trust His real intentions towards us.[5] Therefore, we insist on our way because of unbelief.

If God does anything, it will be according to His character and plan. In most cases, He will do the very thing we would never expect. If we are stubbornly waiting for Him to do it according to our assumption, we will end up missing His intervention.

Most people fail to grow in God, because they will not allow their perception of God to be exposed, challenged, and enlarged. As a result, few are able to receive a greater measure of God's character and ways. They fail to mature in their Christian life, as different aspects of their life are never fine-tuned through the testing of their faith.

We have considered four vulnerable areas within humans. We have the need to belong to some unit. This need has to do with identity and purpose. Only God can fill such a need with His life and presence.

---

[4] Romans 12:3
[5] Jeremiah 29:11

We have our weaknesses. These weaknesses vary with people. The Apostle Paul was very much aware of his weaknesses. Consider what Jesus said to him about this very subject, "My grace is sufficient for thee; for my strength is made perfect in weakness" (2 Corinthians 12:9b).

As a result, the Apostle Paul told of the attitude that he developed towards his weaknesses, "Most gladly, therefore, will I rather glory in my infirmities, that the power of Christ may rest upon me" (2 Corinthians 12:9c). Obviously, we are able to experience the very strength of Jesus in our vulnerabilities.

We have our flaws in our character to contend with. They can cause failure, hurt, and depression. However, if we look to Christ, we can find mercy, grace, and healing. He will fill these flaws up with His wisdom, righteousness, sanctification, and redemption. Flaws remind us that we have nothing to glory in but the glorious reality of the abiding love, authority, and power of our God.[6]

The next area of vulnerability is our source of reliance. Faith is the choice of the will. I choose to believe regardless of the trial, crisis, and darkness that may engulf my soul. Job said it best, "Though he slay me, yet will I trust in him; but I will maintain mine own ways before him" (Job 13:15).

This brings us to a vital area of vulnerability. It has to do with time and energy.[7] There can be a couple of different tests in this area: that of being idle or being too busy. Single people who have idle time on their hands can get into mischief. Those who are too busy can lose sight of what is important.

Idle time and idle hands often lead to self-serving practices that are destructive. One example of such practices is pornography. It is not unusual that people who are idle fall into some type of perverted lifestyle. In their attempt to fill their life with something, they end up being entrapped into practices that are addictive, dangerous, and destructive.

The other aspect of being single, especially in ministry, is becoming too busy with religious matters. Most people mistakenly think that if a person is single in ministry, he or she has the time, money, and energy to pick up any slack in a matter. After all, these individuals have free time, and appear as if they do not have any other obligations. However, this is not true. Single Christians in the ministry are running the race as well. They have daily responsibilities and obligations to meet. They must guard their time to ensure that God remains their center focus. They have to learn how to redeem their time like any other person. In fact, their responsibilities can double as they struggle to maintain daily responsibilities, work, and fulfill ministerial obligations.

Therefore, single people must learn how to discipline their time, energy, and resources. They must look to God concerning their time in order to discipline their energy in the right way. They must consecrate all resources to God to ensure wisdom and multiplication of such resources.

---

[6] 1 Corinthians 1:29-31
[7] Ephesians 5:16

Consider the following areas of vulnerability. Although we have already covered some of these areas or made reference to them in previous chapters, they must be considered in light of weaknesses. Prayerfully ask God to show you how vulnerable you are in each area. Write down your conclusions.

1) Needs

2) Weaknesses

3) Character Flaws: Source of Reliance:

4) Time/Energy/Resources:

# 15

# TORMENTOR OF THE SOUL

The greatest challenge for some people when it comes to being in the single lane is loneliness. Loneliness is a state that often torments the soul. It is vital to understand this state, because many people have found themselves in compromising relationships or situations to try to avoid this torment.

As previously stated, I have never really been alone. However, even when there are people and activities surrounding a person, he or she can experience loneliness. Some of the loneliest people are the busiest people. Obviously, loneliness is a state of the soul and not always a result of the outward environment.

It is important to point out that some people choose to be alone, but others are forced into such a state. You would think that those who have a gift of being single would be spared from experiencing such anguish. However, everyone will probably, in some way, come face to face with this tormentor. In fact, they may never know when they will have to confront this covert enemy, but somewhere along the way they will. It usually happens during one of the different identity crises that people experience.

For the single Christian, this tormentor will raise its head when he or she feels abandoned by God in a situation. King David had such experiences. You can read about his various struggles with this tormentor in the beautiful book of Psalms. As you follow David through different conflicts he had with loneliness, you realize that the one virtue that delivered him from such a foul state was his faith in God. In each struggle, David made the same conclusion. He would choose to trust the ever abiding, faithful character of His God.

Studying the concept of loneliness, I came to this conclusion. Loneliness manifests itself in the feelings of hopelessness and desolation. Such feelings cause one to feel abandoned and lifeless, devoid of warmth and comfort. In summation, nothing in such a person's present environment gives a sense of belonging, security, purpose, or hope.

Such a state causes a couple of reactions. One is fear. For some people even the very thought of being alone causes them to panic. And, one has to question what the person really fears, especially if he or she is a Christian. After all, fear is the opposite of faith. There are a couple of possible reasons for such fear.

The first one is that loneliness can serve as a mirror to our very soul. Jesus came to give us abundant life.[1] To possess an abundant life means to possess a complete life. The one aspect of the soul is that it proves to be a spiritual vacuum that can suck everything out of our environment. To avoid facing the possible spiritual leanness or emptiness of the loneliness of our soul, we can resort to feeding its appetites to silence its many nagging insecurities that take center stage at such times. Ultimately, the mirror of loneliness will show us the worth of our life, as to whether there is any real substance or purpose to our being and existence. This will bring into examination our significance in the scheme of things.

Once the vacuum of our soul is exposed, we must silence its mocking. This is when we can fall into the second trap of fear: that of compromise. We will try to silence that spiritual vacuum by filling up our lives with things or relationships. Keep in mind, things can make us temporarily feel good about life. However, the reality is this temporary euphoria will be snatched away from us, leaving us emptier than we were before.

Relationships can give us a sense of belonging and purpose. However, the wrong attitudes towards relationships can expose our loneliness once again. Granted, we may not be alone physically, but we can be tormented by the reality that relationships cannot fill the vacuum in our soul.

At this point you might wonder what that vacuum represents. Clearly, loneliness can be a temporary feeling, but for people with this vacant space in their soul, it is a state. This state is void of life, companionship, and purpose. Any state that is void of life represents a state of death. The state of loneliness is a place of death and despair.

Most people avoid facing this state of death. What this state represents is the fact that at the end of all of man's attempts and devices lays absolutely nothing. Therefore, loneliness is the expression of people coming to naught in their life. We would all like to think we create, establish, and add to our lives, but in reality we are unable to change these different aspects of life. Granted, we can determine the quality of our life by the attitudes we adopt towards God and life, but we cannot create the life we desire, establish the life we pursue, or add any real meaning to our life. The harsh reality about life is that it comes from outside of our attempts and conclusions.

God has been gracious to bring two co-laborers into my life. I trust these two individuals. I know their strengths and weaknesses as they know mine. We have the same vision, know our place of agreement, and are willing to give way to that which is worthy of all exaltation. Although we have had our challenges along the way, we have always had the same source and place to come back to get our bearings.

These two people do not fill my life, but they enlarge and add to it in immeasurable ways. However, when I go through the valley of the

---

[1] John 10:10

shadow of death, neither one of them can go with me. When I experience the dark night of the soul, they cannot take away the feelings of despair that engulf me. The reason for this is because in such times, God wants me to come to the place where He fills my life with a greater revelation of Him.

We intellectually may know that God is the only one that can fill the vacuum in our lives. But, how many of us have allowed ourselves to face that mirror of our own soul. The vacuum of our soul is insatiable and endless in its demands. It will not be silenced. However, we must honestly face the tormentor of our souls if God is going to be our source and substance in our lives. There are so many people running here and there to avoid facing the vanity of their soul. They fear what the mirror will reveal about their own personal agendas and activities. They fear what it might say about their worth and purpose in the scheme of things.

The state of loneliness can make us desperate. We cannot fill it up, but we can temporarily placate or silence it. However, all attempts are temporary, and we become even more vulnerable as we try to become established on the false foundation of sand. Needless to say, this faulty foundation will not withstand challenging circumstances. Circumstances are always causing life to change underneath us. It is only by being established on the immovable Rock of Jesus that we can remain sure in whatever situation we may be in.[2]

Desperation not only makes us vulnerable, but it makes us foolish. Instead of looking upward for God to fill the void in our lives, we look elsewhere. Although we may placate this loneliness for awhile, it will eventually catch up with us. And when it does, the hope we are seeking will turn into despair, the comfort we are looking for will turn into disillusionment, and the warmth we desire will prove to be illusive, and is often replaced by cruelty and rejection.

The second cause of loneliness is our need to have our life count for something. This need can translate into two extremes: Those who are needy and those who need to be needed. Those who are needy, cling to people, while those who need to be needed can begin to consume people's time, energy, and life.

Those who cling to others will not only demand that the individuals fill their need, but they will suck the life out of people. Eventually, the ones who are being sucked dry want to escape the bondage of the person whose need is insatiable and unrealistic.

People who are needy manage to cling to you due to the fact that they appear fragile. Such an appearance requires them to be handled with care. Therefore, you must avoid any kind of appearance of abandonment because it will devastate them. You cannot afford to be too honest about your attitude towards their neediness, because they cannot deal with it in their fragile state. You cannot call them to accountability because they give the impression that they are not strong enough to handle it. However, this appearance is a game. They are not fragile;

---

[2] Matthew 7:24-27

rather, they do not want to face their real state and be forced to do something about it. They need to grow up, face life head on, and seek God to fill the insatiable vacuum in their narrow existence of selfishness and loneliness.

Those who consume people's lives because they need to be needed do so through good deeds. The motive behind their deeds is to become indispensable. Their logic is that the more they do good deeds, the more the recipients will grow to depend upon them. Such dependency ensures that they will always be in the inner core and that they will not be abandoned. However, these people eventually become burned out and lose patience with those who are on the receiving end. They also become irritable, and display an indifference and cruelty at times. Ultimately, they end up pushing people away as their nobility is stripped off to reveal selfishness, fear of abandonment, and loneliness.

When the recipients feel the sting of these people's cruelty or indifference, they begin to back away. Needless to say, this is translated as abandonment to the one who was in search of being needed. This produces the victim syndrome where the individual now feels used and will go into self-pity. Such a person cannot understand why he or she is receiving such treatment. But, the reality is that both types of people ultimately set themselves up to be rejected or abandoned because the relationship is not built on the right foundation. Rather, it is established on the basis of selfishness that is often being driven by loneliness.

It is not unusual for those who are needy to hook up to those who need to be needed. Sometimes this relationship can continue for a long time, but eventually it will become parasitic. In other words, both parties feed off of one another in one way or another. Obviously, such a relationship is very perverted and is doomed for collapse. After all, the needy one is looking for a savior and the one who needs to be needed will be glad to oblige them. However, there is only one Savior. He is the One who died on the cross. He is a jealous God who will not share His position or work with anyone else.

In our vulnerable state, we must not give way to either mentality. God alone will meet our need, and there is no way we can meet the need of others without miserably failing them. We must be open to help lift others' burdens if possible, but we must be aware that we cannot meet their needs or solve their problems.[3] I had to learn this lesson in many different ways. The reality is I still can fall into the same trap, but I now have enough experience to recognize the vanity of it all.

It is hard to explain to people who are caught up in these different situations that what they are running away from is not a feeling of being alone, but the state of their own soul. The biggest ingredient that is missing is faith towards God. These people have failed to learn that the first place they must go to gain a healthy perspective is God. They may have to wait to gain the right perspective, but the reality is God will fill up those who are open to receive with a greater revelation of Himself.

---

[3] Galatians 6:2-5

The real challenge is that we must allow the reality of God to fill our souls. He is the One who meets our needs, walks through the valleys of uncertainty, and brings satisfaction to our longing soul.

What about your state? Have you faced the vanity of your soul, or have you allowed the life of Jesus to fill you up to overflowing? Prayerfully ask the following questions, and write down your conclusion.

1) Have you faced the mirror of your soul or are you running from it? Explain your answer.

2) Do you fear being alone? If so, why?

3) Have you allowed God to fill your needs with Himself or are you looking elsewhere? If you are looking elsewhere, explain the source of your focus and how it is affecting your life with God and others.

4) Have you found yourself compromising because of loneliness? If so, do you need to repent?

# 16

# LIFE AFTER MARRIAGE

We have dealt with the challenges of having the gift of being single. There are various aspects of our selfish disposition that we must guard against. We must protect ourselves from a wrong spirit, put to death any attractions to the world to avoid any unholy influences, and ignore the essence of self as far as its selfish demands to determine how our life is to be established in Christ. However, we must consider another type of individual when it comes to walking in the single lane. These are the individuals that find themselves single again due to the loss of their mate through death or divorce.

Depending on their attitudes about God and experiences with life will determine how the loss of their mates will affect them. There are various emotions that both groups of people must wade through. Loss is loss no matter what arena it takes place in. For those who lose their mate to death, there can be anger and betrayal. A big gapping hole can clearly be evident in their life that requires healing and change. Loneliness will often loom in front of these people with unbearable torment.

For those who experience the death of a marriage through divorce, it appears as if the matter is open-ended. In other words, there may have been the death of a marriage, but nothing has been resolved. There is no final closure because the parties involved are still living. Fear of uncertainty and loneliness can loom in front of these people as it mocks and tears at their resolve. Some people attempt to look back and try to figure out what happened in order to avoid the same scenario, while others live in delusion and denial about their part in the failed marriage.

One of the biggest challenges people in this position must face is that they have tasted of the intimate fruit of marriage. Needless to say, sexual desires are often heightened for some after they have partaken of this fruit. These heightened desires do not simply go away. They must be kept in perspective, as well as disciplined. After all, they can lead to fornication.

Marriage also points to coming into agreement with someone in a manner that no one else is meant to. When that agreement is broken through some form of loss, there are nagging and persistent feelings of betrayal and anger.

Separation or loss of this nature also points to establishing a different life. People develop habits, as well as lifestyle patterns in their relationships with others. Their attitudes, thinking, and way of doing something has been greatly influenced by their relationship with their mate. For some, they have to devise a whole new way of living. For others, they must adjust their patterns. In many cases, people actually have to find out who they are because their relationship with their spouse has defined them in many different ways. It can throw them into a personal identity crisis where they are not sure who they are. This can be a fearful time for many of them, as they feel vulnerable.

For some, the loss of a mate leaves a terrible hole. As a result, some have fallen into destructive relationships or habits while trying to fill that void. The idea of being alone drives them mad with insecurity and uncertainty.

For others the relationship represented an unpleasant time; therefore, they are glad they are out of the situation. Nevertheless, this means that unresolved issues loom in their life. These unresolved issues can cause these people to make the wrong decisions about their future and any relationships they might come along the way.

Let us consider both forms of loss. After all, many of these people can "fall through the cracks" if the Church fails to address their unique problems.

# Death of a Mate

As previously stated, depending on the relationship, the loss of a mate can be a very devastating time. It leaves a big gaping hole in one's life that must be confronted. Memories can prove to be taunting. Vacant spots in the house can become unbearable as they remain silent and almost mocking. In the end, the person will have to redefine his or her life outside of the participation, companionship, advice, and presence of his or her mate.

During the time of loss, decisions can prove to be overwhelming, and responsibilities depressing. How do you fill a gap left by a person that took care of certain aspects of the household and business affairs? How do you redefine your life to include these responsibilities?

These can be daunting questions that can haunt a person as he or she is forced to make decisions that he or she is not ready for. Moreover, on top of that, everyone seems to be an expert about what needs to be done. Some advise comes from personal agendas, others give advise in ignorance, while there are a few that seem to recognize what is really going on, and quietly lift the burden where possible.

A person who has just lost a mate needs to go through a process that involves three stages. Until the person goes through this process, people need to give them space, constructive support, and be sensitive in how to lift burdens.

The first stage of this process is shock. It is the initial emotional response to any real loss. It is like being in an emotional bubble. Although things are going on, it does not seem real. Shock is a natural way for a person to emotionally handle death. It protects a person from the full emotional impact of the loss. Even though people may know someone is dying, it is still a shock when it happens. Part of the shock has to do with the unknown. It is not that all people, especially saints, are necessarily concerned about the unknown aspect of death itself; rather, fear may come because of the unknown impact such a loss will have on their life and environment. In shock, the finality of one's life does not seem real; it is almost a stage of denial until the emotions are ready to face what the mind knows. However, the mind cannot yet comprehend the loss because the emotional impact has not connected with the mind to bring about understanding.

The second stage in this process is mourning. There appears to be a historical tradition in place for mourning, especially when it came to leaders.[1] After all, the loss of a person that influenced people in a constructive way will be felt at every level. A life once was, but is no more.

The mourning for the children of Israel in regard to losing a leader was to last 30 days. It is amazing that there is a time limit on mourning. I do not understand it, but I do know that our Creator allowed for mourning since He knows our frame.[2] He also knows what it will take to let go of something precious and valuable.

Mourning allows the person to graduate from the shock mode, in order to face the loss. As I consider the month for mourning, I realize that there is a strong message about mourning.

First, it is necessary. It is a time for people to say good-bye. This allows people to let go of the person or the former way of life. The problem is that some people never let go. However, to go on to the new life, that which represents the old must be laid to rest.

In this mourning, a person must face the emotional impact. There will be anger. This anger can be directed at God, as well as the departed mate. At times the anger will take on deep, tormenting feelings of betrayal and abandonment. How could his or her mate leave him or her in this mess? How can this person now face life alone in this manner?

In the mourning process a person is allowed to come to terms with his or her loss. I refer to this as emotionally landing. Many people run from facing reality head on. However, they must face reality to be able to confront life. To face life, they must land physically and emotionally to confront a matter on the spiritual level. During this time my advice to people is that they do not make decisions that will affect their future well-being or testimony. Do not try to deny or ignore the feelings that are boiling under the surface. These people must be brutally honest before God about how they feel. After all, He can only comfort those who honestly mourn.[3] Sadly, I have watched people get themselves into compromising and devastating consequences because they have not properly landed.

The impact of the loss must be faced to bring resolution. Resolution is the place where one accepts the reality of the loss, allowing for the

---

[1] Numbers 20:29; Deuteronomy 34:8
[2] Romans 12:15
[3] Matthew 5:4

person to go on. Advancement is the next step in this process. After the necessary days of mourning, the children of Israel were prepared to pick up their camp and move on. Of course, the cloud of the Spirit of God led them.[4]

This brings us to a very important godly principle. Christians, who have lost their mates, must only move on according to the leading of the Spirit.[5] It is the Spirit that will bring the person into his or her new life in God. It is also the Spirit of God who will help such individuals make the right decisions in regard to their lives.

The Bible suggests that people who once again find themselves in a single status consider serving God. They are no longer tied into a worldly relationship. They can consecrate their lives to serving as a temple in which the glory of God can manifest itself in greater ways. Perhaps, due to years, some do not have the strength behind them, but they have wisdom established in their lives through experience and lessons. They may not be as an attractive vessel as they once were, but they can allow the beauty of their Lord's countenance to shine through their lives, bringing forth a greater, eternal attraction.[6]

There are also instructions for young people who find themselves in this type of loss. If they cannot use their time wisely or if they burn with lust, it is wise to remarry, to once again redirect time and energy. [7]

Whatever the situation, the Bible shows us there is life after great loss. Even though such loss challenges our resolve to go on, as Christians we must choose life. We choose life not because we are noble or because life is wonderful, we choose life because it is a gift from God that one day must be handed back to Him.[8]

Are you struggling with great loss at this time? Make the choice to choose the life God has for you. This will allot you the necessary opportunities to discover a greater measure of life in Christ.

# The Bitter Pill of Divorce

Divorce is one subject that is shrouded in conflict in the Church. In many Christian camps, divorce is almost treated as the unpardonable sin. It becomes a terrible stigma that follows believers wherever they go. In some bodies, divorced believers are barely tolerated or are shunned altogether, but they rarely receive the ministry they need to develop healthy lives.

It is clear that God is against divorce. Divorce shows a breaking of a covenant. When the children of Israel went after other gods and came into agreement with them, God wrote a bill of divorcement.[9] The sin did

---

[4] Exodus 13:21-22; Psalm 78:14
[5] Romans 8:13-14; Galatians 5:16-18; 1 Corinthians 7:39
[6] 1 Corinthians 7:8, 32-33, 37
[7] 1 Corinthians 7:7-9, 39-40; 1 Timothy 5:3-16
[8] Deuteronomy 30:19
[9] Jeremiah 3:7-14; Matthew 19:4-9

not rest in God divorcing Himself from the children of Israel, but it rested with the people of Israel because they had long broken the covenant with God. He simply made it official.

If God can divorce Himself from being associated with fornicators (spiritual adulterers), so can His people in similar situations. That is why divorce is acceptable when adultery is the issue. However, covenants are not just maintained at a physical level. To keep the integrity and intent of a covenant it must be kept at three levels: spirit, principle, and practice. This is why Jesus stated if a man looks on another woman with lust, he has committed adultery in his heart.[10] In such a case the spirit was compromised, betraying the principle or purpose of marriage. Today, many Christian marriages have already been compromised and betrayed, breaking the covenant.

The reality is that God is against all sin. Divorce is a symptom of a hard heart.[11] If you do a study on a hard heart, you will find that pride serves as its platform. There is also a stiff-necked attitude towards truth, and a shallow commitment towards God. Ultimately, the hard heart will manifest itself in indifference or cruelty, which is a lack of love. Without genuine love, there can be no godly submission or honor in a relationship.

When you break sin down, you will see that the greatest sin in the Church is not divorce, which has soared to the high rate of 50%, but unbelief. So many Christians do not really believe the Word of God. In reality, they pick and choose what they will believe. If Christians truly feared the Word of God in the right way, many of them would be doing things differently. This includes how they treat one another in marriage and the Body of believers.

The problem with divorce is that it often serves as a legal means to commit fornication. As you study the culture in the Old and New Testaments, it was the man who usually wrote the bill of divorcement. He could hide behind various excuses for his ungodly attitude towards his wife, when in reality he was lusting after someone else.

Usually, the reason people seek a divorce is selfish in nature. They do not want to personally put into practice the principles of godly marriage to ensure a right spirit and environment. In many cases such people refuse to humble themselves, neither will they choose to love their spouse in a godly manner. Ultimately, they have become disillusioned because they had self-serving expectations about marriage that were not being met.

The Bible clearly establishes that the only reason the covenant of marriage can be nullified is due to the breaking of the actual covenant. However, when you understand covenant, it is quite easy to break. It takes integrity and commitment to maintain the intent of this agreement.

There are people who are willing to pay the necessary price to see that this covenant is maintained. It takes self-denial and sacrifice of one's

---

[10] Matthew 5:27-28
[11] Mark 10:2-5; Hebrews 3:8-19

right to have life on his or her terms. However, the environment of the world that is promoting selfishness in every area of the self-life is invading the Church, taking captive the hearts and minds of Christians.

The Church has adopted much of the world's selfish attitude towards marriage; therefore, those who call themselves Christians are not interested in denying self and choosing the way of personal sacrifice. As a result, the state of marriage finds itself in shambles. It takes only one party with pride and indifference who lacks the necessary vision and scriptural accountability to break the back of this covenant.

For many Christians, divorce has been forced upon them through the indifference or disrespect of their mate. It is important to note that those who seek the actual divorce may have been forced into that position by their spouse's ungodly attitude and actions. Remember it was God who wrote the legal bill of divorcement because the children of Israel forced it upon Him by their adulteress agreements and practices.

Divorced people are labeled with the stigma of being a failure. Yet, we must question how much the Church has failed to properly deal with this matter in the right spirit, within excellent principles, and according to godly practices that should govern every Christian marriage. Has the Church confronted the hard hearts, arrogant expectations, and self-serving agendas of its people? Has it turned on the searchlight of Scripture to expose, contend, and challenge wrong, worldly attitudes about this subject? What has it done to establish the right foundation and attitude to ensure the right environment to establish healthy marriages? Granted, the Church has its platitudes and its rules, but in light of the various practices that are found behind closed doors in marriages such as adultery, perversion, pornography, drugs, and alcohol, to name a few, there is no substance behind what the visible Church offers to properly address the problem.

The marriage bed is being defiled from every angle.[12] Many mates feel they are prostituting themselves with their spouse as they share his or her affections with unholy alliances. In fact, pornography, drugs, and alcohol are included in forms of fornication or unholy agreements and practices.

The Apostle Paul dealt with the issue of divorce in 1 Corinthians 7. Once again, Paul upholds the intent of marriage—that of agreement. If a Christian is married to an unbeliever who wants to be set free from the covenant, so be it to maintain peace.

If a person is bound to a spouse, he or she should not seek to be loosed. But, if a person is loosed from a spouse, he or she is not to seek another. However, Paul recognizes that some people have a problem in the flesh, meaning self-control over their fleshly appetites. In this case, it is better to marry than to burn.[13]

However, before divorced Christians even consider the issue of remarriage, they must thoroughly examine their position, attitude, and

---

[12] Hebrews 13:4
[13] 1 Corinthians 7:9, 27-28

God's will for their lives. Do they have the gift of marriage or of being single? I am divorced, but I discovered after my divorce that I possess the gift of being single. As Paul stated, let every man abide in his present state in God with contentment.[14]

If you find that you have the gift of marriage, but for reasons beyond your control, you have found yourself in a divorce, there are some precautions you must take to ensure you are not falling into the same traps.

Give yourself at least a year's span from your divorce before you even consider entering into another relationship. It is dangerous and unwise for divorced people to rush into another relationship before they have been healed. In that year or so, you need to learn the lessons of your past marriage. For example, what went wrong in your marriage? What was your part in the failure of the relationship? What does God want you to learn? It is necessary that you get rid of the immature exercise of the blame game. Both parties are responsible for the death of a marriage. Ask yourself whether you failed to initially seek God in the matter, and broke the spirit of the covenant by failing to have agreement with a likeminded person. Perhaps, you broke the principle of the covenant by failing to maintain a right attitude towards your spouse, regardless of what was going on in the relationship. Or, maybe you did not preserve the integrity of your relationship in godly practices. It is important that the lessons are learned to bring about healing, resolution, restoration, and wisdom to avoid a similar situation.

Seek God's face about your place in the kingdom of God. It is hard to discern the right mate if you do not know who you are in Christ. Many marriages fail because one spouse is looking to the other for purpose. It puts undue pressure on the mate who feels the need to give his or her spouse a purpose for living.

Finally, you need to make sure that God chooses your mate, and that you are prepared to make the necessary commitment to see through the good and bad times in your marriage. God does not only ordain marriage, but He has given it as a gift to humanity. It must be valued and honored in a right way.

The other aspect in relationship to divorced people is the Church's attitude towards them. The Church is meant to be a hospital, not a courtroom. Divorced people have a lot to wade through. They need understanding, proper challenge, and godly instruction.

Most people have no clue what goes on behind the closed doors of a marriage. Granted, individuals may have solid suspicions and some inside information, but that does not mean they understand the real dynamics of someone's marriage. It does not mean they have a right to judge.

It is natural for most people to take sides based on who they like the most or whom they dislike the most. However, it is better to remain quiet

---

[14] 1 Corinthians 7:24

about what you think you know than to let your opinions flow out to reveal that you are not only judgmental, but you are ignorant.

People who are going through a divorce do not need to be kicked some more by the cruel, opinionated judgments of others. There needs to be healing and instruction. These people need quiet leadership and space to come to terms with their feelings. They definitely do not need to be put in with some group of other divorced people to mope in self-pity or be paired off so they do not feel so lonely. They need to be restored back into the flow of God's people. They need contrast and instruction. They need to discover or rediscover who they are in Christ.

If you ask me who or what is failing the most when it comes to marriage and divorce, I believe in so many ways that it is the Church that is failing to establish and instruct its people in the ways of God. Rather than calling for distinction, much of the Church adjusts Scriptural principles and instructions to the platitudes and selfish philosophies and practices of the world. As a result, many Christians are falling through the cracks of indifference, prejudice, and sin. This is a bitter pill to swallow indeed.

What about you? Are you struggling with life after marriage? There is life after marriage, but it can only be found in Jesus Christ. If you are struggling with this issue, consider the following questions, and be sure to write down your conclusions.

1) Is your gift that of being married or being single?

2) What direction do you sense God is leading you as far as discovering your life in Christ?

3) What lessons are you learning or need to learn in regard to your former life in preparation for a new life?

4) Are you taking the necessary time to land emotionally and spiritually, or are you pushing it back because of fear and loneliness?

5) Have you chosen to trust God with your future?

6) What do you hope God will do with your present life?

7) Are you learning to be content in your present state, so that you can embrace a new life in Christ?

# 17

# FOR HIS SAKE

Although this manual for single Christians is not dealing with new issues, it does bring back into focus godly matters that have been conveniently forgotten, adjusted to fit a more liberal environment, or done away with to make room for new, acceptable philosophies of the world.

It is not unusual to hear Christians talk about pursuing or experiencing some aspect of the world before they die. Obviously, what is missing is any real consideration for what Christ wants to accomplish. As a result, people throw Jesus the leftovers while feasting on what they consider to be the best the world has to offer them. As you consider their miserable sacrifice, you realize they believe that God wants them to feast on the "so-called" best. In their blatant selfishness they cannot perceive that God has not given them abundance to feast on, but to offer it back for the sake of His kingdom.

My goal is to bring Christians back to one reality—that we are here for the sake of Christ. We are not here to live unto ourselves. The concept of finding a life that will make us happy and satisfied in this present world is humanistic in nature and unscriptural. However, this is the concept most chase after in the Christian realm. First they seek happiness, and then they will add, tack on to, or adjust Christ to their life to make it acceptable to their religious palates.

Such an attitude has caused many to become lost or disillusioned with their life in Christ. Rather than blame it on a mixture that is religious in nature and influenced by the spirit of the world, they blame God for their miserable state. After all, they logic that they are in this state because they were trying to do it God's way, when in reality, they were doing it their way, while attaching Christianity to it in some form or the other.

This false presentation of the Christian life is simple. These people are simply conforming to a religious idea to convince themselves that they are okay. They are outwardly performing good deeds to ignore the sin that lurks behind their works. They work at reforming the sinful disposition by rehabilitating it, while remaining unchanged in the inward man. It is all the outward pretense of hypocrisy. After all, we must be transformed before we can conform outwardly to the image of Christ, perform according to the righteousness of God, and ensure reformation of the inner state of our being.

As Christians, we must keep our focus in line with eternity. We are here for the sake of Christ. We do everything for His sake. The whole of our life is ordained for the sake of our Redeemer. In addition, if we miss sight of all that must be done, in light of, and in agreement for the sake of the Son of God, then we begin to live for ourselves. We pursue after Christ via our happiness. We serve Christ via our terms. We seek Christ via our agendas. We pervert, adjust, and change all matters to fit our lifestyle in the name of Christ. Ultimately, we offer profane offerings that lack sacrifice, and will prove to be full of worldly religion and nonsense.

Today, the problem with many Christians in America is that they are here for themselves. They add Christ to their life. He is placed in a nice compartment and only brought out on Sundays and/or Wednesdays. Once the religious duty is fulfilled, Christ is put back into His religious compartment, while everything goes back to the normal way. Nothing changes, as Jesus remains a religious notion and Christianity a doctrine of good deeds and religious rituals.

This manual is to show that married or single, all aspects of our lives must be considered in light of the heart, mind, and will of God. All must be done for His sake to ensure that He is glorified in our lives.

As I have worked with Christians, I have discovered that the biggest point of failure for them is that whatever religious activity they are doing, it is not being done for the sake of Christ. They are selfish enough to delude themselves that it was what God wanted for their lives. They are arrogant enough to believe that God would agree with them. However, their premise is idolatrous and self-serving. As a result, sacrifices from these people's lives have been perverted and rendered useless on the altar of God.

This manual will not be considered pleasant for the "Demases" of Christianity. Demas had been under the auspice of Paul. However, he loved the world more than Christ; therefore, he went back to the world.[1] There are many Christians who are trying to maintain their status in this present world. However, this manual will not let Christians feel good in their selfishness or live in delusion about their right to have personal happiness in life or have life on their terms in this present world. It will expose the profane sacrifices that are being offered up by worldly Christians, because they refuse to consecrate their lives for the glory of God. It will reveal the feeble commitments of Christians that want to tack Christ on to their pursuit to taste of the tree of knowledge of good and evil, while they offer crumbs back to God to sooth their religious conscience.

The goal of this manual is to reveal and present the challenge that regardless of our lot in life, as Christians, we must ensure it is from the premise that everything that we do in this earthly tabernacle is being done for His sake. This is why people must first seek their gift as to their marital status to understand the sacrifice they must offer up for His sake. If marriage is their gift, then they must seek God to bring a right mate to ensure a consecrated life and a sanctified marriage for the sake of Christ.

---

[1] Colossians 4:14; 2 Timothy 4:10

If a person has the gift of being single, then he or she must give up all rights to live his or her life for the sake of finding life according to personal designs or worldly living. Such believers must consecrate their life for the purpose and glory of God.

Today, many are calling for revival. However, I believe the great call needs to be one of repentance and faith. We need to repent of our weak testimonies, worldly ways, and unholy sacrifices. We need to choose the life of faith, that no matter what we have to sacrifice or experience in this present world, we need to desire a greater resurrection. We need to live such a distinct life above the world, that it is not worthy to witness it.[2] We need to do whatever it takes to bring the proper glory to our wondrous Lord. As those around His throne will declare in Revelation 5:12b, "Worthy is the Lamb that was slain to receive power, and riches, and wisdom, and strength, honor, and glory, and blessing."

To come back to this place of true repentance and faith we need the cleansing of the truth of His Word and the purging of the Holy Spirit. We need to be awakened by the fires of adversities, and exposed through and through by the two-edged sword of the Word. And, when we finally have been laid bare by the glorious reality of Christ, perhaps we will realize that what we value in this present world is dung in comparison to gaining the life that was ordained for us before the foundations of the world.

My prayer is that this manual has challenged every reader to consider if the whole of his or her life is designed for one purpose: that all that was done and is being done is truly for the sake of Christ.

---

[2] Hebrews 11:35-39

Book Four

# PARENTS
# ARE PEOPLE
# TOO

(How to Raise Your Parents and Survive)

Copyright © 2006

# INTRODUCTION

There are many books about how parents are to raise children or deal with rebellious children. However, there are very few resources, if any, that deal with unhealthy relationships of adult children with their parents. It seems that there is an automatic assumption as to how this issue is to be handled based on a few Scriptures. As a result, it is rarely addressed. This leaves some adult children in a precarious position.

Many parents rightfully refuse to accept what they consider disrespect from their children. However, it appears that as adults, these very same children must silently accept disrespectful attitudes, demands, and conduct from their parents. It is as if they have no rights to demand respect in this relationship. Because of their initial position as a child under their parents' authority, they are expected to accept their parents' ungodly responses towards them in the name of honor.

Many Christians have asked me this question, "How do I raise my ungodly or unreasonable parents, and survive the heart-breaking ordeal?" This book is hopefully an answer to this very question. There are many Christians out there with unreasonable parents. They want to be responsible Christians towards their parents, but all too often, they end up drinking from a bitter cup of guilt, hurts, and struggles. The Church, as a whole, has failed to address this problem. Any advice that is offered seems empty in light of the emotional and spiritual struggles these people experience because of this issue.

My scriptural research has resulted in interesting conclusions. I do not know if every conclusion will fit every scenario. I do know that those who struggle with this issue will be encouraged and uplifted to learn that God has provided us with decisive principles by which we can evaluate each situation.

Now, I will answer the question as to how to raise parents. You cannot raise your parents, but you can make peace with your scriptural responsibility towards them. And, like Joseph, you can make a similar declaration, "What was intended for evil, God intended for good to accomplish what is now being done in my life and in those I love." (My paraphrase of Genesis 50:20.)

# 1

# WHAT AM I TO DO?

"I know something about you." I felt the blood rushing to my face. I sensed I was about to have some kind of confrontation with my father.

He continued, "I have ways of finding out about these things."

My unprepared response was simply, "So?"

"I found out you changed your name back to Kelley." I knew this was a sore subject with him even though it had never been mentioned until now. I even understood his attitude. I had officially taken my stepfather's name "Kelley" when I was 18. I had used that name since my mother remarried when I was ten. It was not a hidden fact because even by his own choice, my biological father had initially addressed all correspondence to my brother and me by using our stepfather's last name, instead of our birth name.

In my mind, I was Rayola Kelley. My identity had been established in my stepfather's love and commitment. My biological father had not made such an investment. Emotionally, this man had never been there, and financially, he never paid any child support. Everyone excused his irresponsible actions because of his handicaps. He was considered legally deaf and blind, although he could somewhat hear and see with the aid of glasses and a hearing aid.

It had seemed to me that everyone came to his rescue. People constantly made excuses for his sarcastic comments and his irresponsibility. His brother always bailed him out of any major trouble, and another man had ended up raising his two children without any support from him.

At the time his crude comment was made, I was suffering through an unpleasant divorce. I had requested my former name back. It was apparent that my biological father was upset because I had not asked to return to my birth name.

My non-committal attitude to his findings made him more irritable. He looked at me and said, "I could put you in a garbage can." In a flash, I perceived the meaning behind his statement as discarding an unwanted child—an abortion. It was as though I was insignificant, and could be put in the nearest trashcan at his will.

I knew his statement was demonically inspired, but I had determined long before not to put up with any of his crude comments. I looked at him and replied, "If you try, I will never speak to you again."

He flew into a rage and screamed, "Get the h__l out of my house and never come back!" My maternal grandmother, who had come with my friend and me for a friendly visit, somehow beat both of us out the door, and stood waiting by the car. As I hurriedly walked through the door, he stood there, screaming. I remember looking back as the whole house violently shook with his uncontrollable anger as he swung the door back and forth. Although he later apologized for his actions, I was left with a dilemma. As a Christian, how was I to respond to this situation?

My father did finally succeed in aborting our relationship. His jealousies, sarcasm, anger, game playing, and demands had ripped at the heart of what relationship still existed after years of neglect. His last display of disrespect and cruelty finally snuffed out what little life remained.

"What am I to do God? I am supposed to honor this man, but he has dishonored our relationship. He has basically killed it." I did not realize that God was about to answer a question I had struggled with for years.

People seem to make this issue simple. However, it is never simple to those who struggle with it. In my mind, this simplicity could not wipe away the reality that I had tried to be a daughter, only to encounter emotional slams. He only appeared to lay claim to being my father when it served his purpose. Otherwise, he was conspicuously missing most of my life.

As a Christian, I had witnessed to him about Jesus, only to get a glimpse of his personal warped, perverted perception of himself. I had tried to hold the line of respect between us, only to taste jealousy, mockery, bitterness, and anger. I realized he did not understand what it meant to have a healthy relationship with anyone, but he had not striven to establish one that was realistic. It seemed that all relationships had to be on his terms.

"What am I to do God?" I knew I had to guard my heart. Foolishly, I had thought that I was beyond hurt when it came to him, but this man's cruel comments found their way into my spirit. I was wounded because I was in a vulnerable time of my life. I knew that the wounds could fester if I denied their existence or try to put on a Christian front of forgiveness and fake nobility to impress others. I was angry for the vicious attack, and I dared not pretend my emotions were not stirred in all of the wrong ways. Festering wounds produce bitterness as unresolved anger results in hatred. I was not about to let the enemies of my soul win. God was the only one who could resolve not only the issues that plagued me over my responsibility towards him, but my feelings about him.

I knew I had to wrestle with this subject until it was clear in my heart. My first goal was to keep my relationship right with God. This meant that the wound had to be taken care of and the anger resolved. As long as my relationship was right with God, the matter of other relationships would be resolved.

Little did I know that dealing with the wound and anger was just the beginning of this journey into the dichotomy associated with this relationship. Before this struggle was resolved, I would have to face the impact of indoctrination, cultural influences, and attitudes. It would not only be a time of revelation, but one of personal examination and spiritual growth that would change how I perceived my life in God.

# 2

# BROKEN ILLUSION

It is a traumatic shock for children to learn that their parents are not perfect. Small children have an inborn belief that their parents are special, and will never do wrong. They assume, in their innocence, that their role models are trustworthy, and have a noble commitment to ensure their safety and well-being. The sad truth is, parents are often as human and selfish as the child is.

I first encountered this harsh truth in my biological father. He found another woman to take his attention and time from his family. My brother and I were left on the back burner as he openly pursued this new love. My mother did not attempt to stop the affair because she saw it as a way out of their dead marriage.

After a divorce was obtained, my father was completely absent from our lives until his new love began to see that his two children were being neglected and dropped him. Suddenly, he came back into our lives and wanted his family back.

This is when I first became a victim of his game playing. He withheld money from my mother in the hope of forcing her back. We never went hungry because my mother worked, and eventually received government assistance when she emotionally caved under the mounting pressure. Times were tough, and I do remember going to school with the sole of one of my shoes flopping loose, exposing my sock. A teacher felt sorry for me and bought me a pair of shoes.

Strangely, I never questioned my father's love for me, but I ceased to respect him. I did not appreciate being a pawn in his sick game. I could tell he had no idea that he was affecting his children in a negative way. It was obvious he was only interested in pursuing his selfish agenda. I feel this perception kept me from developing bitterness or resentment towards him.

I also encountered my mother's human frailties during this time of my life. My mother always seemed so responsible for our well-being before the divorce. Suddenly, she was faced with not only the overwhelming responsibilities of being a single parent, but she came face to face with a new freedom and a loneliness that drove her to fill the vacuum. Her pursuit often left my brother and me alone on the weekends, or at night, to contend with our own feelings of misery, loneliness, fear, and neglect.

It was at this time in my life that I realized my parents were people too. In the right situation, they could display incredible irresponsibility, especially in parenting. As the commitment of parenting gives way to selfishness, the innocence and well-being of children are sacrificed. This leaves immature and confused offspring to somehow pick up the pieces of a life they did not ask for nor choose.

Sadly, parents still have the Adamic disposition in them regardless of their age. This selfish condition makes them sinners who are in bondage to the flesh and pride. Their world becomes small as they focus on their own needs. And, their perspective becomes limited as they cease to look at the fruits and consequences they are causing for themselves and others. Why should this surprise us?

Romans 3:23 tells us that all have sinned and come short of the glory of God. Parents need to come to the salvation of Jesus like any other lost human being. They need to make Him Lord to stop sinful cycles and destructive lifestyles. The problem with unrepentant parents is that their sins will always devastate their children. Whenever flesh serves as lord, children become victims of destruction.

For instance, the flesh always serves as a relentless tormentor, driving people into greater slavery. This slavery will pervert the judgment of those falling into its snares, causing devastation for the innocent parties. Pride is at the heart of all flesh. It is the essence of selfishness. Selfishness will always sacrifice those who do not serve its present purposes or pursuits.

Divorce is a decisive way to unveil human failings. The stories that have come out of broken families are heart wrenching. The heartache is often similar. It is always caused by selfishness. Like many children from divorced homes, I tasted the bitterness and depravity of this selfishness at a young age. The divorce of my parents was the hard instrument that not only brought an end to a family, but also exposed the frailties of each of my parents. In the end, we all became victims.

One of my friends shared how her mother went from a caring mother to a person who constantly partied after her divorce. Her mother actually exposed my friend to drugs, alcohol, and sexual immorality. At the tender age of nine, my friend began to shut down emotionally. Today, she cannot remember much of her childhood.

This friend admits that she also established mindsets and erected protective walls that were destructive to her in her adult relationships. She started on a path of promiscuity, alcohol, and drugs at a very tender age. She quickly discovered that even though her mother had been on the same route, it turned out to be a dead end. This realization brought my friend to Christ.

We have a term for troubled families today. They are called dysfunctional families. This is nothing more than a nice psychological term for the harsh reality and the consequences of sin reigning in family life. God intended for man to have the best, but as a result of his disobedience in the Garden of Eden, man has become depraved and families "dysfunctional." Even in the Christian realm, many families fall into this category. The reason is clear. Until Christ takes His rightful place as Lord, man remains a slave to sin and families continue to become casualties.

It took me years to make peace with the events that surrounded and followed my parents' divorce. The path in my relationship with my biological father hit a traumatic climax on that fateful day when he was screaming for me to get out of his sight. All the futility of his past games and forms of manipulation exposed themselves in that final scene. The relationship had truly proved to be nothing more than a dead-end with no meaning or purpose.

What was I to do about my relationship with my father? God's words were sure. "Walk away and do not look back." His words seemed contradictory to what I had been taught. After all, this man was my father. It dawned on me that my Lord was releasing me from looking back at what was already dead. This was necessary if I was to follow Him into a new life. In a way, I was being severed from something that had clearly burdened me down. However, being released from something and coming into a place of freedom can prove to be worlds apart.

A couple of months after being released from entanglements with my father, I realized that I still had some unresolved issues about the past. I was now 35, and these unresolved issues had turned into mental and emotional cycles. I discovered they had inspired some destructive decisions. My relationships with others were also affected.

I was surprised to come face to face with these problems, but I realized that Jesus wanted to bring healing to my life. Even though I had been a Christian at this time for fifteen years and felt stable in my life, the tentacles of the past had cleverly rooted themselves into my mental and emotional patterns. I recognized the destruction of these entanglements, and I wanted no part of them. Therefore, I gladly embraced the healing of Jesus, rather than the misery of selfishness.

Today, many people feel sorry for themselves because their childhood carries pain and destruction. This is unnecessary. God has provided each of us with a Great Physician. His name is Jesus. He came to right that which is wrong in our lives. But, first, we must make the decision to allow Him to resolve issues and heal us. This takes honesty on our part. We must be willing to let the hidden wounds be brought to the surface. We must let go of our rights and excuses to be victims and choose to become victors through Christ.

I have met many people who would rather cry about their past life than be healed. It actually serves as a sick cop-out from responsibility for present attitudes and actions that are ungodly and destructive.

Perhaps you can relate to this chapter. You might fit into the category of being a victim of parents who acted very much like selfish children. You feel you have come from a "dysfunctional" family and the tentacles are now reaching into your life and present relationships. Jesus is still the only answer.

Your parents may have not changed through the years because their flesh and pride remains lord of their life, but you can change your life and outlook. You can ensure that Jesus is your Lord and Savior. Ask Him to walk on the scene and resolve any slavery or residue that may be left from your past. Let Him bring the necessary healing, because in doing so, you will begin to make peace with your past. This, in turn, will allow you to make peace with your present relationships.

# 3

# INGRAINED PATTERNS

The Lord released me from trying to maintain some type of relationship with my biological father. The relationship had proved to be a burden too great to bear. As previously stated, being released from a matter and coming to a place of freedom are not the same. I was no longer under a burden, but I did not have the liberty of the soul to experience freedom.

At the core of family relationships are ingrained patterns. I had to face these patterns before I could sort out the different issues that were plaguing my relationship with my parents. Such patterns are developed by influences and a need to survive and to belong. These ingrained patterns are similar to the one established by geese. Apparently, the behavioral pattern and flight patterns are established in goslings by following the example of the parents. This is true for people. Individuals are born with a clean slate. They look to others to write on their slate to establish identity and purpose. As a result, people unsuspectingly are conditioned to respond a certain way in order to survive and belong.

There are two ways people survive in worldly relationships: 1) They play the game with outward compliance, or 2) they rebel against that which would try to control or manipulate them. The outward compliance is a way of keeping peace. On the other hand, outward rebellion, is the way an individual declares independence in order to maintain individuality. This rebellion not only comes out of a struggle to discover one's personal identity, but to maintain it outside of the identity that parents or authorities try to put upon those they are overseeing.

Parents are to train a child in the way he or she should go.[1] Such training points to developing healthy behavioral patterns. To encourage constructive behavioral patterns, attitudes must be properly challenged. By challenging attitudes, proper conduct is encouraged. Conduct brings about contrast and will unveil motivation and expose thought patterns. The problem is that there is a fine line between training a child in the way he or she should go and conditioning a child.

The differences are decisive. Training a child is the same as teaching him or her how to walk the walk through example and discipline. It is a form of cultivating and nurturing. On the other hand, conditioning a child is trying to influence, manipulate, and control him or her in his or her way of thinking. Training influences thought patterns by understanding what constructive behavior is. Conditioning determines thought patterns according to the authoritative figure. Training allows the child to develop his or her own personality, while conditioning aligns the

---

[1] Proverbs 22:6

child to become the expression of those who are in charge. Therefore, the child who is conditioned has the same prejudices and opinions as those who are overseeing him or her.

It is not unusual to see this conditioning going on in families. In fact, everything in our society conditions people, from culture, entertainment, and education, to information sources. This conditioning will determine how people will respond to life and authority. Either they will outwardly conform to an idea of life, while inwardly rejecting authority, or, they will rebel against authority in order to maintain a separate identity and keep control of their life. Nevertheless, in both cases, conditioning is taking place as individuals react to the people who have power over their lives.

As we study human behavior and attitudes, each of us will realize we are being conditioned in some way. The desire to determine the quality of life is not found in avoiding or reacting to being conditioned, but in choosing in what way we allow ourselves to be conditioned. This is why parents are told to train their children. Godly training allows children in their adult life to think outside of the box, and consider what they want their life to personally say about them. Training of this nature allows the person to take responsibility for his or her life and to determine in what way he or she will be conditioned or influenced. For example, I can allow people to influence me to their way of thinking, the world to conform me to its way of being, or God to transform my mind, aligning me to His ways of righteousness. [2] In each situation, I am taking accountability for the environment of my life by choosing what I will expose myself to. Such exposure is going to condition me in my way of thinking, living, and being.

Sadly, conditioning children encourages emotional games. For those who are compliant, they learn how to play games in order to get desired responses from others. This gives them a false sense of power over others. They perceive that all they have to do is play people and they will get the desired responses. Many discover that this is not realistic when they face life as an adult. Not all people can be played, especially in the same way. As a result, these people's games backfire, leaving them bitter and skeptical.

Those who are rebellious learn how to push the emotional buttons of others to come out on top. They perceive their rebellion as a way of controlling their lives. If they can get those who are in authority to react, they see themselves as having the upper hand. This gives them a sense of control. However, these individuals fail to realize that pushing buttons of the lines of authority can result in devastating consequences.

Conditioning ultimately sets up patterns in relationships. For example, those who have been conditioned respond to unspoken attitudes. I know of people who automatically know what their parents want without any communication. They were conditioned as children to know their parents' expectations and how to act accordingly. Sadly, this is carried into a person's adult life. Parents continue to expect their

[2] Romans 12:1-2

children to always know and comply with these unspoken expectations. Problems arise when the adult child sees such expectations as non-applicable and unhealthy.

It is hard for parents to recognize unhealthy patterns in their relationship with their adult children. The reason for this development is due to the fact that in most parents' minds they will always see their children as immature, disadvantaged, and in the position of always needing their ongoing guidance about matters regarding life. Such parents fail to see that if they do not recognize these unhealthy patterns, they will provoke their adult children to anger, and drive them away from having a relationship with them.[3] Ultimately, they fail to see that their adult children have changed, and that their relationship with them must adjust to include this change. Without such change, the relationship becomes unhealthy.

Facing these unhealthy patterns is hard for parents. They have always perceived themselves as being in the position of knowing what is best for their children. This may be true when their children were under their care, but there comes a time when they must allow their adult child to actually grow up and discover his or her own identity and life outside of their perceptions and worlds.

Most parents also want the best for their children. Therefore, they cannot understand how their ideas or conclusions about life may not be considered acceptable or practiced by their adult children. Since these parents never emotionally allow their children to grow apart from their guidance to develop their own identity and life outside of "so-called" acceptable boundaries, they see any struggle against their interference as rebellious.

Instead of focusing on the struggles, parents need to acknowledge that their adult child is demanding equal respect from them. For example, most parents would not tolerate their adult child telling them how to live or think, but they think nothing of demanding that their adult children agree with them. Parents would become angry if their children expected them to adjust their lives to their whims, and yet parents often expect their adult children to drop personal interests to adjust to their whims or demands. Obviously, such parents automatically expect their adult children to react as they always have while under their authority, especially when it serves the parents' personal agendas. When the adult child refuses to respond to the parents' conditioning their disagreement or conflict ends in misunderstanding, hurt, rejection, and anger.

Regardless of how children respond to their parents' conditioning, they eventually hit an identity crisis. They do not know who they are because they have reacted to the conditioning instead of discovering their own personality. They have not been trained to think outside of their conditioning. Often this drives them into extreme situations that set them up for defeat.

---

[3] Colossians 3:21

Since these people may have played games to get their way, they do not know how to properly deal with people on an individual level. They do not understand the virtues of integrity because either they practiced a false way of deception to get certain results, or they walked in the ways of darkness to maintain a false sense of control over their lives.[4]

An Identity crisis always causes confusion that turns into fear or resentment such as in the case of a young girl who was the model of a compliant child. She understood her mother's expectations and moods. She outwardly complied, while she inwardly saw herself as being wise. As she grew older, her mother began to become more involved with her life. As the mother became increasingly caught up with her daughter's life, she pushed her towards the young men her daughter liked. The pressure became so great that the young woman became resentful. She was not her mother. She did not think or react like her mother. In fact, she had no intention of being like her mother. Eventually, she escaped and hit rebellion that took her down a rocky road.

Although different in actions and pursuit, rebellious children have similar problems when they face adulthood. In their mind, they were trying to develop independence and identity. In their adult life, some gain wisdom and learn that their reasoning was a lie. They were not trying to establish identity; they were simply rebelling against the identity and authority that was being put upon them. This rebellion drives these people into destructive patterns and hopeless despair. In the end, as adults, they still react to situations in the same way. Instead of knowing who they are, they find themselves in a maze that leads to one dead end after another.

Sadly, these scenarios are not unusual. Ingrained patterns follow children into their adult life. In some cases when they begin to step outside of the patterns as adults, they find their parents still consider them children. As they struggle to develop their own life as adults, they discover that they still must contend with the attitudes and expectations of their parents. It is at this point that some begin to realize that their parents are playing a game as well.

In the mind of most people it does not matter that a game is being played. All that counts are the results. Most parents want their way with their children. If they allow their offspring to play the game, it matters little as to how dishonorable it may be, as long as they get the desired results. If they have to use devices such as guilt or intimidation to get their way, so be it. After all, it is all part of the game.

There is a price to such games. The greatest price is a loss of respect, honor, and healthy relationships. For example, usually the compliant son or daughter discovers that he or she has played the games at the expense of healthy boundaries and respect in relationship to their parents.

There was a young man who had been a compliant child while his brother had been more independent. His parents bragged about his

[4] Psalm 119:104; 128

conduct. He realized that he had played the game of compliance just to keep them off his back. He had felt smug about his accomplishments while growing up, but as an adult it backfired. As he endeavored to establish his own life, his parents were constantly trying to influence his decisions, while they left his brother alone. He began to realize that even though his brother had fought against their parents' control, he had actually established boundaries in his life that their parents respected. After all, they knew how far they could go with him before he would bluntly tell them to butt out.

The young man realized that if he was going to have a healthy relationship with his parents, he would have to establish such lines. This would not be easy, since ingrained patterns and attitudes were already firmly incorporated in his relationship with them. He not only had to discipline himself to be honest with them, but he had to keep from falling into the little boy syndrome when his parents were around him. He also had to let them know when they were overstepping boundaries in regards to his personal life.

I was a compliant child. This caused problems for me in my teenage and adult life. I never realized how ingrained the patterns were until I was away from my family for a number of years. When the Lord finally brought me back to my home state, I had established my own life in Him. Obviously, I was different, but the way some members of my family regarded me was the same as before. It was as though I was expected to fall back into the old patterns that I had left behind.

Amazingly, I did fall back into some of the patterns, but God began to reveal how perverted they were. They were not only unhealthy, they never allowed for growth or change in people or relationships. It was as if I was that little girl or teenager all over again who needed to conform to what others perceived, regardless of the person I had become.

As a Christian, I wanted healthy relationships, but I had to pay the price. Was I willing to be misunderstood as I refused to play the games? Would I accept being falsely accused, since my actions would cause confusion and hurt to those who were enslaved to these patterns? Was I willing to risk any and all relationships that were not healthy? After all, not being compliant and subjected to the "so-called" righteous demands of others does not correspond with the concept that Christianity is about presenting an outward show of love, compassion, and tolerance. However, such a presentation of Christianity is contrary to the example of Jesus. He did not comply with the religious groups, downplay sin, give way to His family, or was concerned about the impression He left on others. Clearly, Christianity is not a surface impression, but the life of Christ being manifested in a person. People must see His very character being lifted up in a person before they can be saved. As I consider the price and the prize, there could be no other answer for me but "yes." I would gladly pay the price no matter how dearly it cost me.

Sadly, healthy relationships in families are being greatly hindered by the attitude that most of society, including Christianity, promote about it. The idea of the family is being exalted to a dangerous state of idolatry in many arenas. I have even seen this in my own family. Regardless of the type of relationship, the consensus is that one must be willing to do anything for the sake of family. For example, a person must be willing to compromise what is right in order to have peace with others. He or she must be willing to play the game so that the idea of family can remain intact, regardless of how unhealthy it is. And, who will be required to make all the necessary concessions? It has always amazed me that it is not the people causing the problems who are pressured to comply. Rather, it is the person who is considered the most reasonable or pliable who is asked to give in to the whims and demands of those who are being stiff-necked and stubborn. And, what reasoning is being exalted? It all comes down to doing it for the sake of maintaining some type of peace in family relationships.

Sadly, all such compliance is simply an outward façade. It gives the impression of peace and harmony, when in fact it is a downright lie. It is hypocritical, but it allows people to continue on in their unhealthy perceptions or patterns in relationships. Unhealthy perceptions allow people to walk in delusion or denial about their personal ungodly attitudes and patterns that are present. Compliance also serves as a point of control for such people. If everyone properly complies according to the perception of those who are most dominate, then there will be peace, and all will be happy. This is a fantasy. The one who is maintaining such a fantasy will become disillusioned, dissatisfied, and angry when the fantasy never materializes according to their expectations. The one who is forced to compromise will harbor resentment towards those who selfishly insist on their own way. Eventually, such a person will emotionally close down and back out altogether.

One has to be honest about what is really going on in a relationship. Relationship for the sake of relationship is a lie. Such a lie may be acceptable to the world, but Christians need to insist on integrity in their relationships. They must ensure that their part in any relationship is honorable.

I have struggled over the emphasis put on family relationships. As a minister of the Gospel, my main goal is to finish the course that God has set before me. When He brought me back to my home state and placed me in the middle of some of my family, I was aware that He brought me here to this particular harvest field to serve Him and not to play the family games.

This has caused some hurt feelings and anger with some of my family members, especially my mother at different times. It is not that I have cut off relationships with my biological family, but my life has taken me down a different course. This course has changed what I value and how I look at life. Paul said of his past life that he counted it all dung in order to gain Christ. He did not look back to see who was following him down this course. His focus was decisive and clear.[5] The question is will

---

[5] Luke 9:57-62; 1 Corinthians 3:6-9; Philippians 3:7-9; 2 Timothy 4:7

my family accept how this change may manifest itself in my life, or will I be judged?

In this struggle, I have had to honestly ask myself where is the balance? Some people would maintain that my family is part of this harvest field and that I must invest in them. The truth is, those who are located close to me already claim they are Christians, and those who are unbelievers have already heard the Gospel.

I have struggled with the issue of family for much of my Christian life. With the help of God and His Word, I have made peace with much of the inward conflict. Needless to say, my family has no clue about the intense struggle that has taken place over this issue, but they see the results. According to some reports that have made their way back to me, they see me as unfeeling, misguided, and a judgmental stranger. Some of these reports have been fueled by misunderstanding and hurt feelings of others who have personally taken on the cause to bring me back into line with the rest of the family.

How does one come to peace when the war rages around him or her about personal matters? It comes down to acceptance. I accept that the Christian walk will bring a separation between family members. I would love my family to share in my present life, but the reality is that we are walking different paths, and they cannot go where I have been called to walk. Abraham's extended family could not go where God called him.[6] This was true even for Jesus.

Because people encounter different experiences, their outlook on life changes. This results in there being no basis for real fellowship with others who do not share similar experiences. Since there is no basis of real fellowship, some family members and friends use the only other point of association they have, that of memories. Certain family members have tried to use memories of past events to stir up my sentiment towards the family. Granted, I have some memories that are precious, and can bring laughter to my soul, but memories vary as to what people remember and how impacted they were by them.

Healthy relationships are not established on memories, but on present investment. To drag people back into the past is to avoid the fact that there will be no future for that relationship without coming to terms with the present. People change and so must relationships. We may be comfortable with the past relationship, but we will miss knowing the person if we insist they adjust to our past perception of them. Constructive change is necessary and good for people and relationships. However, to avoid coming to terms with the change, (whether good or bad) means missing out on the process of maturity.

The changes in my life have been healthy. The life I now live is no longer mine, but has been totally dedicated to God. It is a life separated unto Him to do His bidding. This requires me to run a race. I am also

---

[6] Acts 7:1-4

aware that time is short, and my first and foremost responsibility is to God and those He has entrusted to me.[7]

When you run the race, you cannot look back or you will lose ground.[8] You cannot be concerned about who is behind you, beside you, or in front of you, for it will cause you to take a detour. You are not responsible to drag along those who have ceased to run, nor are you responsible to run backwards to contend with those who refuse to run. The goal of this race is to complete the course. No one can run this race for me, and I cannot run it for others.

It has taken me years to get the correct focus. I value my life in God; therefore, I guard it. I am satisfied in my life in Christ, and there is no lack or desire that would cause me to look back. In fact, I have a complete life in Christ. To some this steadfast vision makes me appear unfeeling or uncaring, but I have learned what I can change and where my responsibility lies. It has set me free from the ingrained patterns and the sins that easily beset me, to pursue my life in Christ. And, it has been a glorious pursuit. [9]

Do you see yourself in the game playing, the identity crisis, and the frustration caused by ingrained patterns? Do you have unhealthy relationships because of these patterns? Are you suffering from an identity crisis because you have been conditioned to think in terms of family and culture, instead of your life in Christ? Are you struggling with what your godly responsibilities are towards your parents and family? I trust my personal struggle with this issue will help you to understand God's perspective about this subject. Once you gain the heavenly view, you will be able to develop a proper disposition and establish an upright and realistic attitude about your earthy family.

---

[7] 1 Corinthians 6:20; 7:23-24; 9:26-27; Galatians 2:20; Ephesians 5:15-17; Hebrews 12:1

[8] Genesis 19:26

[9] Psalm 16:11 refer to Acts 2:32-34 and Hebrews 8:1; Luke 9:51-53; John 8:32-36; 10:10; Hebrews 12:1

# 4

# HONOR AND AUTHORITY

Relationships between parents and adult children appear to be complicated. It is hard for some parents to let their children become individuals outside of their authority and way of thinking. After all, since they gave them birth and raised them, they feel their children owe them something. Some see their children as an insurance policy for when they get old. In other words, they will always have someone to take care of them. It seems to some adult children as if the whole purpose for their existence was and is to make their parents proud and to serve them.

Incorrect perspectives often cause hardships, resentment, and breakdowns in relationships. This brings us to the main issue the adult child must wrestle with, and that is the issue of respect. Probably one of the greatest challenges facing Christians is how to honor an unreasonable parent. The confusion surrounding this issue can be overwhelming.

It is not unusual for parents to remind their grown children that they must honor them. Sadly, the concept of honor in this relationship is often unrealistic, self-serving, and idolatrous. I have seen this often used by parents who want to manipulate or control their offspring. This tactic is usually effective because it causes guilt or intimidation.

I first encountered this form of control and manipulation from my biological father. As previously stated, he was for the most part absent from my life, that is, until I became an adult. Suddenly, he appeared as if he had always been an active part of my life. He began to ensnare me into the subtle trap of guilt. He somehow made me feel responsible for his well-being. This guilt caused confusion.

Eventually, a friend broke through the confusion and began to question my feelings of guilt and responsibility. She reminded me that my father had relinquished his responsibility and rights as my father years before. Later, I was reminded that I did not ask to be born; therefore, I was not responsible for something I did not choose nor have a part in.

As I waded through all the facts, I found myself becoming quite angry at my father's manipulative attempts to make me responsible for his well-being. I thought to myself, "What audacity this man has to think he can suddenly come into my life and act as if he has the right to use me because I am his daughter."

It is in times such as these that a person could conclude that the main purpose for his or her birth was to grow up to serve his or her parents. It is as though you owe your parent for your life, which has not always been a blessing. If all else fails to get the desired results, you usually encounter the famous self-righteous clincher, "You must honor your parents."

It was during this time of struggling with the issue of honoring my biological father that the Lord reminded me of what I had learned about honor and authority in the United States Navy. I was commanded to honor and come into subordination to my superiors. I had a hard time reconciling the idea of honoring a superior whom I did not respect. I resented the Navy for allowing men to be in superior positions who were inferior in character and leadership abilities. The struggle was intense until a wiser second-class petty officer gave me a special insight into honoring my superiors. He told me that I had to separate the person from his or her position or rank. As long as I recognized the position and showed honor to his or her position, I was safe. I even had the right to go up and express any negative personal opinions I had about the individual's character as long as I showed the proper respect to a person's rank.

I never did attempt such an exercise. Technically, I may have been able to get away with it, but I also knew this person's position carried authority. This authority would give the person the final say, and he or she could make me pay for my personal opinions.

This struggle over the honor issue in the Navy reminded me of the situation with my father. As an individual, I did not respect him. He represented more of a nagging thorn in the side than a respectable father. I knew I had to resolve the issue of honor once and for all.

I looked up the word "honor" in *Strong's Concordance* in both the Old and New Testaments. The Hebrew meaning implies that honor is like receiving a burden that can be grievous or glorious. This burden makes an individual chargeable or, we should say, accountable and responsible. In the case of children, they were being entrusted with the burden, grievous or glorious, of honoring their parents by becoming accountable to them and responsible to become subordinate to their authority.[1]

In the New Testament, Paul reaffirmed this Old Testament command that children should honor their parents. It is interesting to note that the word "children" is missing from the Ten Commandments. Although children can include any offspring, it often is in reference to a child who is still under the authority of his or her parents.[2] Honor in the New Testament has a different meaning than the one in the Old Testament. It means to prize or value your relationship with your parents.[3]

The question is how does one bring all of this together to develop a godly perspective, to ensure uprightness towards parents and be pleasing to God? It is quite simple. You must consider your responsibility to your parents in light of authority.

---

[1] # 3513
[2] Ephesians 6:1; Exodus 20:12
[3] Strong's Concordance, # 5091 & 5093

Jesus actually gives us the first clue to understanding honor and authority in Luke 2. He was twelve years old when his parents accidentally left Him in Jerusalem. They later found Him sitting in the temple conversing with the doctors of the law. Mary shared with Jesus the concern that she and Joseph had over His absence. Jesus told her that He had been about His Father's business. We are then told in Luke 2:51 that He went down to Nazareth with them and became obedient to them.

As a child, Jesus had to come into subjection to His earthly parents. This subjection means that He recognized and valued the authority they had over His life. We are told that within righteous authority there is protection and peace. This is true for a child as well. Like Jesus, we may not understand in our tender years what seems like endless and petty concerns of our parents, but there is much protection and peace within the authority of decent and responsible parents.

When did Jesus finally cease to be responsible to the authority of His parents? After all, He has left us a righteous example that we can trust. Scripturally, we must always honor our parents, but there will be a time when we will move out from underneath their authority. When this happens, our responsibility towards them will change.

This is where the confusion lies. People feel that honoring parents means obeying them or adhering to their whims. If you consider the meaning of "honor," you will not find the word "obedience" in its definition. You will find reference to responsibility. As a child, there must be obedience, but such obligations change as he or she takes on new positions in life.

In studying the Bible, you will find that we will become subjected to others. For instance, when we become adults, our authority becomes the law of the land and those we work for. In my case, God became my final authority. Even though I lived with my parents and honored their wishes concerning their home, I knew that God had the final say over my life.

Marriage also will remove people out from underneath their parents' authority in order for them to cleave to their spouse. Once the authority over them changes, so will their responsibility towards their parents. For example, there were many ranking officers in the Navy, but my main responsibility rested with the superior who was immediately over me. Although I was quite aware of the authority of others, they did not directly affect me; therefore, I did not have the burden of pleasing them.

As Christians, our main obligation will be to those whom we are directly under or have a responsibility towards. We must be aware of our parents and honor them accordingly, but we are no longer required to be in subordination to them. I believe by understanding the basic foundation of honor and authority, it will begin to set confused Christians free to accept the other principles and examples given by Jesus.

As you will see, some of Jesus' very statements and examples could easily throw people into confusion about their responsibility to their parents and family. In some cases, it appears as if He is contradicting the command to honor parents when in reality, He is actually defining it.

What about you? Have you suffered confusion over the issue of what it means to honor your parents? Examine why there is confusion and make sure there is not some form of control and manipulation behind it. Ask the Lord to rip up wrong indoctrinations, or patterns, and give you His perspective.

# 5

# SEPARATION!

Once the authority over a person changes, a separation should follow. This separation is necessary to ensure healthy relationships. For instance, if a husband or wife fails to make the transition to separate him or herself from parents, it will hinder a healthy relationship with his or her spouse.

Separation forces a person to rely on those whom they are now responsible too. I realized this when I joined the Navy. I was no longer responsible to please my parents, but my superiors. This forced me to realign my thinking and my response towards those over me, causing me to grow up in some areas.

We see this in Jesus' life. At age 12, we see Him coming into submission to His parents, but in John 2, we must acknowledge that there is a definite change taking place in His relationship to His mother. This incident involved Jesus' first miracle. He had been baptized and was tempted in the wilderness for forty days and nights. He was a man who was now solely under subjection to His Father. He had a destiny that would lead Him to a terrible encounter with a rugged cross.

There is no way that Mary could understand what her Son had encountered in the wilderness. His experiences alone would bring a separation between them. This happens a lot in parent and child relationship when a parent or an adult child experiences different challenges that bring inward change, which cannot be shared with even with those whom they are close to.

Jesus' destiny to die at Calvary would even bring a greater separation with His biological family as He got closer to the cross. He was the only one who could walk this path, and the cost would be great.

In John 2, we see Jesus' reaction to His mother. It was at a wedding. The host had run out of wine, and Jesus' mother turned to Him to help them in their plight. Jesus' response to her was, "Woman, what have I to do with thee? mine hour is not yet come" (John 2:4). Notice how Jesus addressed her: *"Woman."* It surprised me that Jesus did not address her as *"Mother."* Perhaps this was a proper response for the culture He lived in, but I feel it goes beyond culture. There was a separation occurring. Jesus was not of this world, and His very statement was a prelude to the separation that would occur.[1] The term "woman" implies that there was no real identification or personal attachment.

---

[1] John 3:31; 16:28

Even in the midst of this separation, we see Jesus giving us an example by honoring His mother. He adhered to her request to provide the wine by turning water into the proper substance even though He claimed that His time had not yet come to perform miracles.

Since Jesus was not of this world, earthly entanglements would have to recede into the background. His family represented such entanglements. He knew these attachments could cause divided loyalties and detours. This is why He probably made this hard declaration, "If any man come to me, and hate not his father, and mother, and wife, and children, and brethren, and sisters, yea, and his own life also, he cannot be my disciple" (Luke 14:26).

This statement would put a different light on earthly responsibilities. As Christians, we are not of this world. We have a high calling and our responsibility is foremost to God. The call of God will always lead us away from earthly ties.

We see this in the life of Abraham. God told Abraham to leave his country, people, and father's house and go to a land He would show him.[2] It was in the heart of God to separate Abraham to Himself in order to fulfill a plan to bring forth a holy nation.

This separation is seen in the life of Joseph, Moses, Samuel, David, and Elisha, to name just a few. In the case of Joseph, we see how God allowed him in his separation from his family, to taste the bitterness of slavery at a young age, the sting of false accusation, and the confinement of prison in order to save his father, brothers, and their families from famine.[3]

The biological family of Moses did not raise him; rather, he was raised in the household of Pharaoh. Later, he fled the courts of Pharaoh to preserve his life only to encounter a different type of death, that of the wilderness experience. He tasted the desolation of the land, encountered harsh obstacles as a lowly shepherd, and felt the intense loneliness of separation and silence for forty years. Moses had no idea that these different experiences of separation were to prepare him to become one of the greatest leaders of Israel.[4]

Samuel was an answer to the silent and desperate prayers of his mother, Hannah. She wanted a child, and promised to dedicate the child back to God. God heard her prayers. After she weaned Samuel, she dedicated him to the Lord, where, at a young age, he served the priests. Samuel not only served as the last judge of Israel, but he was also a great prophet.[5]

David found himself running for his life when Saul purposed to kill him. This took him from home, family, and friends. He hid in dark caves

---

[2] Genesis 12:1
[3] Genesis 50:15-21
[4] Exodus 2-4
[5] 1 Samuel 1-2, 12

and tasted the desolation of deserts. However, in his ordeal, God took a shepherd who had a heart for Him and made him into a great king.[6]

Elisha was a farmer until a man by the name of Elijah threw his cloak around him. Elisha then left his oxen, kissed his parents good-bye, burned his plowing equipment, slaughtered his oxen, and fed the meat to the people. After this, he followed Elijah into a life of service to God. Here we see Elisha burning all the bridges to earthly attachments in order to become the man God had designated him to be.[7]

We see in Scripture that Jesus often led the crowd away from the business of the world.[8] His goal was to lead people away from the idols, the defilement, and the constant demands of the world in order to teach, challenge, and feed the people the real manna from heaven.

Jesus' call is the same to all of us. Deny self. Pick up your cross and follow Him.[9] He is trying to separate each of us to Himself in order to bring us to our spiritual potential and give us an eternal perspective.

The reason that Christians are often confused over their relationship with their parents is because it remains an earthy attachment that is never properly put in an eternal perspective. This causes divided loyalties and double-mindedness. Matthew 6:24 tells us that we cannot serve two masters. James 1:8 states that a double-minded man is unstable in all of his ways.

Jesus does offer us liberty, but that liberty can only come when we are following Him.[10] It is His perspective that shows us what our earthly responsibilities are to family and friends. This is why He commanded us, "But seek ye first the kingdom of God, and his righteousness; and all these things shall be added unto you" (Matthew 6:33).

Having the right perspective by first seeking God's kingdom is the key to maintaining our sanity. I have also experienced a change in perspective and spiritual liberty in my separation from my family. This separation has always been evident in the area of my biological father, but my mother is a different story. My mother became a Christian shortly after I looked to Jesus for my salvation. At first, we grew spiritually together, but eventually, our paths began to go in different directions.

There was a point when Jesus finally called me into full-time ministry. I realized that I had to set my face like stone if I was to follow Him.[11] This led me further away from my mother and family into uncharted territories. The challenges I faced were indescribable. They brought a spiritual depth into my life that established different priorities and perspectives.

Even though I looked the same, I was not the same person. The problem was that my mother's understanding of me had not grown. This is not unusual, but if people are not willing to allow for change, it can cause misunderstandings and hurts in relationships. I sensed my

---

[6] 1 Samuel 24
[7] 1 Kings 19:18-21
[8] John 6:1-10
[9] Luke 9:22-25
[10] John 8:32-36
[11] See Luke 9:53

mother's hurt at times when I did not enter into her world and take up her causes. I felt there was even speculation as to why I was responding differently.

As I studied the life of Mary, I felt she could have experienced such hurt as her Son set His face towards Calvary. She probably could not understand His change towards her. Jesus knew her hurt and confusion. Like me, His love for His mother had not changed, but His emphasis and direction had taken Him another route. In the end, Mary would share in her Son's sufferings. We know that she stood at His cross. We also have insight into what she experienced based on Simeon's prophecy in Luke 2:35a, "(Yea, a sword shall pierce through thy own soul also,) that the thoughts of many hearts may be revealed." One thing was certain; nothing would ever to be the same between these two people once Jesus set out to fulfill His mission on earth.

Even in Christian families, separation occurs. This separation can cause misunderstandings and hurts, but the difference is Jesus. He can bring understanding if believers will turn to Him for wisdom. It is important that Christian families allow God to have His way in the lives of His people, even if it means bringing separation. It is vital that Christians allow for change and growth in family members. Such liberty will prevent any strain or unfair demands, and give room for more mature, godly relationships to be established.

There are still times that I feel the tugging of earthly attachments. They can be subtle, but I remind myself of what Paul told Timothy in 2 Timothy 2:3-4, "Thou therefore endure hardness, as a good soldier of Jesus Christ. No man that warreth entangleth himself with the affairs of this life; that he may please him who hath chosen him to be a soldier."

I know Jesus has chosen me. He has bought me with a price; therefore, my life is not my own.[12] My loyalty must totally rest with Him. This has stopped personal confusion and brought me liberty concerning separation from my old life, which includes family. I do appreciate the work God has done in me. I understand the purpose behind both the separation and the challenges.

What about you? Are you divided in your loyalties because you have not decided to follow Jesus? Are you still entangled with earthly affairs causing double-mindedness? Let go of the worldly entanglements, deny self, pick up your cross, and follow Jesus. You will find liberty, purpose, and clarity of mind.

---

[12] 1 Corinthians 7:23

# 6

# A PROPHET WITHOUT HONOR

You may be asking, "What is my Christian responsibility towards my parents?" Keep in mind that our Lord established what our responsibility is to our family. We need to adhere to His instructions. Scripturally, we have two responsibilities towards our family. We are to be living, loving epistles of Christ, and we must preach the Gospel to those who are not saved.

The first responsibility can prove to be the hardest obligation. Being a living epistle, or letter, which serves as an open expression of Jesus to those who have known us best, can prove to be the greatest test. This was true in Jesus' life. He went to His hometown Nazareth. He challenged the people's concept about Him. They were impressed with Him at first, but their response and acceptance were limited because such reactions were based on their past knowledge of Him, "Is not this Joseph's son" (Luke 4:22)? In the minds of these people, Jesus was a mere man; therefore, they did not have to take Him seriously. It was at this time that Jesus began to expose their comfortable, self-righteous attitude, which caused an uprising. These people tried to throw their hometown boy over a cliff. Jesus simply passed through their midst.[1]

Jesus had declared that no prophet is accepted in his own home. In Jesus' case, He simply used the truth.[2] Truth has a way of not only causing a separation, but also stirring people to wrath.

It is hard to be a living, effective witness to our own family. They remember the way we used to be, and have a hard time seeing any change or validity to our claims. Even positive change can be ignored and resented because it will challenge habits and comfort zones that have been established in your relationship with them. As believers who must represent the uncompromising truth of Jesus, others can become stirred up.

Truth has a way of unveiling a person's life. It challenges comfortable beliefs and exposes sins. It is merciful and long-suffering, but it is not tolerant towards that which is unholy. It will not condemn, but neither will it soft peddle that which is motivated by darkness and deception.

This is why Jesus made this statement in Matthew 10:34-36,

Think not that I am come to send peace on earth: I came not to send peace, but a sword. For I am come to set a man at variance against his father, and the daughter against her mother, and the

---

[1] Luke 4:18-31
[2] Luke 4:24

daughter in law against her mother in law. And a man's foes shall be they of his own household.

The separation Jesus is talking about is one of betrayal and devastation. It is hard to think that truth would cause such a gap between family members, but it can and it does.

I have witnessed to my family members, including my biological father. According to my brother, he even said the sinner's prayer, but there was no indication of real change in his life. I can see how, through the years, truth did lead to the sword finally coming down through my relationship with him. I had made a decision that I would not let my father get away with jealousy towards others in my life, as well as his sarcasm and crude comments. I felt that because people never held him accountable for his rudeness and cruelty in the past, he had become a bitter and angry man. He was a slave in a small world of "me, myself, and I."

Before our relationship had been totally aborted, I found myself confronting him many times about his comments, jealousy, and judgmentalism of others. My relentless determination to not let him get away with anything produced much frustration in him. This frustration came out with momentum and anger one day while my brother and I were visiting him. I could tell he was agitated with me. We were talking about something insignificant when suddenly he attacked me about an issue that was not even being discussed. I don't know if my brother was confused about his outburst, but I know he said something to him about the situation while I waited in the car. I could tell my father felt embarrassed and possibly ashamed about his obnoxious outburst. It was as though his frustration and anger took control of his tongue. I allowed this particular outburst to slide, but I continued to call him to accountability.

As previously related, the second and final angry outburst was over my taking back the name of "Kelley." It was during this confrontation that God brought the sword down between our relationship for good. The sound of his cursing and screaming still echoed in my head when I asked the Lord, "What am I to do?" I am still surprised at His answer to walk away and never look back.

God's answer was a relief to me. My father's form of communication with me seemed to border on harassment. There was nothing uplifting or encouraging in our conversations. He usually started out by mocking me in a high shrill voice, *"Hello, millionaire."* I used to cringe every time I heard his voice. My name was Rayola, and I resented the fact that he would not simply address me. I don't know if he was nervous when he called me, but to me it was like he was always trying to make some type of statement. I sensed he could hear my immediate irritation over his greeting, but I think he chose to ignore it. Eventually, after I asked him several questions, his voice became normal and our conversation tolerable.

I must admit, I did question God over His reply to walk away and not look back. I had to make sure it was not a convenient excuse to leave a burdensome relationship behind me. "Lord, must I walk away from my father and never look back?"

The answer was, "Yes."

"I don't understand Lord, he is my father." I was then reminded that light cannot have fellowship with darkness, and that there is no agreement between the temple of God and the temple of Satan.[3] Then, this particular invitation echoed through the corridors of my mind, "Wherefore come out from among them, and be ye separate, saith the Lord, and touch not the unclean thing; and I will receive you, And will be a Father unto you, and ye shall be my sons and daughters, saith the Lord Almighty" (2 Corinthians 6:17-18).

This type of separation is devastating. I know for me, I had to test out my motives and emotional levels to make sure I did not harbor any bitterness towards my father. I realized that he did manage to strike a powerful blow to me. Although emotionally there was not much attachment, such an attack can leave wounds and implies rejection. I found myself going through mourning that I did not understand for our relationship. However, I knew comfort was waiting for me.[4]

I know for my father, the sword that God brought between our relationship was a tragedy. He had always managed to get away with his obnoxious outbursts by saying, "I'm sorry." His remorse managed to prevent possible consequences, but it never brought lasting change to his life. I believe he felt all he had to do was show his typical remorse and everything would be okay between us. How wrong he was!

As I evaluated the events around my relationship with my father, I found myself actually feeling sorry for this man. I still can see all of my brother's and my dusty school pictures sitting in frames in his house. It was as though he had made a shrine out of us. I believe he wanted a relationship with us, but he did not know how to make the proper investment. I feel he may have wanted to communicate, but he did not know how to get past his small, selfish world.

I eventually realized that my father could make a shrine out of me, but he could not honor me. He could not just accept me or the state of our relationship. He wanted something from our relationship that did not exist, and he was forever trying to adjust my world to his own.

I could understand this man and even feel compassion for him, but I could not have any agreement or fellowship with him. He was motivated by another spirit and in subjection to the spirit of the world. I was of a heavenly kingdom and in submission to the King of kings and Lord of lords.

The separation from my father was not instantly cut and dried. I found myself facing many challenges. I have had to go to the Lord many times to gain His perspective and reassurance about this matter. Praise God, He has been faithful to show me.

---

[3] 1 Corinthians 10:21; Ephesians 5:9-13
[4] Matthew 5:4; Hebrews 12:15

I knew that there could be no reconciliation between my father and me until he came to the One who has a ministry of reconciliation in repentance and need. I knew that if such reconciliation were to take place between us, it would be according to Jesus Christ and not based on either of our pathetic attempts.[5]

How about you? Has your Christian life made you unacceptable to family members? Has God tried to bring the sword down between unholy relationships with a parent or family member? Are you holding on to it because of selfish reasons? As Jesus said to all of His followers, "Count the cost." [6]

---

[5] 2 Corinthians 5:17-19
[6] Luke 14:28-33

# 7

# COUNTING THE COST

I felt relieved that God was releasing me from my responsibilities to my father. I had tried to be a witness before him and even shared the Gospel with him. I knew I could not save him or change him. I also felt the urgency to not toy with the idea of looking back or going back into the unhealthy relationship. I felt that if I went back, it would be like a dog returning to its vomit. I also could hear the Lord's words in Luke 9:62, "No man, having put his hand to the plough, and looking back, is fit for the kingdom of God." I knew if I looked back, I would become another casualty like Lot's wife when she looked back on God's judgment of that which was unholy.[1]

My determination was set, but I had no idea of the entanglements and snares that would try to pull me back into the unhealthy relationship and challenge my Christian life. The first attempt came from Satan. Satan's first device is to put doubt in your mind by pointing to the suspicious parts of your own character. We are quite human and always fall short of perfection.

Satan threw his first dart at me by reminding me that I made a determination to call my father to accountability over his jealousy, crude comments, and game playing. He then asked me who gave me the right to straighten out my father. If I kept my mouth shut and just played along with his sick games, he would have never attacked me. By trying to make him accountable, I was actually trying to be God.

It was as though I came under a strong hand of condemnation. I could agree with the accusation, but I also felt sure about God telling me to walk away from the relationship and to not look back. I went to God. "Lord was I out of line by trying to call my father to accountability in regard to our relationship?" I was reminded that love never rejoices in iniquity but in the truth, and that the truth makes a person free.[2]

"God, the truth did not set my father free."

The Lord replied, "But, the truth has been setting you free."

"But Lord, I could have just been a quiet Christian and let him get away with his verbal nonsense."

The Lord then asked me why I didn't simply go along with it. As I evaluated my motivation for not keeping quiet, I realized I was trying to avoid playing his game. I did not want to be party to his sin of unkind and immature attempts to control me, or his way of becoming a poor victim

---

[1] Genesis 19; 2 Peter 2:22
[2] John 8:32: 1 Corinthians 13:6

because of the consequences that his own actions had brought upon him.

"Thank you, Lord. Your truth once again has set me free."

I happily left the issue behind only to be confronted with another. This time people were involved. My father had contacted relatives to be mediators and to bring reconciliation. One of the individuals that talked to me about the incident was my mother. She was concerned for my spiritual well-being. She wanted to make sure that my decision was not based on unforgiveness. Since my strong reaction to her concern revealed unresolved hurt, back to the drawing board I went.

"Lord, do I have any unresolved hurt that will give way to unforgiveness and bitterness?" I knew that in every trying situation in your life, there is a spiritual test. Unforgiveness and bitterness mean that you have flunked a fundamental test of Christianity. I could not allow such failure. I started to test my feelings and emotions about my father. I did feel some raw spots that were not completely healed, but I did not sense any of them were giving way to unforgiveness.

"Lord, why did I have such a strong reaction towards my mother's concern for me?" God began to unveil something that turned out to be quite shocking. In fact, it was downright sinister. I began to realize that there is a price for my determination to follow Jesus. The first price was my reputation. I began to see how people would perceive my actions as unforgiving. I hated to admit it, but I was a religious prig.

I wanted to feel obedient and noble about my response to follow Jesus, but did I want to be misunderstood by others? I could see that many people would not really understand my actions. The attitude of most Christians is to turn the other cheek. Such actions are bound to show that you are a bigger person by being forgiving and tolerant regardless of how unholy something may be.

I started to realize that following Jesus could mean going against the grain of accepted Christian philosophies and practices. In the midst of counting the cost, I was reminded that the Lord went against the religious leaders and practices of His day. He was misunderstood and eventually crucified.

I reminded the Lord that a reputation was important to a valid testimony. He reminded me that He became of no reputation. He gave up His sovereignty as God, so that I could be made rich in Him.[4] My spiritual bubble was losing air fast. Suddenly, I realized that the sword that came down between my father and me was not about my relationship with him. Rather, it was more about my relationship with God.

I was coming face to face with pride, and I did not like what I was seeing. I knew that God was using the situation with my father as a sword to expose my own hidden agendas. It was a hard mirror to look into, and I felt it was just a prelude to what God was going to reveal to me.

---

[4] Philippians 2:7; 2 Corinthians 8:9

My next battle came from an unexpected source. I never realized that your sense of responsibility or duty could put you in bondage. For the most part, people will tell you that I am a responsible person. I believe in keeping my word, paying my bills, and fulfilling my obligations to the best of my ability.

My father had sent an apology to me via my brother. I began trying to figure out what my Christian response should be to my father's apology. According to the Word, I must forgive him. However, what is forgiveness?

I had already forgiven him, but my idea of forgiveness is that once a person asks you to forgive him or her, you have a responsibility to be reconciled to him or her to prove that you have no hard feelings. I realized that this belief was contrary to the Lord's command for me to separate from my father.

This was another lesson in forgiveness. God wanted to reveal what constitutes forgiveness. Forgiveness has two aspects to it. The first is that of release. Forgiveness in this arena has to do with releasing the individual personally from paying restitution for offense. This release is the means of guarding one's own personal attitude against bitterness and hatred.

The other type of forgiveness results in reconciliation. For the Christian, reconciliation can only occur at the point of Jesus. In other words, the offender must seek God's forgiveness. God is then able to step on the scene, and pardon the offender in order to bring forth reconciliation that leads to restoration of relationships.[5]

I wanted to be a responsible Christian and fair about this whole matter. As I considered reconciliation between my father and me, I came to the conclusion that it could not be, because there was no evidence of understanding or change on his part. Without this change, our relationship would remain unhealthy. My responsibility was to release my father from personal restitution, but there could be no reconciliation until he truly repented and became converted to the ways of righteousness.

I was also aware that I did not miss this man. Since God had set me free from his irritating phone calls, I no longer felt a cloud hanging over me. I should have felt guilty over such an attitude, but I enjoyed my newfound freedom.

I debated about what to do. I did not want a relationship with him until it could be right, but I needed to let him off the hook. I thought about writing him occasionally to show him I did not have hard feelings. Yet, I did not want him to see it as an invitation to run in and act as if all was well.

Finally, I decided that I needed to talk to the Lord about my dilemma. "Lord, I know I have forgiven him, but what should I do? Doesn't forgiveness mean reconciliation?" This is where I was reminded that

---

[5] 2 Corinthians 5:18-19

forgiveness was an act of releasing a person, but it did not necessarily lead to restoration of a relationship.

"Lord, I am willing to write him, but I do not want a relationship with him until I know it will be different." The Lord showed me that writing him without the intention of restoring our relationship would be a cruel game. My father would take any correspondence from me as an indication that all was well, and that he had a right to play his role as father again.

"Lord, what must I do?"

His answer was simple, "Follow me."

I began to think about the future. "Lord, if my father passes away before I do, people will expect me to go to his funeral. If I don't, they will think I am an unforgiving daughter."

His answer was clear, "Let the dead bury the dead, you follow me."[6]

"Lord, why do I have such a problem with sticking to what you told me in the first place?" The Lord exposed some more pride. My pride cared more about what people thought about me personally than whether or not I was pleasing my Lord. I had to repent once again. Proverbs 29:25 came to mind, "The fear of man bringeth a snare: but whoso putteth his trust in the LORD shall be safe."

The last battle I fought over this issue was major. I spent Christmas with my parents. My mother and stepfather lived in the same town as my biological father. During my visit I had no intention of contacting my estranged father. One day my parents took me to the Senior Citizens Christmas dinner. I was ready to walk towards the table when my mother began to call out to me. She was pointing behind me while saying, "Your father."

I was confused because I knew my father (stepfather) was behind me paying for the meals. She kept pointing behind me. I went up to her and she said, "Your father, Harold, is behind you." My response was, "*So?*" This shocked her. She asked me if I was going to say hello to him. I told her no.

My biological father had missed this scene between my mother and me because he could no longer see or really hear. He had to be led around. Since there was a lot of noise, he did not hear my mother trying to get my attention. In fact, I was within a couple of feet of him, and he had no idea.

My mother looked at me with exasperation. "Please tell him hi for my sake." This surprised me. I did not know if her statement was a matter of impulse or whether she was influenced by the thought of how people would perceive my actions, or her, since she was my mother. The situation was not about her, nor did she have to contend with my father, especially since she escaped their relationship years earlier. I was also aware that as a child, I had been very compliant. My mother possibly assumed things had not changed, but she did not realize that God had already resolved the situation.

---

[6] Luke 9:59-60

I knew that if I said "hello" to my father, it would open up a door that I would not be able to close. My father was persistent, and if you gave him an inch, he would take a mile. He never learned to respect the lines and boundaries of others. This had caused a major breakdown in our relationship. It all culminated in our last confrontation. I knew that he would pursue restoration with me with a tenacity that knew no limits. I was not about to subject myself to such an ordeal for anyone's sake, including my mother's.

My ordeal was not yet over. I sat at a table with my grandmother and my great aunt and uncle. My great aunt observed the interaction between my mother and me. My aunt is a religious person. She made a point to express her opinion. She felt that I needed to act like nothing had happened and say "hello" to him. I gave her a brief summary of what had happened that fateful day four years before. She then informed me that my father had told her that the confrontation was over religion. My maternal grandmother, who had witnessed the confrontation between my father and me, quickly spoke up and denounced it as a lie.

I realized that my father was up to his old tricks. He could not be man enough and admit that he blew it big time. Somehow, he had to justify his shameful actions at my expense. His lie simply sacrificed my reputation and intention so that he could once again become the noble victim.

I looked at my great aunt and flatly stated that I did not like liars and on that basis alone, I would have nothing to do with him. I was thankful to discover his lie because I felt it was God's gentle reminder that He had brought the sword down between us for good reasons. I knew that no one had a right to separate what God has put together, but I also learned that no one has a right to try to put something back together that God has separated.

We all sat quietly at the table as my father and his girlfriend passed within a foot of me. I can still hear his obnoxious voice, as he was trying to be funny.

My father did find out that I was in town and persistently pursued me. He first called a mutual acquaintance of my parents and asked him to intervene on his behalf. The man asked my stepfather to have me call my father. On the day I left, my father called my maternal grandmother and told her to have me call him. After I was long gone, even his girlfriend finally called my mother with the same request.

As I looked back on these events, I wondered what lesson was to be learned from it all. I questioned the Lord about it. He asked me if I could be coerced into playing some game. My answer was, "No."

"Did you care about what people thought about your actions?"

"No, I did not care what my mother, grandmother, and great aunt thought."

The Lord finally revealed to me the real purpose behind the whole ordeal. "Well, Rayola, you withstood and passed the test."

Galatians 5:1 tells us, "Stand fast therefore in the liberty wherewith Christ hath made us free, and be not entangled again with the yoke of bondage." It is so easy to become enslaved because the snares are many and subtle.

I have learned to appreciate my freedom and fight to hold onto it. I realize that the battle is not as fierce when you are following Jesus. The problem is that subtle devices entrap many Christians. They are being hindered from following Jesus who, not only leads them into spiritual freedom, but also enables them to maintain it.

What about you? Are you ensnared? Make a determination to follow Jesus by counting the cost. The cost may be considered initially high, but the liberty of Christ is well worth the price.

# 8

# IDENTITY AND INHERITANCE

It is easy during times of emotional fervor to declare that you are willing to pay the price in relationship to your spiritual life, but it can become a different story when the payment comes due. I have found that many Christians are miserable because they have failed to pay the price at the required time. They continue to hold onto the personal attachments that were part of the spiritual payment. These people usually want all that God has for them, but on their terms.

I have seen this in the relationships of Christians. For example, God may desire to bring separation between some Christians and their parents and family members for a season, but instead of letting go, some Christians hold onto them. This will cause frustration, misery, and eventually devastation.

As Christians, we have a higher calling. We must adhere to Jesus' voice. If He chooses to lead us away from that which is familiar to us, we must follow. If we fail to follow, we come into opposition to God's will for our lives.

Why won't Christians allow God to have His way in their lives? Granted, the cost may be high. It may mean separation from family members or missing the benefits of a normal way of life, but it will also mean liberty and obtaining the complete life that is available in Christ.

The answer to this question can often be found in identity and inheritance. So much of who we are and what we have in the way of security is wrapped up in our earthly associations. After all, our identity and inheritance are often associated with our relationship with our parents. This is why it is so hard for some Christians to let go.

I have watched many adults, including, Christians, strive for the love, acceptance, or recognition they never received from their parents as children. This pursuit comes out of the need to belong, to have purpose, or identity. To have this identity elude them means personal rejection.

I remember dealing with a young woman who came face to face with walking away from her mother (worldly identity), so that she could be set free to follow Jesus. Her mother had shown no real maternal love. She basically used her. This young woman had experienced much rejection in her life from her mother, but she had an obsession to gain her mother's approval. As she was brought to the place of deciding to walk away from her mother and choose Jesus, she actually chose her mother. What a great tragedy. It showed where her heart was, and it was not with the Great Deliverer. In the end, this woman lost what she refused to give up for Jesus, as well as face the vanity of her foolish sacrifice.[1]

Many Christians are trying to avoid possible rejection by their parents. Even though they have the promise of Psalm 27:10, "When my father and my mother forsake me, then the LORD will take me up," the idea of the unseen God of the universe receiving them in a fatherly manner is not received by faith. I watch these Christians keep hoping and struggling with rejection, thinking things will change. Sadly, they never will change until Jesus steps on the scene. He will not step on the scene until the Christian lets go and steps out of the way.

Many Christians are standing in the way of God's intervention. They are trying to be the Holy Spirit in such matters, instead of letting God do His job. Don't get me wrong, rejection is crushing, but Jesus can heal a wounded heart.[2] Otherwise, individuals remain in bondage to something that is cruel and unfair.

Christians who find themselves in this situation need to re-evaluate their perspective. If they are more concerned with earthy identity and inheritance, it simply means that their focus is on the world, and not on Christ. Our identity as Christians is found in heaven, not on earth. It is based on a person by the name of Jesus Christ, and not on earthly parents.

Colossians 3:1-3 puts our identity in this perspective, "If ye then be risen with Christ, seek those things which are above, where Christ sitteth on the right hand of God. Set your affection on things above, not on things on the earth. For ye are dead, and your life is hid with Christ in God." To me, this is the most beautiful summary of the secret to our Christian life. First of all, we need to remember that we are citizens of heaven. Our heavenly citizenship makes us sojourners when it comes to the world.[3] As sojourners, we should have no earthly attachments. Since our citizenship is heavenward, we answer to another king and a different set of rules.

Even though we are in the world temporarily, we still have a responsibility to represent our King in a worthy manner. After all, each of us carries the official title of ambassador, who is a diplomatic official of the highest rank. It also means an authorized representative or messenger who represents goodwill on behalf of another country.[4]

The question is, why do many Christians try to do a balancing act between the world and heaven? The answer is simple; their affection and thoughts are not heavenward. They want to have a place in this world. They want to have an earthly identity. They want to belong to an earthly family. However, such compromise makes them displeasing to their King.

---

[1] Matthew 16:25-26
[2] Luke 4:18
[3] Philippians 3:20; 1 Peter 2:11
[4] 2 Corinthians 5:20-21

Jesus is the only One who can give us our much-desired identity. Sadly, many Christians rarely look His way for this identity because they are so busy trying to keep their tangible world together.

It is during times of divided loyalties that Christians become frustrated because nothing falls into place and nothing makes sense. There seems to be much compromise without any results. It appears that they are losing more than they gain. Why is this happening? It is because they have ignored a very basic principle in the kingdom of heaven that is found in Matthew 16:25-26, "For whosoever will save his life shall lose it: and whosoever will lose his life for my sake shall find it. For what is a man profited, if he shall gain the whole world and lose his own soul? Or what shall a man give in exchange for his soul?"

The life Jesus is talking about in Matthew 16 is our identity. Everything of value and importance is wrapped up in who we think we are or what we want to be. This search to secure an earthly identity puts a person in bondage and sucks the life out of him or her. It is unmerciful in its demands and never gives the person a sense of belonging or purpose.

Oh, if we could be like the Apostle Paul. He was so singular in his vision. He was so free to live for Christ because he laid no claim to the world, and it laid no claim to Him. This is why he made this statement,

> But what things were gain to me, those I counted loss for Christ. Yea doubtless, and I count all things but loss for the excellency of the knowledge of Christ Jesus my Lord: for whom I have suffered the loss of all things, and do count them as dung, that I may win Christ (Philippians 3:7-8).

Paul made this statement in light of losing all his worldly attachments for the sake of Christ, in order to come to a greater knowledge of Him. He weighed the cost, and he knew what was important. He counted the cost in light of two kingdoms and reasoned that only one kingdom would last forever. He considered the cost of religious prestige that would fade away in light of a King who would reign forever. Paul made the decision and reckoned his worldly associations as dung. With reckless abandonment, he pursued the Eternal King and His everlasting kingdom.

The Apostle Paul understood the nature of his spiritual inheritance. It is important to realize that Paul's earthly inheritance was a rich one. He was an Israelite and steeped in tradition. He was a Pharisee educated under one of the greatest Jewish teachers of his time, Gamaliel.[5] In fact, Paul had it all, according to the world's standards, but what would he profit if he gained a worldly inheritance, only to lose his soul? Paul knew his worldly inheritance was nothing in light of his spiritual inheritance. He described the believer's inheritance in Ephesians 1:13-14,

> In whom ye also trusted, after that ye heard the word of truth, the gospel of your salvation in whom also, after that ye believed, ye were sealed with the holy Spirit of promise, Which is the earnest of

---

[5] Acts 22:3; Philippians 3:5-6

our inheritance until the redemption of the purchased possession unto the praise of his glory.

Our inheritance is God Himself. Oh, to possess Jesus. To know Him as the Bread of Life and Giver of Living Water is to know the One who sustains us, not only now, but also forever. To encounter Him as the resurrection and life is to experience the complete life, abundant for today and eternal forever. To know Him as our strength in times of weakness is to know His unlimited grace. To let Him become our all and all means that we find our sufficiency in Him alone.[6]  To know His faithfulness is to realize that our inheritance will remain intact for eternity. Therefore, we cannot lose it, only gain it.

Abraham understood that his real inheritance was not the Promised Land, but the Lord Himself.[7]  This is why his vision was heavenward. Hebrews 11:10 tells us, "For he looked for a city which hath foundations, whose builder and maker is God."

As Christians we have received a spiritual inheritance from Abraham, that of faith. We have so much in Christ, and yet when we lose sight of Him, we immediately become caught up with the world.[8]

There was a man who was upset with his Christian father over the issue of an earthly inheritance. Apparently, he had worked hard for his father without much compensation and recognition. One day, his father informed him that he was going to give all of his money to Christian organizations. This may have been a noble gesture on the part of this man's father, but it came at a high cost.  His son walked away from him and the Christian God he advocated.

My co-laborer in the Gospel, Jeannette, tried to share with this man that if his father had been obedient to the Word of God, he would leave him an inheritance. This truth is confirmed in Proverbs 13:22 which states, "A good man leaveth an inheritance to his children's children." An unsuccessful attempt was made to point this man back to a loving God who secured an eternal inheritance for him through Jesus Christ. It was pointed out to this poor soul that this priceless inheritance could never be taken away from him because God would remain faithful towards him.

If only we could see what we have in our great God, we would be glad to give up our earthly identity and inheritance. We will be praising Him for eternity for the rich and glorious inheritance that has been obtained by the precious blood of Jesus. Why don't we pursue it with the same reckless abandonment as the Apostle Paul?

The answer is simple. We do not trust our Lord because we do not love Him. We are told to love God with all of our heart, mind, soul, and strength, but we cannot, as long as the things of the world pull at our hearts.[9] We must choose to love God and ask Him to set us free from all

[6] John 6:35; 10:10; 11:25-26; 2 Corinthians 12:9-10; Ephesians 1:22-23
[7] Genesis 15:1
[8] Romans 4:11-18
[9] Mark 12:29-30

worldly entanglements in order for the Holy Spirit to set our hearts and minds on the real Lover of our soul.

What about you? Are you holding onto a worldly identity and inheritance? Are you pursuing acceptance among those of the world? Are you miserable because you are divided in loyalties? Is the life being sucked out of you because your pursuits lead to dead ends? Cry out for the Lord to meet you, and give Him permission to bring the sword down. And, each time He brings it down, declare, "Amen, so be it, Lord Jesus."

# 9

# THE PEOPLE OUR PARENTS MARRY

Stepparents can become another challenging heartache for some Christians. Once again, children are rarely considered when a divorced parent chooses to remarry. As I look back on my life, I see God's intervention when my mother married my stepfather. I could not have asked for a better father. He is an honorable man in every way possible. He wanted to be a father, and he took to having children like a duck takes to water. He was a good example to us and sacrificial in his provision. He strove to make my brother and me responsible and honest. He expected respect from us, and, in turn, he showed us respect.

I know that I found my identity in my stepfather. Our relationship helped me understand my Heavenly Father's commitment to me. I realized that it was a two-way street, and that I had a responsibility to invest in this intimate relationship to make it work properly.

I also know of incidents where this co-operation is missing on the part of the child. Some children will not even give their stepparent a chance. They resent anyone taking the place of their parent. They have not resolved the issue in their minds, and resent change in their lives. This not only causes hardship on the stepparent, but the marriage relationship, as the other parent must juggle between spouse and children.

My mother also realized that my stepfather was a blessing from God. Such a person is a rare gem in today's world and should be highly valued by both the spouse and the children. She could have ended up with a dishonorable man who would not have chosen to love her children or play an active part in their lives.

Too often the opposite scenario is true in the case of stepparents. Children become victims of dishonorable people who, at best, tolerate the unwelcome offspring, or, at worst, neglect and/or physically, emotionally and/or sexually abuse them. In some cases, stepparents who lack both the maturity and understanding of children find themselves inexperienced and unwise in their handling of them. Their immature attempts will backfire as they lose credibility.

I have witnessed the heartbreak of many Christians whose parents married dishonorable people. These people had no intention of being a parent. They were only interested in the prospect of companionship. They could care less about their stepchild or stepchildren because they had their own selfish agenda.

One of the suggestions I hear coming from those who work with the fallout of divorces and remarriage is that a person with children should not remarry until the children are out of the home. This allows the divorced parent to get a proper perspective without jumping into another bad situation. It will also force this parent to put his or her attention in the right place until his or her duty as a parent is completed. After all, children should never be made victims because of the selfishness and irresponsibility of parents.

I know of an incident where a Christian got the short end of the stick with both of her stepparents. Her mother's husband was greedy. His greed exposed the selfishness and greediness of her mother. As her mother grew in her greed, she became hard and self-serving. She expected her daughter to honor the expectations she had towards her, even though she showed no natural love or concern for her offspring. Eventually, her mother and stepfather justified stealing her inheritance from her through lies and manipulation. The tragedy is that this Christian woman is the last of her family, and it appears what inheritance has not been lavishly spent for lust will be given to his children.

In the case of her father, he married a woman who belonged to a cult. She led this Christian woman's father down a path of delusion and control. This woman had two children. Her son was an absolute son of Belial. He blew his mind on drugs, was abusive and threatened her father's life, but his unrealistic mother was very protective of him. Her son became incapable of being responsible for himself. She became his guardian, and guess who paid all of his bills to keep him alive? This woman's father went along with it to keep the peace in his marriage. He allowed her control, but inwardly resented it.

This single Christian woman became deathly ill. Her mother never came to visit her and she never received any financial help from either of her parents. Her mother and stepfather were too selfish and greedy to show real care or concern, and her stepmother had convinced herself that this Christian woman's illness was due to her bad "karma."

My friend's stepmother even tried relieving herself of some guilt by showing an act of kindness, but she had a selfish motive behind it. She gave this Christian woman a health product from her latest multi-level marketing business. She then encouraged her to sell this miracle-working product to not only reap from it physically, but use it to get out of the debt that was incurred by her illness. All the while, this stepmother was hiding behind sick nobility, knowing in the end that she would receive a benefit at her stepdaughter's expense and plight.

Is this fair? Of course not! How can people get away with it? It is simple. They are full of self. This makes them hypocritical in their practices as they become blind to their personal cruelty and delusion.

Divorced parents are vulnerable. They are searching for something to make their life less lonely and hard. This is an opportune time for Satan to send in the wrong person to undermine the present or future work of God in their lives, as well as their children's lives. It happens all the time.

The Christian woman we were discussing has been hindered through much of her Christian life. Her mother resents her commitment to Christ. This resentment is confirmed when the mother's ungodly spirit rises up at times and brutally strikes at my friend. Her stepmother has lied about her and caused hurt feelings between her and her father. Sadly, this is not unusual for people to experience.

In another incident, a Christian, at a very young age, was exposed to various abuses of stepfathers. Her mother chose to be blind to the effects it was having on her children. She lived totally for self, and when her children were almost old enough, they were told to move out so that she and her latest boyfriend could have the house to themselves.

This young woman knew that she was nothing more than a commodity that could be used when needed and quickly discarded for the sake of "so-called" love. This young woman dealt with a lot of resentment and had to be set free from perversion that was established by the ungodly, self-serving example of her mother.

Another popular scenario is that of the gold digger. How many fools have married a person who was after their money, and never bothered to secure it for their offspring? The stories are varied and many. Somehow, the victim truly believes that this person really loves him or her. I am sure that not only pride gets in the way, but there is some delusion as well. This type of individual chooses to ignore obvious warnings, and the results are always devastating, especially to the children who are left holding the empty bag.

Children who are to be the heritage of the Lord often become victims of ungodly, selfish practices of their parents. Parents will sacrifice the well-being of their children in order to justify their selfishness. After all, they deserve to be "happy." They have worked all their life. However, such happiness is a pipe dream. It eludes them and leaves them empty and miserable. Nevertheless, they insist that it can be found in the next relationship or situation that promises pleasure.

These people lack eternal perspective, living only for the present so that they can feed their insatiable appetites. They often appear to be void of common sense or fair play. They have, in reality, cheapened their own quality of life by abusing the heritage that God has entrusted to them, their children. These individuals will sell their soul for a fleeting relationship or for a short moment of pleasure.

We wonder why this generation is bent on destruction. Vanity is their predominate trait. Parents often pursue vain and useless objects, while young people are sacrificed on these altars to the gods of illusive happiness, selfishness, greed, and lust.

The sad truth is that many Christian parents do not regard the welfare of their children when they remarry. They are as guilty of falling into the same selfish traps as the world. Christian parents have exposed their children to the same abuses that are found in the world. I realize that many of these parents felt they had a good deal for their children, but how many earnestly sought the Lord? The package that stood before them may have looked good and talked the talk, but the Lord could see their hypocritical heart.

I would think that the main goal of parents would be to marry honorable people who would show their children proper respect and maintain their rightful inheritance. After all, if a person will not honor your children, they will not honor you in a proper way. I admit there may not be many honorable individuals out there, but God knows who they are and will uphold a person who takes their scriptural responsibility seriously. After hearing some of these heartbreaking stories, one must conclude that it is far better to remain single, than to become involved in a disastrous relationship, which leaves you and your children victimized.

Satan does use stepparents to bring devastation and destruction to the lives of children and Christians. It is sad that biological parents are partakers of these activities. It is a tragedy that they do not realize the damage they are inflicting on their children. They justify or believe that all will turn out well, but it never does.

As a scriptural counselor, I pick up the many pieces of people's lives who have been sacrificed on the altars of vanity. They find themselves in destructive cycles that affect their present families. In turn, their children continue in these cycles unless Jesus steps on the scene and delivers them.

If you are a Christian, as well as a victim of the dishonorable parent syndrome, let me encourage you. This destructive cycle can be stopped. Ask the Lord to step on the scene and heal you from all of your wounds. Ask Him to fight for what is rightfully yours, and trust Him whether you ever see your earthly inheritance or not.

Keep in mind that there is a day of reckoning. Stepparents who have proven to be advocates of Satan in your life will stand before the righteous Judge in shame. Parents who have sacrificed you on the altars of vanity will come face to face with the darkness of their soul and the uselessness of their ways. It will be a sad time indeed. Our only hope is that they will recognize their failings before it is too late.

Meanwhile, do not let anyone stand in your way. God has many promises for you. Enter into His fullness, and embrace each of His promises. They will take the bite out of neglect and abuse, and the sting out of rejection.

Finally, choose to value God's love and commitment towards you. Look into Jesus' wonderful face, and the things of the world will grow strangely dim. Take heart, He will not let you down, nor will He always leave your welfare in the hands of the dishonorable.

# 10

# THE NIGHTMARE OF HOLIDAYS

What is the first thought that comes into your mind when you think about holidays such as Thanksgiving or Christmas? We like to think about wonderful family gatherings that are pleasant, memorable times. We perceive it as a time when we get reacquainted and catch up on the latest happenings of those who represent family roots and heritage.

The truth is that for many people, holidays represent a nightmare. Instead of bringing pleasant thoughts to a person, they actually create anxiety. Instead of being a day to look forward to, they produce dread. The reason for this dread is because holidays often turn out to be someone's platform to try to live out the fantasy that has been created in his or her mind about family. It is as if holidays become a time when all manner of selfishness must be put aside for one day to ensure that this one individual's fantasy can be realized. Of course, this is all done in the sacred name of family.

Needless to say, the person who is doing all the planning does not see that he or she is promoting the epitome of selfishness as well. To this individual, it is reality. After all, everyone should be sacrificial at least once or twice a year to try to live out this fantasy about being a close, loving family. Since people are people, these fantasies rarely turn out, causing disillusionment and conflict.

For many families, celebrating holidays means tolerating a "grinch" or a "whiner." Most families have at least one "grinch." This longfaced individual sits and remembers how rotten his or her former holidays were, or perhaps he or she is unhappy because he or she prefers to be somewhere else. This individual's miserable attitude permeates the house, causing discomfort for everyone. Such an individual actually robs others of enjoying the celebration.

Then there is the "whiner." These people are always unhappy about something. They stir the pot with complaints. Their spouse is usually tone deaf to their voice, and their children are climbing the walls. These people expect those around them to somehow change their life or make them happy. Needless to say, no one can, and most have given up trying years ago.

There are also the families that really have no agreement. It is not that they necessarily dislike each other, but to avoid fights, everyone must keep the conversation light. You have to stay away from politics, religion, or any subject that would stir up the selfish, prideful beast to avoid bad scenes. Therefore, you leave your opinions outside the door, and you quietly walk around the outskirts to keep peace. By the time it is over, you are exhausted, and feel the whole day was a waste of time.

In many incidents, holidays are nothing more than a family brawl. There are those who are looking for a fight to stir up the pot. They know their target and what buttons to push. For others, there is no celebration unless they are looking to alcohol to make them happy. Alcohol has the ability to unleash hidden hurts and offenses. It is unpredictable and often causes arguments.

Holidays also can serve as a time for promotion or causes. I know a Christian who hated to participate in holiday dinners because her stepparent used the celebration as a platform to sell the latest product she was promoting. Needless to say, it never went well with the turkey.

In many cases, holidays seem as if they have been demoted into a time of torment and an exercise in futility. There is no real celebration. Granted, I have met a few families that truly enjoy each other, but you can tell that there are no unrealistic ideas about the concept of family.

Israel celebrated various holidays.[1] These were happy times for the nation as a whole and for the people as individuals, because it brought them all to one central focus, God.

Families today rarely enjoy celebrations and holidays because they lack a central focus. Even though Thanksgiving is a holiday set apart to thank God, few do. Most people gather for the big meal, but usually, it is impossible to do much in the way of thanking God or enjoying a time of family sharing. Why? Because of competition with such things as football games or some form of mindless entertainment.

Christmas may be about Christ's birth and the good will and peace it presumes to promote, but in most situations, this simple message, at best, is "tacked on" and is not the center theme of celebration. It has been misplaced in the midst of commercialism and selfishness. Its meaning has been lost, as Christmas has become a point of competition, producing overwhelming burdens as people try to outdo each other in the areas of gifts and decorations. By the time Christmas rolls around, many have lost what sense of humor they may have had in the first place.

As you can see, holidays are nothing more than burdensome duties to some people. Today, many people are being pulled in different directions because the family has become fragmented due to divorce. Instead of having to please one set of parents, you may have to keep two sets happy. If you are married, you may have to keep as many as four sets of parents happy. Your only hope is that they do not live in the same town; that in fact, they live miles apart. Even in such cases, people who have this scenario to contend with usually have the overwhelming burden of juggling demands and commitments. They know that their decision will most likely hurt someone's feelings. They almost feel helpless in their plight. Instead of holidays being a pleasant time, they often produce unwanted guilt, as people brace themselves for the onslaught of accusations and tearful manipulations.

---

[1] Leviticus 23

I remember a Christian telling me that she ended up eating two Thanksgiving dinners in one day, just to keep all the families happy. She was so miserable from all the food that she had eaten, she just knew death was imminent!

If this is not enough, you may have the incredible burden of ensuring that the celebration meets the expectations of one of your parents or other family members. You know how people can be. Perhaps you are one of them. The person who is in charge of planning the activities has his or her own definite ideas of how things should go. In fact, this person has planned every detail in his or her mind, right down to how others will respond, and how it will make him or her feel. There is even an unwritten script, and somehow, you are supposed to know your part. Usually, you do not have a clue, even though you sense that there is some kind of expectation. You have simply come to enjoy other family members, not to ensure that some fantasy goes off without a hitch. All goes well until the one who planned it becomes frustrated and disillusioned because it did not go as planned. You then find yourself contending with a hurt, insulted person. Oh, the joy of holidays!

For the most part, the American attitude about celebrations is merely selfish. Selfish parents act as if the holidays were made especially for them. Many children act ungrateful, rather than thankful during these celebrations. Unhappy individuals act as if the world should revolve around them. And, guess who is caught in the crossfire? You guessed it—the responsible person who tries to make everyone happy!

I have witnessed this nightmare many times. As a result, I have learned the secret behind what constitutes celebration. True celebration occurs when people simply learn to enjoy each other. It is not the big dinners that set a celebration apart, nor is it the gifts, but the freedom to enjoy the day.

It does not matter what kind of name you tack onto a day or holiday. A true celebration is so much more than a name. Celebration is about being together, not out of duty, but out of love. A real celebration is not about activities. Rather, it is about taking time out and taking stock of your life.

Many in America do not know how to celebrate; therefore, we have managed to make it miserable for others. We need to get back to the grass roots of how God views celebrations. There is joy and fellowship. There is excitement, and at times, gifts. However, God's celebrations went one step further. They were not about a celebration of happiness, but a celebration of life. As the Jews would say, "L'Chaim" *To Life!"*

The Jewish people had learned how to appreciate every aspect of life. They were delivered from slavery in Egypt. They ate of the manna and drank water from the rock. They were able to enter the Promised Land after wandering in the wilderness for forty years.[2] They had experienced both greatness and destruction as a people. They knew that all life came from their God. They also knew that He was the sustainer

---

[2] Numbers 33

of the type of life that held purpose and sustenance. Through their struggles, they learned the meaning of real celebration, that is, life itself.

If you think about the three major holidays Christians celebrate, they are not about happiness or fun, but about life. Thanksgiving is about observing and celebrating the way of life God has given us in America. Christmas is about the Giver of eternal life coming into the world. Easter, or Resurrection Sunday, is about the reality of the new powerful life, miraculously coming forth.

Celebrations in the Old Testament did not surround gifts, but sacrifices. These sacrifices not only reminded the Israelites of God's intervention, but that it costs something to possess life that has quality. As I watch the demands that people put on others (including Christians), I rarely see sacrifice of self. People compete for the attention of others. They put unfair expectations on those they love. In the end, no one enjoys each other.

I appreciate people who understand the demands their adult children face around the holidays. I watch parents adjust schedules to give their children freedom from unfair expectations. Rather than putting stock in a particular day, they set aside a day where they can freely enjoy celebrating life with their family. This is the secret of enjoying holidays.

We Americans need to learn to celebrate life not only on holidays, but at all times. We need to start with God and end with Him. After all, He is the essence of life. We need to learn to enjoy each other in whatever time frame has been allotted. In fact, we need to value every day our Lord has set aside as a celebration of life. We need to quit looking back at lost opportunities to establish special memories, and be quick to make memories when the present opportunity presents itself. We need to be ready to include all those who come into our midst in this special celebration.

How about you? Are you putting unfair demands on your loved ones when it comes to the holidays? Do you use holidays as a platform so that you can live out some personal fantasy about family? Do you have unrealistic expectations that leave you disillusioned and insulted? You need to ask the Lord to bring down your demands and expectations. You need to allow God to change your view and priority about holidays. Holidays are not about families and fantasies, but about the life God has given to each of us. In this life, there is the gift of time, moments, and memories. Give yourself a break, and you will be able to give others a break, and learn to celebrate life.

Perhaps you are the one who suffers the dreadful nightmares because of holiday demands? Do you want to run away from home around the holidays because you feel like the rope in a tug-of-war match? Do you feel miserable and guilty because no one is ever happy about the decisions you make during these times, including you?

I want to welcome you to a growing class of people. I have struggled with this issue, and have felt guilty for wanting to enjoy a time of rest during the holidays. As a minister of the Gospel, I pour out on a continual basis. In most cases, the only days I have off are the holidays. The last thing I want to do on these days of celebration is surround myself with people.

This concept runs contrary to the image created by our society about family and holiday celebrations. To me, there is nothing like quietly celebrating the holidays with those who simply accept me for who I am. At these times, I can relax from my demanding schedule and enjoy my life. I can commune with those who agree, and partake of fellowship as we enjoy communion at the table of the many blessings God has allotted. To many people, this would seem selfish. I personally had to conclude that it is not a matter of selfishness, but a matter of enjoying the gift and quality of life that God has given me. This celebration is like putting gas in my tank. Such times allow me to continue on in the many serious demands of life.

If you are struggling with this matter, you need to ask the Lord for His direction. He will show you, and give you liberty to pursue it. Granted, other people may not be happy with the direction you take, but you can be confident. In your desire to properly embrace the gift of life, you are pleasing your God by enjoying the life He has given you. He will, in turn, give you peace, and you will be able to appreciate your life. This will allow you to make the proper toast to life with the appropriate declaration of thankfulness, joy, and excitement, "L'Chaim, *To Life!*"

# 11

# A NEW FAMILY

Jesus understood what it was like to have problems with His earthly family. John 7:5 tells us that his brothers did not believe in Him. We know that Jesus felt the bitter sting of rejection from His own. John 1:11 tells us, "He came unto his own, and his own received him not."

If you feel like an orphan or a loner who does not fit in your family, Jesus understands. You are not alone in your plight. There are many people in your situation. However, if you are a Christian, you need to take heart. Jesus speaks of being part of a new family. His mother and brothers stood outside the door to have a word with Him. The crowd informed Jesus of the presence of His family. Let His words both comfort and excite you,

Who is my mother? And who are my brethren? And he stretched forth his hand toward his disciples, and said, "Behold my mother and my brethren! For whosoever shall do the will of my Father which is in heaven, the same is my brother, and sister, and mother (Matthew 12:48-50).

Jesus did not drop everything to talk to His biological family. Instead, He redefined the family. The family tie would not come down to physical associations, but to doing the will of the Father. People can claim that they belong to this spiritual family, but unless they are doing the will of the Father, it is simply a verbal expression and not a reality.

What is the will of the Father? Jesus tells us in John 6:39-40,

And this is the Father's will which hath sent me, that of all which he hath given me I should lose nothing, but should raise it up again at the last day. And this is the will of him that sent me, that every one which seeth the Son, and believeth on him, may have everlasting life: and I will raise him up at the last day.

The will of the Father is that a person comes to terms with Jesus and His redemption. Ultimately, the Father's will is to see each of us possess the life of His Son. This will make a person part of an unseen kingdom.[1]

Being a part of the kingdom of God not only guarantees you eternal life, but a new family. We are introduced to the idea of a new family at the point of salvation. John 1:12-13 says, "But as many as received him, to them gave he power to become the sons of God, even to them that believe on his name: Which were born, not of blood, nor of the will of the flesh, nor of the will of man, but of God."

---

[1] John 18:36

400

We see that salvation establishes us as children of God. It implies that we can enter into the sweet relationship of a child to the father. This intimate father and child relationship can only be established through Jesus. He said, "I am the way, the truth, and the life: no man cometh unto the Father, but by me" (John 14:6).

Jesus is leading each of us into a complete life, but it can only be obtained through intimacy with the Father. Jesus' ultimate goal as God Incarnate is to restore that which was lost in the Garden of Eden. What exactly was lost in this beautiful paradise? Many would say man's soul was lost due to man's rebellion. The truth is that the relationship between God and man was broken. Man lost communion with God, who is the essence of real life. Being devoid of real life, meant that man no longer would experience well-being. He was separated from life, and would taste the bitter cup of death, both spiritually and physically.

The Son of God has provided the means by which to reconcile lost man back to God.[2] In fact, Jesus is the only *way* back to this intimate relationship. What does it mean for Jesus to be the way to this relationship? According to *Vine's Expository Dictionary of Biblical Words*, "way" is not only a passageway, but it is a way of thinking and conduct.

Philippians 2:5-7 commands us to have the mind of Christ. 1 John 2:6 tells us that we must walk as Jesus did. Romans 8:29 instructs us to be conformed to the image of Christ. Philippians 2:8 describes the mind of Christ by showing how Christ became a humble, submissive servant who became obedient to His Father, even unto death.

The Word of God shows us how He walked. He walked with determination to the cross in obedience to the will of the Father.[3] He not only left an example, but distinct footprints for us to follow. They are not hidden from man's sight, but they can be ignored as a person puts his or her focus elsewhere.

The Bible's main goal is to unveil Jesus to us. It is a mirror that allows us to see the righteousness of Christ in His humanity, His sacrificial servitude in light of the cross, and His power in line with His deity. This revelation ultimately reveals His glorious position in the kingdom of God.

Jesus leads by example. His example is that of personal regression. This must happen before spiritual progression can take place. Regression of this nature involves self-denial and the application of the cross. Self-denial always gives way to truth, and the cross brings forth new life.

For us, regression leads to child-like faith. Unfeigned faith is pure and simple. It actually allows a person to see God.[4] In this simplicity, an intimate relationship is established between God and the believer. This is where life in Christ is realized.

---

[2] 2 Corinthians 5:16-18
[3] Luke 9:51
[4] Matthew 5:8; 18:2-4

The Christian life produces the fruit of the Spirit.[5] It will display confidence in the worst of times, joy in the face of crises, and an abiding peace in the midst of trials. No wonder Jesus said, "Blessed are the peacemakers: for they shall be called the children of God" (Matthew 5:9).

It is only as we come to God with child-like faith that we will experience true freedom to know and love Him. For this reason the Apostle Paul made this statement in Romans 8:15-16, "For ye have not received the spirit of bondage again to fear; but ye have received the Spirit of adoption, whereby we cry, Abba, Father. The Spirit itself beareth witness with our spirit, that we are the children of God."

Notice how Paul referred to not being in bondage again because a person fears an intimate relationship with the Father. Such fear hinders people from experiencing God's power, knowing His love, and possessing a sound mind.[6]

We find our identity within an intimate relationship with the Father. His children learn who they are, and they also discover the place that they hold in His heart and kingdom. This is vital to ensure maturity.

As you may conclude, Christians are not only suffering identity crises, (because of trying to juggle two worlds), but because they do not know their position in Christ. We are children of God. Because we are His children means that we have an inheritance and certain rights.[7]

Our inheritance is secured because of our relationship with the Father through Jesus Christ. Colossians 1:12-13 tells us, "Giving thanks unto the Father, which hath made us meet to be partakers of the inheritance of the saints in light: Who hath delivered us from the power of darkness, and hath translated us into the kingdom of his dear Son."

1 Peter 1:3-4 gives us this insight into the inheritance our precious Heavenly Father has given us,

> Blessed be the God and Father of our Lord Jesus Christ, which according to his abundant mercy hath begotten us again unto a lively hope by the resurrection of Jesus Christ from the dead, to an inheritance incorruptible, and undefiled, and that fadeth not away, reserved in heaven for you.

I have often stated that I have had the privilege of having three fathers. I had a biological father who gave me physical life, a stepfather who gave me an earthly identity, and a Heavenly Father who has given me both life and identity. Not only has my Heavenly Father given me eternal life and a glorious identity, but He has also given me an inheritance that will never perish.

I realize that many Christians are in bondage because of the paralyzing fear they have towards their Heavenly Father. They can only relate to Him according to their relationship with their earthly father. Some earthly fathers have been far from honorable and loving. They have been harsh and unfair. They may have produced life, but they have

---

[5] Galatians 5:22-23
[6] 2 Timothy 1:7
[7] Ephesians 1:13-14

failed to give their child identity. This causes the child to grow up resisting the Heavenly Father's love, placing him or her far from the heart of the Father. This person may desire this relationship, but the fear of reaching towards Him and ending up with empty arms could be too great a risk.

I honestly do not know how I would feel about my Heavenly Father if the only example I had were my biological father. I was blessed with a stepfather who stepped into my life at a critical time and showed me love, protection, respect, and purpose. He challenged, encouraged, and nurtured me. I knew my place in both his heart and home. I realized this man actually changed the whole face of our family life. When I think of my Heavenly Father, I think of Him in terms of the love and commitment of my stepfather.

I know my place in the heart of the Father because of Jesus and the cross. I know my position in His kingdom because my life is established and hidden in His Son. I also realize that the Father has changed the face of my life. He has challenged and nurtured me with His Word, and encouraged me with His Spirit. What a precious Father He is!

As I look back, I recognize that it was my stepfather who left me with a real heritage. This legacy encouraged me, and made room for me to embrace my Heavenly Father with child-like sincerity and confidence. This is the type of legacy that parents should leave their children, but in many cases, they fail to do so. Christians are in bondage and unable to receive the fullness of their spiritual life because of the perverted heritage that has been established by their earthly family.

If you are a Christian in this bondage, give Jesus permission to lead you into a complete reconciliation with the Father. Take the sword, the Word of God, to any fear that crops up, declaring your rights as a child of the Living God, against every lie you encounter. Keep your focus on Jesus. He will lead you all the way, and you will know the truth about your Heavenly Father's heart towards you. You will rejoice as you find your place within your new family and the kingdom of your great God.

Let me leave you with this final challenge. A few years back, the Holy Spirit reminded me of how the Father introduced Jesus as His Son during His water baptism and on the Mount of Transfiguration.[8] An image came to my mind where I found myself standing in front of Jesus in the courts of heaven with the entire heavenly host silently looking on. All of a sudden, the voice of the Father was heard. A provoking challenge was posed to me, "Based on your present relationship with the Father, would He introduce you as his daughter?"

What about you right now? Based on your present relationship with the Father, would He introduce you as His child?

---

[8] Matthew 3:17: 17:5

# 12

# CAN YOU ENTRUST YOUR PARENTS TO ANOTHER?

I don't know about you, but all my feelings of responsibility towards my parents and family have caused much confusion in my life. It is hard to know where to draw the line in light of scriptural duty. At times, these struggles have caused feelings of guilt and despair. However, the greatest damage this struggle inflicts on my spiritual life is that it takes my focus off of Jesus.

One incident that has always amazed me happened when Jesus was on the cross. As I meditated upon this scene, I found a tremendous release concerning my parents and family. Let me set the scene up for you. Jesus is on the cross. Near the cross, stands His mother, His mother's sister, Mary, the wife of Cleopas, Mary Magdalene, and John, the Beloved. Jesus looks at His mother and says: "Woman, behold thy son!" (John 19:27)

Here we see Jesus taking care of a very important detail, the welfare of His mother. He was actually entrusting His mother to another person. We know that Jesus had brothers and sisters, but John was not a sibling.

There is some indication that John could have possibly been a cousin of Jesus, but we also know from Scripture that John was very close to Jesus. He was the one who laid his head on Jesus' breast. He was also part of the inner core of men who witnessed great miracles, including Jesus' transfiguration on the mount.[1] This man appeared to be trustworthy, and he was part of the new heavenly family and spiritual kingdom that were being established on earth.

It amazes me to think that Jesus reached down through His suffering and despair to take care of His mother by entrusting her to someone else. What an example of love and commitment.

I must once again point out that Jesus addressed her as "woman" and not "mother." This reminds me of the separation that was about to be completed. Jesus was definitely going down a path that His mother could not follow at that time, but He did not leave her comfortless or unprotected.

You may wonder why this gave me a release from my family. As stated before, Jesus will often lead you away from your family. He did me. He led me down a path that my family could not follow. However, He also left me with a very descriptive example concerning my responsibility towards my family.

---

[1] Matthew 17:1-8; John 13:25

We do have a duty to ensure our parents' well-being. The only way we can do this is by entrusting them to another. This will allow us to freely take the path that Jesus leads us down. Look around and see whom you can entrust with the welfare of your parents. Obviously, it cannot be just anyone. They must be trustworthy like John. After all, the Word tells us that John took Jesus' mother into his house from that time on. History tells us that John probably took her to Ephesus where he served as an overseer of a church. I recently read that because Mary lived with John, she probably was instrumental in the writing of the Gospel of John, as well as in the establishing of the new church in Ephesus. This is where most historians believe she probably died, still under John's protection.

This responsible person needs to be part of the kingdom of God with a committed heart, strong character, and the ability to comfort. Do you know any man that fits such a criterion? I do. His name is Jesus Christ.

I have found a great release to follow Jesus because I have entrusted the welfare of my parents and family to Him. I learned a long time ago that I couldn't change my circumstances nor solve my family's problems. I am not able to heal them or comfort them in great sorrow. I cannot change their life, mind, or direction. In fact, I cannot save them.

Like the Apostle John, Jesus is the man for this job. He is able to ensure the well-being of family members. He has sent the best possible representative to contend with my family. His name is the Holy Ghost. He is able to convict people of sin, righteousness, and judgment. He is able to comfort, change hearts, and solve problems.[2] He is faithful, gentle, and committed.

I have realized over the years that I can actually stand in the way of what God wants to do in the lives of my loved ones. It is natural to try to play god in the lives of others. We play god by trying to solve their problems, make others happy, or save their souls. The end result of such attempts will simply prove what everyone knew all along: We are not God.

When we play God, we only make things worse. Relationships become strained, life less enjoyable, and the burdens overwhelming. We lose our sense of humor, while our family becomes more demanding that we fulfill the role we have foolishly or arrogantly taken on.

Jesus released Himself from His earthly attachments by entrusting His mother to another. He did this as an example, so that we will release our earthly attachments to Him.

You need to notice where Jesus officially entrusted His mother to John. He did it from the cross. Self-denial and the cross provide the freedom to finally let go of earthy responsibilities. Being identified with the cross implies that you no longer belong to this world, and you are now adhering to a higher calling.

However, as long as you maintain your personal rights and insist on being a part of your earthly family's well-being, you will never be able to

---

[2] John 14:26; 16:7-13

let go of them completely. These unhealthy attachments will keep drawing you back into the traps of guilt and ungodly duty.

I have truly found liberty in Christ.[3] Every time I have denied self, I have cut more earthly strings. Every time I apply the cross, it adjusts my focus on Jesus and brings much needed discipline to my life. Like Jesus, I am aware that I have a responsibility to my family, but the cross reminds me that because of my death to the old life and the world, all I can do is entrust their welfare to another.

Are you still attached to your earthly family? Do you find yourself being drawn back into the clutches of guilt and unreasonable duty? If you have answered "yes" to any of these questions, you need to take the following actions. First of all, cling to the truth of Galatians 5:1, "Stand fast therefore in the liberty wherewith Christ hath made us free, and be not entangled again with the yoke of bondage."

The next decisive action you must take to experience and maintain freedom is to follow Jesus.

---

[3] John 8:36

# 13

# FOLLOWING JESUS

I have discovered that by simply obeying Jesus' command, "Follow Me," any confusion in my spiritual life can be solved. These two words are tremendously liberating. Confusion is dispelled, and godly perspective and direction are readily available. These words disperse worldly standards, bring down personal judgments, and release people from unobtainable demands.

Jesus looked at twelve men and said, "Follow me, and I will make you fishers of men" (Matthew 4:19). These men left the "normal life" and followed Jesus into a life that wrought change, miracles, and a cross for them. They left families and jobs to spread a message that turned the world upside down.[1]

Following Jesus means that I do not have to question my responsibilities or debate my direction. All I need to do is obey Him and I can be sure of my walk and confident about being part of the family of God.[2]

As I meditated upon following Jesus, I knew that He would lead me away from the world, my family, and personal rights. We can see this pattern in the lives of great men. Jacob was sent away from his family as a young man and did not return until 20 years later. Joseph was separated from his way of life over a decade. Samuel was dedicated to begin a life of service in the temple as a child. From all appearances, John the Baptist grew up in the wilderness for a good part of his life without the influence of his parents. There must be a separation if there is going to be greatness on the part of the saints. This separation is to alleviate all gods and unhealthy attachments, whether they are to the world or to family.

Today, some parents seem to be more than a guide or counselor; they have become gods to their children. The tragedy is that many parents unsuspectingly strive to be in a place of control, exaltation, and worship in their children's lives. They want to be served, rather than encourage and allow their children the freedom to serve God. They do not realize that they are in competition with God. God will not allow any gods before Him or beside Him. He is jealous and He is the only One who deserves worship, commitment, and undivided loyalty and service.[3]

Parents, make sure you are not competing with God in your children's lives. Jesus has bought your children with a high price;

---

[1] Mark 10:28-30; Acts 17:6
[2] Mark 3:35
[3] Exodus 20:5-6

therefore, they do not belong to you. God has entrusted you with these precious gifts for a time. Like the Heavenly Father did with Jesus, you need to lay them on the altar and allow God to establish them in a life of service. It will not be easy to let go, but in due season, God will honor your sacrifice and raise up a new and godly relationship between you and your offspring.

As parents, there are two great legacies you can leave your children. The first one has to do with your eternal destiny. My friend was talking to another individual after her father's death. She shared with the lady that the greatest legacy her father could have left her was the assurance that he would be in heaven for eternity. Can you leave your children with this type of legacy?

The second heritage has to do with the well-being of your children's souls. You need to encourage and allow them to love God with all their heart, soul, mind, and might. You need to deny your own agenda for their lives and give way to God's will for them.

Sons and daughters, the greatest service you can do for your parents is to realize that they are people and not gods. Like you, they need to bow their knees in true repentance seeking mercy and forgiveness, allowing Jesus to become their Lord and Savior.[4] Meanwhile, make sure you are not standing in the way of God having His way in your family's lives, as well as in your life. Entrust each of your family members into the capable hands of Jesus, and begin to follow Him.

Following Jesus will ensure you the liberty to be all that God intends you to be. You will have peace of mind where your family is concerned. You will be able to do right by them, instead of finding yourself in the midst of conflict, confusion, guilt, and frustration. You will have confidence in God's ability to bring the necessary changes into their lives, solve their problems, and bring them instruction and hope.

You can begin to enjoy life, as you enter into an intimate, growing relationship with the Father, through Jesus Christ. You will become stronger in character as you realize your place in God's heart and kingdom. You can rejoice, as you begin to grasp the reality of your eternal inheritance.

Let me conclude with this challenge to Christian parents, offspring, or both. God told the Israelites to choose between life or death, and blessings or cursing. He told them that they could find life if they would seek Him and do good. Joshua reinforced the choices available to people when he told Israel to choose whom they were going to serve, Jehovah God or the false gods of the Amorites.[5]

Every day Christians are faced with this choice. They must decide whom they are going to serve, Jehovah God or the many gods of this world. The decision we make will determine whether we will experience eternal, abundant life or everlasting ruin and devastation.

---

[4] Philippians 2:10-11
[5] Deuteronomy 30:19; Amos 5; Joshua 24

When Jesus was calling His disciples to "follow Him," He was calling them into life and blessings. This high calling is not really optional and requires a decision on the part of the individual. My prayer for Christian parents and offspring is that your daily choice will be as decisive as Joshua's when he told the Israelites, "But as for me and my household, we will serve the Lord" (Joshua 24:15.)

Following Jesus daily means that you will be serving the Lord. This is the only choice that leads to a place of freedom, joy, and peace.

I leave you to meditate upon and embrace these words of Jesus,

> *Who is my mother? And who are my brethren? And he stretched forth his hand toward his disciples, and said, Behold my mother and my brethren! For whosoever shall do the will of my Father which is in heaven, the same is my brother, and sister, and mother (Matthew 12:48-50).*

# Bibliography

Strong's Exhaustive Concordance of the Bible; World Bible Publishers.


Vine's Expository Dictionary of Biblical Words; © 1985 by
    Thomas Nelson, Inc., Publishers


Webster's New Collegiate Dictionary; © 1976, G. & C. Merriam Co.


The 1st Church of the Program by Robert L. Rees, article


Jewish Faith and the New Covenant; Ruth Specter Lascelle; © 1980


The Power of the Spirit; William Law; © 1971; CLC Ministries
    International

# About the Author

Rayola Kelley, a seasoned minister of the Gospel, was born again and saved out of a cult in 1976 while serving in the U.S. Navy. Her spiritual journey continued through extensive discipleship, before following the Lord's call upon her life into full-time ministry over 30 years ago, when, with Jeannette Haley, founded Gentle Shepherd Ministries.

Through the years, Rayola's gift of teaching the Word has opened many doors for her to teach adult Sunday school, oversee a fellowship for over 30 years, hold evangelistic meetings in churches, conduct seminars, and speak at retreats. She has served in jail ministry, and is well known for her gift of spiritual insight and counseling. Upon being called to be a missionary in America, Rayola, along with Jeannette Haley established different fellowships where intense Bible Studies and discipleship training were conducted to equip believers for the ministry. These different mission fields in America entailed working in various churches as well as working with other cultures such as Korean and Hispanic nationalities.

Rayola, along with co-laborer Jeannette Haley, (professional artist, author of Christian novels, Bible Studies and stories for children) began sending out a monthly newsletter containing articles for the Body of Christ in 1997 which continues to grow. Ms. Kelley has authored over 55 books, and numerous Bible Studies including an advanced Discipleship Course (available in both English and Spanish) that is being used in countries such as Africa, Bulgaria, Israel, Ireland, India, Cuba, and Pakistan. Among her many books is *"Hidden Manna"* which deals with destructive cycles in people and relationships, and *"Battle for the Soul"* which presents a clear picture of the battle that rages in the soul. She has written six in-depth devotional books, including both the Old Testament and New Testament devotional study which takes the reader through the entire Bible in one year. All of her books are hard-hitting, bottom-line spiritual food for the hungry and thirsty soul to "chew" upon in order to *"grow strong in the Lord, and in the power of His might."*

Rayola currently resides in Oldtown, ID where she continues to fulfill Christ's commission to make disciples through teaching, spiritual counseling, and writing.

Please visit Gentle Shepherd Ministries Web Site at: www.gentleshepherd.com for further information, and to access her challenging and informative audio sermons.

# Other books by Rayola Kelley:

Hidden Manna
Battle for the Soul
Stories of the Heart
Transforming Love & Beyond
The Great Debate
Post to Post: (1) Establishing the Way
Post to Post: (2) Walking in the Way
Post to Post: (3) Meditations Along the Way

## Volume One: Establishing Our Life in Christ
My Words are Spirit and Life
The Anatomy of Sin
The Principles of the Abundant Life
The Place of Covenant
Unmasking the Cult Mentality

## Volume Two: Putting on the Life of Christ
He Actually Thought it Not Robbery
Revelation of the Cross
In Search of Real Faith
Think on These Things
Follow the Pattern

## Volume Three: Developing a Godly Environment
Godly Discipline
Prayer and Worship
Don't Touch That Dial
Face of Thankfulness
ABC's of Christianity

## Volume Five: Challenging the Christian Life
The Issues of Life
Presentation of the Gospel
For the Purpose of Edification
Whatever Happened to the Church?
Women's Place in the Kingdom of God

## Volume Six: Developing Our Christian Life
The Many Faces of Christianity
Possessing Our Souls
Experiencing the Christian Life
The Power of Our Testimonies
The Victorious Journey

## Volume Seven: Discovering True Ministry
From Prisons and Dots to Christianity
So You Want To Be In Ministry?

## Devotions
Devotions of the Heart:  Books One and Two
Daily Food for the Soul:  Books One and Two

**Gentle Shepherd Ministries Devotion Series:**
Being a Child of God
Disciplining the Strength of our Youth
Coming to Full Age

**Nugget Books:**
Nuggets From Heaven
More Nuggets From Heaven
Heavenly Gems
More Heavenly Gems
Heavenly Treasures

## Gentle Shepherd Ministries Series:

**The Christian Life Series**
What Matter Is This?
The Challenge of It
The Reality of It
**The Leadership Series**
Overcoming
A Matter of Authority and Power
The Dynamics of True Leadership

## Books By
## Jeannette Haley
**Books co-authored with Rayola Kelley:**
Hidden Manna (original)
The Many Faces of Christianity (Volume 6)
Post to Post 3: Meditations Along the Way

**Other Books:**
Rose of Light, Thorn of Darkness (Volume 7)
Interview in Hell (Volume 7)
Interview on Earth (Volume 7)
The Pig and I
Reflections of Wonder (Devotional)

**Children's Books:**
Little Stories for Little People
Traveler's Tales
The Adventures of Zack and Mira
The Adventures of Paul and Dana
(A House on the Beach)
The Monster of Mystery Valley